ECONOMIC GLOBALISATION AND HUMAN RIGHTS

Economic globalisation is one of the guiding paradigms of the twenty-first century. The challenge it implies for human rights is fundamental, and key questions have up to now received no satisfying answers. How can human rights protect human dignity when economic globalisation has an adverse impact on local living conditions? How should human rights evolve in response to a global economy in which non-statal actors are decisive forces? Economic Globalisation and Human Rights sets out to assess these and other questions to ensure that, as economic globalisation intensifies, human rights take up the central and crucial position that they deserve. Using a multidisciplinary methodology, leading scholars reflect on issues such as the need for global ethics, the localisation of human rights, the role of human rights in WTO law, and efforts to make international economic organisations more accountable and multinational corporations more socially responsible.

WOLFGANG BENEDEK is Professor of International Law at the Institute of International Law and International Relations, University of Graz.

KOEN DE FEYTER is Professor of International Law at the University of Antwerp.

FABRIZIO MARRELLA is Professor of International Law at the University "Cà Foscari" of Venice.

ECONOMIC GLOBALISATION AND HUMAN RIGHTS

Edited by

WOLFGANG BENEDEK, KOEN DE FEYTER,
FABRIZIO MARRELLA

CAMBRIDGE
UNIVERSITY PRESS

CAMBRIDGE UNIVERSITY PRESS
Cambridge, New York, Melbourne, Madrid, Cape Town, Singapore, São Paulo, Delhi

Cambridge University Press
The Edinburgh Building, Cambridge CB2 8RU, UK

Published in the United States of America by Cambridge University Press, New York

www.cambridge.org
Information on this title: www.cambridge.org/9780521878869

© Cambridge University Press 2007

First published 2007
Reprinted 2008

Printed in the United Kingdom at the University Press, Cambridge

A catalogue record for this publication is available from the British Library

ISBN 978-0-521-87886-9 hardback

CONTENTS

CONTRIBUTORS

Wolfgang Benedek is professor of international law and international organisations at the University of Graz, Austria. After having graduated from the University of Graz in law and in political economy he has worked at the Austrian Foreign Ministry and the Max-Planck-Institute for International Law in Heidelberg and taught at American and German universities as well as in international Master programmes in Venice and Sarajevo. He is also director of the European Training and Research Center for Human Rights and Democracy in Graz. His research priorities are international human rights law, law of international economic organisations, human security etc. Recent publications include 'Global Governance of the World Economy' (in P. Koller (ed.), *Die globale Frage, Empirische Befunde und ethische Herausforderungen* [*The Global Question, Empirical Findings and Ethical Challenges*] (Vienna: Passagen-Verlag, 2006), pp. 257–274, in German), *The European Union and the Dispute Settlement Procedure of the WTO* (Vienna/Graz: NWV/Schulthess/BWV, 2005, in German), 'Democratisation of International Economic Organisations, the Example of the WTO' (in H. Kopetz et. al. (eds.), *Sozio-kultureller Wandel im Verfassungsstaat, Phänomene Politischer Transformation* [*Socio-cultural Change and the Constitutional State, Phenomena of Political Transformation*] (Vienna/Graz: Böhlau, 2004), pp. 225–238, in German), and, with A. Yotopoulos-Marangopoulos (eds.), *Anti-terrorist Measures and Human Rights* (Leiden: Martinus Nijhoff, 2003).

Laurence Boisson de Chazournes is professor of international law and head of the Department of Public International Law and International Organization at the faculty of law of the University of Geneva (Switzerland). She is also Visiting Professor at the Graduate Institute of International Studies (Geneva) and the University of Aix-Marseille III (France). She holds a Ph.D. in international law from the Graduate Institute of International Studies (Geneva, Switzerland), a Masters Degree in private law and a Diploma in political science from the

University of Lyon II and Lyon III (Lyon, France). Between 1995 and 1999, she was senior counsel with the legal department of the World Bank. A consultant and a member of groups of experts with various international organisations, including the World Bank, WHO, UNDP and ILO, she is the author of a large number of publications dealing with international law, international organisations and international environmental law. Recent publications include: with E. Brown Weiss and N. Bernasconi-Osterwalder (eds.), *Freshwater and International Economic Law* (Oxford: Oxford University Press, 2005); with R. Mehdi, *Une société internationale en mutation: quels acteurs pour une nouvelle gouvernance?* (Bruxelles: Bruylant, 2004); 'Taking the International Rule of Law Seriously: Economic Instruments and Collective Security', in *Policy Papers*, October 2005, International Peace Academy, New York, USA.

Koen De Feyter is professor of international law at the law faculty of the University of Antwerp. He holds a Ph.D degree from the same university. He has worked at the University of Maastricht and at the European Interuniversity Centre for Human Rights and Democratisation (Venice). His research priorities include international development law and human rights. He is the author of *Human Rights. Social Justice in the Age of the Market* (London: Zed Publications, 2005) and *World Development Law* (Antwerp: Intersentia, 2001).

Francesco Francioni is professor of international law at the European University Institute of Florence (Italy) and at the University of Siena (Italy). He is a graduate in law of the University of Florence and holds an LL.M. from Harvard Law School. He has been a visiting professor at the University of Oxford, Cornell and the Texas Law School. His research priorities are in the field of public international law, especially in the area of environmental law, human rights and cultural heritage. He is general editor of the Italian Yearbook of International Law and a frequent member of Italian delegations to international negotiations and diplomatic conferences.

Fabrizio Marrella is professor of international law at the University of Venice 'Cà Foscari' (Italy) where he teaches international law, international investment law, international business law and maritime law. A member of the Board of Administrators of the European Interuniversity Center for Human Rights & Democratisation, he lectures in the European Master program on Human Rights and Democratisation with particular emphasis on Corporate Social Responsibility. He holds the highest Doctorates in Law with top grades (summa cum laude) from the University of Paris I-Sorbonne and Bologna Law Schools. He also holds the Diploma from The Hague Academy of International Law. He participates at international conferences and has given invited lectures at a range of universities both in Europe and abroad. His main research interests centre on arbitration and international economic law, also in connection with human rights issues. Prof. Marrella is the author of books and several articles published in English, French, Italian and Spanish.

Davinia Ovett was (at the time of writing) Programme Officer on Intellectual Property and Human Rights at 3D -> Trade – Human Rights – Equitable Economy and now is an independent consultant on trade and human rights. She graduated with an LLB in European Law from the University of Warwick, has an LLM in International Business Law from London School of Economics and a Postgraduate Diploma in Legal Practice (LPC) from the College of Law, UK. She has worked on human rights issues at Article 19 – the Global Campaign for Free Expression, Interights, the International Commission of Jurists (ICJ) and the International Labour Organization (ILO). Her areas of expertise include international human rights law and mechanisms, international economic law and World Trade Organization Law and processes. Recent publications include a Policy Brief on Intellectual Property, Development and Human Rights, 'How Human Rights Can Support Proposals for a World Intellectual Property Organization (WIPO) Development Agenda,' 3D -> Trade – Human Rights – Equitable Economy, February 2006.

Adalberto Perulli graduated in law from the University of Bologna. He is chair ('professore ordinario') of Labour Law at Cà Foscari University of Venice (Italy). In November 2000 he was elected head of the Law Department of the University of Venice. He is visiting professor at the University of Paris X-Nanterre. His research interests center on the situation of economically dependent workers, self employment, outsourcing and transfer of undertakings, social rights and the global market, social clauses and codes of conduct. He has published widely on a variety of topics in civil law, labour law and comparative labour law.

Jernej Pikalo is lecturer in political theory at the faculty of social sciences, University of Ljubljana, Slovenia. He graduated from the University of Ljubljana and holds a PhD from the same university. In

2001 he was a Marie Curie Visiting Research Fellow at the Centre for the Study of Globalisation and Regionalisation, University of Warwick, UK. His main research interests include theories of globalisation, political concepts, human rights, theory of the state, and interpretative methodology. He is author of *Neoliberal Globalisation and the State* (Ljubljana: ZPS, 2003) and Assistant Editor of the *Journal of International Relations and Development*.

George Ulrich has, since 2003, been Secretary-General of the European Inter-University Centre for Human Rights and Democratisation, where he has also served for three years as the Academic Coordinator and Acting Programme Director of the E.MA programme. Prior to this, he was Senior Researcher at the Danish Centre for Human Rights and Research Fellow at the University of Copenhagen's Institute of Anthropology. He has published widely on issues of ethics and human rights, and lectured throughout Europe and Africa. He holds a Cand. Mag. degree in social anthropology and history of ideas from Aarhus University and an MA and PhD in philosophy from the University of Toronto.

SERIES EDITORS' PREFACE

The present book is the first in the new series of EIUC Studies in Human Rights and Democratisation. The European Inter-University Centre for Human Rights and Democratisation in Venice, Italy is the principal European Human Rights and Democratisation Centre supported by almost 40 renowned European universities, the European Union, the Region of Veneto, the City of Venice and other strategic partners. Professors, researchers, teachers and experts from all over Europe and from different scientific disciplines and partner organisations are active in the Centre's programmes and teaching activities. One of the main objectives of the EIUC is to create a fertile environment for research and research cooperation and the transformation of the results of that cooperation into realistic policies. The EIUC studies aim to publish the best scholarly work on Human Rights and Democratisation resulting from that process of academic cooperation in the Venice Centre and its member universities. The series is not limited to lawyers' discourse alone. It encompasses the scientific disciplinary and interdisciplinary dialogue on Human Rights and Democratisation as practiced in research and teaching in the Centre's activities.

The first book reflects in approach and outcome the overall aim of the EIUC series to enrich the academic discourse on Human Rights and Democratisation with innovative contributions which also facilitate the transfer of academic and institutional expertise into the public sphere. By means of a multidisciplinary methodology the authors identify the relevance of human rights for economic globalisation. The contributions as well as the introduction and conclusions provide a comprehensive and original guidance on the interrelation between areas of international commercial activities and institutional responsibilities as well as the normative environment in which such activities are embedded. EIUC owes gratitude to the volume editors and the authors of the present volume. Wolfgang Benedek, Koen de Feyter, Fabrizio Marrella have been able together with the other EIUC professors to collaborate successfully in the process of multidisciplinary research on a new, fragmented and ever-changing subject setting a significant example for future project cooperation in the field. We would also like to express our thanks to the EIUC Board and the EIUC Assembly members who have been supporting the project of a new series with dedication and patience.

The series would not exist without the support of Finola O'Sullivan from Cambridge University Press. We would like to thank her for her guidance, encouragement and assistance.

Horst Fischer
Fabrizio Marrella
Florence Benoit-Rohmer
Michael O'Flaherty

PREFACE

The challenge that economic globalisation as one of the 21st century's guiding paradigms implies for human rights is fundamental. While the scientific discourse on globalisation has intensified and an ever growing body of research in economic globalisation can be ascertained, key questions have up to now found no satisfying answers.

Economic Globalisation and Human Rights sets out to address this gap. Questions that delimitate the multifaceted impact of globalisation on the very conception of human rights, and on their future, include: How can human rights protect human dignity when economic globalisation has adverse impacts on local living conditions? To what extent and into which direction should human rights evolve in response to a global economy in which non-statal actors are decisive forces? In this collection leading scholars assess these and other questions. Using a multidisciplinary methodology the contributors aim at ensuring that, as economic globalisation intensifies, human rights take up the central position that they deserve as a global value system. Reflecting on issues ranging from the need for a global ethic to the localisation of human rights, from the role of human rights in the WTO and the World Bank to efforts to make international economic organisations more accountable and multinational corporations more socially responsible, the contributors show that economic globalisation cannot be an end in itself, but is shaped and enriched by the globalisation of human rights.

We are proud that this volume is the first in a series initiated by the European Inter-University Centre for Human Rights and Democratisation in Venice, Italy, and coordinated by Horst Fischer, to whom we are grateful for his tireless efforts. We would also like to extend our thanks to Finola O'Sullivan of Cambridge University Press for her support and assistance. Gratitude is further owed to Julie Self for her thorough and thoughtful copy-editing. We also gratefully acknowledge the valuable contribution of our editorial assistant,

Matthias C. Kettemann of the University of Graz, for the completion of this book.

October 2006   Wolfgang Benedek
                                                      Koen De Feyter
                                                    Fabrizio Marrella

ABBREVIATIONS

3D	3D → Trade – Human Rights – Equitable Economy (NGO)
AB	Appellate Body of the WTO
ACHR	American Convention on Human Rights
AComHPR	African Commission on Human and Peoples' Rights
ACRWC	African Charter on the Rights and Welfare of the Child
ACtHPR	African Court of Human and Peoples' Rights
ADI	American Declaration of Independence
ADRDM	American Declaration on the Rights and Duties of Man
AI	Amnesty International
AU	African Union
BIICL	British Institute of International and Comparative Law
BTA	Bilateral Trade Agreements
CA	Appeal Court (several jurisdictions)
CAAU	Constitutive Act of the African Union
CAS	Council of Arab States
CAT	Committee Against Torture/Convention against Torture and Other Cruel, Inhuman or Degrading Treatment or Punishment
CCRF	Canadian Charter of Rights and Freedoms
CDES	Centro de Derechos Económicos y sociales
CEDAW	Committee on the Elimination of Discrimination Against Women/Convention on the Elimination of All Forms of Discrimination against Women
CERD	Committee on the Elimination of Racial Discrimination
CESCR	Committee on Economic, Social and Cultural Rights
CETS	Council of Europe Treaty Series
CHR	Commission on Human Rights
CLAS	Council of the League of Arab States
CMW	Committee on Migrant Workers
CoE	Council of Europe

CP-Tech	Consumer Project on Technology
CRC	Committee on the Rights of the Child/Convention on the Rights of the Child
CS	Civil Society
C-SAFE	Consortium for Southern Africa Food Security Emergency
CUP	Cambridge University Press
DFID	Department for International Development
DPPED	Declaration on the Protection of all Persons from Enforced Disappearance
DSB	Dispute Settlement Body
DSU	Dispute Settlement Understanding
ECHR	European Convention on Human Rights and Fundamental Freedoms
ECJ	European Court of Justice
EComHR	(former) European Commission of Human Rights
ECtHR	European Court of Human Rights
EEC	European Economic Community
EFTA	European Free Trade Association
EIUC	European Inter-University Centre for Human Rights and Democratisation
EPO	European Patent Office
ETC	European Training and Research Centre for Human Rights and Democracy, Graz
ETS	European Treaty Series
EU	European Union
FTA	Free Trade Agreement
GA	(United Nations) General Assembly
GATS	General Agreement on Trade in Services
GATT	General Agreement on Tariffs and Trade
GEO	Global Environmental Outlook
HAI	Health Action International
HIV	Human Immunodeficiency Viruses
HIPC	Heavily Indebted Poor Countries
HRC	Human Rights Committee/Human Rights Council
HRW	Human Rights Watch
HURIST	Human Rights Strengthening: UNDP/OHCHR
IAComHR	Inter-American Commission on Human Rights
IACtHR	Inter-American Court of Human Rights
ICC	International Criminal Court

ICCPR	International Covenant on Civil and Political Rights
ICEDAW	International Convention against all forms of discrimination against women
ICERD	International Convention on the Elimination of All Forms of Racial Discrimination
ICESCR	International Covenant on Economic, Social and Cultural Rights
ICISS	International Commission on Intervention and State Sovereignty
ICJ	International Court of Justice/International Commission of Jurists
ICPD	International Conference on Population and Development, Cairo, 1994
ICPD+5	International Conference on Population and Development Five-year review, 1999
ICPD+10	International Conference on Population and Development Ten-year review, 2004
ICRC	International Committee of the Red Cross
ICRMW	International Convention on the Protection of the Rights of All Migrant Workers and Members of Their Families
ICSID	International Center for Settlement of Investment Disputes
ICTR	International Criminal Tribunal for Rwanda
ICTSD	International Centre for Trade and Sustainable Development
ICTY	International Criminal Tribunal for the former Yugoslavia
IDLO	International Development Law Organisation
IFRC	International Federation of Red Cross and Red Crescent Societies
IGBC	Intergovernmental Bioethics Committee of UNESCO
IGO	Intergovernmental Organisation
IHRR	International Human Rights Reports
ILA	International Law Association
ILM	International Legal Materials
ILO	International Labour Organisation
IMF	International Monetary Fund
INGO	International Non-Governmental Organisation
IO	International Organisation

IP	Intellectual Property
IPRs	Intellectual Property Rights
IRIN	Integrated Regional Information Networks (part of OCHA)
ITO	International Trade Organisation
LDC	Least/less developed country/countries
MDGs	Millennium Development Goals
MIGA	Multilateral Investment Guarantee Agency
MNC	Multinational corporation
MSN	Médecins sans Frontières
NALEDI	National Labour and Economic Development Institute
NGO	Non-Governmental Organisation
NIEO	New International Economic Order
OAU	(former) Organisation of African Unity
OCHA	UN Office for the Coordination of Humanitarian Affairs
OECD	Organisation for Economic Co-operation and Development
OHCHR	High Commissioner for Human Rights
OIC	Organisation of the Islamic Conference
PTO	Patent and Trademark Office (United States)
SACC	South African Constitutional Court
SACU	Southern African Customs Union
SARS	Severe Acute Respiratory Syndrome
SC	(United Nations) Security Council
SCC	Supreme Court of Canada
SCI	Supreme Court of India
SCR	Supreme Court Reports (Canada)
SG	(United Nations) Secretary-General
SIPCs	Severely indebted poor countries
TAC	Treatment Action Campaign
TPRM	Trade Policy Review Mechanism
TRALAC	Trade Law Centre for Southern Africa
TRIPS	Trade-Related Aspects of Intellectual Property Rights
UDHR	Universal Declaration of Human Rights
UK	United Kingdom
UN	United Nations
UNAIDS	United Nations Joint AIDS Programme
UNAMIR	United Nations Mission to Rwanda
UNCTAD	United Nations Conference on Trade and Development

UNDHA	United Nations Department of Humanitarian Affairs
UNDP	United Nations Development Programme
UNEP	United Nations Environment Programme
UNESCO	United Nations Economic, Social and Cultural Organisation
UNFPA	United Nations Population Fund
UNICEF	United Nations Children's Fund
UNPR	United Nations Press Release
UNRISD	United Nations Research Institute for Social Development
UNTS	United Nations Treaty Series
UNUP	United Nations University Press
UNW	UN Wire
USA	United States of America
USAID	United States Agency for International Development
USIP	United States Institute of Peace
USSC	United States Supreme Court
VCCR	Vienna Convention on Consular Relations
VCLT	Vienna Convention on the Law of Treaties
VDPA	Vienna Declaration and Programme of Action of the World Conference on Human Rights
WB	World Bank
WCHR	World Conference on Human Rights
WHO	World Health Organisation
WIPO	World Intellectual Property Organisation
WTO	World Trade Organization

Introduction

KOEN DE FEYTER

This book analyses the relationship between economic globalisation and human rights. It raises two main issues. How can human rights provide protection whenever economic globalisation threatens human dignity? Secondly, should human rights themselves evolve in response to a changing global economy? The main purpose of this opening section is to indicate how subsequent chapters address these questions.

Defining the terms

While the authors in this book use a common concept of human rights, it is less certain that they share a common understanding of economic globalisation. This is not surprising. Although both concepts are contentious, there is at least a legal definition of human rights around which all contributors can rally. For many authors there is no need to explicitly define economic globalisation, as they only deal with a specific aspect (such as the liberalisation of trade, or the human rights impact of companies) rather than with the phenomenon as a whole.

By human rights, the contributors mean the rights included in the core international human rights instruments adopted by the United Nations.[1]

---

[1] Apart from the Universal Declaration of Human Rights, GA Res. 217A (1948), UN Doc. A/810 (1948), which was the starting point of the codification of human rights at the international level, the UN High Commissioner for Human Rights now embraces seven treaties as core international human rights treaties: the International Covenant on Civil and Political Rights of 16 December 1966, 999 U.N.T.S. 171; 6 I.L.M. 368 (1967) (156 States parties); the International Covenant on Economic, Social and Cultural Rights of 16 December 1966, 993 U.N.T.S. 3; 6 I.L.M. 368 (1967) (153 States parties); International Convention on the Elimination of All Forms of Racial Discrimination of 21 December 1965, 660 U.N.T.S. 195, 212; 5 I.L.M. 352 (1966) (170 States parties); the Convention on the Elimination of All Forms of Discrimination against Women of 18 Dec 1979, 1249 U.N.T.S. 13; 19 I.L.M. 33 (1980) (170 States parties); the Convention against Torture and Other Cruel, Inhuman or Degrading Treatment or Punishment,

With the exception of the Migrant Workers' Convention, these treaties have been widely ratified. Non-ratifying states are still bound by human rights law to the extent that human rights have become part of customary international law. Both the International Court of Justice and the international criminal tribunals have asserted in their case law that (a number of) human rights have achieved the status of international customary law.[2] The normative development of international human rights law still continues, but it can safely be said that a comprehensive body of international human rights law now exists that entails binding obligations for all states.

The United Nations' approach to human rights is based on a commitment to the indivisibility and interdependence of civil, cultural, economic, political and social rights. *George Ulrich* explains that in the post-Cold War era a shift occurred in human rights thinking from conceiving human rights as a set of norms designed primarily to curb the abuse of State power as epitomised by the protection of the lone dissident, to a broader conception of human rights as a set of tools to advance social justice on a global scale. It is this expanded human rights agenda that underlies the contributions in the present publication.

One could take a different view, dear to proponents of economic globalisation that mobilise economic arguments to select specific human rights or aspects of human rights on the basis of their usefulness to the establishment of a global free market. Inevitably, the result is a prioritisation of some aspects of civil and political rights over other rights. This approach is not in line with the insistence, in current international human rights law, that all human rights must be treated globally in a fair and equal manner, on the same footing, and with the same emphasis. Although it is not shared by the authors in this book, the selective approach enjoys considerable support, particularly among economists.

Dec. 10, 1984, 1465 U.N.T.S. 85, 113; 23 I.L.M. 1027 (1984) (141 States parties); the Convention on the Rights of the Child, Nov. 20, 1989, 1577 U.N.T.S. 3; 28 I.L.M. 1456 (1989) (192 States parties) and the International Convention on the Protection of the Rights of All Migrant Workers and Members of Their Families, GA Res. 45/158, annex, 45 UN GAOR Supp. (No. 49A) at 262, UN Doc. A/45/49 (1990) of 18 December 1990 (34 States parties). Status of ratification on 8 May 2006, except that of the Migrant Workers' Convention: status of ratification on 17 July 2006 (Cf. http://www.ohchr.org/english/law).

[2] See J. Oraa Oraa, 'The Universal Declaration of Human Rights' in F. Gomez Isa and K. De Feyter (eds.), *International Protection of Human Rights: Achievements and Challenges* (Deusto: University of Deusto, 2006), pp. 123–127.

One of the difficulties with defining globalisation is that the phenomenon can be approached from various disciplinary angles. Depending on the discipline, different types of evidence attesting to the reality of globalisation are brought forward. They include increased economic interdependence, technological change, cultural homogenisation or the growing importance of global institutions. Research on the human rights impact of globalisation fits within a large research agenda that focuses on the impact of globalisation on governance. Governance can be understood as the planning, influencing and conducting of the policy and affairs of institutions (including of the state). These processes determine how power is exercised, how citizens are given a voice, and how decisions are made on issues of public concern. A leading volume on globalisation and governance describes globalisation as:

> . . .a set of processes leading to the integration of economic activity in factor, intermediate, and final goods and services markets across geographical boundaries, and the increased salience of cross-border value chains in international economic flows.[3]

The authors of the volume identify three categories of views on how globalisation may impact on the state. The first view is that the state will wither away, not physically, but in terms of policy options it can effectively exercise in the economic realm. The second perspective is that existing instruments of economic policy, perhaps with some modifications, are sufficient to handle the challenges posed by globalisation. The third is that states will rearticulate themselves by shedding some political and economic functions and adopting new ones.[4] In his contribution to our book, *Jernej Pikalo* argues that economic globalisation will not lead to the demise of the state, but to a system of multi-level governance, with agents at different levels (global, regional, national, local) ideally working together to achieve common goals. From a historical perspective, the result may nevertheless be that the State exercises less control over the regulation of the market than before, a situation that may require compensatory protection action at other regulatory levels.

Nevertheless, as Pikalo argues convincingly, economic globalisation is not something 'that is happening to us.' States consciously decide, in the exercise of sovereignty, to participate in the process. Some speak of

---

[3] See A. Prakash and J. Hart, 'Introduction' in A. Prakash and J. Hart (eds.), *Globalization and Governance* (London: Routledge, 1999), p. 3. [4] *Ibid.*, pp. 11–17.

the 'internationalization of the state', a shift in the state's priority away from the domestic constituency in favour of transnational market interests.[5] States choose to subscribe to the neo-liberal ideology that underpins the current, hegemonic form of economic globalisation. The aim of the neo-liberal approach is to secure the free flow of trade in goods and services, to liberalise foreign direct investment, to remove capital controls, and to allow labour to move to where it is most productive. A variety of public and private actors that promote the approach, encourage the state to use its sovereign powers to allow these free flows in and out of its territory. The state remains sovereign on its territory, but it is increasingly influenced by organisations and companies that operate across borders.

Both the project of economic globalisation and the project of the international protection of human rights are incomplete. Neither has been fully achieved. Both projects impact on the exercise of the power, and on the relationship between the domestic state and internal and external public and private actors. The theme of the book then is to discover how these two processes interact, and how they shape emerging forms of global governance.

Linking economic globalisation and human rights

On the eve of the fiftieth anniversary of the Universal Declaration of Human Rights, the UN Committee on Economic, Social and Cultural Rights adopted a Statement on Globalisation and Economic, Social and Cultural Rights.[6] The Committee was concerned that governments were too focused on promoting globalisation, while 'insufficient efforts are being made to devise new or complementary approaches which could enhance the compatibility of those trends and policies with full respect for economic, social and cultural rights.'[7] In the Committee's view, globalisation was not incompatible with human rights, but:

> . . . globalisation risks downgrading the central place accorded to human rights by the Charter of the United Nations in general and the International

---

[5] Cf. F. Quadir, S. MacLean and T. Shaw, 'Pluralisms and the Changing Global Political Economy: Ethnicities in Crises of Governance in Asia and Africa' in S. MacLean, F. Quadir, and T. Shaw (eds.), *Crises of Governance in Asia and Africa* (Aldershot: Ashgate, 2001), p. 8.

[6] UN Committee on Economic, Social and Cultural Rights, 'Statement on Globalization and Economic, Social and Cultural Rights' (11 May 1998), reproduced in *International Human Rights Reports*, 6 (1999) 4, p. 1176.　　[7] *Ibid.*, para. 4.

Bill of Human Rights in particular. This is especially the case in relation to economic, social and cultural rights. Thus, for example, respect for the right to work and the right to just and favourable conditions of work is threatened where there is an excessive emphasis upon competitiveness to the detriment of respect for the labour rights contained in the Covenant.[8]

As exemplified by the Statement, the most obvious link between economic globalisation and human rights is in the area of labour rights. This was also the argument for the inclusion of the only contribution in this book (by *Adalberto Perulli*) that focuses on a single set of rights, i.e. social rights. Economic globalisation aims at organising the labour market in a specific way (primarily by encouraging labour mobility across borders), and thus impacts directly on domestic employment levels. Immediately, the issue of whether governments are ready to abandon international levels of protection of labour rights, in order to attract investment and maintain employment comes to mind. In any case, as Siegel argues, 'it is likely that no other sphere of social or economic human rights has been, or will be, as strongly affected by globalisation as employment-related rights.'[9]

Nevertheless, economic globalisation impacts on the whole range of human rights, as a host of recent publications demonstrate.[10] The opposite is equally true. Since human rights are also a global project, they can be used to shape economic globalisation.

Ulrich suggests that human rights are increasingly being cast in the context of a global ethical commitment, and offers as evidence the

---

[8] *Ibid.*, para.3.

[9] R. Siegel, 'The Right to Work: Core Minimum Obligations' in A. Chapman and S. Russell (eds.), *Core Obligations: Building a Framework for Economic, Social and Cultural Rights* (Antwerp: Intersentia, 2002), p. 25.

[10] An impressive number of recent publications deal with various aspects of the relationship between economic globalisation and human rights. They include: F. Abbott, C. Breining-Kaufmann, and T. Cottier (eds.), *International Trade and Human Rights, Foundations and Conceptual Issues* (World Trade Forum, Vol. 5) (Ann Arbor: University of Michigan Press, 2006), G. Anderson, *Constitutional Rights after Globalization* (Oxford: Hart Publishing, 2005), C. Breining-Kaufmann, *Globalisation and Labour Rights* (Oxford: Hart Publishing, 2006), R. Brownsword (ed.), *Global Governance and the Quest for Justice. Volume IV: Human Rights* (Oxford: Hart Publishing, 2005), T. Cottier, J. Pauwelyn, and E. Bürgi Bonanomi (eds.), *Human Rights and International Trade* (Oxford: Oxford University Press, 2005), K. De Feyter, F. Gomez Isa (eds.), *Privatisation and Human Rights in the Age of Globalisation* (Antwerp: Intersentia, 2005), K. De Feyter, *Human Rights: Social Justice in the Age of the Market* (London: Zed Books, 2005), O. De Schutter (ed.), *Transnational Corporations and Human Rights* (Oxford: Hart Publishing, 2006), A. Gearey, *Globalization and Law: Trade, Rights, War* (New York: Rowman & Littlefield Publishers, 2005), S. Skogly, *Beyond National Borders: States' Human Rights Obligations in International Cooperation* (Antwerp: Intersentia, 2006).

campaign for human rights launched by the former UN High Commissioner for Human Rights, Mary Robinson under the heading of 'ethical globalisation'. Human rights are presented as a normative framework that should guide the outcome of globalisation. Other contributors echo this view. Pikalo argues that human rights can serve as a moral code for institutions, agencies and networks according to which they can judge and regulate processes of economic globalisation on all levels, from the village to the supranational organisation. *Fabrizio Marrella* takes the view that the integration of economic globalisation and the globalisation of human rights could result in 'sustainable globalisation'.

A similar approach underlies the contributions of *Wolfgang Benedek* and *Davinia Ovett* on the World Trade Organization (WTO). Ovett argues that the WTO (and agents at other levels) should ensure that trade agreements allow for sufficient flexibility so that they do not undermine the capacity of States to honour their human rights commitments. International human rights law should operate as a benchmark and framework for trade agreements. Benedek adds that strengthening the interface between WTO and human rights is needed to address the lack of coordinated global governance. There is an unavoidable link between human rights and trade agreements, and therefore the human rights impact of trade agreements is an issue of legitimate concern that needs to be addressed by global institutions.

Human rights continue to offer protection in a global economy

Both proponents of economic globalisation and human rights advocates have specific expectations of the state. In human rights law, the state is the principal duty holder. In the law of economic globalisation, the state's role is primarily to facilitate the operation of market forces. This leads to the question of whether there is any contradiction between these two sets of expectations. Is the state still able to fulfil its human rights obligations while at the same time enabling market forces to take responsibility for many sectors of the economy that are human rights sensitive, such as the exploitation of natural resources or the provision of services of general interest?

In law, it is clear that economic globalisation, as of itself, has no impact on the state's human rights obligations. A state cannot retract its consent to be bound by human rights treaties, simply by arguing that it no longer has the capacity to comply with these obligations due to globalisation. The rules on termination and suspension of the operation of treaties in the Vienna Convention on the Law of Treaties of 23 May 1969 (VCLT) are strict, and they cannot be invoked when lack of compliance with human rights obligations results from a deliberate decision by the state to open up to economic globalisation. In such a case, the VCLT does not allow a defense based on a state of necessity,[11] the impossibility to perform the treaty or on an unforeseen fundamental change of circumstances.

The UN bodies that monitor human rights treaties, and the UN's political human rights bodies thus insist that economic globalisation in no way diminishes the legal obligations of the state to respect, promote and protect human rights. But, as Benedek shows, UN bodies are increasingly worried about the impact of globalisation and of trade in particular, on human rights. Reports and resolutions on the human rights impact of globalisation have multiplied at the UN Commission on Human Rights over the last decade, and, as Benedek points out, a number of new mechanisms were created to deal specifically with this issue. They include the initiative of the UN Sub-Commission on the Promotion and Protection of Human Rights to annually call a meeting of the 'Social Forum', or the appointment by the UN Secretary-General of a Special Representative on Business and Human Rights.[12] In addition, Ovett reviews the efforts of the UN human rights treaty bodies to deal with intellectual property rights from a human rights angle. She encourages the treaty bodies to approach the issue more systematically, and to produce recommendations that are clearer and more precise.

Although economic globalisation does not as such affect the state's human rights obligations, more complicated legal issues arise when states commit in law to integrate into a process of economic globalisation. The international financial institutions and the WTO certainly encourage or offer incentives to states to accept international legal obligations in this area. From a globalist perspective, it is preferable that states provide legal security under international law to those availing themselves of the opportunities that arise from the opening up of domestic markets. Obligations under international law ensure that domestic positions cannot simply be reversed by a change of direction in national politics. The large majority of states have now committed themselves, under international economic law, to liberalise trade in goods and services, to facilitate foreign direct investment, etc. – albeit to varying degrees.

[11] Compare International Court of Justice, *Gabcikovo-Nagymoros project* (Hungary v. Slovakia), Judgment of 25 September 1997, para. 57.
[12] See UN Commission on Human Rights resolution 2005/59 (20 April 2005). In July 2005, the UN Secretary-General appointed US expert John Ruggie to the position.

Consequently, there is a potential for conflict between a state's obligations under international human rights law and its obligations under international economic law. Examples include a loan agreement with an international financial institution, under which a state commits to cuts in public social expenditure, a regional trade agreement guaranteeing protection of intellectual property rights far beyond what is required by WTO law, or a bilateral investment treaty unconditionally opening up the market in services of general interest to foreign private investors. These may all lead to conflicts with a state's obligations under international human rights law.

Ideally, conflicts between treaty obligations are settled by reading the treaties in such a way that the conflict no longer exists. This solution is envisaged in Article 31, para. 3 (c) of the VCLT that stipulates that when interpreting a treaty, reference can be made to any other 'relevant rules of international law applicable in the relations between the parties'. The WTO Doha Declaration on TRIPS and public health, as discussed by Ovett, could perhaps serve as an example of a WTO effort to interpret the TRIPS Agreement in such a way that it does not conflict with the obligations of WTO member states under international human rights law. Treaties can also be amended to eliminate the potential for conflict, but, as *Adalberto Perulli*'s discussion of WTO debates on the social clause (i.e. the proposal to extend Article XX of GATT to all fundamental social rights) shows, there are limits to the willingness of States and of the WTO to apply a human rights rationale at a trade negotiations forum.

If reconciliation of treaties proves impossible, intricate legal issues arise under Article 30 of the VCLT on the application of successive treaties relating to the same subject matter. Article 103 of the UN Charter, providing that in the event of a conflict between obligations under the Charter and obligations under other agreements, the Charter obligations prevail, and the *ius cogens* provisions in the Vienna Convention introduce elements of hierarchy that may be helpful in ensuring that human rights protection takes precedence.

An additional drawback is that the issue of conflicting treaty obligations is less likely to emerge before an international human rights body (or even before a judicial body settling disputes under general international law), than before an economic dispute settlement body. WTO Member States, for instance, agree to submit trade disputes to the WTO dispute settlement system.[13] The WTO dispute settlement bodies have

---

[13] Article 23 of the Dispute Settlement Understanding of 15 April 1994 (DSU).

a specific competence to settle disputes under WTO agreements, and can only consider public international law in order to clarify the existing provisions of those agreements.[14] Under those conditions, it appears unlikely that, should a conflict arise, a WTO dispute settlement body would ever apply a human rights treaty *contra* a provision in a WTO agreement.

Efficient human rights protection depends on the ability of the holders of the rights to claim their rights – at the domestic or if need be at higher levels of regulation – before mechanisms with the requisite enforcement powers. One of the main achievements of human rights law has been to contribute to the recognition of individuals as subjects of international law, e.g. as entities having international personality, and thus capable of possessing international rights and duties, and having *some* capacity to maintain their rights by bringing international claims. Individual complaints procedures attach to a number of international and regional human rights treaties.

Access for individuals to international economic dispute settlement systems is limited, even when the decisions of these bodies may have a substantial impact on human rights. From a human rights perspective, the delocalisation of trade disputes creates a problem whenever the litigation affects the human rights of persons, e.g. because they are the consumers of a life-saving drug, or the users of a water distribution system. The persons affected are, however, not parties to the relevant trade agreement or contract and thus they will not have direct access to the competent economic dispute settlement body. One of the parties to the dispute will need to make the human rights argument on their behalf, thus leaving the individual with no active recourse.

The WTO dispute settlement mechanism is available to WTO members only, i.e. states and customs territories as defined in the Agreement establishing the World Trade Organization of 15 April 1994. In his contribution, Benedek discusses the possibility for non-governmental organisations to act as friends of the court in the public interest by submitting *amicus curiae* briefs. Such briefs have been accepted in the WTO dispute settlement system, and thus offer a possible entrance for human rights concerns. Benedek also points out, however, that no panel report has so far explicitly referred to an *amicus curiae* brief. On the other hand, Ovett notes that the United States dropped a case before the WTO dispute settlement system against Brazil on the compulsory licensing of HIV/AIDS drugs under the pressure of international civil society.

---

[14] Article 3, para. 2 of the DSU.

Koen De Feyter addresses possibly more promising developments in international arbitration proceedings which provide for *amicus curiae* petitions by non-governmental organisations on human rights grounds. Marrella offers a full discussion of the increasing importance of human rights in international commercial arbitration, including in the area of procedural requirements.

Laurence Boisson de Chazournes perceives the World Bank's Inspection Panel as a 'vehicle for public participation'. The World Bank's Inspection Panel is an administrative, rather than a judicial body, competent to receive requests for inspection presented to it by an affected party demonstrating that its rights have been or are likely to be adversely affected as a result of a failure of the World Bank to follow its operational policies with respect to projects financed by it. The Inspection Panel is limited to reporting on World Bank compliance with its own policies. The Panel therefore does not rule on violations of international law, including human rights law. On the other hand, nothing prevents the requesters from arguing that their *human* rights have been adversely affected by World Bank action, and this has occurred in a number of cases. Notably, the World Bank's management and the Inspection Panel responded substantively to the human rights claims.

On the need to adjust human rights to new economic realities

Even in situations where there is no doubt that the state is fully bound under international human rights law because no conflict with other treaty obligations arises, the impact of non-state actors on the actual implementation of human rights is probably much more important now than could be envisaged when the core human rights treaties were drafted.

International human rights law developed at a time when States monopolised international relations. The international human rights system was similarly state-oriented. In today's world, however, human rights violations often occur as a consequence of the behaviour of a variety of actors, including inter-governmental and private economic actors.

One option is to construct human rights duties for every actor whose actions have an impact on human rights. The other option is to maintain the state as the sole duty holder[15] under human rights law. The latter option is discussed first.

---

[15] With the possible exception of individuals, given the developments in international criminal law.

Maintaining the emphasis on the state arguably makes sense because of all the entities that participate in international relations, only states (governments) have a specific responsibility to take into account the public interest. This is the reason why they are – at least ideally – subject to democratic control. In contrast, under traditional international law, intergovernmental organisations are responsible only to the member states of the organisation, while corporations are mainly accountable to their proprietors (shareholders). Both entities are therefore bereft of mechanisms placing them under direct control of the population of a specific territory. If these institutions are not subject to democratic control and have no responsibility towards the population as a whole, how can a human rights responsibility be constructed on their behalf?

If there is a need for human rights to adjust to economic globalisation, the way forward is through clarifying state obligations. State duties to protect human rights, i.e. to provide protection against abuses by third parties, need to be refined. States need to ensure that they dispose of sufficient legal instruments that allow them to intervene in the domestic economy for the purposes of human rights protection, even after having opened up to the global economy. Perhaps the area of privatisation of services of general interest that are covered by human rights (anything from access to drinking water to humane prison conditions) offers the clearest example. After privatisation, the state will only be able to provide protection, if it disposes of instruments for overseeing the human rights impact of service delivery by the private actor, and for stepping in when human rights are abused. Prior attention to the maintenance of regulatory capacity even after privatisation is therefore essential. Likewise, it will be hard in the context of international arbitration to raise human rights as a justification for post-investment measures that impact on the investor's profitability, if the rules, – i.e. the law and/or the contract – applying to the investment did not, at the time of the conclusion of the investment agreement, refer to human rights[16] as an objective the investment was deemed to achieve, or did not include specific protection clauses on issues that are sensitive from a human rights perspective (e.g. on indigenous rights, or priority access to services for the poor . . .). This leads to the conclusion that certain branches of domestic law, such as administrative law, the law of contracts and tort law become increasingly important as a means to protect human rights.

---

[16] Or 'human development', or 'social and environmental objectives' – or any such formula creating an opening for the consideration of human rights.

States will also need to apply a precautionary approach when they act as members of economic or financial intergovernmental organisations (IGOs). Barring the establishment of direct human rights obligations for IGOs (discussed below), it should at least be clear that the human rights obligations of states extend to their participation in IGOs, and that states should therefore 'use their influence to ensure that violations do not result from the programmes and policies of the organization of which they are members'.[17] If governments apply such a precautionary approach when negotiating trade or investment agreements, conflicts with human rights treaties will not arise.

Concerns about both the willingness and/or the ability of states to take up these new forms of human rights protection lead to the second option, i.e. the construction of human rights responsibilities of non-state actors. The contributors to this publication appear ready to travel down this road, and to favour or, at least, consider the construction of human rights duties for non-State actors.

Marrella discusses self-regulation as a possibility for transnational corporations to actively integrate human rights concerns. Observance of human rights is becoming a part of responsible business conduct, or, put otherwise, it is an element of corporate social responsibility (CSR). Marrella argues that CSR should be taken seriously, because codes of conduct can be enforced through the market, and, in specific circumstances, even in the courts or through international commercial arbitration. Perulli also recognises the usefulness of corporate self-regulation in the field of social rights, but emphasises a number of substantive and procedural criteria that the codes need to fulfil if they are to provide real human rights protection.

Francesco Francioni goes beyond self-regulation by companies, and addresses state regulation. Direct liability of the corporation under international law is only one of the aspects discussed in his contribution. He also investigates the responsibility of both the home and the host state when they fail to prevent human rights abuses by companies, and analyzes to what extent corporate officials can be held individually responsible for serious violations of human rights by their companies, an idea that goes back to the Nuremberg trials.

The issue of the relative merits of State regulation and self-regulation (i.e. non State regulation) also figures prominently in the debate on the

---

[17] Maastricht Guidelines on violations of economic, social and cultural rights (26 January 1997), para. 19.

human rights responsibility of IGOs. That debate focuses particularly on IGOs with a strong field presence that engage in human rights-sensitive activities on the ground, such as peace-keeping, law enforcement and reform, or major industrial projects and exploitation of natural resources.

The existence of direct human rights obligations of international financial institutions can be derived from their status as subjects of international law. As such, they are capable of possessing rights and duties under international law. In its advisory opinion on the *Interpretation of the Agreement of 25 March 1951 between the WHO and Egypt*, the International Court of Justice clarified that international organisations are bound by 'any obligation incumbent upon them under general rules of international law, under their constitutions or under international agreements to which they are parties'.[18] Consequently, IGOs are subject to the reach of international human rights law, insofar as human rights are incorporated in international customary law or in the general principles of law. As a minimum, they are under an obligation not to violate or to become complicit in the violation of general rules of human rights law by actions or omissions attributable to them.

In her contribution to this volume, *Boisson de Chazournes* limits herself to self-regulation by the institutions in the area of human rights. She argues that the World Bank in particular, due to its increased attention to the social dimensions of its operations, has developed over time a number of normative and institutional instruments which play an important role in operationalising human rights in the field.

Clearly human rights need to respond to changes in the economic field. Economic globalisation, too, cannot be conceptualised without being firmly rooted in human rights. The two questions mentioned at the beginning – firstly, how human rights can protect human dignity in times of economic globalisation; and, secondly, whether human rights should evolve in response to the emergence of new actors in the global economy – are of fundamental importance for scholars and practitioners, in both economic globalisation, and in human rights. This book hopes to provide some answers on the compatibility of economic globalisation and human rights.

---

[18] International Court of Justice, *Interpretation of the Agreement of 25 March 1951 between the WHO and Egypt*, Advisory opinion of 20 December 1980, paras. 89–90.

Bibliography

Abbott, F., Breining-Kaufmann, C. and Cottier, T. (eds.), *International Trade and Human Rights, Foundations and Conceptual Issues* (World Trade Forum, Vol. 5), (Ann Arbor: University of Michigan Press, 2006)

Anderson, G., *Constitutional Rights after Globalization* (Oxford: Hart Publishing, 2005)

Breining-Kaufmann, C., *Globalisation and Labour Rights* (Oxford: Hart Publishing, 2006)

Brownsword, R. (ed.), *Global Governance and the Quest for Justice. Volume IV: Human Rights* (Oxford: Hart Publishing, 2005)

Cottier, T., Pauwelyn, J., Bürgi Bonanomi, E. (eds.), *Human Rights and International Trade* (Oxford: Oxford University Press, 2005)

De Feyter, K. and Gomez Isa, F. (eds.), *Privatisation and Human Rights in the Age of Globalisation* (Antwerp: Intersentia, 2005)

De Feyter, K., *Human Rights: Social Justice in the Age of the Market* (London: Zed Books, 2005)

De Schutter, O. (ed.), *Transnational Corporations and Human Rights* (Oxford: Hart Publishing, 2006)

Gearey, A., *Globalization and Law: Trade, Rights, War* (New York: Rowman & Littlefield Publishers, 2005)

Oraa Oraa, J., 'The Universal Declaration of Human Rights' in F. Gomez, K. De Feyter (eds.) *International Protection of Human Rights: Achievements and Challenges* (Deusto: University of Deusto, 2006), pp. 73–133

Prakash, A., Hart, J., 'Introduction' in Prakash, A., Hart, J. (eds.), *Globalization and Governance* (London: Routledge, 1999), pp. 1–24

Siegel, R., 'The Right to Work: Core Minimum Obligations' in Chapman, A., Russell, S. (eds), *Core Obligations: Building a Framework for Economic, Social and Cultural Rights* (Antwerp: Intersentia, 2002), pp. 23–52

Quadir, F., MacLean, S., Shaw, T., 'Pluralisms and the Changing Global Political Economy: Ethnicities in Crises of Governance in Asia and Africa' in MacLean, S., Quadir, F., Shaw, T. (eds.), *Crises of Governance in Asia and Africa* (Aldershot: Ashgate, 2001), pp. 3–30

Skogly, S., *Beyond National Borders: States' Human Rights Obligations in International Cooperation* (Antwerp: Intersentia, 2006)

PART I

Inter-disciplinary Perspectives on Human Rights and Economic Globalisation

Economic Globalisation, Globalist Stories of the State, and Human Rights

JERNEJ PIKALO

Introduction

In the early years of the state/globalisation debates it had become almost a fashion in certain intellectual circles to speak of the demise of the state as a response to the pressures of globalisation.[1] Government policy papers and newspaper reports were (and sometimes still are) full of accounts of the state/globalisation relationship.[2] It was contended that globalisation of culture, communication, and, especially, capital had led to a point where the state was no longer capable of steering its own course. It was argued that irreversible historical changes had occurred, which would have a major impact on the nature and capabilities of the state, as it has been known since the eighteenth century. The state as an institutional form was helpless when faced with the processes of economic globalisation, and therefore also redundant. New forms of global governance that transcended traditional division of the world into state-units were being envisaged.[3]

Such theories provoked an explosion of academic literature, contending that they were wrong in many different ways and on numerous

---

[1] V. Cable, 'The diminished Nation-State: A study in the loss of economic power', *Daedalus* 124 (1995) 2, 23–53; J. Dunn, *Contemporary Crisis of the Nation-State?* (Oxford: Blackwell, 1995); M. Horsman and A. Marshall, *After the Nation-State: citizens, tribalism and the new world disorder* (London: HarperCollins, 1994); S. Strange, 'The defective State', *Daedalus* 124 (1995) 2, 55–74; K. Griffin, 'Economic globalisation and institutions of global governance', *Development and Change* 34 (2003) 5, 789–807.

[2] See, among many, *e.g.* C. Crook, 'The future of the state', *The Economist* 344 (20 September 1997) 8035, 5–7 and D. Rupel, 'Uveljavljanje slovenske identitete v procesih globalizacije' [Asserting Slovenian Identity in the Processes of Globalisation], in D. Rupel, *Prevzem zgodbe o uspehu* (Ljubljana: Zaloûba Mladinska knjiga, 2004), 570–574.

[3] For analysis of new forms of global governance as a consequence of globalisation, see J. Bartelson, 'Three Concepts of Globalisation', *International Sociology* 15 (2000) 2, 180–96.

counts,[4] and also of literature commenting on the allegedly competing relationship between the state and globalisation as a false, artificial opposition.[5] Weiss systematically identified four hypotheses about the relationship between state and globalisation, the first one belonging to the first wave of literature, and the rest to the second:[6]

a) strong globalisation leads to state power erosion;[7]
b) strong globalisation leaves state power unchanged and holds that the state never had the macroeconomic planning powers it is said to have lost, and that those powers it continues to have are still (regrettably) significant;[8]
c) weak globalisation (strong internationalisation) leads to a reduction of state power in scope;[9]
d) weak globalisation (strong internationalisation) leads to an emphasis of state power adaptability and differentiation.[10]

Theories of the 'decline', 'retreat' and 'obsolescence' of the state that were popular a decade ago are today, in Scholte's words, 'widely discounted'.[11] There is a great deal of empirical research available suggesting that states, especially stronger states of the world's northern regions, retain substantial capacities in terms of industrial policy, welfare delivery, environmental regulation, and military intervention, despite the 'pressures' of globalisation.[12] But that is not to say that things have not changed; substantial and far-reaching changes have occurred in all areas of human life

---

[4] E.g. P. Hirst and G. Thompson, 'Globalization and the future of the nation state', Economy and Society 24 (1995) 3, 408–442; L. Panitch, 'Globalisation and the State', in R. Miliband and L. Panitch (eds.), Socialist Register 1994: Between Globalism and Nationalism (London: Merlin Press, 1995), pp. 60–93; J. Zysman, 'The myth of "Global" economy: enduring national foundations and emerging regional realities', New Political Economy 1 (1996) 2, 157–184.

[5] E.g. L. Amoore, R. Dodgson, B. K. Gills, P. Langley, D. Marshall and I. Watson, 'Overturning "globalisation": Resisting the theological, reclaiming the "political" ', New Political Economy 2 (1997) 1, 179–195; J.-A. Scholte, 'Global capitalism and the State', International Affairs 73 (1997) 3, 427–452.

[6] L. Weiss, 'Globalization and the myth of the powerless State.' New Left Review 225 (1997), 6.

[7] As suggested in the works of Reich, Horsman and Marshall: R. B. Reich, The Work of Nations (London: Simon & Schuster, 1993); Horsman and Marshall, After the Nation-State.

[8] E.g. C. Crook, 'The future of the state', The Economist 344 (20 September 1997) 8035, 5–7.

[9] E.g. Hirst and Thompson, 'Globalization and the future of the nation state', 408–442.

[10] Weiss, 'Globalization and the myth of the powerless State'. 6–7.

[11] J.-A. Scholte, 'Governing economic globalization: A response to Keith Griffin', Development and Change 35 (2004) 5, 1052.   [12] Ibid.

because of the processes of globalisation. Humanity is daily faced with new problems, stemming from new global awareness, advancement of the capitalist mode of production, new technologies, new contagious diseases, environmental problems, etc.

Human rights are constantly tested for their efficacy in the global environment. Economic globalisation has brought about developments that are hard to describe as 'a positive sum game' for the whole of humanity. New human rights applications will have to be established, to harness global capitalism and to provide global governance that will work for the benefit of all.

This chapter will argue that in the world of multi-scalar and multi-dimensional globalisation there is a fundamental need for a common ground on which global actions can be judged. Human rights have the potential to become a universal moral code for those global actions that escape the traditional control of the state system. The chapter will begin by analysing the so-called 'globalist' discourse of the state/globalisation relationship, which is widely regarded as one of the most salient analyses of the current human condition. The next part will present the negative aspects of globalist prescriptions for development and human rights, whilst the final section will advocate alternative ways for approaching global governance through human rights.

Globalist analysis

Let us illustrate the so-called 'globalist' thinking on globalisation with some quotes. First, from the Socialist International Declaration of Paris:

> Humankind is witnessing a new change of era marked by the phenomenon of globalisation . . . Macroeconomic policies which are disciplined by the operation of the global financial markets have been constrained in what they can attempt to achieve and compelled to meet stringent requirements relating to public deficits, inflation etc.[13]

Next, from Sir Leon Brittan, in his capacity as Vice-President of the European Commission:

> Globalisation is a fact of life, and will continue irrespective and independent of the activities of government. The issue is not whether we can accept

---

[13] Socialist International, 'Declaration of Paris – The Challenges of Globalization' The XXI Congress of the Socialist International, Paris, 8–10 November 1999, http://www.socialist-international.org/5Congress/XXI-PARIS/DeclParis-e.html (accessed: 25 September 2005).

or reject it, but how to ensure it is channelled in positive directions. It is vital that national and international organisations acknowledge the impact of globalisation and respond accordingly.[14]

Janez Drnovšek, then the Prime Minister of Slovenia:

> Globalisation is a fact of life. Processes of globalisation have been going on for some time and a question has arisen as to what is the best policy for an individual or a small state such as Slovenia with regard to globalisation. We cannot be global players and actively influence these processes. To a far greater extent, these processes influence us and create an environment in which we are striving to establish the best possible existence.[15]

And finally Mojca Drčar Murko, columnist for the Slovenian daily *Delo*:

> The logic of uninhibited trade and free-flowing capital, based on great technical innovations and technological novelties and encompassed in the term 'globalisation' has fundamentally changed world politics. We are witnessing an era of changes, and do not know where they will end. Social pacts – the outcomes of the great political battles of the twentieth century – have been annulled by this process, to the same extent as the traditional ranking of countries based on power.[16]

The people and organisations mentioned come from a variety of personal and institutional ideological positions. Yet strangely, they speak almost a similar language, based on similar ideas and preconceptions. Uniform thinking has advanced to the stage that one can speak of speak of the orthodoxy of a certain view. One can discuss a new universal spirit of our time, a new ecumenical evangelism that is being spread by a cohort of statesmen and politicians, officials of international organisations, managers, civil servants and journalists. Academics usually, though not entirely, exclude themselves from this enterprise. The discourses on globalisation, as presented above, have some common features, which now fall to be discussed: technological change, inevitability, convergence, instrumentality, globalisation's status as a benign process; further, the processes of globalisation are 'non-actor driven'.

---

[14] L. Brittan, 'The contribution of the WTO Millennium Round to globalization: an EU view', in C. Baudenbacher and E. Busek (eds.), *Europa im Zeitalter der Globalisierung: Vorträge des 1. DDr. Herbert Batliner Symposiums* (Vienna: Manz, 2000), p. 82.

[15] J. Drnovšek, 'Strateški svet za nacionalna vprašanja: Vstop Slovenije v NATO ne bo ogrozil slovenske nacionalne identitete', 22 July 2002, http://nato.gov.si/slo/novinarsko-sre-disce/sporocila-za-javnost/1573/ (accessed: 1 June 2006). Translated by author.

[16] M. Drčar Murko, 'En sam svet, če nam je prav ali ne', *Delo*, 17 September 2002, 1.

Technological change is presented as the driving force of globalisation, i.e. changes in science, technology, and production methods essentially determine the future of workers, managers, and the state, and their inter-relationships.[17] In discourses on globalisation, internet and computer-based technologies are increasingly seen as its main driving force;[18] technology is supposed to lead to a better future. Mike Moore, former Director-General of the World Trade Organization (WTO), has expressed this view as: 'Technology can be the friend of the people. Nobody wants yesterday's medicine.'[19] Technological change is seen as a 'golden cage'[20] and it is presumably beyond control.[21]

Globalisation is framed *as inevitable*,[22] with no viable alternatives, and is described as a state of affairs that increasingly sets parameters of political and economic processes: 'Globalisation is unavoidable. Globalisation cannot – even if we wanted – be resisted, because it is already a fact.'[23]

Globalisation is described as a process leading towards *convergence*. From divergent starting points and diverse institutional bases, it is thought, states and societies will become increasingly alike using the same set of formulae. This development is seen as a linear universal process that will, in all cases, follow the same path. States and societies are seen as objects, leaving aside their historical and socially-specific developments.

---

[17] Cf. C. Crook, 'The future of the state', 5; M. Mann, 'Has globalisation ended the rise and rise of the nation-state?' *Review of International Political Economy* 4 (1997) 3, 473; R. Langhorne, *The Coming of Globalization: Its Evolution and Contemporary Consequences* (Basingstoke/New York: Palgrave, 2001), p. xi; V. Cable, 'The Diminished Nation-State: A Study in the Loss of Economic Power', *Daedalus* 124 (1995) 2, 25–26.

[18] Cf. Scholte, 'Global Capitalism and the State', 74–86.

[19] M. Moore, 'In Praise of the Future', Speech to the Canterbury Employers Chamber of Commerce, Christchurch, New Zealand, 14 August 2000, http://www.wto.org/english/news_e/spmm_e/spmm34_e.htm (accessed: 10 November 2001).

[20] In the words of Thomas Friedman 'golden straitjacket': T. L. Friedman, *The Lexus and the Olive Tree* (New York: HarperCollins, 1999) p. 18.

[21] R. J. Barry Jones has noticed that discussions on technological change that are driving globalisation are taking the form of technological determinism. He pointed out that not all technological changes do necessarily bring about development in certain directions. R. J. Barry Jones, 'Globalization and change in the international political economy: Overview', *International Affairs* 75 (1999) 2, 360.

[22] L. Amoore *et al.*, 'Overturning 'Globalisation'', 183; J. Weldes, 'Globalization is Science Fiction,' *Millennium: Journal of International Studies* 30 (2001) 3, 651; cf. N. Fairclough, 'Language in the New Capitalism', http://www.cddc.vt.edu/host/lnc/papers/fair_lnc.doc, 2000 (accessed: 12 May 2006); J. M. Hobson and M. Ramesh, 'Globalization makes of States what States make of it: between agency and structure in the State/Globalisation debate', *New Political Economy* 7 (2002) 1, 7.

[23] D. Rupel, 'Uveljavljanje slovenske identitete v procesih globalizacije', 572.

Globalisation processes will release their immanent similarities and lead to convergence.

Globalisation is presented *instrumentally*.[24] There is a tendency to simplify the description of change in order to prescribe a set of formulae to manage change. The picture of globalisation is painted with broad strokes of a brush; such a picture is invariably impressionistic, despite making claims to cross-subjective objectivity. Globalisation is seen as a tool for a variety of unpopular (in the literal sense of the word) decisions that are being prescribed for states and societies, with policies which look 'as if they were dictated by matters of fact (thematic patterns) and deflect consideration of values of choices and the social, moral and political responsibility for such choices'.[25] Technical discourse is employed to present a complex process in shorthand numerical terms, which are seen in our societies as value-neutral, objective, 'facts' on the basis of which decisions can be made 'objectively'.[26]

Globalisation is presented as a *benign* process, with mild or positive effects. Ohmae[27] saw in globalisation a process that could lead to a brighter future:

> Now that the bitter ideological confrontation sparked by this century's [now already last century] collision of 'isms' has ended, a larger number of people from more points on the globe than ever before have aggressively come forward to participate *in* history. They have left behind centuries, even millennia, of obscurity in the forest and desert and rural isolation to request from the world community – and from the global economy that links it together – a decent life for themselves and a better life for their children.[28]

The social conflict that is generated by new modes of capitalist production and its organisation is, from this point of view, confined to the adjustment phase, and is seen only as a temporary by-product of restructuring.

The representation of globalisation in such discourses takes place without a human agent, without an actor. The human (or any other) agent is either inanimate or abstract. Globalisation processes are thought to be *non-actor driven*. To the reader this gives an impression that the processes of globalisation are driven by the natural condition of things

---

[24] L. Amoore *et al.*, 'Overturning "Globalisation"', 184.

[25] J. Lemke, *Textual Politics: Discourse and Social Dynamics* (London: Taylor and Francis, 1995), p. 60.   [26] N. Fairclough, 'Language in the New Capitalism'.

[27] K. Ohmae, *Borderless World* (London: HarperCollins, (1996), p. 1.

[28] *Ibid.*

themselves and are not dependent upon the views people have of the There is hardly anything that can be done or changed except to adjust to the reality of globalisation; it looks as though globalisation is just happening to us. In the philosophy of science, this is called objectivism:

> The world consists of objects that have properties and stand in various relationships independent of human understanding. The world is as it is, no matter what any person happens to believe about it, and there is one correct "God's-Eye-View" of what the world really is like. In other words, there is a rational structure to reality, independent of the beliefs of any people, and correct reason mirrors this rational structure.[29]

If there is no agent, it is hardly surprising that there is no will. Will is absent from such discourses on globalisation. There is no discussion about how multinational companies seek unrestricted access to world markets; there is no talk about free trade, a minimal state, etc. Absence of will stems from seeing globalisation as a process without agents, as a 'natural' thing, as if globalisation were a consequence of a natural condition or some divine plan, and not of human making. Globalists present globalisation as a *consequence* and *not* as an *initiative* or a *will*.[30] It is not something some agents want to do or have wanted to do, it is rather something that is happening to us. Anonymous forces of globalisation are apparently beyond our reach and scope, and are therefore not manageable.[31]

Globalist views of the State

With all the structural features of the discourse in mind, one wonders whether globalist discourse presents the whole picture of globalisation; is it just this, or can it be something else? Can it mean something else? Do hermetically-sealed concepts and there-is-no-alternative approaches

---

[29] M. Johnson, *The Body in the Mind: The Bodily Basis of Meaning, Imagination, and Reason* (Chicago: University of Chicago, 1987), p. xi.

[30] See, among enormous literature, e.g. Cable, 'The diminished Nation-State: A study in the loss of economic power'; Ohmae, *Borderless World*; Langhorne, *The Coming of Globalization: Its Evolution and Contemporary Consequences*; S. Sassen, *Losing Control? Sovereignty in an Age of Globalization* (New York: Columbia University Press, 1995).

[31] The difference between globalisation and universalisation can be interpreted through will. Universalisation has predominantly been seen as a process of unification, a process of will, while globalisation is a project without common goal, without common base, and without a will to achieve both. Universalisation is thought to lead to common rules, while globalisation dwells on its diversity.

describe the whole picture? Because doubts and questions remain with us, we can try to look beyond the picture, and see the whole exhibition; we want to put the picture in its context.

A frame is not just a simple decoration for a picture. It frames the picture's contents, sets them in relationship with the background and acts as an intermediary between the picture and the background. A frame can be considered as a context to the picture that is in correspondence with the background of epistemic reality. It is an integral part of it, giving it structure and existence.

The globalist discourse on globalisation paints a picture without a frame. There it is, the sole picture, hermetically sealed, not needing nor wishing any correspondence with the contextual frame, speaking about itself and for itself. It is real because it proclaims itself to be real, without situating itself in a wider discourse. But is it possible to recover the frame, to look behind and beyond the simple picture in order to gain a better understanding of it? Can a frame, that has been silenced and down-graded, tell a story that is different from the message of the picture itself? Can recovering a frame lead the way to a fuller picture of the processes of globalisation? Can it change the perception of a picture of globalisation? Does the key to a proper understanding of globalisation processes lie in recovering a will that has been silenced? There have undoubtedly been many interests behind the globalisation discourse, and it has repeatedly been used as a scapegoat for many economic and political measures that would otherwise not have taken place.

Before we proceed to the contexts of the globalisation discourse, there is an issue about discourses that we need to note. Discourses may seem to be merely mediums for presenting the world more or less accurately, but there is a second, not secondary task, for discourses: that is constructing the reality.[32] In other words, discourses both describe and ascribe, present and construct the reality. This issue is important since the globalisation discourse as presented tends to omit the 'constructivist' function of discourses. This stems both from the objectivist and foundationalist convictions of a 'given world' out there.

Globalisation is presented in the globalist discourse as unintentional. This may seem as a rather benign point in analysis, but it has deep roots and more far-reaching consequences than most of us are able to predict.

---

[32] W. E. Connolly, *The Terms of Political Discourse*, 3rd ed. (Oxford: Blackwell, 1993); J. Milliken, 'The Study of Discourse in International Relations: A Critique of Research and Methods', *European Journal of International Relations* 5 (1999) 2, 225–254.

There are several reasons for seeing globalisation as unintentional actions. The disciplinary division of labour between modern social sciences has caused a vast array of different analyses that tend to describe situations or processes in the most minute detail. In doing this, they tend to forget to take into account a bigger picture, and what is even more important, they forget that social and political concepts are relational and not physical/material. They take precisely the concepts we need to explain – globalisation, states, markets, individuals – as their ready-made starting points, and do not see them as relational and historically embedded, but rather as a direct and one-dimensional mirror-like reflection of natural entities, as something fixed, constant over time and space. By thinking about them as natural, as something that is not worth questioning and redefining again and again, as something that is historically nonspecific, something that represents a starting point, they are of course thought of as unintentional, as just being there by their nature.

One of the ways to rescue independent thinking on political concepts from fixed relations among 'natural' entities is it to dissolve political forms of the state, the individual, and the market back to historically specific relations between the people who constitute them. Focusing on the state in the globalisation processes, there can be other answers besides nothing-can-be-done-because-of-globalisation.

It may be one of the consequences of the long-time Anglo-American ideological hegemony in political science that the state was put aside, since it has never found a proper place in the Anglo-American political science thinking, despite theoretical efforts to 'bring the state back in'.[33] According to Evans, 'statelessness [is the] dominant global ideology and potential institutional reality.'[34] But what is even more striking in these accounts of the state/globalisation relationship is the easy and nonreflective position of how the concepts of state and globalisation are dealt with, as if the debate about the state started only recently. In Abrams's words, 'We have come to take the state for granted as an object of political practice and political analysis while remaining quite spectacularly unclear as to what the state is.'[35]

The huge debates that have sprung up in the last decade have mainly focused on whether the state has lost its sovereignty because of the

---

[33] Cf. P. Evans, 'The Eclipse of the State? Reflections on Stateness in an Era of Globalization', *World Politics* 50 (1997) 1, 62–78.   [34] *Ibid.*, 64.

[35] P. Abrams, 'Notes on the Difficulty of Studying the State', *Journal of Historical Sociology* 1 (1988) 1, 59.

processes of globalisation, and what were and are the forces that influence
the sovereign state. Sovereignty is an important concept for the state, since
it was through the concept of sovereignty that states were internally pacified
and externally 'given' the right to pursue whatever is within their national
interest (in Realist terms), it was through the concept of sovereignty that
the state became the centre of authority and the origin of law, and became
the source of individual and collective security.[36] But the concept of the sovereignty of the state is all too easily dealt with in the state/globalisation
debate. I will put forward three objections to the views that sovereignty of
the state is being eroded in the processes of globalisation.

*Sovereignty is presented in the globalist state/globalisation discourse as an
ideal type concept.* A question that we should ask ourselves is not whether
the nation-state and with it sovereignty as its main attribute is endan-
gered; the question is rather, has there ever been a nation-state that was
actually, completely and fully sovereign in the exclusivist sense? Is there
any nation-state today that is similarly sovereign? There have always been
external challenges to the sovereignty of territorial states, and international co-operation amongst them.

Sovereignty as presented in the globalist discourse[37] is an ideal type theoretical concept, sanitised of any historical sediments and disembedded. It
is used as a 'fact'[38], as a ready-made starting point for the debate of which
genealogy is silenced. Definitions of sovereignty are amnesiastic about
their historically and socially specific character. One should not forget, for
example, that from the outset sovereignty, in practical terms, was never
more than a claim to authority[39] and that it never meant absolute control,
but only a claim to it.[40] This also does not mean that sovereignty is a static
concept and that understandings of it have not changed over the centuries;

---

[36] R. Devetak and R. Higgott, 'Justice unbound? Globalisation, states and the transformation
    of the social bond', *International Affairs* 75 (1999) 3, 485–86; J. Bartelson, *A Genealogy of
    Sovereignty* (Cambridge: Cambridge University Press, 1995).
[37] Cf. Sassen, *Losing Control? Sovereignty in an Age of Globalization.*
[38] The word 'fact' has its roots in Latin *facere*, to do, which implies that 'facts' are made.
[39] In the tradition of the Cambridge school of interpretation one must strive to recover an
    author's complex intention. See e.g. Q. Skinner 'Meaning and understanding in the
    history of ideas', in J. Tully (ed.), *Meaning and Context: Quentin Skinner and his Critics*
    (Cambridge, Polity Press, 1988), pp. 29–67. A question appears about the legitimacy of
    such a claim and what was the purpose behind it.
[40] Y. H. Ferguson and R. W. Mansbach, 'History's Revenge and Future Shock', in M. Hewson
    and T. J. Sinclair (eds.), *Approaches to Global Governance Theory* (Albany: SUNY Press,
    1999), p. 199; A. B. Murphy, 'The sovereign state system as political-territorial ideal: his-
    torical and contemporary considerations', in T. J. Biersteker and C. Weber (eds.), *State
    Sovereignty as Social Contruct* (Cambridge: Cambridge University Press, 1996), p. 87.

Bartelson has shown how the understanding of the concept of sovereignty has changed with the production of knowledge.[41]

The globalist position on sovereignty draws on elements from the theoretical postmodern supermarket. At its most obvious it is ontologically and epistemologically foundationalist and positivist, believing that sovereignty out there is a 'given' and that the only way to attain an understanding of it is through empirical experience. On the other hand, in terms of globalist ideology, it is quietly constructivist, prescribing how it should be viewed. It does not (want to?), however, ask questions from the constructivist repertoire about sovereignty itself: is it socially constructed or are the ideas about it socially constructed? Or both? What are the relations among these social constructions?

The concept of sovereignty is taken out of historic context. This mental operation is usually done by defining what sovereignty is[42] and then this view of sovereignty is, without any doubt or scepticism, compared to all possible empirical data, theses, etc in order to be able to see it in the desired light:

> Concepts are given definitional value, with it they are linked to other knowledge or concepts, they become part of a dense web of concepts that are defined in each other's terms. This is the way conceptual analysis typically begins – by closing the concept, while opening up its field of application to divergent interpretations.[43]

What we must realise is that the meaning and references of words are not constant through the ages and that it is necessary to recover the context in which various works were written in order to understand them.[44] With regard to the sovereignty of a state this operation is done by defining what the concept of sovereignty is, without addressing, or at least pointing at, special historical circumstances that surrounded its development. Definitions of sovereignty are usually based on a sixteenth and seventeenth-century reasoning about the situation when nation-states first became sovereign through the military control of a particular space, and the aspirations of rulers about its absolute control.[45] Such mental operations are methodologically doubtful since they describe today's situation in seventeenth-century terms. It is then very easy to say that states are no longer fully sovereign, when faced with contemporary

---

[41] Bartelson, *A Genealogy of Sovereignty*.
[42] F. H. Hinsley, *Sovereignty* (Cambridge: Cambridge University Press, 1986).
[43] Bartelson, *A Genealogy of Sovereignty*, p. 14.   [44] *Ibid.*, p. 61.
[45] See A. Giddens, *The Nation-state and Violence* (Cambridge: Polity Press, 1985).

social circumstances (such as the appearance of globalising forces). Concepts appear as if they are defined once and for all, while the world and social circumstances change constantly. Such reasoning juxtaposes evolutionary circumstances to static concepts. The concepts, which are defined *a priori*, should not aspire to *posteriori* values or, better still, we should not think in these terms.

This is, of course, not to say that states in their institutional arrangements do not change. Globalisation may have major repercussions not only for capitalism, such as a supraterritorial mode of organisation (transnational corporations, global strategic alliances and worldwide business associations[46]) but also for its institutional arrangements, since with a change in economic role states tend to change in their institutional form as well.[47] But this does not go to say that states are withering away because of globalisation processes. It has been shown in numerous accounts and with different types of arguments that the state is not withering away.[48] In empirical terms this can be identified through the rise of states' budgets during the 1990s, through facilitation by states of global firms' operations and profits with suitably constructed property guarantees, tax regimes, labour laws, investment codes, currency regulations and police protection.[49] The growth in importance of the international markets does not mean that the state is doomed because it is ever more dependent on international trade.[50] Evans argues that although higher shares of trade may increase a state's vulnerability, a larger public sector (which is associated with a stronger state) provides an efficient counterweight.[51] Examples of East Asian strong states have shown that 'high stateness' can be a competitive advantage in a globalising economy. Singapore is the most obvious case in point.[52]

---

[46] Scholte, '*Global Capitalism and the State*', 429.
[47] See B. Jessop, *State Theory: Putting the Capitalist State in its Place* (Cambridge: Polity Press, 1990), p. 355; P.G. Cerny, 'The dynamics of financial globalisation: Technology, market structure, and policy response', *Policy Sciences* 27 (1994) 4, 319–342.
[48] E.g. M. Mann, 'Has globalisation ended the rise and rise of the nation-state?' *Review of International Political Economy* 4 (1997) 3, 472–496; Weiss, 'Globalization and the myth of the powerless State', C. Hay and D. Marsh, 'Introduction: demystifying globalization', in C. Hay and D. Marsh (eds.) *Demystifying Globalization* (Basingstroke, Palgrave, 2000), 1–17.   [49] Scholte, 'Global Capitalism and the State', 442
[50] Evans, 'The Eclipse of the State?', 67.   [51] *Ibid.*, 67–68.
[52] Evans, 'The Eclipse of the State?', 69–70; K.-H. Chen, 'Not yet the postcolonial era: the (super) nation-state and transnationalism of cultural studies: Response to Ang and Stratton', *Cultural Studies* 10 (1996) 1, 37–70; D. Lam and C. Clark, 'Beyond the developmental state: the cultural roots of 'guerrilla capitalism' in Taiwan', *Governance* 7 (1994) 4, 412–430; Z. Önis, 'The logic of the developmental state', *Comparative Politics* 24

Economic globalisation and development

Globalists tend to agree that economic globalisation is a positive-sum game.[53] Property markets, if unencumbered, will produce global economic growth and maximise social returns, based on some notion of Pareto optimality; markets as self-standing entities that operate by inertia would be disrupted in the most efficient allocation of resources if political interference occurred.

The globalists' view of economic globalisation draws from the classical and neoclassical economic philosophy that argue that unencumbered markets are the natural condition, while state-regulated markets are artificial. Contrary to that, Polanyi argued that '[t]he road to the free market was opened and kept open by an enormous increase in continuous, centrally organised and controlled interventionism.'[54] Thus, markets have a tendency towards regulation and all markets in history have been regulated. It is the power of the regulator (i.e. the power of the state) that keeps markets free so that they do not lapse into monopolies.

The same pattern can be observed on the global level. '[G]lobal laissez-faire doesn't just come into being by the process of evolution. It has to be introduced by acts of political power just like protectionism.'[55] One can observe this in acknowledging the role of the World Trade Organization as a controller of free trade on a worldwide scale, or by acknowledging the role national governments play in enacting policies such as lifting the controls on capital. The power of states in international trade organisations is the power that keeps free trade functioning; actors in global markets cannot operate without some kind of regulation from the outside, i.e. externally to the markets themselves. What is required is at least some system of law, or its equivalent, which guarantees the performance of contracts.

Economic growth due to economic globalisation is consistently conflated with development. Globalists maintain that spill-over effects occur

(1991) 1, 109–126; R. Wade, 'State intervention in 'outward-looking' development: neoclassical theory and Taiwanese practice', in White, G. (ed.), *Developmental States in East Asia* (London: Macmillan, 1988), 30–67; G. White and R. Wade, 'Developmental states and markets in East Asia: an introduction', in G. White (ed.), *Developmental States in East Asia* (London: Macmillan, 1988), pp. 1–29.

[53] See, e. g. Horsman and Marshall, *After the Nation-State*; Ohmae, *Borderless World*.
[54] K. Polanyi, *The Great Transformation: The Political and Economic Origins of Our Time* (Boston: Beacon Press, 1944), p. 140.
[55] E. Hobsbawm, 'The big picture: the death of neo-liberalism', *Marxism Today*, November/December 1998, 5.

from the economic growth to other areas and that eventually there will be
a trickle-down effect of globalisation that will be of benefit to all people.
Li and Reuveny have empirically assessed the effects of economic globalisation on the levels of democracy from 1970 to 1996 for 127 countries.[56]
They analysed effects of four aspects of economic globalisation: trade
openness, foreign direct investment inflows, portfolio investment
inflows, and the spread of democratic ideas across countries, and found
that trade openness and portfolio investment inflows negatively affect
democracy. The effect of trade openness is constant over time, whilst the
negative effect of portfolio investment strengthens. Foreign direct inflows
positively affect democracy, but the effect weakens over time. The spread
of democratic ideas promotes democracy persistently over time.[57]

   It is hardly any secret that unencumbered economic globalisation does
not deliver the benefits of development equally to all; there is a persistent
need for regulations that would harness global markets and compensate
for the asymmetrical costs and benefits of economic globalisation.[58]
Political will is crucial in order not to succumb to the 'there-is-nothing-
that-can-be-done' position. There have been many suggestions on how to
govern economic globalisation, from unilateralism of a hegemonic
nature, to global governance based on global democratic institutions or
even cosmopolitan democracy. Common to all approaches is the assertion that since we have a global economy there is also a need for global
polity that would deliver global public goods.

   Debates about global governance of economic globalisation have
developed in many directions, though most of them differ on two
issues: the extent, and the nature, of global governance. Many authors
feel that regulatory mechanisms for global governance are not yet in
place and that there is a need for a set of institutions that would work
towards delivering global public goods.[59] Others point out that global
regulatory mechanisms already exist in the form of more than 3600
multilateral treaties concluded mainly in the second half of the twentieth century, governing all spheres of global activities:[60] in the form of

---

[56] Q. Li and R. Reuveny, 'Economic globalisation and democracy: an empirical analysis',
   British Journal of Political Science 33 (2003) 1, 29–54.   [57] *Ibid.*, 30.
[58] For example, Griffin, *'Economic Globalisation'*, p. 792, mentions that there is continuing
   discrimination against products of particular importance to low income countries, where
   as a rule slower processes of liberalisation of trade occur (for products like food, textiles,
   clothing, footwear, leather products – in general labour-intensive products).
[59] Cf., *inter alia*, Griffin, *'Economic Globalisation'*, pp. 789–807.
[60] See, among many, Scholte, 'Governing economic globalization: a response to Keith
   Griffin', 1050.

transgovernmental regulation of global economic affairs, which has emerged since the 1970s;[61] and in the form of private mechanisms[62] and their role in global economy.[63]

Authors also differ in their opinions regarding the nature of global governance mechanisms, with some seeing similarities between the early stages of nation-building and what is happening today on the global level, and calling for the establishment of a similar set of institutions to those within the nation-state, which provide global public goods as we know them on nation-state level.[64] Others insist that governing the global economy is qualitatively different from governing the national economy.[65] Scholte suggests that:

> The global economy is not giving rise to a unitary, centralised governance apparatus (a "global state") in the way that the national economy previously stimulated the growth of the territorial state. On the contrary, regulation of global economic activities is a polycentric and multi-scalar affair, involving multiple and widely dispersed agencies across subnational, national and supranational spheres.[66]

A fourth democratic wave (*pace*: Huntington[67]) will not be a simple transposing of patterns of national democratic institutions to the global level. There are several practical (e.g. one person/one vote or one country/one vote) and philosophical issues underlying operations of the nation-state that would need different elaboration for the global level. New ways for democratisation of global governance will have to be found, based on different values.

All this having been said, it is important to note that global governance is not necessarily in contradiction and competition with the state. Global governance can work best on the multi-scalar basis, applying different approaches for different levels of problems arising. Global governance works best when agencies of different scales and dimensions cooperate for the common goal.

---

[61] Group of Eight (G8), Group of Ten (G10), Group of Twenty (G20).
[62] For example the Internet Corporation for Assigned Names and Numbers (ICANN).
[63] Scholte, 'Governing economic globalization: a response to Keith Griffin', 1050.
[64] Cf. J. Galtung, 'Imagining Global Democracy', *Development and Change* 35 (2004) 5, 1073–1079; Griffin, '*Economic Globalisation*', pp. 789–807.
[65] E.g. Scholte, 'Governing economic globalization: a response to Keith Griffin', 1049–1056.
[66] *Ibid.*, 1052.
[67] S. P. Huntington, *The Third Wave: Democratization in the Late Twentieth Century* (Norman: University of Oklahoma Press, 1991).

Democratic global governance and human rights

However, global governance is faced with yet another challenge, more
fundamental and salient than the practical issues of who does what, and
in what manner. It is the question, on what grounds should humanity
build a set of global institutions capable of supplying global public
goods?[68] What can be a common moral ground on which to base (democratic) global governance?

States are, in my opinion, still the prime bearers of responsibility
for human rights protection. The popular post-World War II thesis of
engines of development that argued that the economic development
of states will automatically generate improved human rights practice[69] has
in many instances proven false.[70] It has been shown that economic development does not bring improved human rights practices on its
own. Current trends in globalist thinking argue that transnational corporations will generate better human rights records because of the international pressures of global civil society on them.[71] But neither individuals
nor transnational corporations are signatories of international treaties
defining and protecting human rights; states are ultimately the only agents
held legally accountable for violations of human rights standards.[72] The
discussion referred to above has shown that states are far from 'withering'
away, in some cases growing even stronger, institutionally, in the era of economic globalisation. Stronger states have, in fact, proved to be a mixed
blessing for human rights protection (with the level of protection and exercise of power of the state depending upon the cultural context).

Yet that does not mean that states are satisfactory agencies for the protection of human rights in the era of economic globalisation, which has
brought about issues that are outside the traditional division of the world
into states. Human rights are of such a character, as envisaged in the 1948

---

[68] By 'global public goods' I mean peace, equity, security, healthy environment, etc.

[69] For positive correlation between MNCs and human rights in the third world, see
for example W. H. Meyer. 'Human rights and MNCs: theory versus quantitative analysis', *Human Rights Quarterly* 18 (1996) 2, 368–397 and W. H. Meyer, 'Confirming,
infirming, and "falsifying" theories of human rights: reflections on Smith, Bolyard,
and Ippolito through the lens of lakatos', *Human Rights Quarterly* 21 (1999) 1,
220–228.

[70] See J. G. Smith, M. Bolyard, and A. Ippolito, 'Human rights and the global economy: a
response to Meyer', *Human Rights Quarterly* 21 (1999) 1, 207–219.

[71] Griffin, '*Economic Globalisation*'.

[72] Smith, Bolyard, and Ippolito, 'Human rights and the global economy: a response to
Meyer',

Universal Declaration of Human Rights[73] and stressed again in paragraph 5 of the 1993 Vienna Declaration and Programme of Action of the World Conference on Human Rights;[74] not just international, but also global, insofar as they are norms that transcend the state-system of the world. Human rights are global in their nature and should be protected and enforced globally, in a multi-scalar and multi-dimensional way. Dispersed agencies of global governance must be entrusted with a role in protecting human rights.

Human rights can serve as a framework for national and global policy choices: 'When poorer countries are tempted or pressured (for example, in the course of structural adjustment reforms) to cut social spending and social budgets or reduce the provision of health care, education, or food security for the poor, the human rights framework affirms that economic, social, and cultural rights must be respected.'[75]

Human rights can serve as a framework for a set of supranational institutions, agencies and networks that are able to deal with a range of transnational issues. They can be a moral code for institutions, agencies and networks according to which they can judge and regulate processes of economic globalisation on all levels, all dimensions, all scales, from village to supraterritorial integration.

The European Union has taken a step in this direction by signing and proclaiming the Charter of Fundamental Rights of the European Union.[76] Integration on a supranational level demands a catalogue of rights that are aimed at protecting citizens not just against workings of their own states, but also against supranational institutions. Romano Prodi, president of the European Commission, has expressed this thus:

> In the eyes of the European Commission, by proclaiming the Charter of Fundamental Rights, the European Union institutions have committed themselves to respecting the Charter in everything they do and in every

[73] United Nations, 'Universal Declaration of Human Rights' (1948), http://www.un.org/Overview/rights.html (accessed: 12 May 2006).
[74] United Nations – World Conference on Human Rights, 'Vienna Declaration and Programme of Action' (1993), http://www.unhchr.ch/huridocda/huridoca.nsf/(Symbol)/A.CONF.157.23.En?OpenDocument (accessed: 12 May 2006).
[75] M. Robinson, 'Shaping Globalization: The Role of Human Rights', Annual Meeting of the American Society of International Law (Washington: American Society of International Law, 2003), 11.
[76] European Commission, 'Charter of Fundamental Rights of the European Union' (2000), http://ec.europa.eu/justice_home/unit/charte/index_en.html (accessed: 12 May 2006).

policy they promote ... The citizens of Europe can rely on the
Commission to ensure that the Charter will be respected . . .[77]

Conclusion

Seeing human rights as a framework for a set of global institutions, agencies and networks will inevitably spark criticism of advocates of cultural
relativism of human rights. Overexerted Western influence on global institutions in the form of 'Western' human rights will be identified. The West
will be accused of steering global governance mechanisms according to its
moral code. But human rights as a framework for global governance should
not be seen as an end-state of affairs. They should be looked at as a process,
in the constructionist sense, constantly in the making, being enriched by
different local, regional, national, and supranational experiences.

If seen in this way, human rights have the potential to become a universal moral code for those actions that escape traditional control of the
state-system. The multiscalar, deregulated and decentred world of today
needs global public goods and equal development delivered by global
institutions. Relying solely on the fortunes and misfortunes of market
mechanisms will not solve the problems. Concerted global political
action and innovative thinking might.

Bibliography

Abrams, P., 'Notes on the Difficulty of Studying the State', *Journal of Historical
Sociology* 1 (1988) 1, 58–89
Amoore, L., Dodgson, R., Gills, B. K., Langley P., Marshall, D. and Watson, I.,
'Overturning "Globalisation": Resisting the Theological, Reclaiming the
"Political"', *New Political Economy* 2 (1997) 1, 179–195
Barry Jones, R. J., 'Globalization and Change in the International Political
Economy: Overview', *International Affairs* 75 (1999) 2, 357–367.
Bartelson, J., *A Genealogy of Sovereignty* (Cambridge: Cambridge University Press,
1995)
'Second Natures: Is the State Identical with Itself?' *European Journal of
International Relations* 4 (1998) 3, 295–326
'Three Concepts of Globalisation', *International Sociology* 15 (2000) 2, 180–96
Becker, T. C. and Slaton, C. D., *The Future of Teledemocracy* (Westport, CT/
London: Praeger, 2000)

---

[77] R. Prodi, 'Statement by the President of the European Commisission' (2000), http://www.
europarl.eu.int/charter/default_en.htm (accessed: 14 November 2005).

Brittan, L., 'The contribution of the WTO Millennium Round to Globalization: An EU view', in Baudenbacher, C. and Busek, E. (eds.), *Europa im Zeitalter der Globalisierung: Vorträge des 1. DDr. Herbert Batliner Symposiums* (Vienna: Manz, 2000)

Cable, V., 'The Diminished Nation-State: A Study in the Loss of Economic Power', *Daedalus* 124 (1995) 2, 23–53

Cerny, P. G., 'The Dynamics of Financial Globalisation: Technology, Market Structure, and Policy Response', *Policy Sciences* 27 (1994) 4, 319–342

Chen, K.-H., 'Not Yet the Postcolonial Era: The (Super) Nation-State and Transnationalism of Cultural Studies: Response to Ang and Stratton', *Cultural Studies* 10 (1996) 1, 37–70

Connolly, W. E., *The Terms of Political Discourse*, 3rd ed. (Oxford: Blackwell, 1993)

Crook, C., 'The Future of the State', *The Economist* 344 (20 September 1997) 8035, 57

Devetak, R. and Higgott, R., 'Justice Unbound? Globalisation, States and the Transformation of the Social Bond', *International Affairs* 75 (1999) 3, 483–498

Drčar Murko, M., 'En sam svet, če nam je prav ali ne', [One World – Whether We Like it or Not], *Delo*, 17 September 2002, 1

Drnovšek, J., 'Strateški svet za nacionalna vprašanja: "Vstop Slovenije v NATO ne bo ogrozil slovenske nacionalne identitete" ', [Strategic Council for Security Issues meeting: 'Slovenia's national identity will not be threatened by joining NATO'], 22 July 2002, http://nato.gov.si/slo/novinarsko-sredisce/sporocila-za-javnost/1573/ (accessed: 1 June 2006)

Dunn, J., *Contemporary Crisis of the Nation-State?* (Oxford: Blackwell, 1995)

European Commission, 'Charter of Fundamental Rights of the European Union' (2000), http://ec.europa.eu/justice_home/unit/charte/index_en.html (accessed: 12 May 2006)

Evans, P., 'The Eclipse of the State? Reflections on Stateness in an Era of Globalization', *World Politics* 50 (1997) 1, 62–87

Fairclough, N., 'Language in the New Capitalism', http://www.cddc.vt.edu/host/lnc/papers/fair_lnc.doc (accessed: 1 June 2006)

Farr, J., 'Understanding Conceptual Change Politically.' in Ball, T., Farr, J. and Hanson, R. L. (eds.), *Political Innovation and Conceptual Change* (Cambridge: Cambridge University Press, 1989), pp. 24–49

Ferguson, Y. H. and Mansbach, R. W., 'History's Revenge and Future Shock', in Hewson, M. and Sinclair, T. J. (eds.), *Approaches to Global Governance Theory* (Albany: SUNY Press, 1999), pp. 197–238

Friedman, T. L., *The Lexus and the Olive Tree* (New York: HarperCollins, 1999)

Galtung, J., 'Imagining Global Democracy', *Development and Change* 35 (2004) 5, 1073–1079

Giddens, A., *The Nation-state and Violence* (Cambridge, Polity Press, 1985)

Gray, J., False Dawn, *The Delusions of Global Capitalism* (London: Granta Books, 1999)

Griffin, K., 'Economic Globalisation and Institutions of Global Governance', *Development and Change* 34 (2003) 5, 789–807

Harrison, G., 'Why Economic Globalisation is Not Enough,' *Development and Change* 35 (2004) 5, 1037–1047

Higgott, R. and Payne, A., 'Introduction: Towards a New Political Economy of Globalization', in Higgott, R. and Payne, A. (eds.), *The New Political Economy of Globalization*, (Cheltenham: Edward Elgar Publishing, 2000), pp. ix–xxiv

Hinsley, F. H., *Sovereignty* (Cambridge: Cambridge University Press, 1986)

Hirst, P. and Thompson, G. 'Globalization and the Future of the Nation State', *Economy and Society* 24 (1995) 3, 408–442

Hobsbawm, E., 'The Big Picture: The Death Of Neo-Liberalism', *Marxism Today* (November/December 1998), 4–8

Hobson, J. M. and Ramesh, M., 'Globalization Makes of States What States Make of It: Between Agency and Structure in the State/Globalisation Debate', *New Political Economy* 7 (2002) 1, 5–22

Horsman, M. and Marshall, A., *After the Nation-State: Citizens, Tribalism and the New World Disorder* (London: HarperCollins, 1994)

Huntington, S. P., *The Third Wave: Democratization in the Late Twentieth Century* (Norman: University of Oklahoma Press, 1991)

Jessop, B., *State Theory: Putting the Capitalist State in its Place* (Cambridge: Polity Press, 1990)

Johnson, M., *The Body in the Mind: The Bodily Basis of Meaning, Imagination, and Reason* (Chicago: University of Chicago, 1987)

Lam, D. and Clark, C., 'Beyond the Developmental State: The Cultural Roots of "Guerrilla Capitalism" in Taiwan', *Governance* 7 (1994) 4, 412–430

Langhorne, R., *The Coming of Globalization: Its Evolution and Contemporary Cosequences* (Basingstroke/New York: Palgrave, 2001)

Lemke, J., *Textual Politics: Discourse and Social Dynamics* (London: Taylor and Francis, 1995)

Li, Q. and Reuveny, R., 'Economic Globalisation and Democracy: An Empirical Analysis', *British Journal of Political Science* 33 (2003) 1, 29–54

Mann, M., 'Has Globalisation Ended the Rise and rise of the Nation-state?' *Review of International Political Economy* 4 (1997) 3, 472–496

Milliken, J., 'The Study of Discourse in International Relations: A Critique of Research and Methods', *European Journal of International Relations* 5 (1999) 2, 225–254

Meyer. W. H., 'Human Rights and MNCs: Theory Versus Quantitative Analysis', *Human Rights Quarterly* 18 (1996) 2, 368–397

Meyer, W. H., 'Confirming, Infirming, and "Falsifying" Theories of Human Rights:

Reflections on Smith, Bolyard, and Ippolito Through the Lens of Lakatos', *Human Rights Quarterly* 21 (1999) 1, 220–228

Moore, M., 'In Praise of the Future,' Speech to the Canterbury Employers Chamber of Commerce, Christchurch, New Zealand, 14 August 2000, http://www. wto.org/english/news_e/spmm_e/spmm34_e.htm (accessed: 10 November 2001)

Murphy, A. B., 'The Sovereign State System as Political-Territorial Ideal: Historical and contemporary considerations', in Biersteker, T. J. and Weber, C. (eds.), *State Sovereignty as Social Contruct* (Cambridge: Cambridge University Press, 1996), pp. 81–120

Ohmae, K., *Borderless World* (London: HarperCollins, 1996)

Offe, K., *Contradictions of the Welfare State* (London: Hutchinson, 1984)

Önis, Z., 'The Logic of the Developmental State', *Comparative Politics* 24 (1991) 1, 109–126

Panitch, L., 'Globalisation and the State', in Miliband, R. and Panitch, L. (eds.), *Socialist Register 1994: Between Globalism and Nationalism* (London: Merlin Press, 1995), pp. 60–93

Polanyi, K., *The Great Transformation: The Political and Economic Origins of Our Time* (Boston: Beacon Press, 1944)

Prodi, R., 'Statement by the President of the European Commission' (2000), http://www.europarl.eu.int/charter/default_en.htm (accessed: 14 November 2005)

Reich, R. B., *The Work of Nations* (London: Simon & Schuster, 1993)

Robinson, M., 'Shaping Globalization: The Role of Human Rights', Annual Meeting of the American Society of International Law (Washington: American Society of International Law, 2003)

Rupel, D., 'Uveljavljanje slovenske identitete v procesih globalizacije ['Asserting Slovenian Identity in the Processes of Globalisation'], in D. Rupel, *Prevzem zgodbe o uspehu* (Ljubljana, Zaloûba Mladinska knjiga, 2004), pp. 570–574

Sassen, S., *Losing Control? Sovereignty in an Age of Globalization* (New York: Columbia University Press, 1995)

Scholte, J.-A., 'Global Capitalism and the State', *International Affairs* 73 (1997) 3, 427–452

Scholte, J.-A., 'Governing Economic Globalization: A Response to Keith Griffin', *Development and Change* 35 (2004) 5, 1049–1056

Skinner, Q., 'Meaning and Understanding in the History of Ideas', in Tully, J. (ed.), *Meaning and Context: Quentin Skinner and his Critics* (Cambridge: Polity Press, 1988), pp. 29–67

Smith, J. G., Bolyard, M. and Ippolito, A., 'Human Rights and the Global Economy: A Response to Meyer', *Human Rights Quarterly* 21 (1999) 1, 207–219

Socialist International, 'Declaration of Paris – The Challenges of Globalization'

The XXI Congress of the Socialist International, Paris, 8–10 November
    1999, http://www.socialistinternational.org/5Congress/XXI-PARIS/ DeclParis-
    e.html (accessed: 25 September 2005)
Strange, S., 'The Defective State', *Daedalus* 124 (1995) 2, 55–74
Wade, R., 'State Intervention in "Outward-looking" Development: Neoclassical
    Theory and Taiwanese Practice', in White, G. (ed.), *Developmental States in
    East Asia* (London: Macmillan, 1988), pp. 30–67
Walker, R. B. J., *Inside/Outside: International Relations as Political Theory*
    (Cambridge: Cambridge University Press, 1993)
Weiss, L., 'Globalization and the Myth of the Powerless State.' *New Left Review* 225
    (1997), 3–27
Weldes, J., Globalization is Science Fiction.' *Millennium: Journal of International
    Studies* 30 (2001) 3, 647–667
White, G. and Wade, R., 'Developmental States and Markets in East Asia: an
    Introduction', in White, G. (ed.), *Developmental States in East Asia* (London:
    Macmillan, 1988), pp. 1–29
Zysman, J., 'The Myth of "Global" Economy: Enduring National Foundations and
    Emerging Regional Realities', *New Political Economy* 1 (1996) 2, 157–184

Towards a Theory of Global Ethics in Support of Human Rights

GEORGE ULRICH

'Linking human rights with ethics and globalisation represents a connection whose time has come. And yet the task is daunting.'

Mary Robinson, 2002[1]

Introduction

The vision articulated by Mary Robinson, then UN High Commissioner for Human Rights, in a lecture presented at the University of Tübingen in January 2002, epitomises an important turn in the contemporary concept of international human rights. This is the close linking of human rights with a project of global ethics, indeed the framing of human rights as a vehicle and expression of a global ethic.

A predominant feature of international relations in the post-World War II era is the codification of human rights in the form of international law.[2] Following the adoption of the Universal Declaration of Human Rights (UDHR)[3] in 1948, the International Convention Against All Forms of Racial Discrimination (ICERD),[4] the International Covenant on Civil and Political Rights (ICCPR),[5] the International Covenant on Economic, Social and Cultural Rights (ICESCR),[6] the International Convention Against All Forms of Discrimination Against Women (ICEDAW),[7] the

---

[1] M. Robinson, 'Ethics, Human Rights and Globalization', Second Global Ethic Lecture, The Global Ethic Foundation, University of Tübingen, Germany, 21 January 2002, p. 1; available at http://www.weltethos.org/dat_eng/st_9e_xx/9e_144.htm#top (last accessed: 25 January 2006).

[2] For a comprehensive overview of international human rights law and protection mechanisms, see M. Nowak, *Introduction to the International Human Rights Regime* (Leiden: Martinus Nijhoff Publishers, 2003). [3] GA Res 217 A (III) of 10 December 1948.

[4] GA Res 2106 (XX) of 21 December 1965, entered into force 4 January 1969.

[5] GA Res 2200A (XXI) of 16 December 1966, entered into force 23 March 1976.

[6] GA Res 2200A (XXI) of 16 December 1966, entered into force 3 January 1976.

[7] GA Res 34/180 of 18 December 1979, entered into force 3 September 1981.

Convention Against Torture (CAT),[8] and the Convention on the Rights of the Child (CRC)[9] all mark milestones in a process of human rights standard-setting, which has now been largely accomplished, if not entirely completed.[10] Parallel developments have occurred in a regional context in Europe, the Americas, and Africa with the European Convention on Human Rights (ECHR), the American Convention on Human Rights (ACHR), and the African Charter on Human and Peoples' Rights (ACHPR), respectively.[11] Since the end of the Cold War period, the emphasis of the international community has increasingly shifted to realising the established human rights standards in practice.[12] The International Criminal Tribunals set up after the genocides and crimes against humanity in the Former Republic of Yugoslavia (ICTY)[13] and in Rwanda (ICTR),[14] the Special Court in Sierra Leone,[15] and the International Criminal Court (ICC),[16] all mark highly important recent steps towards reinforcing legal protection mechanisms for human rights. The European Court of Human Rights and the Inter-American Court of Human Rights have over a period of several decades developed an even more advanced body of human rights jurisprudence and present the most advanced examples of legal enforcement of human rights at the regional level.[17]

[8] GA Res 39/46 of 10 December 1984, entered into force, 26 June 1987.
[9] GA Res 44/25 of 20 November 1989, entered into force 2 September 1990.
[10] The International Convention on the Protection of the Rights of All Migrant Workers and Members of Their Families, adopted in 1990 and entered into force in 2003, is an example of continued standard-setting within the UN context; this convention has, however, not yet been sufficiently widely ratified to be generally counted among the 'core' UN human rights instruments (GA Res. 45/158, annex, 45 UN GAOR Supp. (No. 49A) at 262, UN Doc. A/45/49 (1990)).
[11] 1950 European Convention for the Protection of Human Rights and Fundamental Freedoms as amended by Protocol No. 11, available at http://conventions.coe.int/treaty/en/Treaties/Html/005.htm (last accessed: 25 January 2006); American Convention on Human Rights, adopted on 22 November 1969, OAS Treaty Series No. 36, entered into force July 18, 1978; African Charter on Human and Peoples' Rights adopted June 27, 1981, OAU Doc. CAB/LEG/67/3 rev. 5, 21 I.L.M. 58 (1982), entered into force 21 October 1986.
[12] The practices of the UN treaty monitoring bodies and non-conventional mechanisms are especially indicative in this regard. Details are available at http://www.ohchr.org/english/bodies/index.htm (last accessed: 25 January 2006). The Vienna World Conference on Human Rights in 1993 likewise epitomises this tendency, as does the creation of the UN Office of the High Commissioner for Human Rights (OHCHR), also in 1993.
[13] SC Res 827 of 25 May 1993.   [14] SC Res 955 of 8 November 1994.
[15] For information, see http://www.sc-sl.org/about.html (last accessed: 25 January 2006).
[16] UN Doc. A/CONF.183/9 of 17 July 1998, entered into force 1 July 2002.
[17] For an overview of the European and American Courts case-law, see, respectively, C. Ovey and R. White *The European Convention on Human Rights* (Oxford: Oxford University Press, 2002, 3rd ed.) and A. A. Cançado Trinidade, 'The Inter-American System of

Viewed in a global context it is evident, however, that human rights norms do not function exclusively, or even predominantly, as legal norms. There are several notable reasons for this, spanning from the scarcity and relative weakness of international adjudication mechanisms to the frequent assertion of human rights claims in contexts where they have no legal force, such as vis-à-vis states that have not ratified a given convention, or have done so with reservations; vis-à-vis so-called non-state actors (transnational corporations, intergovernmental organisations, etc.); and vis-à-vis governments and populations in affluent countries in respect to the realisation of human rights in other parts of the world (so-called 'international obligations'). Such a tendency to assert human rights outside of established legal contexts is not in and of itself surprising, for, after all, human rights demand vigilant attention especially in contexts in which they are not well protected. Yet this indicates a pattern whereby human rights are asserted with a primary ethical or moral[18] appeal, serving first and foremost to add legitimacy to policy objectives at the national and international levels.

There is another contemporary development, closely related to the proliferation of extra-legal ways of invoking and instrumentalising international human rights, which needs to be brought into focus in the present context. This has to do with a certain shift in the underlying concept of human rights, as championed in widespread circles of the international human rights community in the post-Cold War era. Stated in abstract terms, this may be characterised as a shift from conceiving human rights as a set of norms designed primarily to curb the abuse of state power and epitomised by the protection of the lone dissident to conceiving human rights more broadly as a set of tools to advance social justice on a global scale. Such an expanded human rights agenda – as reflected in countless speeches by prominent UN personalities, in the UN Millennium Development Goals,[19] and in Amnesty International's

---

Protection of Human Rights: The Developing Case-Law of the Inter-American Court of Human Rights (1982–2005)' in I. F. Gomez and K. De Feyter (eds.), *International Protection of Human Rights at the Dawn of the Twenty-First Century* (Bilbao: University of Deusto/EIUC, 2005).

[18] It should be noted that I make no systematic distinction in the present chapter between ethics and morals. The two concepts (and their various derivatives) tend in practice to be used interchangeably, and whatever distinctions are sometimes introduced do not clearly apply in the present context.

[19] United Nations Millennium Declaration, GA Res 55/2, 18 September 2000. Further information is available at http://www.un.org/millenniumgoals (last accessed: 25 January 2006).

expanded mandate,[20] just to mention a few examples – retains the classical focus on protecting civil liberties and the integrity of the individual person but in addition mobilises human rights in relation to issues such as social and economic development, global poverty reduction, universal access to essential medicines, and as a consequence of such objectives, also in relation to enhanced international peace and security.[21] In earlier decades, these agendas were not unified to the same degree, and certainly not under the banner of human rights. To the contrary, the political left which ostensibly spearheaded social justice and solidarity with the impoverished South was openly suspicious of the 'bourgeois' ideology of human rights, if not directly hostile to it. This may in part have been due to the strictures of established Marxist doctrine, but the schism was also more fundamentally a matter of seeing the predominantly legal protection of human rights and the pursuit of global social justice as two distinct causes.

It should be noted that the development that I am here trying to get into focus is not only a matter of insisting on the conceptual and practical unity of the different so-called generations of human rights, i.e. civil and political rights on the one hand and economic, social and cultural rights on the other hand. Certainly this is part of the picture, but it is also a matter of putting human rights norms to work in areas beyond the core nexus of state and individual. Human rights thus come to serve as a reference point for horizontal relations between individual citizens as well as for defining social responsibilities of private actors in the economic realm, of international organisations in shaping global policies and development opportunities, and of affluent nations in facilitating the realisation of human rights world wide.

It is sometimes said that human rights have come to resemble a new religion. However, human rights defenders widely resent this analogy – and I tend to agree with them – on the grounds that human rights are not

---

[20] Over the years Amnesty International has expanded its mandate to include human rights violations committed by non-state actors as well as to include focus on the realisation of economic, social and cultural rights. Further details are available at http://web. amnesty.org/pages/aboutai-faq-eng; (last accessed: 25 January 2006).

[21] In a much quoted passage from his recent proposal for UN reform *In larger Freedom*, UN Secretary-General Kofi Annan note that 'we will not enjoy development without security, we will not enjoy security without development, and we will not enjoy either without respect for human rights. Unless all these causes are advanced, none will succeed' (*In larger freedom: towards development, security and human rights for all*. Report of the Secretary-General, UN Doc. A/59/2005 of 21 March 2005, at 17; available at http://www.un.org/largerfreedom (last accessed: 25 January 2006).

a matter of faith, do not address nearly the range of life issues covered by religion, and are at any rate intended to be compatible with diverse religious commitments. This point will be taken up in further detail below. Another way of capturing the shift in question would be to view human rights as a political platform for pursuing social justice after the decline of socialist ideologies No doubt this interpretation has some merit, yet the operative contemporary concept of human rights is not explicitly political in a partisan sense (which would anyhow run into confrontation with an underlying presumption about political neutrality in the sense that human rights norms are presumed to be sufficiently general to be binding upon all parties across the political spectrum and thus to establish a framework within which legitimate political disagreement can unfold rather than constitute a particular political agenda).

What we are witnessing, I would suggest, is multiple mutually supporting indications that human rights are increasingly being cast in the context of a *global ethical commitment.* Robinson, as we have seen, has given voice to this trend by baptizing the campaign for human rights launched upon her retirement as UN High Commissioner for Human Rights as an initiative for 'ethical globalisation'.[22] Underlying this agenda is a perception of globalisation processes as inherently ambiguous. They contribute to an unprecedented increase of wealth on a global scale, yet co-produce widespread impoverishment and deepening social imbalances. Economic globalisation and the expansion of communication technologies facilitate the integration of individuals and institutions over great distances, but at the same time marginalise large segments of the world's population from vital flows of goods and information in ways that have a detrimental impact on these communities' affluence, well-being, and security. The exponentially expanding dissemination of knowledge and information on a global scale at the same time serves as a powerful vehicle for disinformation, and the inter-communal understanding and tolerance that one should hope would result from increased contacts and exposure is sometimes overshadowed by manifestations of fundamentalism, ethnic and religious intolerance, and new patterns of discrimination, which also seem to be characteristic by-products of globalisation.[23] In this historical context, there is therefore a vital need to

---

[22] See www.eginitiative.org (last accessed: 25 January 2006).

[23] The Declaration and Programme of Action emerging from the World Conference against Racism, Racial Discrimination, Xenophobia and Related Intolerance, Durban 2001, display a heightened degree of concern about the ambiguities of globalisation. The Preamble thus '[recognises] both the challenges and opportunities presented by an

forge a normative framework within which to guide the outcome of globalisation. 'We are at the edge of a big idea', Robinson asserts, '– the shaping of ethical globalisation.'[24]

The view that human rights as codified in international law may be found to supply the required normative framework for an ethical shaping of globalisation is not peculiar to human rights advocates such as Mary Robinson; it increasingly finds support among business leaders and political elites, as well as within bureaucracies and institutional structures entrusted with the exercise of public authority.[25] However, the aspiration to assert human rights as a global ethic, while evocative, is not straightforward. In order to render the undertaking viable there is a pressing need to draw explicit attention to the ethical commitment underlying and informing the current human rights discourse. There are several important reasons for this. One is that the discourse needs to be revitalised. The flip side of articulating an agenda for global change in the form of a short collection of legal articles is that such articles may take on a formulaic character and tend to become regarded with complacency and fatigue. We therefore need to periodically reconnect with the underlying nerve of human rights law. It must be acknowledged, furthermore, that the expansion of the contemporary human rights agenda occurs in tandem with a rising scepticism about human rights in many circles. Such scepticism sometimes manifests itself in reservations about the very status and validity of the international law of human rights, sometimes in general complaints about 'rights talk' and the bureaucratisation of human rights, and sometimes in calls to prioritise human rights and thereby scale back the scope of their application. Human rights advocates

increasingly globalized world in relation to the struggle to eradicate racism, racial discrimination, xenophobia and related intolerance'; para. 11 of the Declaration emphasises the need to 'prevent and mitigate the negative effects of globalization' and ensure that 'globalization [is] made fully inclusive and equitable'; para. 105 invokes 'a collective responsibility to uphold the principles of human dignity, equality and equity and to ensure that globalization becomes a positive force for all the world's people'; and para. 152 of the Programme of Action, similarly, makes explicit reference to the need 'to address within existing mechanisms, or where necessary to put in place and/or develop mechanisms, to address those aspects of globalization which may lead to racism, racial discrimination, xenophobia and related intolerance'; see http://www.un.org/WCAR/durban.pdf (last accessed: 25 January 2006).   [24] Robinson, 'Ethics' (2002), p. 1.

[25] A primary manifestation of this trend is the United Nations Global Compact, in which numerous private companies from all regions of the world, international labour and civil society organizations, academic institutions, and even cities, are engaged in promoting human rights, labour standards, the environment and anti-corruption; see http://www.unglobalcompact.org (last accessed: 25 January 2006).

often display an unfortunate inclination to flatly dismiss such voices of scepticism simply as political reaction. In my view they must be taken seriously, as expressions of real concerns that resonate widely in most parts of the world, but also as a welcome occasion to focus on what is in fact implied by commitment to human rights. To this end it will be helpful to focus our attention on the values and ethical commitment underlying the international law of human rights.

The purpose of the present chapter is to examine the concept and theory of global ethics, both on its own terms and as an implicit under-current to the contemporary discourse on human rights. While this is expected to provide a potential source of support and inspiration for human rights, it is also conceivable that a critical examination of the theory of global ethics may help us to see how rights-based approaches to social issues need to be complemented by a broader normative commit-ment revolving around other core principles such as, for instance, duty, solidarity, empathy, or charity.

In what follows, I seek to outline the contours of a theory of global ethics in support of human rights in the form of an examination of five basic themes, each of which relates to a central point of ambiguity or key feature of ethical reflection in the current era. The first section examines what it means to speak of ethics as global and adopts from Hans Jonas a notion of ethical responsibilities over large temporal and spatial distances. The second section addresses the question of globally shared values and revisits the significance of Hans Küng's famous 'Projekt Weltethos'. The third section, drawing largely on thinkers such as Jürgen Habermas and John Rawls, examines the terms and conditions for establishing ethical norms applicable to interaction in the public sphere in a context of normative pluralism. The fourth section develops four specific categories of norms of relevance in such a context and establishes that these are fundamentally consistent with international human rights. The fifth section, finally, iden-tifies apathy and lack of a sense of agency as central obstacles to the realisa-tion of Robinson's vision of ethical globalisation. It is suggested by way of conclusion that the theory of global ethics, when further elaborated, is equipped to specifically address this problem and in so doing may make an important contribution to the realisation of universal human rights.

Global ethics – a contradiction in terms?

What does it mean to qualify ethics as 'global'? Or phrased differently, *under what circumstances* does it make sense to speak of a global ethics?

From a certain point of view, which in fact is quite prevalent, the very notion is an oxymoron, for the concept of ethics is assumed to pertain to relations of a local nature and to be embedded in a communal context. This position is in particular characteristic of the Aristotelian tradition of moral philosophy,[26] given that Aristotle based his entire practical philosophy on the premise of an inextricable link between ethics and politics, the latter being understood as the affairs of the city state and as such delimited to a contained communal unit that was assumed to be morally and religiously homogeneous. Outside of the political community humans are reduced to contending with the problem of *merely living*, i.e. bare survival, but within the *polis* the possibility arises to dedicate oneself to *living well*, i.e. realising 'the good life'. This is the essential ethical question for Aristotle and ethics, accordingly, is defined as a concern that is intrinsic to the integrated political, moral and religious community.[27] All communitarian moral philosophers retain this basic premise and would therefore not recognise a notion of global ethics as meaningful.

The German moral philosopher Hans Jonas sought in the 1970s and 1980s to demonstrate that the entire classical tradition of moral philosophy, i.e. not only the Aristotelian tradition but all major schools of thought, was restricted in its outlook to thematising relations of proximity in time and space:

> All previous ethics . . . had these interconnected tacit premises in common: that the human condition, determined by the nature of man and the nature of things, was given once for all; that the human good on that basis was readily determinable; and the range of human action and therefore responsibility was narrowly circumscribed. . . . The good and evil about which action had to care lay close to the act, either in the praxis itself or in its immediate reach, and were not matters for remote planning. This proximity of ends pertained to time as well as space. . . . Ethics accordingly was of the here and now.[28]

---

[26] For an influential contemporary exponent of this tradition, see A. MacIntyre, *After Virtue: A Study in Moral Theory* (London: Duckworth, 1985).

[27] These connections are made in several places in Aristotle's opus but occur most notably in the opening book of the *Politics*: 'The partnership finally composed of several villages is the city-state; it has at last attained the limit of virtually complete self-sufficiency, and thus, while it comes into existence for the sake of life, it exists for the good life' (Aristotle, *Politics*, translated by H. Rackham, Cambridge, MA: Harvard University Press/London: William Heinemann Ltd. 1944, 1.1252b).

[28] H. Jonas, *The Imperative of Responsibility: In Search of an Ethics for the Technological Age* (Chicago: The University of Chicago Press, 1984), pp. 1–5.

In the contemporary world this has radically changed. Jonas does not attribute the change expressly to globalisation, as the phenomenon had not been conceptualised as such at the time of his writing. Rather he builds his argument on the related observation of an exponential increase in humanity's technological powers and hence scope of influence. 'The containment of nearness and contemporaneity is gone, swept away by the spatial spread and time-span of cause-effect trains which technological practice sets afoot, even when undertaken for proximate ends.'[29]

In Jonas's analysis the upshot of this change in the condition of human life on earth is that classical ethical categories only retain limited applicability. The new socio-technical reality calls for a rethinking of ethical principles and norms:

> To be sure, the old prescriptions of the 'neighbor' ethics – of justice, charity, honesty, and so on – still hold in their intimate immediacy for the nearest, day-by-day sphere of human interaction. But this sphere is overshadowed by a growing realm of collective action where doer, deed, and effect are no longer the same as they were in the proximate sphere, and which by the enormity of its powers forces upon ethics a new dimension of responsibility never dreamed of before.[30]

In effect, 'novel powers to act require novel ethical rules and perhaps even a new ethics.'[31] Jonas's response to this challenge at the level of theory formation consists in asserting a *principle of responsibility* that has application over great distances in time and space. His primary concern is with the responsibilities of those living in the present towards future generations, the overriding obligation being to ensure that our actions do not jeopardise the possibility for human life as we know it to persist. This is a radical obligation, for as Jonas notes, '[n]o previous ethics had to consider the global condition of human life and the far-off future, even existence, of the race.'[32]

Adopting the language of Jonas, one may define global ethics as a normative framework, within which to address responsibilities that extend over vast distances of time and space and hence are not limited to immediate inter-subjective and intra-communal relations. This may be recognised as involving a dimension of inter-generational responsibilities (as well as responsibilities towards non-human creatures), yet the primary concern in the present context is with

---

[29] *Ibid.*, p. 7.   [30] *Ibid.*, p. 6.   [31] *Ibid.*, p. 23.   [32] *Ibid.*, p. 8.

contemporary ethical responsibilities that are linked with the process of globalisation.[33]

Before turning to the specific nature of such responsibilities, it will be helpful to make a further observation about the context in which they are being asserted. This is that the very notion of global ethics is premised on a perception of *interconnectedness*. Jonas attributes this to the causal impact of technologies across national and regional boundaries, as is obviously pertinent, but interconnectedness can also be viewed as a function of the way in which the critical problems and vulnerabilities facing humanity increasingly assume a global character, and of the way in which powerful actors move freely across continents and exercise influence at the global level. Examples of concerns of a global reach include environmental issues, climate change, the spread of contagious diseases, the stability of the international economic system and hence the flow of vital goods, global trade, peace and geo-political stability, nuclear threats, and international organised crime – just to mention a few. Problems and concerns of this nature transcend regional boundaries and thus confront us with the fact that human beings living far apart are increasingly coming to share a common destiny. However, the degree of interconnectedness that they establish does not generate a global community in any emphatic sense and does not give rise to a shared substantive morality proportionate to the ethical challenges of globalisation. To the contrary, normative pluralism remains a fact of the globalised world. The core tenets of a global ethics must be framed accordingly.

The question of globally shared values

The quest to define responsibilities that are applicable at the global level and well-suited to address the primary problems of humanity in the current era has since the early 1990s been widely associated with the 'Projekt Weltethos' pioneered by the Austrian theologian Hans Küng.[34] Mary Robinson closely aligns her commitment to an ethical moulding of

---

[33] Jonas in fact acknowledges that there is a structural difference between future-oriented responsibilities and responsibilities directed towards contemporaries in other parts of the world, for whereas the former relation is devoid of any aspect of reciprocity, the latter is not. Interestingly, Jonas links the principle of reciprocity closely with a notion of rights, so on this line of reasoning it would make sense for an ethical theory directed at contemporary global relations to align itself with a philosophy of human rights, whereas a theory of ethical responsibilities towards future generations would be likely to invoke different principles. See *Ibid.*, p. 38 *et seq.*

[34] See http://www.weltethos.org (last accessed: 25 January 2006).

globalisation with the vision of Küng and points to the *Declaration Toward a Global Ethic*[35] drafted by Küng and endorsed by the Parliament of the World's Religions in Chicago in 1993 as a statement of parallel significance to the *Declaration and Programme of Action* adopted at the World Conference on Human Rights in Vienna 1993.[36]

The long-standing ambition of Küng has been to demonstrate and solicit public confirmation that all major religions do share a core of common values, and that such values are essential to adequately address problems such as global poverty, conflict, and ecological destruction.[37] The main outcome of Küng's attempt to distil common values from the world's religions is found in four 'irrevocable directives: do not kill, do not steal, do not lie, and do not commit sexual immorality.'[38] These directives, while seemingly rather general, are interpreted, respectively, as a commitment to a culture of non-violence and respect for life; a commitment to a culture of solidarity and a just economic order; a commitment to a culture of tolerance and a life of truthfulness; and a commitment to a culture of equal rights and partnership between men and women. It is this added layer of interpretation, ultimately, that ensures the contemporary significance of a global religious ethic.

The *Declaration Toward a Global Ethic* furthermore proclaims that its message is consistent with international human rights, yet that the real meaning of human rights cannot be realised through legal means alone. It states:

> We recall the 1948 Universal Declaration of Human Rights of the United Nations. What it formally proclaimed on the level of *rights* we wish to confirm and deepen here from the perspective of an *ethic*. The full realisation of the intrinsic dignity of the human person, the inalienable freedom and equality in principle of all humans, and the necessary solidarity and interdependence of all humans with each other.
>
> On the basis of personal experiences and the burdensome history of our planet we have learned
>
> • that a better global order cannot be created or enforced by laws, prescriptions, and conventions alone;
> • that the realisation of peace, justice, and the protection of Earth depends on the insight and readiness of men and women to act justly;

---

[35] Parliament of the World's Religions, *Declaration Toward a Global Ethic*, Chicago, 4 September 1993; available at http://www.weltethos.org/dat_eng/index3_e.htm (last accessed: 25 January 2006).   [36] Robinson, 'Ethics' (2002), 1.

[37] Parliament, *Declaration*, p. 4.   [38] *Ibid.*, p. 8 *et seq.*

- that action in favour of rights and freedoms presumes a consciousness of responsibility and duty, and that therefore both the minds and hearts of women and men must be addressed;
- that rights without morality cannot long endure, and that *there will be no better global order without a global ethic.*[39]

There is obviously something very appealing about global religious leaders beginning to embrace human rights and invest the international human rights project with the moral authority of the major world religions. Nevertheless, I believe that the undertaking is questionable and potentially counterproductive, both with regard to its manner of attributing content and substance to the notion of global ethics and in its claim to providing a normative foundation for universal human rights. For not only is the ambition to produce a catalogue of global consensus values difficult to achieve in a plausible manner with a significant degree of specificity; what is more, the implicit premise of raising culture and religion in a static, timeless sense (already a fiction) to absolute normative authority establishes a criterion that may potentially de-legitimise rather than legitimise human rights. The world's main cultures and religions do not in fact support full gender equality, and much less the equal rights of sexual minority groups, just to mention a few pertinent examples.

However, no such substantive confluence of religious norms is actually required in order to support a theory of global ethics. I shall argue, to the contrary, that a viable theory of global ethics should base itself, not on established cultural or religious authority but rather on certain essential features of the process of social rationalisation and globalisation. The premise of normative pluralism that was established above as an irreversible consequence of globalisation can be heeded not only by attempting to identify shared global values but also by establishing certain overarching and mutually binding norms for how to interact, and what basic protections to ensure, in a context that is no longer determined by traditional world views.

In view of a *secular* contextualisation of global ethics and human rights, it may nevertheless be found that Küng's quest to link human rights with fundamental religious values – and the wider dialogue among world religions that this undertaking fosters – proves itself to be profoundly significant. What it may achieve, however, will not be a normative foundation for global ethics and human rights but rather a pervasive

---

[39] *Ibid.*, p. 5 *et seq.* (Emphasis in the original.)

perception of compatibility between such frameworks of international normativity and local value and belief systems, such as they exist in different parts of the world.

About ethics in the public sphere: the premise of normative pluralism

A defining feature of the process of social modernisation that characterises occidental history and has today become an undeniable reality in all parts of the world, in fact part and parcel of what is understood by globalisation, is a radical delimitation of morality in the public sphere. The entire edifice of liberal constitutional democracy, which too is becoming globalised, is based on the premise that traditional concepts of the good, as sustained by comprehensive religious and/or metaphysical world views, do not provide a legitimate basis for the ordering of social relations and the exercise of political power. Public authority cannot, in other words, be based on a comprehensive moral cosmology, i.e. a system of *objective right*, which legitimises a hierarchical social order, prescribes behavioural norms for different social groups and extensive obligations of the individual towards the community and state, and establishes meaning and purpose in life by embodying a vision of the good life which individual society members may seek to realise in accordance with their own capabilities and social position.[40] In what Jürgen Habermas has styled *postmetaphysical* society, the presence of a shared moral cosmology can no longer be taken for granted, and what does remain of substantive morality is relegated to the private sphere where it becomes a matter of personal commitment made in accordance with individual beliefs and preferences as well as communal affiliations.

In the public sphere normative pluralism must be accepted as a fact. This profoundly affects both law and public morality or ethics. As Habermas observes '[i]n a pluralistic society, the theory of justice can expect to be accepted by citizens only if it limits itself to a conception that is postmetaphysical in the strict sense, that is, only if it avoids taking sides in the context of competing forms of life and worldviews.'[41] Habermas further notes with reference to the work of John Rawls that 'a postmetaphysical theory of justice . . . rests on a weak, that is, merely formally

---

[40] Such visions of the good life may of course be otherworldly in their orientation, as was the case with the medieval Christian appropriation of Aristotelian eudemonistic ethics.

[41] J. Habermas, *Between Facts and Norms* (Cambridge: Polity Press, 1996), p. 60.

defined, concept of the good.'[42] Thus public morality becomes a matter
of predominantly procedural norms, i.e. norms for how to interact in the
public sphere without presuming a common substantive set of values,
but with a view to ensuring a maximum degree of liberty for individual
society members in pursuing their own values and life aims, as long as
this does not infringe on the ability of other society members to do the
same.

In *A Political Theory of Rights*, Attracta Ingram develops an analogous
line of reasoning.[43] She notes that:

> [I]n liberal democracies people subscribe to different, often incompatible
> conceptions of what makes life worthwhile. These may be religious, ethical,
> or philosophical views. Since such views are the subject of disagreement
> and are also sources of the deepest convictions people have about how to
> lay out their lives those facts must be represented as 'givens' in any model of
> the circumstances in which the question of rights arises for us. In other
> words, our thinking about rights takes place against certain background
> beliefs that are not in question within the liberal democratic perspective:
> (1) that citizens are to be treated as equals from the point of view of poli-
> tics; (2) that certain liberties, such as the liberty to practice religion, are of
> fundamental importance; (3) that disagreement about the fundamentals
> of human existence is to be tolerated (even regarded as a good thing) rather
> than stamped out by force. Together these beliefs direct us to find a moral
> basis for an acceptable scheme of rights, one that can be endorsed by all cit-
> izens, in some point of agreement which overarches differences in concep-
> tions of what makes life worthwhile.[44]

Historically, the articulation of norms applicable to a pluralistic society has
tended to be centred on notions of *subjective right* and has therefore
entailed a certain privileging of law over morality in the traditional sense as
the primary structuring principle of public, intersubjective relations.
Hugo Grotius is widely recognised as a pioneer of this intellectual development,[45] yet in fact it is a constitutive feature of all social contract theory.
Habermas expressly links it with a project of liberation of the individual
from an externally prescribed morality. 'By opening up the legal space for
pursuing personal preferences, individual rights release the entitled person
from moral precepts and other prescriptions in a carefully circumscribed

---

[42] *Ibid.*, p. 61.
[43] A. Ingram, *A Political Theory of Rights* (Oxford: Oxford University Press, 1993).
[44] *Ibid.*, p. 97.
[45] See, e.g., W. Edmundson, *An Introduction to Rights* (Cambridge: Cambridge University
      Press, 2004), pp. 17 *et seq.*

manner. . . . With the introduction of individual liberties, modern law – in contrast to traditional legal orders – validates the Hobbesian principle that whatever is not explicitly prohibited is permitted.'[46]

Obviously, the rise of a notion of universal human rights is part and parcel of this historical development, and it is for this reason fundamentally misconceived to treat human rights as a new religion. Human rights do not embody a unified vision of the good life. Rather, they embody claims to essential protections and provisions in the public realm that are necessary in order to empower individual right holders to pursue their own life projects (subject, of course, to the familiar restrictions of not interfering with the ability of others to do the same). The ethical agenda with which universal human rights are associated must accordingly be construed along the lines sketched above as a minimalist agenda defined predominantly in procedural and formal rather than substantive terms. Indeed, it must be framed as potentially consistent with diverse substantive ethical, religious and cultural, commitments. Our primary analytical challenge consists in beginning to furnish such an agenda with concrete content.

Before turning to this challenge, it is relevant to note that the post-metaphysical premise attributed by Habermas to occidental pluralistic society may also be taken to apply to the search for a binding normativity at the global level, and therefore that any theory of global ethics must respect the stricture not to base itself on a framework of substantive morality (even if individuals and communities worldwide remain profoundly influenced by and committed to religion and traditional morality). This theoretical stipulation is supported by a view of human rights as the outcome of a social contract not only within but also between states, as was already prefigured in the eighteenth century idea of perpetual peace which in turn has been associated by Kant with a notion of rights of the world citizen.[47] To function as such, international human rights cannot be seen to embody any particular metaphysical presuppositions

---

[46] J. Habermas, 'Remarks on Legitimation Through Human Rights,' *Philosophy and Social Criticism* 24 (1998) 2/3, 158.

[47] I. Kant, *Perpetual Peace: A Philosophical Sketch* (Cambridge: Cambridge University Press, 1991), pp. 105 *et seq*. It is in this connection no coincidence that one of the main scholars to revive Kant's essay on perpetual peace in a contemporary context is Habermas. See J. Habermas, 'Kant's Idea of Perpetual Peace: At Two Hundred Years' Historical Remove' in J. Habermas, *The Inclusion of the Other: Studies in Political Theory* (Cambridge: Polity Press, 1998), pp. 165–201. John Rawls has for his part established an analogous interpretative framework in his theory of the law of peoples. See J. Rawls, *The Law of Peoples* (Cambridge, MA: Harvard University Press, 1999).

but must instead be open to interpretations that are consistent with diverse metaphysical, moral, and religious commitments.

Without being able to address the matter in significant detail, it must be acknowledged that the separation of public and private, as outlined above, has been contested from many sides and for a variety of reasons. A central line of critique has its origin in feminist theory which notes that the dichotomy tends to leave the private sphere to traditional morality and hence beyond the reach of established legal standards, including human rights standards.[48] This is obviously unsatisfactory, in particular for women who in many social contexts are confined to the private sphere and are almost invariably assigned inferior status in traditional cosmologies. Rawls acknowledges the problem and accordingly takes issue with the underlying premise that the private sphere should be exempt from public scrutiny and regulation: 'If the so-called private sphere is a space alleged to be exempt from justice, then there is no such thing.'[49]

Another objection asserted by feminist scholars, among others, is that the liberal notion of the isolated individual acting autonomously in the public sphere is at odds with real life experience, and in particular the experience of women, who find themselves entangled in intricate webs of concrete (private and public) relationships that are associated with equally intricate non-universalisable ethical obligations. Real life ethical experience is thus better characterised, so it is suggested, in terms of a relation-specific 'ethics of care'.[50] This line of reasoning resonates with

[48] See e.g. C. M. Cerna and J. C. Wallace: 'Th[e] private sphere, which deals with issues such as religion, culture, the status of women, the right to marry and divorce and to remarry, the protection of children, the question of choice as regards family planning, and the like, is a domain in which the most serious challenge to the universality of human rights arises. Certain societies are unwilling to assume international human rights obligations in this private sphere; their own code of conduct, which is informed by their religious or traditional law, already covers this terrain. This tension between the universality of norms in the private sphere and the competing religious/traditional law renders those international human rights norms, which have not become part of *jus cogens*, suspect.' C. M. Cerna and J. C. Wallace, 'Women and Culture', in K. D. Askin and D. M. Koenig (eds.), *Women and International Human Rights Law*, Volume 1 (New York: Transnational, 1999) p. 629.

[49] J. Rawls, *Justice as Fairness: A Restatement* (Cambridge, MA: The Belknap Press of Harvard University Press, 2001), p. 166.

[50] Seminar works developing the notion of an ethics of care include Carol Gilligan, *In a Different Voice: Psychological Theory and Women's Development* (Cambridge, MA: Harvard University Press, 1982) and Annette Baier, 'What Do Women Want in an Ethical Theory?' contained in A. Baier, *Moral Prejudices* (Cambridge: Harvard University Press, 1995). See also T. L. Beauchamp and J. F. Childress, *Principles of Biomedical Ethics*, 5th ed. (Oxford: Oxford University Press, 2001), pp. 369 *et seq.*

the typical objection voiced by non-western intellectuals that the western construction of autonomous individuality is at odds with the experience of more communally-oriented societies, in which ethical obligations too tend to be defined as relative to concrete relationships.[51] I have no intention of taking issue with these observations but only wish to suggest that such relational responsibilities and entitlements cannot form the basis of a public morality, and in particular not in a social context in which normative pluralism is already a 'given', and in which processes of individuation have long since begun uprooting people to a greater or lesser degree from their established communal environments.

Basic norms

The pivotal claim of the present argument is that even if the theory of global ethics must remain minimalist in substantive terms and should in principle not import norms which may be found to be particularistic in origin or content, it is still possible on the grounds established above to assert a relatively comprehensive catalogue of normative commitments. Moreover, this can be shown to be largely consistent with the explicit and implicit ethical content of international human rights. It must be noted from the outset that my purpose in the present context is not to present a philosophical justification for any or all human rights, but simply to sketch the range of normative commitments that are implied by a post-metaphysical public ethics that is asserted at the global level, and in so doing begin to unpack the correlative ethical presuppositions of international human rights.

An important group of norms can be derived without recourse to metaphysical assumptions from the procedural requirement that participants in public discourse must be able to assume from each other a reciprocal recognition of discursive competence and a mutual entitlement to inhabit the public sphere and conduct oneself safely and freely within it. On this basis one can establish familiar human rights principles of freedom of conscience and expression, freedom of movement, liberty, etc., as well as the range of classical political rights – all subject to the limitation that the exercise of one's rights must not infringe on the ability of others to enjoy the same rights. Certain rights, such as notably the freedom of expression, must

---

[51] See, e.g., O. Yasuaki, 'Towards an Intercivilizational Approach to Human Rights' in Ko Swan Sik et al. (eds.), *Asian Yearbook of International Law*, Volume 7 (Leiden: Martinus Nijhoff Publishers, 1997), pp. 57 *et seq.*

also generally be exercised in a spirit of tolerance and respect for others, in particular when deeply held values and convictions come into play. Legal provisions protecting the freedom of expression often make some reference to the need to exercise the right responsibility, yet the horizontal obligation, integral to the very enjoyment of public liberties, to demonstrate tolerance and respect in inter-subjective and inter-communal relations can be articulated much more forcefully within an ethical paradigm.

Another group of essential public norms aims at restricting the exercise of state power and, conversely, at protecting the integrity of the human person. This is of paramount importance in a historical context in which the state exponentially concentrates power and assumes a monopoly on the exercise of violence, ostensibly in the best interest of its citizens. Human rights principles such as the right to life, freedom from torture and degrading treatment, protection against arbitrary detention, the right to a fair trial, etc., reflect this interest.

Thirdly, it can within a postmetaphysical framework be established that law and public morality must protect and facilitate all society members' private pursuit of happiness, life ambitions, and substantive moral commitments, as long as these do not conflict with the legitimate interests and commitments of others. This forms the basis of principles of toleration and non-discrimination in inter-subjective and inter-communal relations and of human rights norms such as the right to privacy and family life (including the rights of sexual minorities), freedom of religion, etc., within the wider societal context.

There is yet another important set of public norms, finally, which cannot easily be construed as formal or procedural yet which must be included within our catalogue of essential standards of a global ethics. These are norms having to do with providing for basic human needs, in particular in situations of extreme privation. A certain obligation to respond to suffering and care for fellow human beings in need is reflected in all major systems of morality and is usually linked with values of charity and compassion. In a contemporary international context this has been taken up by the International Committee of the Red Cross (ICRC) and numerous other humanitarian organisations in the form of the proclamation of a humanitarian imperative.[52] However, commitments to doing good for others typically retain a certain optional character and

---

[52] See The Sphere Project, *Humanitarian Charter and Minimum Standards in Disaster Response*, Geneva 2001, available at http://www.sphereproject.org/handbook/hdbkpdf/hdbk_full.pdf (last accessed: 25 January 2006).

invariably position the recipient of charity or aid in a position of inferiority and moral debt. The ethos of a global public morality that we are here seeking to elaborate is, to the contrary, premised on a reciprocal recognition of discursive competence and seeks to reinforce such competence in one's fellow human beings, when required and within the limits of what is meaningful and feasible. It can be argued that minimal public provisions in areas such as health, education, food security, shelter and employment are necessary to allow human beings everywhere to realise their individual potential and thus to constitute discursive competence in an elusive, yet intricately interconnected global community. Emergency assistance and essential socio-economic provisions must, in other words, be given in a spirit of empowerment and on the basis of an elementary sense of universal entitlement. This, in essence, is the underlying ethical thrust of international economic and social human rights. The realisation of such rights becomes a primary responsibility of the international community, and of all powerful actors in the international sphere, in a context in which the ability of human beings everywhere to have their basic economic and social needs met, and hence to be able to begin to realise their wider life ambitions, is already thoroughly mediated and constrained by global processes, mechanisms and decisions taken in distant international fora. This, in effect, brings us full circle back to the essential premise of global responsibility, as attributed to Jonas in an earlier section.

Taken together, all of the norms outlined above – which clearly are interlinked, thus mirroring the theorem of interdependence and indivisibility of all human rights – reinforce an underlying commitment to the *autonomy* and *dignity* of the human person.[53] Articulated in Kantian terms, this can be construed as a commitment to a vision of a global 'kingdom of ends,' i.e. a socio-historical context in which it is universally recognised as ethically wrong to treat a human being merely as a means to the objectives of others and not also at the same time as an end in his or her own right.[54] Slavery constitutes the most blatant example of such

[53] With regard to autonomy and discursive competence Ingram notes that '[t]he ideal of autonomy flows from the thought that individuals have a moral personality that enables them to discern good and evil for themselves' (Ingram, *Political Theory* (1993), p. 99). The overall thrust of her argument is in fact to establish that a commitment to autonomy lies at the very heart of political theory of human rights – as distinct from a proprietary (i.e. Lockean) conception of rights.

[54] A fundamental premise of Kantian ethics is that 'man and generally any rational being exists as an end in himself, not merely as a means to be arbitrarily used by this or that will,

misrecognition, but all human rights abuses in fact display aspects of denying the human person intrinsic value. The implicit emphasis on autonomy and human dignity might be viewed as indicative of a 'western' bias in human rights, yet inter-cultural consultations demonstrate that these values in fact resonate strongly with all major moral and religious traditions,[55] and it can be argued that they anyhow assume an imperative character in a context of global social modernisation (driven primarily by processes of economic globalisation) which on the one hand rapidly uproots traditional contexts of moral orientation and communal protection, i.e. produces individuation and exposure to existential insecurity, and on the other hand generates unprecedented capacities precisely for violating human dignity and autonomy. By laying principles of human dignity and autonomy at the very foundation of the Universal Declaration of Human Rights,[56] its drafters, in the view of the present author, launched a vision of human rights not as the expression of a particularistic occidental philosophical doctrine but rather as a response to some of the most urgent challenges of our time.

The problem of ethical commitment – indifference, marginalisation, neglect

The weakest point of a theory of global ethics in support of human rights does not, arguably, consist in articulating norms which can meaningfully be asserted in a contemporary context of globalisation. Rather, it consists in making a persuasive case, both cognitively and emotionally, for why such norms should be respected. The Kantian premise that a truly moral agent will act purely on the basis of a cognitive recognition of what is right bespeaks a spurious anthropology. In fact people tend to act on the basis of affectively charged ideas, such as are exploited by nationalism and similarly by the major religions with which people identify in an intensely

but in all his actions, whether they concern himself or other rational beings, must be always regarded at the same time as an end.' Kant (1785), *Groundwork for the Metaphysics of Morals*, Second Section: 'Transition From Popular Moral Philosophy To The Metaphysic Of Morals', translation by J. W. Ellington (Indianapolis: Hackett Publishing Co, 1993, 3rd ed.).

[55] This, indeed, is very valuable outcome of Hans Küng's global ethics project and other similar attempts to promote inter-religious dialogue and establish cross-cultural universals.

[56] Mary Ann Glendon notes that the 'prologue establishes the Declaration's membership in the large family of dignity-based rights instruments that were adopted after the Second World War' (M. A. Glendon, *A World Made New: Eleanor Roosevelt and the Universal Declaration of Human Rights* (New York: Random House, 2001), p. 175).

emotional manner. Notions of cosmopolitanism do not hold a similar sway, nor do values of universal human rights.[57]

In practice the greatest obstacles to the shaping of an ethical globalisation are *apathy* and *indifference*. Even if the argument that ethical responsibilities today pertain over great distances of time and space, as established by Jonas and reiterated in the present chapter, is intellectually persuasive, people are in fact not readily capable of relating across great distances. Thus, while a significant cross-section of the population in the affluent parts of the world as well as many actors and experts directly involved in globalisation processes are supportive of the idea of ethical globalisation, the reality is that large-scale systemic wrongs and preventable or reducible mass suffering are widely treated with passivity and inaction.

Against this harsh reality, the impulse towards articulating and mobilising an ethical response to globalisation needs a vital boost from somewhere. Where? While there is no easy answer to this question, it seems clear that a theory of global ethics needs to pay close attention to, and in a certain sense rediscover, values such as solidarity, compassion and empathy, perhaps even charity, civic duty and a commitment to serving others – all of which are values that tend not to be well supported within a rights-based paradigm. This need not be in contrast to a commitment to universal human rights (the opposition between rights and duties is widely misconstrued in the present-day debate), but should rather be seen as a complementary dimension of the underlying commitment to a global ethics in support of human rights.

Ultimately the problem may have even deeper roots. Rather than reflect a lack of commitment and good intentions, our inaction in the face of injustice and suffering – what might be described as the 'collateral casualties' of globalisation – often rests on a basic perception that there is very little we can do to make a difference. Systemic relations in the age of globalisation assume a character of inescapable fate,[58] and in response people opt to orient themselves not towards perceptions of social justice and global change but rather towards navigating the existing socio-economic structures to their own best advantage, perhaps with a concomitant

---

[57] This is a recurrent theme in P. Cheah and B. Robbins (eds.), *Cosmopolitics: Thinking and Feeling beyond the Nation* (Minneapolis: University of Minnesota Press, 1998).

[58] An analogous argument has been widely made with reference to what was once called late capitalism. A by now classical analysis of the phenomenon is found in T. Adorno and M. Horkheimer, *Dialectic of the Enlightenment* (New York: Continuum, 1976); see in particular 'Excursus I: Odysseus or Myth and Enlightenment'.

commitment to alleviating the need and suffering of others in proximate relations and on a modest scale.[59]

Such reactions confront ethical theory with a need to address the question of agency. Individuals cannot be held directly responsible for the consequences of macro-level systemic structures, but our powerlessness vis-à-vis such large scale structures does not, on the other hand, entirely exempt us from any responsibility in the face of suffering and global injustice. As a genuine ethical response to economic and cultural globalisation, the theory that we are seeking to articulate must therefore define responsibilities that are relevant to actors at all levels, always abiding by the premise that such responsibilities should be proportionate to the feasible agency of the actors in question. Global ethics thus enjoins us to take responsibility for the problems of our shrinking world in ways that show empathy and solidarity towards those marginalised and neglected in the processes of globalisation, in ways that demonstrate openness and a willingness to engage in reciprocal interaction across communal and regional boundaries, and in ways that still remain meaningful and proportionate within the life world or social context that each actor inhabits. Conceivably such an agenda can better be articulated within a framework of ethics than of rights. This, ultimately, may be the most important contribution of ethical theory to the shaping of global socio-economic processes and explains why the appeal to global ethical standards and principles is a vital complement to the quest to realise universal human rights.

Postscript

From 30 September 2005, a series of cartoons depicting the Prophet Mohammed were published in a Danish newspaper, *Jyllands-Posten*,[60] with the clear intent of challenging religiously imposed limits to freedom of expression and testing the commitment among Muslims in Denmark to secular democratic values.[61] The very fact of publishing such images

---

[59] The shrill tenor and apparent lack of direction of the no-global movement may paradoxically be interpreted as a variant reaction to the same general perception of impotence in the face of globalisation processes.

[60] F. Rose (ed.), 'Muhammeds ansigt', *Jyllands-Posten*, 30 September 2005.

[61] For a detailed explication of the motives behind publishing the cartoons, see 'Why I Published Those Cartoons' An op-ed by Rose in the February 19, 2006 *Washington Post*, available at: http://www.washingtonpost.com/wp-dyn/content/article/2006/02/17/AR2006021702499.html (last accessed 17 March 2006).

violated a general prohibition in Islam against portrayal of the Prophet and some of the cartoons were moreover blatantly offensive in content, notably by implying an intrinsic link between Islam and international terrorism. The publication of the cartoons quickly drew international attention – to some extent provoked by Islamist groups seeking to exploit the provocation to their own ends – and by early 2006 (i.e. around the time when the present chapter was being completed) the incident had broken into a fully fledged international crisis. Large-scale protests were staged by Muslims all around the world, religious leaders and diplomats made repeated demands for apologies both from the newspaper editors and from Danish government authorities, Danish products were being boycotted in most Muslim countries, flags and in some cases even embassies were burned and gory threats of retribution brandished in slogans and on placards – and numerous other European newspapers in the meantime reprinted the cartoons with the predictable effect of adding fuel to the fire of outrage.

International leaders did their best to exercise damage control, but with limited effect.[62] Clearly the provocation had touched a raw nerve. Even to many moderate Muslims, the deliberate publication of offensive images of the Prophet was taken to be indicative of a deep seated denigration of Islam in Western society, and the fact that such an offence should be presumed to be protected by freedom of expression only confirmed suspicions of international double standards, as it was widely taken for granted that similar offences to Christianity or Judaism would not have been tolerated. Many commentators viewed the escalation of the conflict as confirmation of Samuel Huntington's prediction of a clash of civilisations, whereas others, to the contrary, took it to confirm all the more strongly the need for constructive inter-civilisation dialogue. The temperate voice of Hans Küng, not surprisingly, was noticeable amongst the latter.[63]

In the present context, what is interesting about the controversy it the way in which it places in relief several important aspects of the theory

---

[62] See e.g. the joint statement of 7 February 2006, by Javier Solana, European Union High Representative for Common Foreign and Security Policy; Kofi Annan, United Nations Secretary-General; and Ekmeleddin Ihsanoglu, Secretary-General of the Organization for the Islamic Conference, calling for restraint and calm after attacks on Danish and other diplomatic missions across the Middle East; available at http://europa-eu-un.org/articles/en/article_5663_en.htm (last accessed 17 March 2006).

[63] See H. Küng, 'How to Prevent a Clash of Civilizations', *International Herald Tribune*, 3 March 2006; available at: http://www.iht.com/articles/2006/03/03/opinion/edkung.php (last accessed: 17 March 2006).

of global ethics as outlined above. The case illustrates, firstly, the importance of maintaining a complementary relationship between ethics and law. As has already been indicated, the newspaper, *Jyllands-Posten*, justified its publication of the cartoons on the grounds of freedom of expression.[64] Much of the ensuing discussion has therefore naturally revolved around what is protected by the freedom of expression, what limitations can legitimately be imposed on this right, also in the interest of safeguarding other rights (notably the freedom of religion), and whether the Danish publishers in fact violated national or international law. A competent Danish court found that it did not,[65] yet parallel steps

---

[64] Section 77 of the Constitutional Act of Denmark (1953) reads: 'Any person shall be at liberty to publish his ideas in print, in writing, and in speech, subject to his being held responsible in a court of law. Censorship and other preventive measures shall never again be introduced.' Available at: http://www.folketinget.dk/pdf/constitution.pdf (last accessed 17 March 2006).

Relevant provisions of international human rights law are:

Article 19 of the ICCPR:

1. Everyone shall have the right to hold opinions without interference.
2. Everyone shall have the right to freedom of expression; this right shall include freedom to seek, receive and impart information and ideas of all kinds, regardless of frontiers, either orally, in writing or in print, in the form of art, or through any other media of his choice.
3. The exercise of the rights provided for in paragraph 2 of this article carries with it special duties and responsibilities. It may therefore be subject to certain restrictions, but these shall only be such as are provided by law and are necessary:
   (a) For respect of the rights or reputations of others;
   (b) For the protection of national security or of public order (ordre public), or of public health or morals;

and Article 10 of the ECHR:

1. Everyone has the right to freedom of expression. This right shall include freedom to hold opinions and to receive and impart information and ideas without interference by public authority and regardless of frontiers. This article shall not prevent States from requiring the licensing of broadcasting, television or cinema enterprises.
2. The exercise of these freedoms, since it carries with it duties and responsibilities, may be subject to such formalities, conditions, restrictions or penalties as are prescribed by law and are necessary in a democratic society, in the interests of national security, territorial integrity or public safety, for the prevention of disorder or crime, for the protection of health or morals, for the protection of the reputation or rights of others, for preventing the disclosure of information received in confidence, or for maintaining the authority and impartiality of the judiciary.

[65] Cf. International Helsinki Federation for Human Rights, Human Rights in the OSCE Region: Europe, Central Asia and North America, Report 2006 (Events of 2005) (Vienna: International Helsinki Federation for Human Rights, 2006), p. 140.

have meanwhile been taken to refer the case to the European Court of Human Rights.[66] The juridical evaluation aside, however, it has rightly been pointed out by many critics that freedom of expression is a right which needs to be exercised in a responsible fashion demonstrating respect for the values and beliefs of others. Thus, while there may not have been valid legal grounds for a censoring of the cartoons, it can still be argued that their publication runs counter to the fundamental tenets of a global ethics, which in addition to defining basic liberties vis-à-vis the state also imposes a horizontal obligation on partners in discourse to mutually recognise discursive competence and hence demonstrate respect for the deeply held values and convictions of others. The central challenge to the theory of global ethics, which in this regard presents itself as an indispensable complement to the law of human rights, is to clarify how to maintain such a spirit of tolerance and reciprocity while also safeguarding the possibility of critical dialogue, and allowing space for bold expressions of disagreement about issues of common concern in the public sphere.

A second central theme brought out by the present case has to do with the feasibility of upholding a broad international commitment to the idea of a delimited secular ethics governing relations in the public sphere. Some reactions to the publication of the cartoons have clearly contradicted such a delimitation of ethics and implicitly or explicitly indicate a wish for the reinforcement or re-introduction of religious authority in the public sphere. This has notably been apparent in repeated demands placed on the Danish government to intervene against the creators and publishers of the cartoons irrespective of whether it might have legal recourse to do so, and similarly in extreme calls for violent retribution (e.g. death by beheading), as might be supported by some religious texts on a fundamentalist reading, yet which even in their very articulation constitute a violation both of existing law and of the core tenets of a secular ethics.

Indeed, it was a determination to expose the prevalence of such anti-democratic sentiments that led newspaper editors in Europe and around

---

[66] On 13 February 2006, the French Regional Council for the Muslim Religion (CRCM) filed a complaint with the European Court of Human Rights (ECHR) to review the conduct behind publishing caricatures of the Prophet Muhammad in French newspapers. See, e.g., http://www.earnedmedia.org/irpp0314.htm (last accessed 17 March 2006). Danish Muslim groups have similarly taken steps to refer the case to the ECHR or, alternatively, to the UN High Commissioner for Human Rights; see 'Muhammed-tegninger til domstolen i Strasbourg', Jyllands-Posten 18 March 2006; available at: http://www.jp.dk/indland/artikel:aid=3625816:fid=11364 (last accessed 20 March 2006).

the world to re-publish the cartoons, and even if one shares the view of the present author that the provocation was misguided, one is bound to acknowledge that aspects of the reaction have been profoundly disturbing. It must, however, at the same time be emphasised that by far the more prevalent reaction, both by Islamic opinion leaders and by Muslim populations in Europe, has been measured and has remained squarely within the bounds of secular constitutional and ethical norms. Contrary to impressions initially conveyed by various media reports, Islamic diplomats confronting the Danish government about the case did not in fact request any form of censorship or restriction of free speech; they simply asked for a public assurance that Danes generally have no intention to offend Islam and that the government does not condone blatantly offensive expressions in the media.[67] There is no good reason why this request should not have been heeded – not as a reluctant concession to the Muslim world but rather as a proactive gesture designed to reinforce a spirit of reciprocity and mutual respect in a global context that is all too often marred by inter-communal prejudices and suspicions. Such a gesture, one might surmise, could moreover help to de-legitimise manifestly hostile and intolerant reactions.

Importantly, the controversy concerning the cartoons appears to be giving rise to a widespread mobilisation of moderate Muslims in Europe and around the world who refuse to allow fundamentalist groups to define the public image of Islam.[68] What this development signals, in effect, is that the primary divide concerning adherence to a secular global ethics in support of human rights is not *between* Islamic and western civilisation but is rather *internal* to Islam, as it is to all other major religious communities as well. While the case considered here by way of conclusion thus highlights the precariousness of maintaining a tolerant, pluralistic ethical and legal order on a global scale, it also underscores the extent to which the aim of forging global ethical standards and reactions defines the current historical moment.

---

[67] Cf. A. Shadid and K. Sullivan, 'Anatomy of the Cartoon Protest Movement; Opposing Certainties Widen Gap Between West and Muslim World', *The Washington Post*, 16 February 2006, A1.

[68] It is telling in this connection that a newly formed Danish organisation *Demokratiske Muslimer* (Democratic Muslims) has seized the cartoon controversy as an occasion to mobilise likeminded Muslim groups around the world in support of democratic values and human rights; see the organisation's website: http://www.demokratiskemuslimer.dk, and similarly the website of the organisation's founder, Naser Khader: http://www.khader.dk.

Bibliography

Adorno, Th., and Horkheimer, M., *Dialectic of the Enlightenment* (New York: Continuum, 1976)

Annan, K., *In Larger Freedom: Towards Development, Security and Human Rights for All*, UN Doc. A/59/2005 of 21 March 2005, available at http://www.un.org/largerfreedom (last accessed: 25 January 2006)

Aristotle, *Politics*, translated by H. Rackham (Cambridge, MA: Harvard University Press/London: William Heinemann Ltd., 1944)

Baier, A., *Moral Prejudices* (Cambridge: Harvard University Press, 1995)

Beauchamp, T. L. and Childress, J. F., *Principles of Biomedical Ethics*, 5th ed. (Oxford: Oxford University Press, 2001)

Cançado Trinidade, A. A., 'The Inter-American System of Protection of Human Rights: The Developing Case-Law of the Inter-American Court of Human Rights (1982–2005)' in I. F. Gomez and K. De Feyter (eds.), *International Protection of Human Rights at the Dawn of the Twenty-First Century* (Bilbao: University of Deusto/EIUC, 2005)

Cerna, C. M. and Wallace, J. C., 'Women and Culture', in K. D. Askin and D. M. Koenig (eds.), *Women and International Human Rights Law*, Volume 1 (New York: Transnational, 1999)

Cheah, P., and Robbins, B. (eds.), *Cosmopolitics: Thinking and Feeling Beyond the Nation* (Minneapolis: University of Minnesota Press, 1998)

Edmundson, W., *An Introduction to Rights* (Cambridge: Cambridge University Press, 2004)

Gilligan, C., *In a Different Voice: Psychological Theory and Women's Development* (Cambridge, MA: Harvard University Press, 1982)

Glendon, M. A., *A World Made New: Eleanor Roosevelt and the Universal Declaration of Human Rights* (New York: Random House, 2001)

Habermas, J., 'Remarks on Legitimation Through Human Rights,' *Philosophy and Social Criticism* 24 (1998) 2/3, 157–171

The Inclusion of the Other: Studies in Political Theory (Cambridge: Polity Press, 1998)

Between Facts and Norms (Cambridge: Polity Press, 1996)

Ingram, A., *A Political Theory of Rights* (Oxford: Oxford University Press, 1993)

Jonas, H., *The Imperative of Responsibility: In Search of an Ethics for the Technological Age* (Chicago: The University of Chicago Press, 1984)

Kant, I., *Groundwork for the Metaphysics of Morals*, translated by J. W. Ellington (Indianapolis: Hackett Publishing Co, 1993, 3rd edn; original publication 1785)

Perpetual Peace: A Philosophical Sketch (Cambridge: Cambridge University Press, 1991; original publication 1795)

MacIntyre, A., *After Virtue: A Study in Moral Theory* (London: Duckworth, 1985)

Nowak, M., *Introduction to the International Human Rights Regime* (Leiden: Martinus Nijhoff Publishers, 2003)

Ovey, C. and White R., *The European Convention on Human Rights*, 3rd ed. (Oxford: Oxford University Press, 2002)

Parliament of the World's Religions, 'Declaration Toward a Global Ethic', Chicago, 4 September 1993, available at http://www.weltethos.org/dat_eng/index3_e. htm (last accessed: 25 January 2006)

Rawls, J., *Justice as Fairness: A Restatement* (Cambridge, MA: The Belknap Press of Harvard University Press, 2001)

Rawls, J., *The Law of Peoples* (Cambridge, MA: Harvard University Press, 1999)

Robinson, M., 'Ethics, Human Rights and Globalization', Second Global Ethic Lecture, The Global Ethic Foundation, University of Tübingen, Germany, 21 January 2002, available at http://www.weltethos.org/dat_eng/st_9e_xx/ 9e_144.htm#top (last accessed: 25 January 2006)

The Sphere Project, 'Humanitarian Charter and Minimum Standards in Disaster Response', Geneva, 2001, available at http://www.sphereproject.org/ handbook/hdbkpdf/hdbk_full.pdf (last accessed: 25 January 2006)

Yasuaki, O., 'Towards an Intercivilizational Approach to Human Rights' in Ko Swan Sik *et al.* (eds.), *Asian Yearbook of International Law*, Volume 7 (Leiden: Martinus Nijhoff Publishers, 1997)

Localising Human Rights

KOEN DE FEYTER

Introduction

Economic globalisation – understood as a process of breaking down State barriers in order to allow the free flow of finance, trade, production and at least in theory, labour – affects human rights. It affects the role of the main duty holder in human rights, the State, both in the world and the domestic economies. Globalism, the ideology supporting economic globalisation, favours the withdrawal of the State from the provision of many services essential to human rights, and its replacement by private actors. It also insists on opening up the economy to products, services and investments originating in countries that enjoy a competitive advantage, and on discipline in taking the advice of international trade and financial organisations.

From a human rights perspective, economic globalisation raises questions about the human rights responsibilities of private actors, of intergovernmental organisations and of third States when their actions have extraterritorial effects. There is also an urgent need to rethink human rights obligations of States. This is often a very technical issue, requiring knowledge of the law of international contracts and arbitration and of domestic administrative law.

Inevitably, a part of the human rights response to economic globalisation needs to take place at the global level – hence the discussions on the human rights accountability of the World Bank, the role of human rights in the World Trade Organization (WTO) dispute settlement system, or the efforts to codify the human rights responsibility of corporations. Maintaining the common language of global rights is also essential for the purposes of identifying common causes of violations in different countries. In the context of economic globalisation, such causes are not purely domestic, but regional and global as well.[1]

[1] My own views on many of these issues are in K. De Feyter, *Human Rights: Social Justice in the Age of the Market* (London: Zed Books, 2005).

67

Nevertheless, whether and to what extent aspects of economic globalisation have an adverse impact on human rights protection will differ from society to society. The human rights needs of slum dwellers who face a private company operating the water supply system are very different from the needs of industrial workers faced with the relocation of their industry to low-income economies. For human rights to be relevant to all, they will need to be situation-specific. They will need to be *localised*. Localisation implies taking the human rights needs as formulated by local people (in response to the impact of economic globalisation on their lives) as the starting point both for the further interpretation and elaboration of human rights norms, and for the development of human rights action, at all levels ranging from the domestic to the global. In order to provide efficient protection against the adverse impact of economic globalisation – itself inevitably a top-down process – human rights need to be as locally relevant as possible. Global human rights need an infusion from below.

Several authors point out that local relevance is essential for the legitimacy of human rights as global norms. Mutua argues that '[o]nly by locating the basis for the cultural legitimacy of certain human rights and mobilizing social forces on that score can respect for universal standards be forged'.[2] Similarly, Baxi conceives of peoples and communities as the primary authors of human rights. Their resistance to (abusive) power 'at a second order level [is] translated into standards and norms adopted by a community of states. In the making of human rights it is the local that translates into global languages the reality of their aspiration for a just world'.[3] Both authors present the need to localise global human rights as a target, rather than as a description of current practice. The objective of this chapter is to investigate how exactly the interplay between local experiences of human rights abuse, and global human rights norms and institutions, can be achieved against the backdrop of economic globalisation.

Inspiration is taken from the field of development studies, where bottom-up approaches enjoy a longer pedigree than in the field of human rights. In discussions on an earlier draft of this chapter, co-editor Wolfgang Benedek pointed out that many of the ideas I was at pains to develop resembled a text adopted fifteen years ago in Arusha. This was the African Charter for Popular Participation in Development and

[2] M. Mutua, *Human Rights: A Political and Cultural Critique* (Philadelphia: Philadelphia University Press, 2002), p. 81.

[3] U. Baxi, *The Future of Human Rights* (New Delhi: Oxford University Press, 2002), p. 101.

Transformation. This Charter does not deal directly with human rights, but stresses the need for popular participation in development, and it emphasises:

> . . . the basic fact that the role of the people and their popular organizations is central to the realization of popular participation. They have to be fully involved, committed and, indeed, seize the initiative. In this regard, it is essential that they establish independent peoples' organizations at various levels that are genuinely grass-root, voluntary, democratically administered and self-reliant and that are rooted in the tradition and culture of the society so as to ensure community empowerment and self-development. Consultative machinery at various levels should be established with governments on various aspects of democratic participation. It is crucial that the people and their popular organizations should develop links across national borders to promote co-operation and interrelationships on sub-regional, regional, South-South and South-North bases. This is necessary for sharing lessons of experience, developing people's solidarity and rising political consciousness on democratic participation.[4]

Along similar lines, this chapter argues that there is a need for more popular participation in human rights, particularly at a time when decisions on economic globalisation are taken at levels remote from the people affected by them.

The continuing validity of the Universal Declaration of Human Rights

By arguing in favour of the localisation of human rights, I do *not* intend to query the validity of the Universal Declaration of Human Rights (UDHR),[5] or subsequent major human rights instruments as a catalogue of global human rights norms. The reasons are pragmatic, rather than profound; so much of value would stand to be lost if a 'clean slate' approach were to be advocated. The proposal is to build upon what exists, rather than to start afresh.

---

[4] Paragraph 11 of the African Charter for Popular Participation in Development and Transformation, Resolution 691(XXV), adopted at the 25th session of the Commission and 16th meeting of the ECA Conference of Ministers Responsible for Economic Planning and Development (19 May 1990). It would be of contemporary interest to examine to what extent the World Bank's commitment to involve civil society in the drawing up of poverty reduction strategies reflects a similar approach.

[5] Universal Declaration of Human Rights, UN General Assembly Resolution 217 A (III), 10 December 1948.

It is true that on 10 December 1948 the United Nations had a much more limited membership than today, and that eight States (the socialist States, Saudi Arabia and South Africa) abstained from endorsing the text. Nevertheless, many non-Western members of the UN Human Rights Commission impacted significantly on the drafting process.[6] Subsequent Declarations adopted at the *world conferences* on human rights in Teheran[7] and Vienna[8] remedied the democratic deficit of the original drafting process, by confirming that the Universal Declaration represented the common understanding of *all* peoples, and constituted an obligation for the members of the international community.[9] Arguments have been made that the UDHR (as a whole or in part) has become part of customary international law.[10]

The Universal Declaration has had, in the words of Richard Falk, 'an extraordinary cumulative impact on the role of human rights in international political life'.[11] The adoption of the UDHR as such boosted the idea that human rights were of universal validity, and the text still enjoys wide support in both governmental and civil society circles. The Universal Declaration has acted as a 'persuasive, liberating force for individuals and groups'[12] in contexts perhaps unforeseen by the drafters of the text (such as decolonisation), lending some credibility to the statement in the Preamble that the UDHR represents the 'highest aspiration of the common people.'[13] In addition, the Universal Declaration has set the direction for the standard-setting and monitoring activities of the United Nations in the field of human rights. Preserving the Universal Declaration as the starting point for discussion on global human rights does justice to this impressive legacy.

Donnelly argues that the UDHR rights can easily be derived from a conception of human beings viewed as free, autonomous persons entitled

---

[6] See S. Waltz, 'Universal Human Rights: The Contribution of Muslim States', *HRQ* 26 (2004) 4, 799–844.

[7] Proclamation of Teheran, Final Act of the International Conference on Human Rights, Teheran, 22 April to 13 May 1968, UN Doc. A/CONF. 32/41 (1968) at 3.

[8] Vienna Declaration, World Conference on Human Rights, Vienna, 14–25 June 1993, UN Doc. A/CONF.157/24 (Part I) (1993) at 20.   [9] Art. 2 of the Proclamation of Teheran.

[10] See A. Eide and G. Alfredsson, 'Introduction' in G. Alfredsson and A. Eide (eds.), *The Universal Declaration of Human Rights: A Common Standard of Achievement* (The Hague: Martinus Nijhoff, 1999), p. xxxi.

[11] R. Falk, *Human rights Horizons* (London: Routledge, 2000), p. 53.

[12] J. Lindgren Alves, 'The Declaration of Human Rights in Post Modernity', *HRQ* 22 (2000) 2, 500.

[13] See Anderson-Gold, *Cosmopolitanism and Human Rights*, (Cardiff: University of Wales Press, 2001), p. 3.

to equal concern and respect. The list, so he argues, is a response to the major perceived threats to human dignity. Those threats are identified as a consequence of political struggle, and the emergence of an increasing number of groups as political actors. He concludes that the UDHR and subsequent key human rights treaties represent 'a widely accepted consensus on the minimum prerequisites for a life of dignity.'[14] It follows from Donnelly's analysis that the UDHR rights remain a relevant, even necessary defence against threats to human dignity *today*. Nevertheless, the UDHR was a response to specific historical circumstances. Circumstances change, and so must human rights. The Universal Declaration is not the omega, but it remains the alpha of human rights.

In achieving the further development of human rights, Habermas' discourse principle may be of assistance. According to the principle, norms are valid when all possibly affected persons agree to them as participants in a rational discourse.[15] The discourse process itself will only be rational if all participants recognise each other's rights as equal contributors to the dialogue.[16] Habermas' discourse principle can be used as a quality control mechanism for the process through which human rights are further developed. If that process takes place at the global level, and the aim is to codify rights that are universally applicable, inevitably the process will have to be cross-cultural.[17]

Human rights allow for plurality

There is no contradiction between maintaining human rights as a global language and allowing for variations in content in order to make human rights protection as locally relevant as possible. On the contrary, global human rights stand to be enriched if they take into account input from varied societies.

Zeleza perceives of the universal human rights regime as a work in progress to which different societies have a role, indeed a right to contribute.[18] He argues for 'contextualisation': universal principles have their

---

[14] See J. Donnelly, *Universal Human Rights in Theory & Practice* (Ithaca: Cornell University Press, 1989), pp. 23–27.

[15] J. Habermas, *Between Facts and Norms* (Cambridge: Polity Press, 1996), p. 107.

[16] *Ibid.*, pp. 118–123.

[17] See B. Parekh, 'Non-ethnocentric Universalism' in T. Dunne and N. Wheeler (eds.), *Human Rights in Global Politics*, (Cambridge: Cambridge University Press, 1999) p. 140.

[18] P. Zeleza, 'The Struggle for Human Rights in Africa' in P. Zeleza and P. McConnaughay (eds.), *Human Rights, the Rule of Law, and Development in Africa* (Philadelphia: University of Pennsylvania Press, 2004) p. 15.

genesis in local situations and traditions, and national insights and experiences will continue to improve and perfect international human rights standards and values.[19] Ibhawoh makes a similar point:

> To enhance its legitimacy, the emerging universal human rights regime must draw upon the cultural peculiarities of each society. . . . [B]ecause different people in different parts of the world both assert and honor different human rights demands, the question of the nature of human rights, must to some extent, ultimately depend on the time, place, institutional setting and the other peculiar circumstances of each society.[20, 21]

Brems develops a theory of 'inclusive universality', which requires efforts on two fronts: within societies, efforts must be undertaken towards cultural, ideological and political change, so as to make those societies more receptive to human rights. And within the international human rights system, flexibility and transformation have to be used so as to make international human rights more receptive to more different societies by accommodating some of their particularist human rights claims.[22] She argues, however, that there is no room for particularities in the context of gross human rights violations that attack the core of human rights. Kjoerum agrees: universality presupposes a differentiation, but variations must not undermine the essence of the norms.[23] But clearly, there is no expectation in international human rights law of absolute uniformity.

At first sight the 'margin of appreciation' technique developed for the purposes of judicial decision-making by the European Court of Human Rights (ECHR) appears appealing if the aim is to localise human rights; the technique has been used in cases where values vary across the region,

---

[19] *Ibid.*, p. 18.

[20] B. Ibhawoh, 'Restraining Univeralism: Africanist Perspectives on Cultural Relativism in the Human Rights Discourse' in P. T. Zeleza and P. McConnaughay (eds.), *Human Rights, The Rule of Law, and Development in Africa* (Philadelphia: University of Pennsylvania Press, 2004), p. 28.

[21] The quote echoes paragraph I. 5 of the Vienna World Conference on Human Rights Declaration: 'All human rights are universal, indivisible and interdependent and interrelated. The international community must treat human rights globally in a fair and equal manner, on the same footing, and with the same emphasis. While the significance of national and regional particularities and various historical, cultural and religious backgrounds must be borne in mind, it is the duty of States, regardless of their political, economic and cultural systems, to promote and protect all human rights and fundamental freedoms'.

[22] E. Brems, *Human Rights: Universality and Diversity* (The Hague: Martinus Nijhoff, 2001), pp. 338, 511.

[23] M. Kjoerum, 'Universal Human Rights: Between the Local and the Global' in K. Hastrup (ed.), *Human Rights on Common Grounds* (The Hague: Kluwer, 2001), pp. 83–87.

and where the Court accepts the government's argument that it is better placed than the regional court to assess the scope of the right in its own society. Brems summarises the Court's case law on the issue as follows:

> The scope of the margin of appreciation and, reversely, that of the control exercised by the Court, is a function of the respective weight of the two scales in the balance. The margin will be wider and the Court's control looser if the threat to the general interest is more urgent or more important and the threat to the individual right is smaller. The margin will be narrower and the Court's control stricter if the threat to the individual right is more serious and the threat to the general interest is smaller. [24]

The application of the technique to specific cases has proven controversial, however;[25] in practice, it functions as a defence instrument for governments, rather than as a device that allows the Court to interpret the Convention in the light of the specific needs of the claimants in a particular society. The technique allows for plurality, not for the purposes of offering more locally relevant protection, but for limiting the scope of individual rights in order to safeguard the general interest as defined by the State.

Carozza suggests that subsidiarity has become a structural principle of international human rights law.[26] He argues that subsidiarity pervades all aspects of human rights law and politics. In the human rights context, the principle requires:

> First, that local communities be left to protect and respect the human dignity and freedom represented by the idea of human rights whenever they are able to achieve those ends on their own . . . Second, subsidiarity supports the integration of local and supranational interpretation and implementation into a single community of discourse with respect to the common good that the idea of human rights represents. And third, to the extent that local bodies cannot accomplish the ends of human rights without assistance, the larger communities of international society have a responsibility to intervene. Insofar as possible, however, the *subsidum* of the larger community should be oriented toward helping the smaller one achieve its goal without supplanting or usurping the latter society's freedom to pursue its own legitimate purposes.[27]

---

[24] Brems, *Human Rights*, p. 366.
[25] J. Brauch, 'The Margin of Appreciation and the Jurisprudence of the European Court of Human Rights: Threat to the Rule of Law', *Colombia JEL* 11 (2004) 1, 113–150.
[26] P. Carozza, 'Subsidiarity as a Structural Principle of International Human Rights Law', *AJIL* 97 (2003) 1, 38–79.   [27] *Ibid.*, pp. 57–58.

The idea that local communities have a primary duty to ensure human rights compliance by their own means is consonant with the idea of local-isation of human rights, but the passage remains ambivalent about the exact identity of the local community. A 'local community' consists of many actors: certainly, both local government and civil society actors, and even in Carozza's view (if my reading of him is correct), national governments. The subsidiarity principle takes on different consequences according to the definition of local community that is used.

Plurality within human rights most clearly results from the coexistence of different regional human rights systems. The major regional human rights treaties have different lists of rights that purport to reflect different regional sensitivities; Falk speculates that the further elaboration and implementation of human rights will take on a regional character.[28] It has for instance been argued that domestic implementation of human rights in Muslim States would improve if the Organization of the Islamic Conference adopted a binding Islamic regional human rights covenant.[29]

The existing American, African and European regional protection mechanisms have approached similar cases differently, whilst all using human rights language. The differences are not a threat to human rights, but a contribution to their effectiveness. Consider for instance the decisions in the Dogan,[30] Awas Tingni[31] and Ogoni[32] cases. Whilst the circumstances of the cases differ, the cases all involve essentially collective claims by politically and economically marginalised communities living off their land, and challenging governmental decisions allowing that land (and its natural resources) to be used in ways with which they disagreed. In the three cases, the regional body finds in favour of the applicants and insists that the relevant government ensures full human rights protection, but the courts opt for a different legal basis. The European Court of Human Rights found that the applicants in the Dogan case, all members of a Kurdish family who were forcibly evicted from an area of political violence, suffered a violation of their individual entitlements to the peaceful

---

[28] R. Falk, Human Rights Horizons (London: Routledge, 2000), p. 52.
[29] M. Baderin, 'Identifying Possible Mechanisms within Islamic Law for the Promotion and Protection of Human Rights in Muslim States', NQHR 22 (2004) 3, 329–346.
[30] European Court of Human Rights, Dogan and others v. Turkey, judgment of 29 June 2004.
[31] Inter-American Court of Human Rights, Mayagna (Sumo) Awas Tingni Community v. Nicaragua, judgment of 31 August 2001.
[32] African Commission on Human and Peoples' Rights, Economic Rights Action Center (SERAC) and the Centre for Economic and Social Rights (CESR) v. Nigeria. Communication No. 155/96, report of 27 May 2002.

enjoyment of their possessions, because an excessive burden was placed on them. In *Awas Tingni*, the Inter-American Court found that the property rights of an indigenous community had been violated by a governmental decision to allow logging activities on indigenous land. The Court stated that property included communal property as defined in accordance with indigenous customary law. The African Commission found, *inter alia*, a violation of the collective right of the Ogoni people to freely dispose of its wealth and natural resources due the to the circumstances under which the Nigerian military authorities allowed oil exploitation in the Ogoni area.

These summaries do not do justice to the wealth of the regional bodies' decisions,[33] and it may be true that institutional differences among the regional systems in part explain the differences in the outcome,[34] but the point remains that the courts achieve the same aim – offering a degree of human rights protection to affected communities – by using different means. Arguably the different approaches reflect the uniqueness of each regional system: a strong emphasis on individual property rights in Europe, a tribute to indigenous conceptions of rights in Latin America, and a reliance on peoples' rights in Africa. The plurality of the approaches reinforces, rather than diminishes the global relevance of human rights. From a global perspective, it is counterproductive to insist on more uniformity, when in reality the human rights responses to challenges on the ground differ in different societies. The human rights regime is well advised to accommodate plurality, in order to address local human rights challenges more effectively.

The view from below

Having established that the human rights regime allows for plurality, the stage is now set for a discussion on how this space can best be used in the interest of extending human rights protection to those most in need. It will be argued that this requires interpreting and further developing human rights in light of the human rights needs as defined by community based organisations.

Why is the contribution of local communities to the interpretation and further normative development of human rights so essential? Human

---

[33] De Feyter, *Human Rights*, pp. 155–166.
[34] See R. Murray and S. Wheatley, 'Groups and the African Charter on Human and Peoples' Rights', *HRQ* 25 (2003) 1, p. 236.

rights crises emerge at the local level. It is at the local level that abuses occur, and where a first line of defence needs to be developed, responses also need to be developed, first and foremost by those that are threatened. It is when people face abuse in their personal experience and in their immediate surroundings that they 'have' to engage in collective action for the defence of their rights,[35] and it is at this time that the efficacy of mechanisms of protection is tested. It is at the local level that the power to enjoy human rights either proves vital or illusory.

The communities which go through a human rights crisis build up knowledge – a usage of human rights linked to concrete living conditions. The recording and transmission of this knowledge (regardless of whether the appeal to human rights was successful or not) is essential if human rights are ever to develop into a global protection tool. Human rights need to develop in light of the lessons learned from attempts to put them into practice at the local level. In a fascinating analysis of five case studies across the globe, based on extensive interviews, Bales shows that the practice of slavery today (defined in the book as the total control of one person by another for the purpose of economic exploitation) is completely different from the old slavery often associated with the American South before 1860.[36] New forms of slavery avoid legal ownership, involve a short-term relationship, and are not based on racial differences. The implication must be that the human rights response to slavery – including the normative response – must change in order to offer effective protection. Without the knowledge of those living as slaves today, such a response can simply not be developed.

There is another argument going beyond efficacy to support an active role for communities facing abuse in the further development of human rights. Olesen criticises the human rights movement for offering a form of solidarity that displays elements of inequality;[37] the movement is based on a one-way relationship between those who offer solidarity and those who benefit from it, and the provider of solidarity is supposed to be stronger than the beneficiary. His analysis echoes Mutua's reference to a savage-victim-saviour metaphor that plagues the human rights movement, where only the saviour is white. Olesen contrasts human rights

---

[35] See R. Lipschutz, *Global Civil Society & Global Environmental Governance* (New York: State University of New York Press, 1996), p. 39.
[36] K. Bales, *Disposable People: New Slavery in the Global Economy* (Berkeley: University of California Press, 2000).
[37] T. Olesen, 'Globalising the Zapatistas: from Third World Solidarity to Global Solidarity', *Third World Quarterly* 25 (2004) 1, 255–267.

solidarity with 'global solidarity', involving a more reciprocal model, 'constructing the grievances of physically, socially and culturally distant people as deeply intertwined.'[38] The textbook example[39] is the transnational solidarity work surrounding the Zapatistas:

> The Zapatistas . . . serve as a source of inspiration and not mainly as an object of solidarity: 'When people come back from a delegation to Chiapas, or an extended stay there, typically they want to figure out ways to apply what they've learned in Chiapas to community organizing here. And when they go down to visit Chiapas in the first place, they aren't going as teachers, but as students.'[40]

Grounding human rights in local experiences offers the human rights movement the opportunity to emphasise similarities between the challenges facing different communities, whilst at the same time respecting and acknowledging local differences.

If the experience of local communities is to inspire the further development of human rights, community-based organisations will have to be the starting point. The World Bank study *Voices of the Poor*[41] describes community-based organisations as 'grassroots organizations managed by members on behalf of members', and distinguishes them from other civil society organisations such as non-governmental organisations and networks of neighbourhood or kin. Kaufman and Dilla Alfonso offer a more detailed description in their study,[42] in which they suggest that community organisations are based at the level of a geographic community, and are founded on common interests (not on political affiliation); they are thus potentially unitary bodies able to express and articulate the felt needs of people in relation to a variety of perspectives. They are mass organisations open to anyone in the community, and represent an attempt to capture more power for the population at the grassroots level. The authors find that community organisations best allow ordinary people to articulate a *holistic* concept of their needs. The World Bank study adds that they are often the only organisations that poor people feel they own and trust, and on which they can rely. Not surprisingly, trust is

---

[38] Olesen, 'Globalising the Zapatistas', p. 259.
[39] See also A. Starr, *Naming the Enemy: Anti-Corporate Movements Confront Globalization* (London: Zed Books, 2005).
[40] Olesen, 'Globalising the Zapatistas', p. 260.
[41] D. Narayan et al, *Voices of the Poor: Can Anyone Hear Us?* (New York: Oxford University Press, 2000), p. 143.
[42] Kaufman, M. and Dilla Alfonso, H. (eds.), *Community Power and Grassroots Democracy* (London: Zed Books, 1997), pp. 9–11.

high when the organisation emanates from within the community, but less so if the organisation is created from the outside, i.e. by government or foreign donors.

Not all community-based organisations will define their work in terms of human rights. *Voices of the Poor* finds that community-based organisations *acting alone have* generally not been a force for change in local power structures. The organisations may remain aloof from the political realm, or may simply not be granted the space by local authorities to engage in political action,[43] and have to work within the ideology of the dominant sector of society (which may not be human rights-friendly at all). From a human rights perspective, community-based organisations are of particular interest when they start using the language of rights as a defence against the threats they face. Of key importance is the perception of a community that a certain practice violates the human rights of the members of the group, even if at the time when the claim is formulated, it may not yet be possible to validate it under the domestic or international legal system. If the general findings of the *Voices of the Poor* study are correct, the likelihood that a community organisation will address an issue in terms of human rights is much higher if the organisation is connected to other, similar, organisations, which facilitates the detection of common causes affecting the communities; and also if it is connected to groups of a different nature.[44] Those 'different groups' in our case are groups with a specific commitment to human rights, i.e. domestic human rights NGOs.

It could be argued that a more natural starting point would be to turn to organisations of victims of human rights violations rather than to community-based organisations. Generally, victim organisations mobilise to seek recognition and influence, in order to promote victim-centred interests.[45] The organisations may take up a variety of tasks: they may offer practical assistance and emotional support to victims; they may assist victims in obtaining compensation by the State or restitution by the offender; they may engage in lobbying to secure an improved role for the victim in the criminal justice system, or may insist on tougher sentencing or a hard-line approach to law and order issues. No doubt, the experiences of victims (and of those who self-identify as victims) are important in order to improve and adjust systems of human rights protection, but

---

[43] Compare P. Uvin, *Aiding Violence: The Development Enterprise in Rwanda* (West Harford: Kumarian Press, 1998), pp. 169–179.   [44] Compare Narajan, *Voices*, pp. 150–151.
[45] J. Goodey, *Victims and Victimology* (Edinburgh: Pearson Education, 2005), p. 102.

there is a risk that their organisations focus narrowly on the defence of the personal interests of their membership, rather than on the need to improve human rights protection as such. It should not be assumed that victim organisations automatically have empathy with other victims of human rights violations who have very different convictions or backgrounds, or that they are committed to the need to extend human rights protection to all. The more inclusive membership of community organisations (which should be open to victims as well) should in principle offer greater chances of a less specific, and perhaps more balanced approach to human rights problems at the local level.

Community-based organisations are only the first link in the chain that is required to ensure that local human rights experiences of human rights impact on the further normative development of human rights. The second link in the chain are local human rights NGOs – private organisations that are independent from the government and the market, and have chosen as their primary aim the promotion and protection of human rights. 'Local' in this context means that they are based in the same country as the relevant community-based organisations. They may well be in the capital, however (and thus physically far away from the community organisations) and be based on expertise, rather than grassroots membership. Local human rights NGOs are important in assisting community organisations in identifying the human rights angle to the situation they face, and in offering them support in the human rights strategy that the community may wish to develop, particularly at the national level. It is worth recalling that the level of municipal law is by far the most important level for the purposes of human rights protection. This is true generally, and in particular if one seeks to address the human rights impact of private actors (such as corporations). Appiagyei-Atua thus describes the 'ideal' (as distinct from the actual) role of human rights NGOs in Africa as 'an organization that forms a vital component of civil society and which devotes its resources to helping marginalized entities on the dependence structure to be politically-conscious so as to be in a position to articulate, organize and assert claims and protect their rights from further abuse'.[46] It is of equal importance, however, that local human rights NGOs learn from community organisations about the reality of human rights-related struggles on the ground, and that they transmit lessons learned to the international level. Very often community

[46] K. Appiagyei-Atua, 'Human Rights NGOs and their Role in the Promotion and Protection of Rights in Africa', *International Journal on Minority and Group Rights* 9 (2002) 3, 289.

organisations will not have contacts with the international human rights regime, and will need to rely on specialised human rights NGOs to establish the connection.

This takes us to the third link in the chain: international non-governmental human rights organisations (INGOs), i.e. organisations with an international membership that act across national borders in defence of the human rights of a wide variety of individuals and groups. The involvement of INGOs is essential when the domestic political space is very limited, and in particular when restrictive domestic legislation curtails the actions of local human rights NGOs.[47] But even when political space is available, Kaldor argues that international involvement is necessary: 'those who are trying to exert a constructive influence over local life in a globalised world, can only succeed if they have outside support and access to those international organizations that can influence governments and global regulatory processes'.[48]

In a globalised world, the causes of human rights violations are increasingly not exclusively domestic. Powerful States take decisions that have extraterritorial effects. Intergovernmental organisations affect standards of living. Companies organise across borders. Domestic actors face constraints in their response because their range is limited geographically. Not only is there a need for global rules, there is also a need for globally concerted action.

Nevertheless, the relationship should not only be top-down – INGOs coming in to assist domestic actors in a human rights struggle whenever such an action fits within the INGO's mission or strategic plan – but also bottom-up. Missions and strategic decisions of international human rights NGOs, including policies on the normative development of human rights, should reflect the perceptions of human rights needs at the local level, where the purported beneficiaries of their actions live. It is not at all certain that this is current practice – accountability to beneficiaries is generally not a great strength of international human rights NGOs. *Voices of the Poor*, for example, reports that organisations 'known worldwide for their excellent work' are mentioned only infrequently by the poor.[49] Amnesty International has been essential in providing information and lobbying global institutions on human rights' violations, but has

---

[47] Compare B. He, 'Transnational Civil Society and the National Identity Question in East Asia', *Global Governance* 10 (2004) 2, 227–246.
[48] M. Kaldor, 'Transnational civil society' in T. Dunne and N. Wheeler (eds.), *Human Rights in Global Politics* (Cambridge: Cambridge University Press, 1999), p. 209.
[49] Narajan *et al.*, *Voices*, p. 131.

little tradition in working closely with domestic human rights NGOs, let alone community organisations, in assisting them to campaign domestically or involving them in Amnesty's own priority setting. Accounts of Amnesty's work at the United Nations provide little evidence of any commitment to support the human rights concerns of local organisations.[50] Amnesty chose the alternative route of trying to set *itself* up as a grassroots organisation in as many (strategically important) countries as possible, but has perennially struggled to flourish in non-Western societies. Gready's comment sums up this discussion of the role civil society organizations: '

Civil society is the engine behind a normative agenda seeking to establish and enforce contracts from below. Ordinary people can, and should, make and monitor laws.[51]

Civil society organisations cannot, however, make law directly. As Rajagopal points out, in international law, their 'texts of resistance' are not a source of law,[52] nor do they have any law-making authority in domestic law. They are able to monitor compliance with laws, but civil society monitoring mechanisms have no powers of enforcement. Nor should they have any – they lack the democratic legitimacy necessary to exact discipline. In the fields of law-making and enforcement, civil society organisations are dependent on alliances with others who do enjoy such competencies, i.e. governments and inter-governmental organisations.

This takes us to the fourth link in the chain. Keck and Sikkink's well-known work on transnational advocacy networks[53] is particularly relevant in this context. Transnational advocacy networks include: '[t]hose relevant actors working internationally on an issue, who are bound together by shared values, a common discourse, and dense exchanges of information and services'.[54] Such networks may include the following actors: international and domestic nongovernmental research and advocacy organisations; local social movements; foundations; the media; churches, trade unions, consumer organisations and intellectuals; parts

---

[50] Compare R. Cook, 'Amnesty International at the United Nations' in P. Willets (ed.), *The Conscience of the World* (London: Hurst & Company, 1996); K. Martens, 'An Appraisal of Amnesty International's work at the United Nations: Established Areas of Activities and Shifting Priorities since the 1990s', *HRQ* 26 (2004) 4, 1050–1070.

[51] P. Gready (ed.), *Fighting for Human Rights* (London: Routledge, 2004), p. 8.

[52] B. Rajagopal, *International Law from Below* (Cambridge: Cambridge University Press, 2003), p. 233.

[53] M. Keck and K. Sikkink, *Activists Beyond Borders* (Ithaca: Cornell University Press, 1998).

[54] *Ibid.*, p. 2.

of regional and international intergovernmental organisations; and parts of the executive and/or parliamentary branches of governments.[55] The authors suggest that such networks are most prevalent in issue areas characterised by high value content and informational uncertainty.

Human rights are one of these issue areas. In his analysis of recent major international human rights campaigns, Gready confirms that most were based on 'mixed actor coalitions', NGO-led but involving a broad range of other parties including business, governments, IGOs, and parts of and personnel within these actors.[56] Alliances with governments proved to be challenging, but the trend is that NGOs increasingly work with sympathetic States, or with sympathetic individuals within States. In the context of international alliances, 'government' primarily means the executive branch – ministers, diplomats, and civil servants, who engage in diplomatic negotiations. At the domestic level, however, it is equally important to be able to rely on judges who are willing to give domestic effect to human rights, and on Members of Parliament, who are willing to take legislative initiatives in the field of human rights.

Transnational advocacy networks, as perceived above, do not necessarily imply institutionalised alliances. They are based primarily on voluntary communication and exchanges, which may be public, but could just as well be unofficial and based on shared convictions between individuals situated in different parts of the network. Individuals have been found to change places in the human rights network as well – moving with ease from governmental to non-governmental organisations or vice versa. In the relationship between non-governmental and governmental actors, informal types of collaboration on human rights are popular, because both actors may worry about the effects on their image of more public cooperation.

In summary, a bottom-up approach to human rights is dependent on the existence of a network consisting of four partners: community-based organisations, local human rights NGOs, international human rights NGOs, and allies in governmental and intergovernmental institutions. Although some such networks may exist, or have functioned in the context of specific campaigns,[57] it is not contended that this type of networking is current general practice. There are plentiful examples of community-based organisations without human rights awareness, of local

---

[55] *Ibid.*, p. 9.   [56] Gready (ed.), *Fighting*, p. 18.
[57] Compare T. Risse, S. Ropp and K. Sikkink (eds.), *The Power of Human Rights* (Cambridge: Cambridge University Press, 1999).

human rights NGOs disconnected from grassroots organisations, of international human rights NGOs that self-define their priorities without any reference to local partners, and of governmental and intergovernmental actors that persevere in perceiving of international relations and international law as the reserved domain of governments. For many actors at the different levels (whether governmental or nongovernmental) becoming receptive to bottom-up networking will pose a challenge, and require a change in their working methods.

Nor does the creation of a network in itself suffice to ensure that human rights will be built from below. A bottom-up approach requires that the human rights experiences of communities set the agenda for the entire network. Whether this will happen depends upon the relationships between the actors in the network, which are ideally based on an egalitarian 'Habermas-like' discourse, resulting in a common understanding of human rights and of the strategy to be pursued. In reality, resources may be divided unequally among the actors, and a top-down hierarchy may set in, unless power balances are negotiated very carefully.[58] Discussions about what it means in practice to give local content to global human rights rules are bound to take place. Writing about environmental networks, Lipschutz warns:

> There is also an inherent tension between these global networks and the local organizations linked into them. By their very nature, the networks of global civil society tend to be cosmopolitan, in the sense that they are driven by Ecology, a shared, global worldview. But, as noted above, the world is characterized by ecological diversity, both physical and social. As a result, there is a continual struggle between the global and the local, as the former tries to impose some part of its vision on the latter, and the latter resists yielding up its particular identity to the former. The local does have leverage, however, since those actors whose reach is 'global' cannot succeed unless they have access to the knowledge, legitimacy, and social capital possessed by the local . . .[59]

It is to be expected that similar discussions will emerge within human rights networks about the tension between the shared global view of human rights, and the vision of local organisations on the reality of human rights struggles on the ground; such discussions are exactly what are required in order to improve the universal relevance of human rights.

---

[58] Compare L. Henry, G. Mohan and H. Yanacopulos, 'Networks as Transnational Agents of Development', *Third World Quarterly* 25 (2004) 2, 839–855.
[59] Lipschutz, *Global Civil Society*, pp. 74–75.

The question of whether network actors are able in practice to manage the model in such a way as to achieve the grounding of human rights in the experiences of local communities goes beyond the reach of the conceptual desk study that I am attempting here. That question can only be answered through interdisciplinary field research on the operation of a specific network over a sufficiently long period of time. Similarly, it is tempting to speculate what the outcome of localisation would be for the future interpretation and further development of human rights norms (particularly on current contentious issues within the human rights movement itself), but again the model proposed in the chapter is that such issues should be decided through the process described above, rather than through abstract reasoning.

A return to the global

Falk's argument that regional organisations are well placed to ensure sufficient plurality within the human rights regime can easily be extended to their superior ability to take into account local human rights experiences. Nevertheless, a need for the involvement of a global institution (the United Nations) in the further elaboration of human rights remains. Sufficiently wide global relevance can, prima facie, be assumed whenever the new human rights norm seeks to address the adverse effects of State, corporate or organisational strategies that affect countries in different parts of the world or have a global impact. The challenge is, however, to ensure that these global norms build on local human rights experiences.

Twenty years ago, Alston argued that 'the application of a formal list of substantive requirements' to the normative development of human rights was unworkable, because decision making at the preferred body for proclaiming new human rights, the UN General Assembly, was not sufficiently rational and objective.[60] Instead, Alston proposed procedural requirements that the General Assembly would need to meet whenever it engaged in drafting new human rights law, including a comprehensive study by the UN Secretary-General incorporating comments from 'governments, relevant international and regional organizations and non-governmental organizations'.[61] Alston's proposal was not adopted – perhaps it was too rational as well. Of course, one could still try to think of procedural devices that would increase the opportunities for hearing

---

[60] P. Alston, 'Conjuring up New Human Rghts: A Proposal for Quality Control', *AJIL* 78 (1984) 3, 618.   [61] *Ibid.*, p. 620.

the voices of those suffering abuse in the context of the UN human rights machinery, but in the end it is the effectiveness of the networking described above that will determine whether the global system becomes more open to a bottom-up approach.

More sensitivity of UN human rights bodies to local experiences could perhaps also result from an increased UN human rights presence in the field, which exposes UN officials to local human rights experiences. At least in theory, lessons learned from working with local communities could be used to detect gaps in the global protection system or to redirect global human rights action.

Thematic Special Rapporteurs of the UN Commission on Human Rights perhaps come closest to using visits, usually short term, for such a purpose. The missions allow direct access to community-based organisations, local non-governmental organisations and benevolent government officials. Country visits may be used for comparative purposes, and thus lead to the identification of a global trend that needs to be tackled from a human rights perspective.[62] There is however, no systematic commitment to learning from below in the missions. Even if a Special Rapporteur takes the initiative to report on the human rights needs of local communities, there is no guarantee (and in fact little evidence) of follow-up at the level of the UN Commission on Human Rights, let alone at the UN General Assembly.

Louise Arbour, the current UN High Commissioner for Human Rights, has made the increased in-country and regional presence of her officers a high priority. As she sees it, her office pursues two overarching goals: protection and empowerment. Empowerment:

> [I]s a broad concept, but I use it in two distinct senses. Experience from many countries teaches us that human rights are most readily respected, protected and fulfilled when *people are empowered to assert and claim their rights*. Our work, therefore, should empower rights holders . . . Additionally, successful strategies to protect human rights depend on a favorable government response to claims that are advanced. Empowerment is also about *equipping those with a responsibility to implement human rights with the means to do so*.[63]

The OHCHR Plan of Action recognises that the Office can 'benefit from the support, analysis and expertise of civil society';[64] it is also prepared to

---

[62] See de Feyter, *Human Rights*, pp. 106–107.
[63] UN High Commissioner for Human Rights (2005), The OHCHR Plan of Action: Protection and Empowerment, A/59/2005/Add.3 at paras 36–37.　　[64] *Ibid.*, at para 111.

offer direct protection for civil society groups facing threats. Clearly, the Plan of Action creates an opening for the UN to act as a global actor that could support the localisation of human rights.

A word of caution is in order, however. Long-term UN human rights field presences often take place in the context of peacekeeping operations, with the initiative coming from New York rather than from Geneva. The need for UN field action may be based on the lack of capacity of the State, and perhaps also of non-State actors, to ensure human rights protection; the State may have 'collapsed', and civil society may not exist. Often this lack of domestic capacity is precisely what triggers UN involvement on the ground: the lack of internalisation of human rights justifies the inter-vention of the external actor.[65] In its most extreme form, the UN itself takes over the administration of a territory (as in Kosovo), and sets itself up for charges that it is violating human rights.[66] A bottom-up approach to human rights may not be self-evident in those circumstances. And as is the case for the Special Rapporteurs, international support (of member States of higher echelons of the UN bureaucracy) for the findings of local UN staff on human rights isues may be less than overwhelming.[67]

However, except perhaps in extreme circumstances when local human rights resources are non-existent, at least on the ground UN human rights field officers should be able to play the role of a temporary catalytic actor: 'The human rights officers work to augment the state's capacity to respect human rights (supply) and increase the citizens' proaction to ensure their rights are respected (demand).'[68] Or in Kofi Annan's words: '. . . the United Nations has a unique bridge-building ability to bring together civil society and Governments, creating opportunities for building trust.'[69]

In a context of economic globalisation, the necessity to take local human rights needs into account is not limited to global human rights institutions. Human rights bodies do not settle disputes on economic

---

[65] T. Risse and K. Sikkink, 'The Socialization of International Human Rights Norms into Domestic Practices: Introduction' in T. Risse, S. Ropp, and K. Sikkink (eds.), *The Power of Human Rights* (Cambridge: Cambridge University Press, 1999), p. 11.

[66] F. Mégret and F. Hoffman, 'The UN as a Human Rights Violator? Some Reflections on the United Nations' Changing Human Rights Responsibilities', *HRQ* 25 (2003) 2, 314–342.

[67] Compare B. Majekodunmi, 'United Nations Human Rights Field Officers' in Y. Danieli (ed.), *Sharing the Front Line and the Back Hills* (Amityville: Baywood, 2002), pp. 137–146.

[68] T. Howland, 'UN Human Rights Field Presence as a Proactive Instrument of Peace and Social Change: Lessons from Angola', *HRQ* 26 (2004) 1, 14.

[69] UN High Commissioner for Human Rights (2005), The OHCHR Plan of Action: Protection and Empowerment, at para 111.

globalization; these are decided in the context of intergovernmental organisations such as the WTO, or through international arbitration. Such institutions are far removed from the communities where the human rights impact of economic decisions is felt, and tend to perceive international trade and investment rules as self-contained systems, allowing for little consideration of human rights. The traditional view of international arbitration, for instance, is that it is essentially confidential, and that arbitrators should not be under public scrutiny, because this would prevent them from giving proper weight to the contractual rights of private investors. So is there really any hope that human rights consequences at the local level will ever play a role in their decision making?

Some cracks in the armour appear. One Arbitration Tribunal of the International Centre for the Settlement of Investment Disputes (ICSID) recently allowed a petition, as *amicus curiae*, by a group of five non-governmental organisations in the *Aguas Argentinas et al v. Argentina*[70] case. It was the first time an ICSID tribunal took such a decision against the wishes of the private companies who act as requesters in the dispute. The ICSID Convention and the arbitration rules are silent on whether non-parties can contribute to proceedings as 'friends of the court'. Interestingly, the ICSID Secretariat has now proposed to change the rules to explicitly enable tribunals to allow submissions by non-disputing parties, and to allow for public hearings.[71] In the context of the North American Free Trade Agreement (NAFTA) arbitration, open proceedings are already quite common.

In the above-mentioned case, Aguas Argentinas, a consortium of which Suez is the largest shareholder, took over the water and sewerage system of Buenos Aires in 1993 from a badly run state-owned water company. The takeover was part of a huge privatisation/deregulation/ decentralisation policy adopted by the Carlos Menem administration, which was under pressure from the international financial institutions in order to obtain relief for Argentina's huge external debt. The relationship between the consortium and official institutions has gone through many ups and downs,[72] and the details of the dispute are not known; but there is little doubt that the consortium argues that it has not received a fair

---

[70] ICSID Tribunal, *Aguas Argentinas, Suez, Sociedad General de Aguas de Barcelona and Vivendi Universal v. Argentine Republic* (ICSID Case no. ARB/03/19), order in response to a petition for transparency and participation as *amicus curiae* of 19 May 2005.

[71] Working Paper of the ICSID Secretariat, Suggested Changes to the ICSID Rules and Regulations, 12 May 2005.

[72] A. Sjölander Holland, *The Water Business* (London: Zed Books, 2005), pp. 46–61.

return on investment, due to the national government's combined decision in December 2001 to devalue the peso, and to convert its debts from US dollars to pesos, and to its refusal to approve tariff increases.

The five non-governmental organisations[73] asserted that the case involved matters of basic public interest and the fundamental rights of people living in the area. They filed for access to the hearings of the case, the opportunity to present legal arguments as *amicus curiae*, and access to all of the documents. The Tribunal accepted that there was a justification for the acceptance of *amicus curiae* briefs in 'ostensibly' private litigation when cases involved issues of public interest, and because decisions in those cases have the potential, directly or indirectly, to affect persons beyond those immediately involved as parties in the case:

> The factor that gives this case particular public interest is that the investment dispute centers around the water distribution and sewage systems of a large metropolitan area, the city of Buenos Aires and surrounding municipalities. Those systems provide basic public services to millions of people and as a result may raise a variety of complex public and international law questions, including human rights considerations. Any decision rendered in this case, whether in favor of the Claimants or the Respondent, has the potential to affect the operation of those systems and thereby the public they serve.[74]

The petitioners were instructed to file a subsequent petition giving details about their identity, their interest and specific expertise to act as friends of the court. The issue of access to documents would be dealt with subsequently. The request for open hearings was denied, as current ICSID rules provide that this is only possible with the consent of the parties of the dispute. The element of consent was missing, given the consortium's objection.

The importance of the Order should obviously not be exaggerated. We are a galaxy away from an ICSID decision that would give precedence to the human rights of the users of a public service in a case where the investor argues that its profitability has been harmed by post-investment government measures. Concerns remain about ICSID as a forum, since the Institute is part of the World Bank Group, and another part of the same group, the International Finance Corporation, is a creditor of

---

[73] Asociacion Civil por la Igualdad y la Justicia, Centro de Estudios Legales y Sociales, Center for International Environmental Law, Consumidores Libres Cooperativa Ltda de Provision de Servicios de Accion Communitaria, and Union de Usarios y Consumidores.

[74] Howland, 'UN Human Rights Field Presence', 19.

twenty percent of Aguas Argentinas international debt, and of five percent of its equity shares.[75] After all, justice must also be seen to be done. On the other hand, it is unlikely that any progress in acknowledging local human rights needs in economic international relations will occur unless community organisations are able to take an active role. In that sense developments at the WTO, NAFTA and ICSID on allowing community organisations to intervene in proceedings as non-parties, matter.[76]

Conclusion

This chapter has argued that if the world economy is globalising, there is a need to localise human rights. Localisation was defined as a process whereby local human rights needs inspire the further interpretation and elaboration of human rights norms at levels ranging from the domestic to the global and serve as a point of departure for human rights action. It was argued that taking inspiration from the local does not require abandoning the Universal Declaration of Human Rights and subsequent international law, but that it will contribute to the universal legitimacy of human rights. Localisation inevitably implies that a degree of plurality is accepted within human rights discourse, but this is a welcome development. In any case, there are no legal obstacles to doing so.

The localisation of human rights depends on cooperation between actors at different levels. Four links in a chain were identified. Community-based organisations are essential in identifying local human rights needs – their experience should provide the direction for the localisation effort. The role of local human rights NGOs is to assist community-based organisations in familiarising themselves with rights approaches, and subsequently to support them in taking their human rights agenda to the domestic level and beyond. Local NGOs also serve as the anchor for connections with international civil society. The involvement of international non-governmental organisations is important, because in a context of economic globalisation, the causes of human rights violations are no longer exclusively domestic. In addition, in countries where the space for political action is very limited, intervention by external actors is vital. Finally, alliances need to be forged with actors enjoying law-making and law

---

[75] As of December 2001.
[76] The work of the World Bank Inspection Panel is also relevant in this context. For some of my own work on this procedure, see my contribution on 'Self-regulation' in W. Van Genugten, P. Hunt and S. Mathews, *World Bank, IMF and Human Rights* (Nijmegen: Wolf Legal Publishers, 2003), pp. 79–137.

enforcement authority, i.e. those committed, in governmental and inter-governmental circles, to a vision of human rights that responds to local needs.

For all actors referred to above, opening up to a strategy of localizing human rights poses a challenge. The final section focused in particular on global actors, and reviewed a number of obstacles, but also of opportunities, in the current practice of UN human rights institutions and of international economic organisations.

Bibliography

Alston, P., 'Conjuring up New Human Rights: A Proposal for Quality Control', *AJIL* 78 (1984) 3, 607–621

Anderson-Gold, S., *Cosmopolitanism and Human Rights* (Cardiff: University of Wales Press, 2001)

Appiagyei-Atua, K., 'Human Rights NGOs and their role in the Promotion and Protection of Rights in Africa', *International Journal on Minority and Group Rights* 9 (2002) 3, 265–289

Baderin, M., 'Identifying Possible Mechanisms within Islamic Law for the Promotion and Protection of Human Rights in Muslim States', *NQHR* 22 (2004) 3, 329–346

Bales, K., *Disposable People: New Slavery in the Global Economy* (Berkeley: University of California Press, 2000)

Baxi, U., *The Future of Human Rights* (New Delhi: Oxford University Press, 2002)

Brauch, J., 'The Margin of Appreciation and the Jurisprudence of the European Court of Human Rights: Threat to the Rule of Law', *Colombia JEL* 11 (2004) 1, 113–150

Brems, E., *Human Rights: Universality and Diversity* (The Hague: Martinus Nijhoff, 2001)

Carozza, P., 'Subsidiarity as a Structural Principle of International Human Rights Law', *American Journal of International Law* 97 (2003) 1, 38–79

Cook, R., 'Amnesty International at the United Nations' in Willets, P. (ed.), *The Conscience of the World* (London: Hurst & Company, 1996)

De Feyter, K. and Gomez Isa, F. (eds.), *Privatisation and Human Rights in the Age of Globalisation* (Antwerp: Intersentia, 2005)

De Feyter, K., *Human Rights: Social Justice in the Age of the Market* (London: Zed Books, 2005)

Donnelly, J., *Universal Human Rights in Theory and Practice* (Ithaca: Cornell University Press, 1989)

Eide, A. and Alfredsson, G. 'Introduction' in Alfredsson, G. and Eide, A. (eds.), *The Universal Declaration of Human Rights: a Common Standard of Achievement* (The Hague: Martinus Nijhoff, 1999), pp. xxv-xxxv

Falk, R. *Human Rights Horizons* (London: Routledge, 2000)

Goodey, J., *Victims and Victimology* (Edinburgh: Pearson Education, 2005)

Gready, P. (ed.), *Fighting for Human Rights* (London: Routledge, 2004)

Habermas, J., *Between Facts and Norms* (Cambridge: Polity Press, 1996)

He, B., 'Transnational Civil Society and the National Identity Question in East Asia', *Global Governance* 10 (2004) 2, 227–246

Henry L., Mohan, G. and Yanacopulos, H., 'Networks as Transnational Agents of Development', *Third World Quarterly* 25 (2004) 2, 839–855

Howland, T., 'UN Human Rights Field Presence as Proactive Instrument of Peace and Social Change: Lessons from Angola', *HRQ* 26 (2004) 1, 1–28

Ibhawoh, B., 'Restraining Universalism: Africanist Perspectives on Cultural Relativism in the Human Rights Discourse' in Zeleza, P. T. and McConnaughay, P. (eds.), *Human Rights, the Rule of Law, and Development in Africa* (Philadelphia: University of Pennsylvania Press, 2004), pp. 21–39

Kaldor, M., 'Transnational Civil Society' in Dunne, T. and Wheeler, N. (eds.), *Human Rights in Global Politics* (Cambridge: Cambridge University Press, 1999), pp. 195–213

Kaufman, M. and Dilla Alfonso, H. (eds.), *Community Power and Grassroots Democracy* (London: Zed Books, 1997)

Keck, M. and Sikkink, K., *Activists Beyond Borders* (Ithaca: Cornell University Press, 1998)

Kjoerum, M., 'Universal Human Rights: Between the Local and the Global' in Hastrup, K. (ed.), *Human Rights on Common Grounds* (The Hague: Kluwer, 2001), pp. 75–89

Lindgren Alves, J., 'The Declaration of Human Rights in Post Modernity', *HRQ* 22 (2000) 2, 478–500

Lipschutz, R., *Global Civil Society & Global Environmental Governance* (New York: State University of New York Press, 1996)

Majekodunmi, B., 'United Nations Human Rights Field Officers' in Danieli, Y. (ed.), *Sharing the Front Line and the Back Hills* (Amityville: Baywood, 2002), pp. 137–146

Martens, K., 'An Appraisal of Amnesty International's Work at the United Nations: Established Areas of Activities and Shifting Priorities since the 1990s', *HRQ* 26 (2004) 4, 1050–1070

Mégret, F. and Hoffman, F., 'The UN as a Human Rights Violator? Some Reflections on the United Nations' Changing Human Rights Responsibilities', *HRQ* 25 (2003) 2, 314–342

Murray, R. and Wheatley, S., 'Groups and the African Charter on Human and Peoples' Rights', *HRQ* 25 (2003) 1, 213–236

Mutua, M., *Human Rights: a Political and Cultural Critique* (Philadelphia: Philadelphia University Press, 2002)

Narajan, D. with Patel, R., Schafft, K., Rademacher A., Koch-Schulte, S., *Voices of the Poor: Can Anyone Hear Us?* (New York: Oxford University Press, 2000)

Olesen, T., 'Globalising the Zapatistas: From Third World Solidarity to Global Solidarity', *Third World Quarterly* 25 (2004) 1, 255–267

Parekh, B., 'Non-Ethnocentric Universalism' in Dunne, T. and Wheeler, N. (eds.), *Human Rights in Global Politics* (Cambridge: Cambridge University Press, 1999), pp. 128–159

Rajagopal, B., *International Law from Below* (Cambridge: Cambridge University Press, 2003)

Risse, T. and Sikkink, K., 'The Socialization of International Human Rights Norms into Domestic Practices: Introduction' in Risse, T., Ropp, S. and Sikkink, K. (eds.), *The Power of Human Rights* (Cambridge, Cambridge University Press, 1999), pp. 1–38

Risse, T., Ropp, S. and Sikkink, K. (eds.), *The Power of Human Rights* (Cambridge: Cambridge University Press, 1999)

Sjölander Holland, A., *The Water Business* (London: Zed Books, 2005)

Starr, A., *Naming the Enemy: Anti-Corporate Movements Confront Globalization* (London: Zed Books, 2005)

Uvin, P., *Aiding Violence: The Development Enterprise in Rwanda* (West Harford: Kumarian Press, 1998)

Van Genugten, W., Hunt, P. and Mathews, S., *World Bank, IMF and Human Rights* (Nijmegen: Wolf Legal Publishers, 2003)

Waltz, S., 'Universal Human Rights: The Contribution of Muslim States', *HRQ* 26 (2004) 4, 799–844

Zeleza, P., 'The Struggle for Human Rights in Africa' in Zeleza, P. T., McConnaughay, P. (eds.), *Human Rights, the Rule of Law, and Development in Africa* (Philadelphia: University of Pennsylvania Press, 2004), pp. 1–18

Globalisation and Social Rights

ADALBERTO PERULLI

Introduction: the social dimension of the global market

The growing economic interdependence between Nation-States, and the fast expansion of global trade, linked to international financial mobility, are at the origin of the extensive debate about the measures needed to protect fundamental social rights from the increased competition of markets and resulting competitive devaluation of national social policies.[1] The latest analyses of the evolving tendencies of globalisation highlight two fundamental implications for national labour law systems. One is linked to the relationship between the economy and the State, and concerns the decline of the nation-state's control of the regulation of the market. The other relates to the de-nationalisation of economic activities by companies, especially multinational ones, in large part influenced by regional differences in labour costs and social security programmes, which transplants the declining of the regulatory capacity of the nation-state and 'deconstruction' into labour law systems.[2]

Both tendencies risk causing a general rush towards an acceptance of a lowest common denominator level in workplace standards; standards which are anyway being threatened by what institutional economists call 'destructive competition'[3] and by the resulting processes of global

[1] See P. Alston, 'Labour Rights as Human Rights: The Not So Happy State of The Art', in P. Alston (ed.), *Labour Rights as Human Rights* (Oxford: Oxford University Press, 2005), p. 3; S. Deakin, 'Social Rights in a Globalized Economy', in Alston (ed.), *Labour Rights as Human Rights*, p. 25; B. Wedderburn, 'Common Law, Labour Law, Global Law', in B. Hepple (ed.), *Social Rights in a Global Context* (Cambridge: Cambridge University Press, 2002), p. 19.

[2] Many scholars have argued that globalisation and new forms of production provoke an 'identity crisis of labour law': see M. D'Antona, 'Labour Law at the Century's End: An Identity Crisis', in J. Conaghan, R. Fischl and K. Klare (eds.) *Labour Law in an Era of Globalization: Transformative Practices and Possibilities* (Oxford: Oxford University Press, 2002), p. 31.

[3] See G. De Martino, 'L'harmonisation des normes du travail dans une perspective internationaliste', *Syndicalisme et société* (1998), 265.

delocalisation of production, phenomena which are followed by the competitive devaluation of internal social policies. The search for greater competitiveness is often carried out, even in the more advanced and consolidated economic systems, through the compromise of social rights and sweatshop-like practices instead of through re-planning of organisational models of production based on making workers responsible and involving them. Thus, these scenes generate a new type of value questions, on the one hand a question relating to the transfer of the functions of governing the market to supranational levels, which, until now, have been carried out by States in national spheres. On the other hand, a new question relates to the possibility of channelling the protection of social standards onto the global level, by placing the obligation to respect workers' minimum standards under the protection of institutions regulating international trade.

The Uruguay Round negotiations and the following Marrakech Agreement constitute a decisive achievement and signal the expansion of the world economy, but they do not provide an adequate reflection of the effects that such liberalisation could have on the labour markets of the contracting Parties. In reality, the constitutive agreement of the World Trade Organization (WTO), in facilitating access to the markets of industrialised countries, and in particular the specific imports of developing countries (DCs), creates strong tensions mainly in the low-salary sectors of the countries with higher social standards and in the higher-salary sectors in the less developed countries.[4] Basically, as a result of the elimination or reduction of trade barriers, the developed Western systems suffer unregulated competition from the emerging countries, which have an inexhaustible 'reserve army' ready to enter the labour market with lower salaries and social standards. It fatally pushes the Western economies towards the retributive systems and conditions of exploitation of the workforce of the competing countries.[5]

These phenomena require the reiteration of globalisation into

---

[4] See M. Vellano, 'Full Employment and Fair Labour Standards in the Framework of the WTO', in P. Mengozzi (ed.), *International Trade Law on the 50th Anniversary of the Multilateral Trade System* (Milano: Giuffrè, 1999), p. 390.

[5] For an analysis on the impact of labour cost on the mobility of capital in Europe, see C. Erickson and S. Kuruvilla, 'Labor Costs and the Social Dumping Debate in the European Union', *Industrial Labour Relations Review* 48 (1994), 28; more generally on the effects of international trade on employment and salaries, see, R. E. Baldwin, *Trade Policy in a Changing World Economy* (Chicago: University of Chicago Press, 1988), p. 181; N. Gaston and D. Trefler, 'Protection, Trade and Wages: Evidence from US Manufacturing', *Industrial Labour Relations Review* 47 (1994), 574.

politically shared schemes that can legitimise the market action. In fact, as it was written by Thurow, 'if the époque of the national economic legislation has been exhausted, world economic legislation has not yet begun'.[6] This statement remains valid. In today's context, a similar regulative perspective can be maintained only as regards supranational sources – or an interstate network maintained by interdependence – instituted to favour cooperation in wider areas than the ones defined by the singular states which regulate economic phenomena on the regional[7] or on the global[8] scale. It means that there are issues where two different but not conflicting *ratios* compete. One such issue relates to the planning and creation of a global economic order, that is not only reduced to the mere juridical creation and institutionalisation of markets but also introduces guarantees against the undesired social consequences of globalisation.[9] The other one entails avoiding 'social dumping', the distorting phenomenon that prevents the optimal allocation of resources on the global scale.[10]

The following analysis attempts to put these two perspectives into correlation. On the one hand, the intention is to inquire about the relationships, historical, logical and functional, that link market liberalisation with labour law, whilst, on the other hand, reconsidering the regulatory options An emphasis will be placed on a perspective which could be capable of connecting the traditional instruments of international labour law with those of economic governance (and especially with international economic law).

Trade liberalisation and labour law: the ambivalences

Trade liberalisation has a very complex relationship with labour law, indicating a hypothesis of both a virtuous link, and an indomitable

---

[6] See L. C. Thurow, *The Future of Capitalism* (New York: William Morrow & Co, 1996), p. 77.

[7] E.g., the European Union (EU), or the North American Free Trade Agreement (NAFTA).

[8] E.g., the WTO.

[9] J. Habermas, *Die postnationale Konstellation. Politische Essays* (Frankfurt am Main: Suhrkamp, 1998); D. Held, *Global Covenant. The Social Democratic Alternative to the Washington Consensus* (Cambridge: Polity Press, 2004).

[10] See A. Lyon-Caen, 'Pérennité d'une interrogation', in *Bulletin de droit comparé du travail et de la sécurité sociale* (1996), 13–20; L. Dubin, *La protection des normes sociales dans les échanges internationaux* (Marseille: Presses Universitaires D'Aix-Marseille, 2003); this link received inputs also from the OECD study on *Trade, Employment and Labour Standards: A Study of Core Workers*, www.oecd.org.

opposition. On the basis of a historical analysis, the link between the two terms is in the very genetic code of labour law. At heart, the 'liberation' of work – and therefore the birth of the 'social question' which leads to the creation of labour law – was made possible by a process of liberalisation of exchanges (trade) that made people free to offer their own work for others: '*il sera libre à toute personne de faire tel ou tel négoce et d'exercer telle profession, art ou métier qu'elle trouvera bon*' [it is permitted/free to all persons to carry out any business or practice any profession, art or job that he or she deems right. *Translation by the author*] as expressed by Article 7 of the Decree of Allarde of 1791.[11] The link between the dimension of exchanges, and the labour law norm, then develops on a functional analytical basis, so that labour law takes part in the 'equalisation' of free competition conditions in the economic contest of the market. This happens to the extent that, according to Lyon-Caen, labour law comes to existence as a *component* of competition law and not as its antithesis; the protection of work represents a by-product of that primary function.[12] From this perspective, labour law and trade liberalisation progress together, a process accentuated by the current context of the globalisation of the economy. The universality of labour law recalls the need for a global governance of social rights also from an economic point of view, which favours the path towards a civil society and a global policy. At last, it can be considered that trade liberalisation and market integration processes include a social dimension, as they open up new areas for comparative studies. Useful elements can be drawn from their development for the resolution of the complex practical problems brought about by the demands of harmonisation and 'alignment' of national legislations.

The opposing connotations between the two terms appear similarly radical. Trade liberalisation is a term of the classical doctrine of economics. It favours freedom of entrepreneurship, free competition, and 'playing the game' of individual initiatives. Shortly, trade liberalisation finds itself in an economic paradigm, contrasted with the idea of the market as a result of a spontaneous confrontation between economic actors.

Labour law, however, adheres to a different rationality that perceives regulation as a necessity that allows for the economic actors to regulate their interaction. It is like saying – to recall the idea of Hayek, one of the greatest

[11] The so-called 'décret d'Allarde', decreed by the French National Assembly on 2 March 1791.

[12] G. Lyon-Caen, 'L'infiltration du Droit du travail par le droit de la concurrence', *Droit Ouvrier* (1992), 313.

representatives of the liberal doctrine – that labour law is composed of organisation rules backed up by public law pursuing the 'mirage of social justice'.[13] It is an opposing relationship, once again, since trade liberalisation is a vector of the neo-liberal strategy aiming at reducing the economic power of the State, and of the public sector, for the benefit of private actors and market mechanisms. Labour law, on the other hand, is closely linked to the idea of the Nation-State and its historical function of mediation and conciliation between mercantilist values of the economy and extra-economic values of solidarity. It is an opposition; ultimately, because trade liberalisation in so far as it takes part in the economic sphere is rooted in the idea of *oikos* and *oikonomia*. It is the organisation of the national economy, which started to develop in the Middle Ages, from the commencement of trade with the outside world to the birth of the capitalistic company. Labour law, however, is rather linked to the idea of *koinon*, represented by civil society, and a political community of noble values, since it participates to the realisation of social, economic and cultural rights indispensable for the dignity of human beings. It is the *moral space* where the multiplicity of private interests is rationalised in the general interest.

The linkage hypothesis

Trade liberalisation and labour law have a single *trait d'union* in the ambit of international trade regulation.[14] This historical link is underlined in the current context of globalisation of the economy, under which the expansion of trade along with the renewed push for economic regionalism represents a fundamental component; an impulse which implies the creation of free trade zones, customs unions and common markets with forms of economic integration that go beyond the trade sector and touch upon areas such as services and investment.

This link between trade liberalisation and labour law, however, constitutes a founding element of international labour law as regards both the construction of normative policy of the International Labour Organisation (ILO), and the relationship between the ILO and international economic organisations. As for the normative policy in particular, it was evident from

---

[13] F. A. Hayek, *Law, Legislation and Liberty. A New Statement of the Liberal Principles of Justice and Political Economy*, vol. II (London: Routledge & Kegan, 1976), p. 10.

[14] A theory of trade linkage has been developed by D. W. Leebron, 'Linkages', *AJIL* 96, (2002), 5; see also P. Alston, 'Linking Trade and Human Rights', *German YIL* 23 (1980), 126, noting that the potential costs of linking trade and human rights may be considerable and calling for a careful weighing process.

the very beginning that the function of international labour law was to contrast the opportunism of those States which would have placed – or were actually placing – the protection of workers below their companies' economic and competition interests. Thus, the Preamble of the Constitution of the ILO states that 'the failure of any nation to adopt human conditions of labour is an obstacle in the way of other nations which desire to improve the conditions in their own countries. On the one hand, this meant the recognition that under the burden of international competition social progress of one State depended to a great extent on the behaviour of others. On the other hand, it also meant that labour law norms, by nature, had an impact on competition.

The recurrent dialectic that links labour law norms with international exchanges later reappeared with greater clarity and accuracy in the wording of the Havana Charter,[15] progenitor of the yet to be created (but at the end never established) International Trade Organisation. It not only expressly stated the obligation of respecting fair labour conditions but it went much further by outlining the need for an institutional link between the International Trade Organisation and the ILO towards a profitable integration of trade law and social standards.

The linkage between trade liberalisation and labour law cannot but reappear with more power under the processes of globalisation, leading to a growing interdependence between economies, favoured by a strong expansion of flows of capital and transnational companies in international trade. In fact, trade liberalisation is the primary component of globalisation, along with other vectors and factors such as the deregulation of capital markets, growth of foreign trade and investment, the enormous reduction of transport and telecommunications costs, the intensification of international competition, the extension of production systems on a global scale, and the unification of financial markets in the framework of a 'financialisation' of the capital system. However, the link between trade liberalisation and labour law in the present form of globalisation should be analysed in light of a fundamental transformation of the national and international system of balance and distribution of power, which until the present day has been mastered by nation-states.[16]

---

[15] The United Nations Conference on Trade and Employment, held in Havana, Cuba, in 1947 adopted the Havana Charter for an International Trade Organisation which was meant to establish a multilateral trade organization. For various reasons, the Charter never came into force. See, for more information, www.wto.org.

[16] U. Beck, *Macht und Gegenmacht im globalen Zeitalter* (Frankfurt am Main: Suhrkamp Verlag, 2002).

In the absence of any multilateral coordination, and prior to a process of internalisation of trade governed by the General Agreement on Tariffs and Trade (GATT),[17] which reinforced competition between social systems and capital mobility of the different countries, the idea of normatively structuring the original relationship between trade liberalisation and labour law on a national and international level, tends to fade away or even disappear in the cry of neo-mercantilism. The global economy, in particular, has developed a meta-power that has been permitted to free itself from the national and territorial power game of which it was prisoner. Two related phenomena emerge: the denationalisation of the economy and the declining of the regulatory capacity of the Nation-State.

The hallmark of the first phenomenon is the growing importance of the 'network company', possessing a complex structure and transnational dimension, and enjoying the consequent phenomena of self-regulation. This powerful non-State actor, present on the global scene, on the one hand compromises the utility and the efficiency of the internal legal norms, since the production strategies and activities of the undertaking are not structured according to the boundaries of national law. On the other hand, it forces upon States a greater opening-up of their markets to facilitate trade, attract foreign capital, and benefit from the presence of these actors on their own territory. The geographical dispersion allows transnational companies to take advantage of the fragmentation of state competences, and to make national states compete by manipulating national norms regarding the conflict of laws, in order to fall under that national law which is most favourable to their interests.

The creation of autonomous systems of spontaneous transnational norms by economic actors is a typical manifestation of the second phenomenon. This is the case with international exchanges between companies, which form the basis of the new *lex mercatoria*; that is, a law organised by companies that extends the radius of their economic action and at the same time opportunistically structures their legal space through uniform contractual models. However, the internationalisation of the sources of production of this post-national law pertain to other fast-spreading experiences and practices, such as international codes of conduct and standard rules of ethical normalisation, which imply self-referential normative powers.

---

[17] See www.wto.org.

The effects of trade liberalisation on labour law

In view of the dismantling of territories by the action of a transnational economic network, and vis-à-vis both what Teubner calls 'self-destruction' of the law in its national dimension,[18] and the creation of an autonomous, transnational law (whose function is to permit the economy its self-legitimisation), the fullness and exclusiveness of State sovereignty is by now almost unreal. Naturally, the question is of a greater importance and concerns the very idea of law as a unitary (*Ordnung, Order, Ordre*) and localised system (*Ortung*), imposingly represented by Schmitt in his work on *Nomos der Erde*;[19] that is, the original and immediate form in which the organisation of a people becomes visible. This deconstruction seems to be closely linked to the questioning of the traditional role of the regulatory State in the economic and social sphere. The processes of globalisation impose a general retreat of state institutions, accompanied by the creation of new institutions, which are equivalent to the already existing ones, to operate on the transnational and local level. Moreover, globalisation favours the progressive shift of regulation to the top (towards new extra-state decision-makers) and to the bottom (levels of regional, local, and company governances) where one witnesses the combination of – without implying a contradiction – mixed processes of deregulation and over-regulation in the framework of the multiplication of actors and levels of regulation within and outside of the territories of the Nation-State. What are the consequences of these processes on labour law?

The answer is evident; as it is considered that the norms of national labour law systems were conceived in function of employment relationships within state boundaries between legal persons actually put under the juridical authority of the State and exposed to its coercive power. Internationalisation, financial globalisation of the economy erode the institutional configuration of labour law inherited from the past, whilst in the new context, new models of regulation emerge based on very different regulatory instruments and techniques from the traditionally *étatiste* ones. We encounter the first effect of globalisation on the national systems of labour law: the deconstruction of the system. As for labour law systems, in the way they evolved during the last century in most Western countries, the assumption of this deconstruction is to question the social

---

[18] G. Teubner, 'Contracting Worlds: The Many Autonomies of Private Law', in *Social and Legal Studies* (2000), p. 402.

[19] C. Schmitt, *Der Nomos der Erde* (Berlin: Duncker & Humbolt, 1997), p. 15.

and political 'Fordist' compromise, under the pressure of a liberalism aimed at the deregulation and competition of social systems. The argument of an exacerbated international competition exercises, in this way, a downward pressure and functions as a discourse on the flexibilisation of the norms capable of redefining consolidated policies and legislative orientations. The risk run by the systems which follow the rule of deconstruction is to fall into a practically unstoppable race to the bottom. Indeed, in the face of the intensification of the competition, companies follow strategies of delocalisation to countries with ever-lower social costs, whilst the levels of productivity of developing (or newly industrialising) countries tends to adjust to those of Western countries, thanks to formidable technological developments. In this strategy of making more flexible the deconstruction of social standards, liberalisation of trade, and foreign direct investment seem to be decisive, since they provide for the normative and material bases of global economic rationality. Production from those companies which have delocalised in order to save on social costs is not for the local market, but for exportation to third countries. Prior to a significant drop of customs rights and the elimination of quantitative restrictions, multinational companies obtain favourable measures for their import of products from branches or suppliers in developing countries. On the one hand, it leads to Generalised Systems of Preferences, thanks to which a quota of customs-free exports is given to developing countries in certain sectors. On the other hand, thanks to outward processing arrangements, the limitation of customs rights to added value is realised for the importation of products with raw materials and components previously exported to developing countries.

This interdependence in the global integration of production, which means the different elements of the national productive system and the development of international exchanges, take us to the second effect of globalisation: competition/concurrence between social systems. Globalisation induces macro-economic policies where the weakness of social protection systems becomes an element of competitiveness: in the absence of internationally-enforced labour standards, employers will resort to a 'sweatshop' business strategy in order to meet international competition;[20] the non-application of social rights becomes an element of generating competition between social systems. In a competitive

---

[20] See, e.g., M. J. Piore, 'Labor Standards and Business Strategies', in A. Herzenberg and J. F. Pérez-Lopez (eds.), *Labor Standards and Development in the Global Economy* (Washington: US Department of Labor Bureau of International Labor Affairs, 1990), p. 35.

relationship between national systems, markets are free to evade local 'rigidities' acting therefore as progressive weakening factors of labour law's rationality and of its structural organisations (welfare state, trade union dimension of employment, etc.). In the face of these phenomena, the traditional regulative prospective looks for remedies in supranational sources, whether they refer to international law (e.g., ILO Conventions with their limited efficiency and effectiveness) or to single macro-regional contexts (e.g., the European Community's social dimension, which now seems to be 'constitutionalised'; and the North-American interstate cooperation within the framework of the North-American Agreement on Labor Cooperation (NAALC),[21] the 'Andean Pact',[22] and the Mercado Común del Sur (Common Market of the South, MERCOSUR[23]).

The regulation between the global and the local: the Social Clause and fundamental social rights

The convergence of these phenomena (deconstruction and competition between systems) raises the question of regulation in order to find a possible conciliation between the sphere of global economy and the strengthening of social rights. As we will see, the question of regulation requires a differentiated treatment which is global and local at the same time. Its elements cannot be provided for by national law; the crisis of sovereignty is evident from the internationalisation of the sources of law by the activity of globalisation actors. Nor can they be provided for by international law, based on the principle of sovereignty of states and affected by structural deficiencies in respect of the efficiency of the ILO's normative action.[24]

Given that globalisation diminishes the efficiency of classical instruments of social regulation, one can envisage two responses. The first is neo-liberal in nature, aimed at deregulating in order to suppress the rigidities of labour markets, which should converge towards the optimum regulated by the 'invisible hand' of the market. In this vision, the spontaneous allocations that take place on the global market are by definition efficient and fair since everyone is paid according to his or her contribution to the overall richness. The promise is rather tempting:

---

[21] See, for more information, see www.naalc.org.
[22] The trade bloc today is known as the Andean Community. Its member states are Bolivia, Colombia, Ecuador, Peru and Venezuela. See, for more information, www. comunidadandina. org.   [23] For more information, see www.mercosur.int.
[24] See ILO report, *Travail décent et économie informelle* (2002), www.ilo.org.

everyone will become rich, and even the poor will end up by benefiting from it.

The other response, of an institutional character, is based on the assumption that all market relations are social constructions and they do not derive from the spontaneous confrontation of economic agents. Social and labour rights are presented as a necessary component of efficient and competitive markets. From this perspective, regulatory factors should be mobilised to substitute market rationality with a rationality based upon normative, axiologically-oriented constructions. This institutionalist approach takes us back to the heart of the problem: the question of the integration of social provisions into the system of regulation of international trade and in particular the problem of rational and moral justification of such integration. In this respect, there are two sets of justifications which can be re-conducted, in line with Weber's logic, to a rational justification as regards scope and value.

The first justification stresses the economic interest of trade, a typically mercantilist interest, and the instruments of regulation in order to overcome market failures, and the limits of rationality of an unregulated market. This operative and instrumental justification of regulation looks into the harmonious development of the market and is based on the idea of fair trade.[25] The protection of the fundamental social norms guaranteed in the framework of international trade is justified when the sense of violation of those standards by the exporting States is likely to damage the economy of those countries which respect the standard of the supranational 'level playing field'. Thus, the notion of fair trade can be considered as a means to complete the game of free trade, guaranteeing to the State and economic actors that none of the global players will take advantage of the unfair benefits that result from the non-application of the national (such as the model of the North American Agreement on Labour Cooperation (NAALC)[26] which does not establish any supranational minimum threshold[27]) or international (as provided for by international labour law: it is the EC's external approach[28]) or 'internationally recognised' social norms (like the model unilaterally applied by the USA). Social standards therefore penetrate in the regulative sphere of

---

[25] See C. McCrudden and A. Davies, 'A Perspective on Trade and Labour Rights', in F. Francioni (ed.), *Environment, Human Rights and International Trade* (Oxford: Hart, 2001), p. 179, suggesting that labour rights that serve to increase freedom of choice and contract are theoretically consistent with the ideology of free trade and may be required by it.   [26] www.naalc.org.   [27] www.naalc.org.
[28] For more information, see: www.europa.eu.int/pol/comm/index_en.htm.

competition law as an instrument of implementation of a principle of fair competition at the international level, aimed at limiting the phenomena of social dumping.

The main instrument of this conditionality is the social clause to be introduced in the international trade agreements, and through which the linkage between work standards and trade liberalisation can be realised. The term 'social clause' indicates peculiar norms having as their object internationally recognised social rights that States (in their productive activity and application of law) and consequently the companies (in their quality of employers) have to respect to be able to enjoy certain benefits induced by liberalisation of international trade, that is to avoid running into economic sanctions.[29] From this perspective, apart from the protestations expressed by developing countries which, until now, have blocked attempts to introduce the issue of labour standards in the WTO agreements, the problem is the very definition of 'social standards'. It is about what minimum rules should be respected so that the *ceteris paribus* clause is fully applied in the framework of fair trade rules. This definition requires an agreement, the adoption of which is more difficult than that of multilateral conventions of the ILO. Similar difficulties arise with the creation of eventual mechanisms put in place of the sanctions in the WTO. It is sufficient to recall that distorting commercial measures authorised by the WTO's Dispute Settlement Body are considered as compensation for commercial prejudices suffered, and not as real sanctions as proposed by the supporters of the social clause.[30]

The problem is open, even if the preferable approach seems to set up a linkage with regard to the formulation of fundamental social rights solemnly declared by the ILO, which asks for the respect of fundamental rights conventions such as the 1998 Declaration of Geneva,[31] regardless of their ratification by all members of the Organisation.[32]

By remaining on a strictly legal basis, a careful analysis of the sources of international law allows for the identification of a hard core of 'unconditional' social rights, which do not depend upon the different economic and cultural situations. Beyond the ILO Conventions, these rights already considered by the Universal Declaration of Human Rights and UN

---

[29] A. Perulli, *Diritto del lavoro e globalizzazione* (Padova: Cedam, 1999).
[30] www.wto.org.
[31] ILO Declaration on Fundamental Principles and Rights at Work, www.ilo.org.
[32] www.ilo.org/dyn/declaris/DECLARATIONWEB.ABOUTRDECLARATIONHOME?var_language=EN (accessed: 15 March 2006).

Covenants of 1966 on civil and political, and on economic, social and cultural rights were recognised as fundamental by the Declaration of Copenhagen on Social Development[33] and finally endorsed by the historical declaration adopted by the 86th session of the International Labour Conference (Geneva, 18 July 1998).[34] These rights are freedom of association, the right to collective bargaining, the elimination of of forced and compulsory labour, the abolition of child labour and the elimination of discrimination in the workplace.[35] This set of core labour standards has to be considered of universal application; the ILO requires their respect by the member states by the mere fact of belonging to the organisation.[36] It is for the very reason of the constitutional value of the fundamental conventions that the Conference declared that 'all Member States, even if they not have ratified the convention in question, are obliged by the mere fact of belonging to the organisation, to respect, to promote and to realise in good faith and in line with the Constitution the principles relating to fundamental rights which are part of the respective conventions'.[37] These are workers' rights which basically 'behave' as internationally recognised human rights, for which there must most probably be an *opinio iuris* by which the international community is obliged to respect these rights. For instance, the use of child labour in employment relationships threatens – by its nature, and because of the conditions in which it is carried out – the physical and moral health of minors; an activity that should fall under the notion of 'cruel, inhumane and degrading treatment'(Arts 1 and 56 of the UN Charter) and it has without any doubt reference to *jus cogens* (under which it can be sanctioned).[38] It is a way of saying that the social clause has a codifying function for the principles which already apply under general international law: trade agreements containing them should therefore be interpreted so as to confirm, enlarge and specify the

---

[33] www.un.org/esa/socdev/wssd/index.html (accessed: 15 March 2006).

[34] ILO Declaration on Fundamental Principles and Rights at Work, International Labour Conference, 86th Session, Geneva, June 1998. The Declaration is subdivided into a preamble, a provision, and an original control mechanism *(mécanisme de suivi; follow-up mechanism)*; for a description, see H. Kellerson, 'La Déclaration de 1998 de l'Oit sur les principes et droits fondamentaux: un défi pour l'avenir?', *Revue international du Travail*, (1999), 244.

[35] For an analysis of these fundamental rights, see L. Betten, *International Labour Law* (Boston: Deventer, 1993).

[36] See F. Maupain, 'Is the ILO Effective in Upholding Workers' Rights? Reflections on the Myanmar Experience', in Alston (ed.), *Labour Rights as Human Rights*, p. 131.

[37] Article 2 of the Declaration on Fundamental Principles and Rights at Work.

[38] See, J. Diller and D. Levy, 'Child Labor, Trade and Investment: Toward the Harmonization of International Law', *American Journal of International Labour* (1997), 673.

already existing customary norms. It is evident that a similar analysis is not universally accepted; for instance, one may think with a certain embarrassment about the views of one author, Bhagwati, who recently wrote:

> [T]his very day, in the field of trade union matters, for example, we can agree on declaring the killing of trade union leaders illegal but not on an agreement on the question of the recruitment of blacklegs or on the dismissal of workers for economic or disciplinary reasons.[39]

The second type of justification privileges the axiological dimension of fundamental social rights.[40] The demand to link trade agreements with social agenda objectives recalls once again the use of general trade sanctions towards violating countries, the use of such strategies as the suspension or prohibition of market access for those products which violate rules or agreements, for example, if they have been produced by using child labour, or prison work. Inasmuch as they are founded on a postulated value, socially fair production and trade not tarnished by the failure to apply core labour standards, highlight the moral dimension of fundamental rights. The approach of putting mercantilist justifications aside and penetrating extra-economic ethics into the *societas mercatorum* – thus limiting the economic freedom of the actors[41] seems homogenous with the one offered by the international public order. It is surprisingly not considered a structuring factor of the *lex mercatoria*, yet it is capable of nullifying the validity of contracts with regard to the immoral character of certain transactions, not only as to corruption but also as to human rights and enslaving practices at arbitral courts.[42] An expansion of these *boni mores* towards imperatives to protect human rights, in their complex notion of civil, economic, social rights consequently requires a careful reflection upon the identification of labour law principles of the *lex mercatoria*, which cannot be modified by different economic and cultural situations and which bear effects similar to *jus cogens*.

---

[39] J. Bhagwati, *In Defence of Globalisation* (Oxford: Oxford University Press, 2004), p. 55.

[40] See M. J. Trebilcock, 'The Fair Trade Debate: Protection of Labour Standards and International Economic Law', in S. Griller (ed.), *International Economic Governance and Non-Economic Concerns: New Challenges for the International Legal Order* (New York: Springer, 2003), p. 299.

[41] J. B. Racine, *L'arbitrage commercial international et l'ordre public* (Paris: LGDJ, 1999), p. 368.

[42] P. Lalive, 'Ordre public international (ou réellement international) et arbitrage international', *Revue de l'arbitrage* (1986), 329.

Levels and subjects of regulation

At this point, the discourse develops according to the different levels and subjects of regulation. First of all, it is necessary to consider the economic forms of trade organised at a global level, which includes multiple or 'multidimensional' juridical areas, meeting and overlapping. Each of these areas should be analysed in accordance with the measure to which it can or does guarantee the operative realisation of a link between trade liberalisation and respect of social norms, each in its own way.

In this regard, four pertinent levels of analysis can be distinguished:

i) The global level, governed by the criteria of decision-making centralisation and a multilateral framework (WTO); at this level, the aggregate and regulative processes typical of social rights are generally absent, or else are very weak and fragmented.

ii) Regional level, governed by multilateral and diversified criteria, which depend on the intensity of forms of integration (according to the usual internationalist model: integrated markets, free trade zones, customs union, etc.). They follow the model of the EC or of the North American Free Trade Agreement (NAFTA) or other forms of regional integrations such as Mercado Común del Sur (MERCOSUR – Common Market of the South) or Association of Southeast Asian Nations (ASEAN) etc., and vary as to whether there are supranational organs with normative and/or judiciary powers having a direct effect on the Member States. At this level, integration ordains labour norms of differing standards, and which are protected by means that are expected to accompany the enlargement, integration and opening up of markets.

iii) Levels unilaterally governed by States or economic aggregations of States; labour issues are often present at this level as the social condition for trade liberalisation

iv) Levels governed autonomously by economic operators. Intra-firm commercial exchanges have allowed for the appearance of non-state norms, calling into being transnational mercantilist spheres. They include the *lex mercatoria*, a network of extra-territorial relations organised by transnational companies; and the Codes of Conduct of specific companies, which are considered to be part of the corpus of *lex mercatoria* and an expression of international customs or general principles recognised by the international community. The social dimension of these Codes of Conduct adopted by multinational companies is also well-known.

If this multidimensional scheme is capable of representing the complexity of the scenarios of the transnational regulation of trade and labour, there are two key words: diversity and interdependence (or inter-relatedness).

One can talk about the diversity of juridical spheres that govern the development of trade, the diversity of actors and the relevant regulation, the diversity of legal techniques that determine the production of norms, the diversity with regard to the modalities governing the link between trade liberalisation and social norms; and, finally, the diversity with regard to the force and the effectiveness of the rules formalising this link. Interdependence, or if one prefers, connection, of the economies and trade actors, interdependence of the logic and justifications at the basis of the norms that govern the functional relation between liberalisation and the promotion of social norms. How to govern, therefore, this pluralism and interrelatedness? By applying the four-level scheme, it is possible to combine the integration experiences on the basis of a mixture of relevant references both under the geographic profile and from a political-institutional point of view.

The multilateral global dimension: the General Agreement on Trade and Tariffs – World Trade Organisation

The first level refers to global multilateral coordination in the framework of the General Agreement on Trade and Tariffs-World Trade Organization (GATT-WTO).[43] This powerful idea, promoted for a period by the doctrine and intergovernmental practices, suggests the insertion of a social clause into the law of WTO, through which the integration of social rights into the level that is supposed to regulate international trade could take place.

As is known, this perspective has not yet brought about concrete results. The reason for the difficulties encountered by the idea of a social clause at the multilateral global level is due to the lack of institutional capability of the international organisations, and largely to the politico-structural factor. It concerns the concept of international division of work suggested by the WTO, strongly based on Ricardo's classical theory of comparative advantages. In the First WTO Ministerial Declaration[44] the parties 'renew their commitment to the observance of internationally

---

[43] www.wto.org.
[44] Art. 4 of the Singapore Ministerial Declaration, adopted on 13 December 1996 during the Singapore WTO Ministerial 1996: Ministerial Declaration WT/MIN/(96)/DEC, Art. 4.

recognized core labour standards' and 'reject the use of labour standards for protectionist purposes, and agree that the comparative advantages of countries, particularly low-wage developing countries, must in no way be put into question.'[45] The principle of comparative advantage is based on the idea of an interpretation of national economies in the international division of labour according to the competences and richness of natural resources, labour force and capital. The WTO therefore inherited – and up till now has jealously maintained – the concept of the safeguarding the application of trade rules, and is consequently unable to remedy trade distortions caused by the diversity of national legislation, in particular by labour cost factors.

Despite the unfruitful results of the debate on the social clause, the pressure coming from the industrialised countries and the critiques by consumers' organisations, trade unions and non-governmental organisations interested in the 'social' failures of trade liberalisation represent a guarantee for the re-launching of the social clause at the WTO. In the meantime, it is also useful to verify the *current* compatibility of a social clause with the GATT principles in force, ensuring the eventual practicability of the restrictive trade measures adopted by individual states against social dumping. In this respect, there is a set of significant dispositions whose analysis produces results which are problematic but possible.

The first problematic aspect derives from the fact that the concept of 'social dumping' cannot be traced back to the notion of 'dumping' as it is meant under Article VI of the GATT. International trade law, indeed, does not recognise the differential cost between producers as a potential cause for dumping, whereas in a market economy system the decrease in the price of a product falls under the classical objectives of free competition. What is relevant, instead, in this respect is that the producer sells the same product at different prices in the domestic market and in the foreign market. If the price of the goods represents the cost of production *in both markets*, there is no dumping. Since dumping does not depend on the difference between the sales price on the domestic market and the sales price of the importing market – because the price is equally low in the first one also – one has to conclude that as a principle, it does not constitute an unfair trade practice under GATT.[46]

[45] See, generally, V. A. Leary, 'The WTO and the Social Clause: Post-Singapore', *EJIL* 8 (1997), 118.

[46] See, WTO Appellate Body, *Japan: Taxes on Alcoholic Beverages*, Report of 4 October 1996, Doc. WTO/OS8/ABIR, and *Canada: Certain Measures Concerning Periodicals*, Report of 30 June 1997, Doc. WTO/OS31/ABIR.

The notion of export subsidies is closer to the practice of social dumping; it is characterised by the fact that the price, which is less than the normal price, results from aids provided directly or indirectly from States to companies. In addition to allowing the disadvantaged States to react by imposing 'compensative' customs duties in such cases, the GATT regulates this phenomenon by limiting or prohibiting the concession of subventions.[47] The question is whether the State that allows national companies to violate social norms by doing so does not concede *de facto* a subvention? It is a suggestive interpretative hypothesis; a similar one has been envisaged in the case of environmental dumping. However, this hypothesis still suffers from some drafting difficulties, since the requirements of a subsidy described in the agreement drafted at the Uruguay Round such as the *financial contribution* from the government and the specificity of the subsidy, are absent. Indeed, an *undifferentiated* aid to companies is not considered a subsidy.

Furthermore, the mechanism of the social clause cannot be compared to the so-called safeguard clauses, conventional dispositions that in certain situations foresee the possibility of temporary derogation from the norms of interstate economic cooperation with the adoption of protective measures such as the increase of customs tariffs, quantitative restrictions or subventions to domestic companies. For example, all GATT countries can temporarily limit their own imports if the national production is susceptible to an influence from low price imports (Art. XIX of the GATT). A perspective that considers the safeguard clause as an instrument to react with protective measures to unfair trade practices for the failure to respect social standards cannot therefore be excluded, given the generic nature of the circumstances that can cause disturbances to the market which can be qualified as 'economic and social differences'. On the other hand, in order to avoid the risk of activating a similar measure provided by the agreement on the European Economic Area, the signatory parties foresaw the modality of harmonisation not only in economic aspects, but also in the social and the environmental field, and in matters such as workers' safety and health, prohibition of retributive discrimination and social dialogue between social partners.

The only norm in the GATT that can be compared to a social clause is established in Article XX, relating to a system of derogations called 'general exceptions' aimed at creating a reservation of domestic

---

[47] Article VI.

jurisdiction in favour individual states, which are authorised to give priority to certain interests of national policy against trade liberalisation. In particular, this norm allows for the parties to adopt justified restrictive trade measures for the protection of public morals, the life and health of humans, animals and plants, the environment and natural resources, the safeguarding of the cultural heritage, the protection of consumers, and for reasons linked to the commercialisation of products made in prisons (Article XX, (e)).

Based on the above, states could adopt restrictive measures of international trade in order to protect their markets from the import of manufactured goods produced at a low labour cost. It is a norm that has not yet been invoked by any country to justify such restrictions but it is theoretically very significant because it authorises states to adopt protectionist measures based on the evaluation of *processes of production* of foreign goods. On the other hand, it is known that Article XX is in principle applicable as regards the intrinsic quality of a certain product and not on the basis of productive processes used for its creation. *De iure condendo*, the main way should lead to the reformulation of Article XX by inserting new exceptions on the failure to respect such fundamental social rights, even if an extensive interpretation of the measures 'necessary to protect the health and the life of persons' could already include at least the prohibition of child labour and minimum norms regarding safety at work, allowing states which suffer social dumping to adopt restrictive measures on imports.[48]

It is worth mentioning Article XXIII of the GATT as it has been widened by the WTO Dispute Settlement Rules. The norm on the 'Protection of concessions and advantages' provides that when a contracting party considers that an advantage resulting from the Agreement is 'nullified or compromised', or the realisation of one of the objectives of the Agreement is compromised because of the behaviour of another party, or if 'there exists another situation' such to nullify or to compromise the said advantages, the party is justified in asking for the activation of an inquiry that could lead to the suspension of concessions or other obligations deriving from the General Agreement. An official document of the United States has declared that 'trade problems stemming from unfair labour standards were

---

[48] Some commentators have suggested that Article XX could be interpreted broadly to allow for the protection of human rights, including collective labour rights. 'An evolutive interpretation of Article XX GATT on general exceptions could be of relevance, which allows addressing conditions of production violating human rights'; see the contribution by Benedek in this volume.

already actionable under Article XXIII',[49] and the same opinion was supported by the Congress of English Trade Unions (TUC) which mentioned the recourse to Article XXIII to impose commercial sanctions on countries which violate international labour standards.[50] This perspective can be easily updated. In fact, on a strictly juridical basis, the reference to the existence of 'another situation', such as to 'nullify or to compromise' the advantage resulting from the GATT seems so undefined as to create a sort of general clause in which a social clause could be inserted, but it does not seem that Article XXIII has ever been invoked for this purpose.

The European dimension

If the operative justification – on which the social clause is based – appears for the moment impracticable on the global multilateral level, it appears however functional to the development of regional integration. We find important examples of this functional vision in the European construction and framework of the North American integration. The European experience is well-known. Social harmonisation was perceived for a long time as being useful to avoid forms of dumping and competition distortions based on the normative disparities in social issues, and the issue of employment considered inappropriate in the project which aimed to guarantee the harmonious development of the internal market.[51] For this reason, European social law witnessed an instrumental rationality in the service of the common market. In a functionalist vision of the integration,[52] the goal of the founders of the common market was

---

[49] U.S Commission on Foreign Economic Policy: Staff Papers, February 1954, 437. On this point see, S. Charnovitz, 'L'influence des normes internationales du travail sur le système du commerce mondial', *Revue international du travail* (1987), 646; J. Perez-Lopez, 'Conditioning Trade on Foreign Labor Law: The US Approach', *Comparative Labour Law* 9 (1988), 257.

[50] See, L. Murray, 'Standard syndicaux équitables en matière de commerce international', *Monde du Travail libre* (1961), 102.

[51] G. F. Mancini, 'Effect of EC Law on Member States' Employment Law', in G. F. Mancini (ed.), *Democracy and Constitutionalism in the European Union* (Oxford: Oxford University Press, 2000), p. 114; G. and A. Lyon-Caen, *Droit social international et européen* (Paris: Dalloz, 1993); S. Deakin, 'Labour Law as a Market Regulation: The Economic Foundations of European Social Policy', in P. Davies *et al.* (eds.), *European Community Labour Law: Principles and Perspectives* (Oxford: Oxford University Press, 1996), pp. 63–94.

[52] On the market as 'the principle vehicle of harmony' see S. Simitis and A. Lyon-Caen, 'Community Labour Law: A Critical Introduction to its History', in P. Davies *et al.*, (eds.), *European Community Labour Law*, p. 5; see also S. Sciarra, 'Market Freedom and Fundamental Social Rights', in B. Hepple (ed.), *Social and Labour Rights in a Global Context* (Cambridge: Cambridge University Press, 2002), p. 95.

to avoid a 'race to the bottom' competition in the application of social standards by contrasting the possibility of deregulation – which have laid always in ambush – due to the structural weaknesses and the absence of a common reference to a minimum threshold of fundamental social rights.[53] Today the functionalist vision of the integration is definitely being abandoned thanks to the treaty-based references – especially after the Treaty of Amsterdam – and constitutionalisation of fundamental social rights. Their domain has been progressively widened and emerging from their original ancillary position in the economic construction of Europe, they have acquired the same position as the basic principles of the economic integration (free movement and competition). In this situation, the Charter of Fundamental Rights approved at Nice, and its Chapter on 'solidarity', reconfirm the autonomy of the European social model and strengthens it, developing an axiological system whose function is to organise differing social representations and logics and integrate them around a common purpose.[54]

Being forced to penetrate into the community legal order through the activity of the Court of Justice, fundamental rights are deemed to become common constitutional references as regards social matters. In this way, the EU's apparently schizophrenic stance, in obliging the respect of fundamental social rights in its external relations without their formal internal recognition, can be avoided.

Certain ambiguous elements, however, are present; in particular, two issues are worthy of being mentioned even if only briefly. The first one concerns the structure of the Treaty establishing a Constitution[55] which confirms the distinction between principles and rights in its Articles II-51 and II-52.

If the aim is to limit the application of the principles of social law, this approach should be strongly criticised, both under the light of the achieved equality between fundamental human rights and economic liberties and on the basis of the principle of the indivisibility of human

---

[53] See S. Sciarra, 'La constitutionnalisation de l'Europe sociale, entre droits sociaux fondamentaux et soft law', in O. De Schutter and P. Nihoul (eds.), *Une constitution pour l'Europe. Reflexions sur les trasformations du droit de l'Union européenne* (Brussels: Bruylant, 2004).

[54] A. Lyon-Caen, 'The Legal Efficacy and Significance of Fundamental Social Rights: Lesson from the European experience', in B. Hepple (ed.), *Social and Labour Rights in a Global Context*, p. 190; M. Weiss, 'The Politics of the EU Charter of Fundamental Rights', in B. Hepple (ed.), *Social and Labour Rights in a Global Context*, p. 73.

[55] Treaty Establishing a Constitution for Europe, OJ 2004 C310/1.

rights. This ambiguity is strong and casts a shadow on the constitutional feasibility of Europe as it re-launches the opposition between rights and programmatic rules, with the imminent risk of de-legitimising some of the rights of the Charter of Nice.

The second ambiguity relates to the use of soft law regimes under the Open Method of Coordination – now preferred to legislation as the means of giving effect to policy – and the pointlessness of harmonisation in face of the enlargement.[56] Will the 'EU-25'[57] be both able and willing to use the new regulatory techniques and governance in a progressive manner by consolidating the acquired rights and widening the social sphere of the market in order to realise new and more advanced levels of integration between trade liberalisation and social and labour law? Or will soft law represent the instrument for a regulatory competition in which the link between the economic dimension, and the instances of social protection, will impose the *raisons* of the first to the detriment of the second without breaking into pieces? For these very reasons, as others have noted, there is still a need for a core of protection based on fundamental rights.[58]

The North American Agreement on Labor Cooperation

Under the North American Agreement on Labor Cooperation (NAALC),[59] negotiated parallel with NAFTA, the functionalist logic similar to the

---

[56] The open method of coordination (OMC), which emerged from the proceedings of the Lisbon European Council in 2000, involves 'fixing guidelines for the Union, establishing quantitative and qualitative indicators and benchmarks as a means of comparing best practice, translating these European guidelines into nation and regional policies by setting specific targets, and periodic monitoring, evaluation and peer review organised as 'mutual learning processes' (Presidency Conclusions, Lisbon European Council, 23 and 24 March 2000, para. 37). See S. Sciarra, 'Fundamental Labour Rights after the Lisbon Agenda', in G. De Burca and B. De Witte (eds.), *Social Rights in Europe* (Oxford: Oxford University Press, 2005), p. 212, where the author suggests that 'the OMC, by insinuating flexible measures into the regulation of employment contracts, may create a potentially less stable environment for the guarantee of fundamental rights'; but see, on the growth of soft law and the lack of effective procedures and sanction for the enforcement of social rights, B. Hepple (ed.), *Enforcement: The Law and Politics of Cooperation and Compliance*, in B. Hepple, *Social and Labour Rights in a Global Context* (Cambridge: Cambridge University Press, 2002), at p. 238; see also the Introduction to the same volume.

[57] This common abbreviation refers to the 25 Member-States of the European Union as of 2006.

[58] See C. Barnard and S. Deakin, 'Corporate Governance, European Governance and Social Rights', in Hepple (ed.), *Social and Labour Rights in a Global Context*, p. 147.

[59] See www.naalc.org.

primitive European community experience is reaffirmed in an ambit characterised by a weak type of integration limited to economic matters. However, the technique and objectives of supranational social regulation vary in the North-American Agreement on Labor Cooperation. The NAALC objective is a procedure of supervision and cooperation between the partner countries, which can lead to real economic and financial sanctions when the failure to respect agreed obligations effectively prejudices competition. This mechanism can therefore be considered a social clause, which does not take into account respect for uniform minimum supranational standards, but has regard instead to the safeguard of effective application of the national social standards of each country, rather than the usual provisions of international trade agreements, and the European integration experience (as well as the normative tradition of international labour law),

In the logic of the agreement, the basis of the social clause is essentially economic: it deals with the regulation of competition and the preservation of comparative advantages at the same time. Indeed, the condition for the application of a sanction is the evidence of a competitive advantage deriving from the failed application of the internal labour legislation of a given country. Article 3 of NAALC expresses the intention of the Parties to promote the 'respect and the effective application of their own labour laws through appropriate government actions'. There is no aim of harmonisation or of achieving uniformity of the levels of social protection, aims which are left to the discretion of the national legislator.

It is true that the agreement identifies some principles in the Annex on Labor Principles, which forms an integral part of the Agreement. However, these principles do not represent supranational social standards, but they do indicate 'guiding values'[60] of labour law, and 'areas of interest',[61] in which each country has established its own level of regulation. The original nature, and weakness of the North American social clause lies, therefore, in the fact that it does not set the limits of fair trade on the basis of respect of international fundamental social rights recognised by international labour law, nor on the harmonisation of norms (as happened in the creation of the social dimension of the EC), nor on the obligation of guaranteeing a standard level of protection (perhaps flexible due to *souplesse* clauses) according to the tradition of ILO Conventions.

The NAALC represents a peculiar case of a social clause adopted in the context of the multilateral free trade agreement between the USA,

---

[60] Preamble of NAALC's Annex 1.   [61] *Ibid.*

Canada and Mexico (NAFTA).[62] It is the first free trade agreement that provides for a specific normative instrument aimed at encouraging labour protection by a procedural mechanism, permitting the striking of a balance between trade liberalisation and the respect of fundamental social rights. By incorporating objectives which differ from those of trade liberalisation, the so-called NAFTA Labour Side Agreement presents itself as a model for the interpretation of social values in supranational processes that regulate economic globalisation.[63]

An area of concern is the different protection ensured by the eleven Labor Principles of the NAALC. The agreement excludes trade union rights (freedom of organisation, the right to strike and to collective bargaining from the stronger level of protection afforded to other rights, allowing only for the activation of ministerial consultations and not the imposition of economic sanctions. Only the violation of some labour standards on health and safety at work, child labour and minimum wage would entail the initiation of the complex review procedure which begins at the level of inter-ministerial consultations, and culminates in the creation of an Arbitral Panel, with the power to impose financial sanctions. The field of application of the sanctions is therefore rigorously delimited: they apply only if the violation of the agreement, as well as being persistent, proves to be 'trade-related' and 'covered by mutually recognized labor laws'.[64] In other words, not all violations can be prohibited, but only the ones that are relevant for the economic and trade integration targeted by NAFTA; that is, the respective legal orders fail to act upon the infractions committed by singular economic subjects in order to attain an unfair comparative advantage. Moreover, the failed application should concern labour law provisions which have been recognised by the contracting parties as actionable.

Paradoxically, however, the procedures of infraction have been all initiated against the violation of trade union rights, whereas the review

[62] North-American Free Trade Agreement, www.nafta-sec-alena.org.
[63] J. Cowie and J. French, 'NAFTA's Labor Side Accord: A Textual Analysis', *Latin American Labor News* (1994), 30; M. A. Moreau, 'La clause sociale dans les traités internationaux: Bilan et Perspectives', Séminaires de la Maison des Sciences de l'Homme, Ange Guepin (Nantes), 20 mars 1995; M. A. Moreau and G. Trudeau, 'La clause sociale dans l'accord de libre-echange nord-américain', *Revue Internationale de Droit Économique* (1995), 395; P. Staelens, 'Les conséquences sociales de l'intégration nord-Américaine sur le Mexique', *Syndicalisme et société* (1998), 97. No consensus exists about the value of the NAALC; references can be found in S. Charnovitz, 'The Labor Dimension of the Emerging Free Trade Area of the Americas', in P. Alston (ed.), *Labour Rights as Human Rights*, p. 155.
[64] NAALC, Article 49, Definitions.

procedure has produced important results thanks in particular to the intervention of those groups involved in the raising of public awareness and the resulting 'media' sanctions.[65] The international cooperation between trade unions organisations is also of relevance, in an area where the prevailing factors do not facilitate international solidarity between trade unions. Such cooperation is stimulated by the the NAALC's requirement that a submission procedure on a country be introduced at an administrative structure (National Administrative Offices) of a country by a foreign organisation.[66] It is important to remember in this regard the link that exists now between independent Mexican,[67] Canadian, and US trade union organisations.

Despite the narrow margins of application, the existence of a social clause, accompanied by a real sanction mechanism (that goes much beyond the 'moral pressure' and 'mobilisation of shame', as essentially happens with ILO sanctions) in a multilateral free trade agreement is without any precedent.[68] It shows, on the one hand, a slight break-away from the past experiences of international regulation of the economy and trade, especially from the GATT. On the other hand, it changes the unilateral approach that has dominated US trade policy until now, by making it more in line with the principles of international law and the multilateral discipline of trade relations.

The Central-American Free Trade Agreement (CAFTA)

The Central-American Free Trade Agreement (CAFTA),[69] signed on 27 July 2005 between Costa Rica, the Dominican Republic, El Salvador, Guatemala, Honduras, Nicaragua and the United States of America, has to be added to the not-too-long list of free trade agreements that address

---

[65] The obligation of the NAO's to make public reports became an important source of public pressure, identifying official culpability, thereby inducing governments and businesses involved to improve their standards and performance: see R. Adam and P. Singh, 'Early Experience with NAFTA's Labour Side Accord', *Comparative Labour Law Journal* 18 (1997), 161. More detailed information on such dispute resolution processes can be found in A. Perulli, *Diritto del lavoro e globalizzazione.*

[66] See Article 4 and Articles 15, 16 of Section C of the NAALC

[67] Such as *Frente autentico del trabajo* and *Sindicato de Telefonistas de la República Mexicana.*

[68] See J. Garvey, 'Trade Law and Quality of Life: Dispute Resolution under the NAFTA Side Accords on Labor and the Environment', *AJIL* 89 (1995), 453, which qualified NAALC as 'revolutionary' under this profile.

[69] www.ustr.gov/Trade_Agreements/Bilateral/CAFTA/Section_Index.html (accessed: 15 March 2006).

the question of workers' rights and conditions of employment, beside the primary aim of trade liberalisation. The Preamble of the Agreement states that the Parties are obliged not only to promote the integration understood in strict economic terms, but also to create new opportunities for social and economic development in the respective territories and to protect and reinforce workers' rights and cooperation in labour issues between the interested institutions, in order to create new employment opportunities and to improve life and employment conditions.

By examining the Chapter dedicated to labour issues in particular,[70] it can be useful, primarily, to note that the CAFTA takes after the model proposed by NAALC and other recent free trade agreements with Australia, Morocco, Chile and Singapore.[71] In this view, there is a line of continuity with former experiences, even if important signs, in the sense of gradual recognition of social rights accompanying economic rationality, are present. The Agreement can ideally be divided into two parts. Whilst the first part contains references to recognised structures of protection for workers, and to functional instruments guaranteeing their effectiveness, the second one aims at emphasising and promoting a participative and collaborative model between the different actors represented in the Agreement.

After an initial reference to the ILO principles expressed in the Declaration of 1998, with the clarification that the Parties oblige themselves to respect the principles as much as in applying internal legislation in order to comply with international labour norms,[72] the text imposes on the participant States the task of not encouraging trade practices through the weakening of protection prescribed by their internal law. In the same way, it prohibits States from allowing work conditions inferior to those guaranteed by the principles of international labour laws, in their efforts to promote trade or encourage investments in their territory, and to therefore become more competitive in the globalised market. In concrete terms, as explained by Article 16(8), when the Agreement refers to 'labour laws' it means norms introduced by the participating countries, directly linked to internationally recognised labour principles such as freedom of association, the right to organise and collective bargaining, the prohibition of all forms of forced labour, minimum age for employment, the prohibition and the elimination of forms of exploitation of child labour, and the right to acceptable work conditions (in particular as

---

[70] Chapter 16 of CAFTA.   [71] For more information, see www.ustr.gov.
[72] Article 16.1 of Chapter Sixteen of CAFTA.

regards the minimum wage, work hours, and health and safety at the workplace).

Article 16(2) introduces a real obligation for the contracting parties:

'The Parties recognize that it is inappropriate to encourage trade or investment by weakening or reducing the protections afforded in domestic labor laws. Accordingly, each Party shall strive to ensure that it does not waive or otherwise derogate from, or offer to waive or otherwise derogate from, such laws in a manner that weakens or reduces adherence to the internationally recognized labor rights referred to in Article 16.8 as an encouragement for trade with another Party, or as an encouragement for the establishment, acquisition, expansion, or retention of an investment in its territory.'

If it is not respected, a procedure foreseen by the Agreement should be activated, which provides for appropriate trade sanctions vis-à-vis the concerned party. As for the instruments introduced to make the provisions on the respect for the ILO principles effective, and the need to strengthen internal legislation to ensure the improvement of the social and professional status of workers, the Agreement provides for a safeguard procedure, and for the responsibility of the State in guaranteeing an impartial access to the judicial authorities for the full exercise of rights.[73] This procedure must be fair, free and transparent. The signatories of the Agreement have to ensure that a person with a legally recognised interest can turn to the judicial authorities in the country of citizenship to make their claim.

The second part of the Chapter reflects the intention of enhancing, as much as possible, the cooperation between participating countries in monitoring the implementation of the agreement and the eventual problematic issues which may emerge in its application. The creation of a Labour Affairs Council (LAC),[74] and the provision of the Capacity Building Mechanism, aimed at promoting and strengthening cooperation, improving work standards and favouring consultations and encounters between the parties,[75] can be seen in this light. For instance, LAC has the task of verifying periodically the status of implementation of the agreement, consultation, and coordination between the signatories.

If we were to draw some conclusions about the impact of the Agreement, we of course cannot ignore the fact that the provisions on labour issues

---

[73] Article 16.3 of Chapter Sixteen of CAFTA.   [74] Article 16.4 Chapter Sixteen of CAFTA.
[75] Article 16.4 of Chapter Sixteen of CAFTA.

fall completely under the Free Trade Agreement. It is not a simple attachment, but an enumeration of Principles, which constitute an integral part of the Agreement. The attention given to labour issues shows, therefore, its importance, even if it has to be linked to the exigencies dictated by the market. Secondly, the Agreement tries to focus on the instruments by which the effectiveness of the safeguards can be ensured. The problem is the concrete application of the norms on the protection of workers, a problem which has become apparent with every previous free trade agreement; although now, as shown in the ILO Report of June 2005, the provisions recognising and promoting the respect of core labour standards are present in the legislation of Central-American countries as well as in the Dominican Republic.[76] It is a problem which provokes an interest in including instruments into trade agreements that could provide additional ways of enforcing social rights.'

Unilateral regulation and the generalised system of preferences

The level of unilateral regulation on the basis of an agreement aimed at linking enlargement, trade liberalisation and values and social rights is illustrated by the European and US experience. Legislatively mandated measures, designed to protect labour rights in foreign countries, constitute an important dimension of US human rights policy.[77] The methods experimented in the US domestic policy are based upon the notion of fairness applied to commercial exchanges; on the other hand, the notion of fairness in the American legal tradition appears to be a key concept in both competition and labour law. In the same way as competition law seeks to achieve the regulation and protection of the national market, by aiming to prohibit companies from having recourse to economically unfair practices and behaviours, so labour law seeks to achieve the protection of the national market against socially incorrect practices carried out by companies. In this regard, Section 301 of the 1974 Trade Act[78] consented to the widening the *champs d'opérativité* of fair trade by including unfair internal practices of States with which the United States has trade

[76] For more information, see: www.ilo.org.
[77] See P. Alston, 'Labor Rights Provisions in US Trade Law: Aggressive Unilateralism?', in L. A. Compa and S. F. Diamond (eds.), *Human Rights, Labor Rights, and International Trade* (Philadelphia: University of Pennsylvania Press, 1996), p. 71; J. F. Pérez-Lopez, 'Conditioning Trade on Foreign Labor Law: The US Approach', *Comparative Labor Law Journal* 9 (1988), 253.
[78] www.osec.doc.gov/ogc/occic/301.html (accessed: 15 March 2006).

relations. These are trade practices categorised by the American legislation as being 'unjustifiable', 'discriminatory' and 'unreasonable'. This last category may include the violation of internationally recognised workers' rights, a notion that does not coincide with fundamental social rights as identified by the ILO.[79] It raises the question of knowing the legal nature of these rights, probably identifiable with an eclectic methodology from the human rights contained in the Universal Declaration and the general principles of international law (e.g. prohibition of degrading and inhuman treatment, etc.).

As for unilateral action, the EU external relations and the use of the conditionality in trade are worthy of mention.[80] By 1994, the Council was advocating EU promotion of core labour standards not only within, but also outside the Union, using for this objective the Generalised System of Preferences (GSP),[81] the EU's main unilateral measure on trade. The preferential and non-reciprocal treatment in international trade that the industrialised countries were asked to concede to the developing ones represent a mechanism of distributive justice. It is an important derogation to the GATT rules in international trade.[82] Beginning in 1971, the EEC has given generalised tariff preferences for completed and semi-fabricated industrial products from developing countries by authorising a more advantageous customs treatment than the one normally applied, and entailing the total or partial abolishment of import customs duties. The Council, by adopting a new GSP on 19 December 1994,[83] ratified for the first time a link between trade and the respect of fundamental social rights, concretising this principle by a trade instrument of the European Community.

The GSP scheme contains incentives as well as sanctions. Previously, under the EU GSP Regulation of 1998,[84] there were two types of

---

[79] See P. Alston, 'Labor Rights Provisions in US Trade Law', *HRQ* 15/1 (1993), 8; Dubin, *La protection des normes sociales dans les échanges internationaux*, p. 56.

[80] See T. Novitz, 'The European Union and International Labour Standards: The Dynamics of Dialogue between the EU and the ILO', in Alston (ed.), *Labour Rights as Human Rights*, p. 229.   [81] www.europa.eu.int.

[82] GSP schemes are, in principle, contrary to the GATT's most favoured nation principle, because they grant preferences to developing countries without extending them to other WTO members. See T. M. Franck, *Fairness in International Law and Institutions* (Oxford: Oxford University Press), 1995, p. 58.   [83] www.europa.eu.int.

[84] The Regulation entered into force on 1 July 1999 and covers the period until the end of 2001. It is the first one to cover all products and all arrangements (such agricultural, industrial, textiles, GSP etc.). It is laid down in Council Regulation (EC) No 2820/98 of 21 December 1998.

measures.[85] The first one was a real sanction, *id est* the temporary, total or partial withdrawal of the advantages incorporated in the scheme of preferences in the case of any form of slavery as defined in the Geneva Conventions[86] and in ILO Conventions No. 29[87] and No. 105,[88] and in the case of products made in prisons. The temporary withdrawal was not automatic, but became effective only at the end of a specific procedure that could be initiated by a Member State or by any physical or legal person or by any non-legal personality association that could prove an interest in the sanction, by reporting the violation directly to the Commission. The second provision of the Regulation was a positive sanction of a promotional nature, a sign of a more cooperative rather than punitive approach. It consisted of the concession of a special 'system of encouragement' with the aim of helping recipient countries to improve their progress by preparing more advanced social policies. The disparity between grounds for granting and withdrawing preferential trade access was an evident basis for concern. Under the Regulation of 2001[89] special incentive arrangements for the protection of labour rights may be granted to countries already admitted to GSP which present a written request by which they prove that they have adopted and effectively applied internal legislation containing the provisions of the four core labour rights laid down in ILO Conventions: freedom from forced labour, freedom from child labour, freedom from discrimination, and freedom of association and the right to collective bargaining.[90] The Council Regulation furthermore provides that the request shall include the measures taken in order to implement and monitor the effectiveness of social legislation, and a commitment by the government to assume full responsibility for the control and execution of the established procedures.[91]

---

[85] Currently governed by Council Regulation 2501/2001 EC, OJ 2001 L 346/1, as amended.

[86] Slavery Convention, Protocol amending the Slavery Convention, Supplementary Convention on the Abolition of Slavery, the Slave Trade and Institutions and Practices Similar to Slavery, Forced Labour Convention, Abolition of Forced Labour Convention, Convention for the Suppression of the Traffic in Persons and of the Exploitation of the Prostitution of Others, For more information, see:www.ohchr.ch.

[87] ILO Convention concerning Forced or Compulsory Labour (No. 29).

[88] ILO Convention concerning the Abolition of Forced Labour (No. 105).

[89] Council Regulation (EC) No 2501/2001 contains the legal provisions for the GSP scheme applicable for the period 1.1.2002–31.12.2005 (as amended). For more information, see: http://europa.eu.int/comm/trade/issues/global/gsp/legis/index_en.htm (accessed: 15 March 2006).

[90] For more information, see: europa.eu.int/comm/trade/issues/global/gsp/legis/index_en. htm (accessed: 15 March 2006).   [91] *Ibid.*

There may be temporary withdrawal of these preferential arrangements in the case of 'practice of any form of slavery or forced labour'[92] and or 'serous and systematic violation of the freedom of association, the right to collective bargaining or the principle of non-discrimination in respect of employment and occupation, or use of child labour, as defined in relevant ILO Conventions',[93] as well as 'export of goods made by prison labour'. In this manner the parity of grant and withdrawal of special preferences is apparently achieved.[94]

Even if GSP is a unilateral and a European instrument, the Council includes additional objective and operative criteria on the basis of internationally accepted ones, takes note of the results of the studies carried out by the ILO, WTO, and OECD. This will thereby promote a new control mechanism based on cooperation among different international organisations, which should serve as a backbone of any future hypothesis about the inclusion of a social clause in international trade agreements.

By taking into consideration the direct reference to the ILO Conventions, the European system is on the whole characterised by being more respectful of the principles of international law than is the American one. As a consequence, one can affirm that the European Union has laid down the foundations of an international trade policy integrating fundamental social rights, which allows the Union to act in total consistency in order to make a social clause acceptable on the universal and on the multilateral level. Of course, whilst this approach is uncontroversial within the EU, it is regarded with suspicion by trade theorists, who are keen to insulate the WTO from extraneous non-trade issues.

The most recent proposal for a new GSP scheme (the so-called GSP+ Arrangement[95]) does not seem to change this underlying philosophy; that is, still requesting that the beneficiary country cumulatively accept the main international conventions on social and human rights, environmental protection and governance [Article 9(1) of the GSP Proposal].

The company dimension and Codes of Conduct

This last level of supranational regulation takes us to the complex dimension of company structure, a powerful non-state actor of international

---

[92] *Ibid.* [93] *Ibid.*

[94] T. Novitz, 'The European Union and International Labour Standards: The Dynamics of Dialogue between the EU and the ILO', in Alston (ed.), *Labour Rights as Human Rights*, p. 231.

[95] COM (2004) 699 Final, October 20, 2004.

relations which aspires to the recognition of having legal personality in international law. In an era of increased transborder commercial exchanges, the preoccupation of states with controlling multinational enterprises (according to a typical view of the 1960s and 70s that saw the emergence of this new economic power as a threat to state sovereignty) changes to a positive evaluation of the role of the enterprise, vector of internationalisation of foreign direct investment on its own territory. In this context, the State is ready to make all sorts of concessions in order to guarantee favourable conditions for the investors, starting from the pro- vision of mechanisms of dispute settlement against the hosting state at international arbitration fora to the creation of free zones where the non- respect of fundamental social rights is justified in the name of world competition. It is clear that such an economically powerful and politically influential subject can modify the normative setup where it is present. Indeed, parallel to its international economic action, the enterprise incorporates norms of good conduct of various origins; not least an internal one, a result of an autonomous regulation that crosses the different levels of the value chain incorporated in the network of a complex structure company.

Codes of conduct for international business operations are proliferat- ing and taking shape as a part of a broader movement of corporate social responsibility. There are two main types of codes:[96] one type is the 'exter- nal' ones, prepared by international organisations such as OECD Guidelines[97] and the Tripartite Declaration of the ILO;[98] the other type is 'internal' codes adopted by multinational enterprises.

External codes, dating back further in time and more widely known, show a low efficiency level. They are instruments of 'soft law' and their provisions are voluntarily adopted without any enforcement and/or sanction mechanism. The latest observation on external codes of conduct demonstrated significant implementation problems with the ILO Tripartite Declaration,[99] and it is at least doubtful whether the OECD Guidelines produced that contribution to the promotion of social welfare that lingers in the document as a programmatic objective. In this regard,

---

[96] See L. A. Compa and T. Hinchliffe Darricarrère, 'Private Labor Rights Enforcement Through Corporate Codes of Conduct', in L. A. Compa and S. F. Diamond (eds.), *Human Rights, Labor Rights, and International Trade* (Pennsylvania: University of Pennsylvania Press), 1996, p. 181; see the contribution of Marrella in this volume; see further the contributions of Benedek and Francioni.   [97] See www.oecd.org.
[98] Tripartite Declaration of Principles Concerning Multinational Enterprises and Social Policy; for more information, see www.ilo.org.   [99] *Ibid.*

the efforts of the UN should be mentioned, such as the Code of Conduct on Transnational Corporations,[100] and the Global Compact,[101] which is not a code of conduct but an attempt to promote the fundamental principles of the UN in a field that is dominated by enterprises. Through cooperation with the UN, trade union organisations, and NGOs, companies are encouraged to adopt a 'good practices' approach, defined by a dialogue between the different stakeholders. The UN Code of Conduct on Transnational Corporations considers that each transnational corporation or other business enterprise shall apply and incorporate these Norms in their contracts or other arrangements and dealings with contractors, subcontractors, suppliers, licensees, distributors, or natural or other legal persons that enter into any agreement with the transnational corporation or business enterprise in order to ensure respect for and implementation of the Norms.

Internal codes, self-written, are communicated to the contracting or sub-contracting companies of the multinational enterprises through the outsourcing or supply contract, which represent a sort of standard clause, included in the text itself, or a reference is made to it. By signing the contract, the contractor obliges him/herself to respect the rules of the code under the threat of punishment by the application of foreseen sanctions, which can even lead to the dissolution of the contract. The major weakness of internal codes lies in the application and monitoring procedures; generally the control systems are carried out by the companies themselves and not by trade union organisations or NGOs that could guarantee the independence and the impartiality of the evaluation. It is necessary to create more advanced and credible regulative instruments on the basis of the Codes of Conduct negotiated by social partners. An example would be the agreement, directed to European enterprises, between the European Trade Union Federation: Textile, Clothing and Leather (ETUF: TCL) and the entrepreneurs' European Apparel and Textile Organisation (EURATEX) in the textile and clothing sector. The reference to the ILO Conventions and the provision of their exact application is the most interesting part of this European code. Normally, indeed, the transnational companies' texts recall only the principles of the mentioned conventions, partially modifying the original wording, which can cause interpretative and applicative distortions, to the detriment of the rights

---

[100] Draft Norms on the Responsibilities of Transnational Corporations and other Business Enterprises with regard to Human Rights, E/CN.4/Sub.2/2003/12/Rev.2, art.15 (accessed: 15 March 2006). [101] www.un.org/depts/ptd/global.htm (accessed: 15 March 2006).

of the workers. The reference to the Export Processing Zones in the Agreement is also fundamental. It is in these areas, where there is the risk of non-application of the Conventions ratified by the country due to the provided derogations. The application of the EURATEX – ETUF: TCL could contribute to guaranteeing the respect of fundamental social rights.

It is desirable that the mentioned models are rigorously applied, overcoming the underlying weaknesses that have become visible during the application of internal codes. Beyond imposing more stringent and precise obligations on the contractors, companies should above all entrust the procedures of application of the codes not only to quality controllers or trade agents (internal monitoring), but also to external and independent subjects, competent in the field of labour law, industrial relations and human rights (external monitoring). The model code drafted by the Apparel Industry Partnership (AIP),[102] an organisation consisting of companies, NGOs and trade unions, represents a measure of progress into this direction. Indeed, the coalition has elaborated the Principles of Monitoring, which regulate the control of the codes, both as regards internal and external monitoring. In the case of internal control, the involvement of experts in the field of employment and human rights is proposed, who would carry out periodical controls on the facilities of the contractors even without prior notice about the controls. A regular consultation with the trade union representatives of the legally established workers' association, and local institutions and organisations working with human rights is also established, and their opinion on the application of the code is sought. The company should also guarantee that the implementation procedures of the code are not contrary to the company collective agreements. Concerning external control, the section on the *Obligations of Independent External Monitors* of the AIP Code also provides for the application of the relevant tasks to associations specialised in human rights or in labour law.[103] It is carried out with the help of clear evaluation criteria, based on both periodic and also unexpected inquiries made of a representative sample of the companies. The evaluation has to include, amongst other things, the level of knowledge of employees on the content of the code, the existence of a claim procedure that does not expose the employees to reprisals, and sample interviews

---

[102] www.itcilo.it/english/actrav/telearn/global/ilo/guide/apparell.htm.
[103] Section II of AIP Code, www.itcilo.it/english/actrav/telearn/global/ilo/guide/apparell. htm#Apparel%20Industry%20Partnership's%20Agreement (accessed: 15 March 2006).

with the workers, undertaken with the assistance of trade union or religious association representatives.

There are different interpretations with regard to Codes of Conduct. For example, one can imagine that respect for these codes represents a functionally weak substitute, for effective interstate regulation, in the absence of such effective regulation. The new institutional rationality then degrades into soft regulation, and becomes eventually subjected to the supervision of NGOs in the absence of a supranational authority capable of controlling economic actors.[104] Can this voluntary, flexible and non-binding regulation have the same efficiency as the legal norm imposed by the nation-state within its boundaries? It is right to doubt it. However, this modern vector of transnationalisation of rights cannot be ignored or underestimated, especially in the light of the internal markets and the commodity chains created by transnational and associated enterprises.[105] The big transnational corporations decide more and more often, for complex reasons, to adopt principles and norms on conduct on environmental and social matters, regardless of where they are based, and they request from their employees – wherever they may be – loyalty to the values of the company, tailored to fundamental principles (equal treatment of men and women, non-discrimination, etc.). In this sense, they represent a path among the many pieces of the puzzle that we are trying to reconstruct, in the search for an embryonic constitutional, multipolar and asystematic network that ratifies the sense of connection between the economy and social values in the era of globalisation.

Concluding remarks: labour law in the post-national puzzle

From the intensification of international competition to the transnationalisation of production activities, the changes brought about by economic globalisation have radically challenged the capability of national legal systems to come up with adequate rules to govern the new dimensions of the markets. Indeed, both in doctrinal and political circles, the

---

[104] As B. Hepple noted, the main weaknesses of all codes is 'the absence of positive obligations on states to require TNCs to observe both core and core-plus standard [... and] the reliance that the international system places on national labour laws at a time when national governments have been disempowered by globalization', 'A Race to the Top? International Investment Guidelines and Corporate Codes of Conduct', *Comparative Labour Law and Policy* 20 (1999), 361.

[105] See Lord Wedderburn, 'Common Law, Labour Law, Global Law', in Hepple (ed.), *Social and Labour Rights in a Global Context*, p. 52.

opinion that the instruments of labour relations should be envisaged on macro-regional levels, thus reconciling the exigencies of global competitiveness with those of social justice and equity, is widely held. In view of a normative action of the ILO, which is rather useful to identify universally recognised social standards but hardly effective as regards efficiency, it is necessary to mobilise institutions that incorporate supra-state communities in order to promote the convergence between the minimum standards of labour regulations.

The task of juridical research is to contribute to the promotion of the adoption of mechanisms capable of efficiently regulating phenomena of social dumping – being harmful to fundamental social rights and distorting international competition at the same time – and promoting social progress and fundamental rights. In this field, a synergy between the institutions and international organs and their regulative capability is required by the link between social justice, economic growth and the regulation of international competition. It is a link that could produce either praiseworthy effects or, on the contrary, which could also lead to an unstoppable race to the bottom. From its beginnings, the very international labour law itself has been closely related to competition preoccupations: those companies that do not internationalise the social costs of production put in place an unfair trade practice and obtain a competitive advantage on the market. Respect for certain social standards capable of guaranteeing a minimum of supranational social citizenship reflects not only the requirements of social fairness and justice but also the regulative function of the competition carried out by labour law norms.

The idea of the social clause, the mechanism that accompanies international trade liberalisation subordinating the enjoyment of tariff benefits to the respect of some fundamental social principles, is now under discussion in the international community. The social clause should overcome the traditional intrinsic limits of international labour law by the help of a higher level of efficiency, guaranteed by trade sanctions which could be imposed on states that disregard the most elementary rules of the protection of fundamental human rights. The identification of basic social rights (*id est* 'fundamental' or 'internationally recognised') through the recognition of the norms drafted by international organisations (*in primis* the ILO and UN) allowed an opportunity for a reconstructive hypothesis to consider social clauses not as instruments of masked protectionism – as denounced by many developing countries that oppose their adoption – but as an operative reinforcement of universally recognised human rights already existing in general international law and, maybe, in *jus cogens* as well. The central point of this social clause is not intended to cancel the competitive advantages (on a comparative basis) of the developing economies, or the ones in transition, but to create the necessary requirements of international trade so that the minimum conditions of social and trade union fairness be respected.[106] Thus, possible action strategies have been identified in the multilateral sphere, testing the compatibility of the social clause with the GATT-WTO rules in force. In this respect, it is necessary to offer a critique of some of the international trade-regulating principles, from a perspective of taking advantage of the GATT's 'public' profiles, by hypothesising the extraterritorial application of the previously identified social standards. For example, the failure to adopt social guarantee instruments by a country could be qualified as a 'subsidy' to the national industry, likely to be considered as a compensatory measure. The GATT rules on safeguard clauses, exceptions and protection of concessions and benefits should be analyzed under the same interpretative line.

However, the social clause is already *de facto* operational, especially at the level of unilateral action. This is especially so in the case of the generalised preferences in the US experience, and, more recently, that of the EU. The US experience is particularly significant for the radical nature of the criteria of social conditionality of trade legislation; however, it shows the limits of a unilateral perspective that reveals a strong political, aggressive, and arbitrary use of the social clause. This does not seem to be the case in the European practice, which is characterised by a higher commitment to the principles of international labour law and avoids any selective and discretional interpretation of the enshrined social rights.

The North American Agreement on Labor Cooperation (NAALC) merits a wider consideration; it accompanied, in a unique way the opening of a regional economic integration phase, marked by the entry into force of NAFTA.[107] It is a very peculiar experience that on the one side does not provide for mechanisms of social harmonisation which would allow Member States to preserve their full sovereignty on juridical-institutional level. On the other side, it establishes institutional surveillance structures and collaboration between States in order to guarantee the promotion of respect for respective internal legislation by providing both for a higher standard and an effective application.

---

[106] See D. Held, *Global Covenant. The Social Democratic Alternative to the Washington Consensus* (Cambridge: Polity Press, 2004).
[107] The NAFTA entered into force on 1 January 1994.

Nonetheless, the protection of the core labour standards can also be implemented by voluntary and consensual solutions, codifying the rules of good ethical-social conduct shared by multinational companies. Among these soft law instruments, the codes of conduct have a primary role, which could be prepared by international organisations such as the ILO or the OECD or by the multinational companies themselves. Whilst the first can be adopted spontaneously by the addressees, the second shows the growing consciousness of the companies to produce and commercialize their products in a 'socially' adequate way. With this regard, a significant role could be played by governments, adopting measures aimed at promoting the transparency of the social conditions of the production. This could be done either by obliging companies to prepare annual reports with information on their productive environment or by the creation of 'social labels' which guarantee to the consumer the respect of certain fundamental workers' rights.

To conclude: this analysis has illuminated some profiles of fundamental social rights, which, under the banner of supranational regulation, reveal problematic relations between values, rights, and the economic dimension of globalisation. At present, the possibly indicative composition of numerous and diverse levels of regulation is witnessed; from one perspective, denying the image of a market unified on the global level, guided solely by an economic logic; from another, there appears to be delicate problems of governance, in the absence of a constitutional framework able to face the challenge posed to labour law by what Habermas defined as a 'post-national constellation'. For the moment, it is possible to confine oneself to noting the formation of a complex and polycentric system of partial legal spaces, involving public and private subjects and global, regional and local levels of deregulation. This pluralism of sources perhaps represents regression, if judged by the traditional categories of a labour law of statutory tradition, but it constitutes a necessary form of regulation of a transnational space in the search for a possible global constitutional panoply.

Bibliography

Alston, P., 'Labour Rights as Human Rights: The Not So Happy State of The Art', in Alston, P. (ed.), *Labour Rights as Human Rights* (Oxford: Oxford University Press, 2005), pp. 1–24

'Labor Rights Provisions in US Trade Law', *Human Rights Quarterly* 15/1 (1993), 1–35

'Linking Trade and Human Rights', *German Yearbook of International Law* 23 (1980), 126–135

'Labor Rights Provisions in US Trade Law. Aggressive Unilateralism?', in Compa, L. A. and Diamond, S. F. (eds.), *Human Rights, Labor Rights, and International Trade* (Philadelphia: University of Pennsylvania Press, 1996)

Baldwin, R. E., *Trade Policy in a Changing World Economy* (Chicago: University of Chicago Press, 1988)

Barnard, C. and Deakin, S., *Corporate Governance, European Governance and Social Rights*, in Hepple, B. (ed.), *Social and Labour Rights in a Global Context* (Cambridge: Cambridge University Press, 2002)

Beck, U., *Macht und Gegenmacht im globalen Zeitalter* (Frankfurt am Main: Suhrkamp Verlag, 2002)

Betten, L., *International Labour Law* (Boston: Deventer, 1993)

Bhagwati, J., *In Defence of Globalisation* (Oxford: Oxford University Press, 2004)

Charnovitz, S., 'L'influence des norms internationals du travail sur le systeme du commerce mondial', *RIT*, (1987), pp. 635–657

'The Labor Dimension of the Emerging Free Trade Area of the Americas', in Alston, P. (ed.), *Labour Rights as Human Rights* (Oxford: Oxford University Press, 2005), pp. 143–176

Compa, L. A., and Hinchliffe Darricarrère, T., 'Private Labor Rights Enforcement Through Corporate Codes of Conduct', in Compa, L. A. and Diamond, S. F. (eds.), *Human Rights, Labor Rights, and International Trade* (Philadelphia: University of Pennsylvania Press, 1996)

Cowie, J. and French J., 'NAFTA's Labor Side Accord: A Textual Analysis', *Latin American Labor News* (1994), 28–37

D'Antona, M., 'Labour Law at the Century's End: An Identity Crisis', in Conaghan, J., Fischl R., and Klare, K. (eds.), *Labour Law in an Era of Globalization: Transformative Practices and Possibilities* (Oxford: Oxford University Press, 2002), pp. 51–63

De Martino, G., 'L'harmonisation des normes du travail dans une perspective internationaliste', *Syndicalisme et société* (1998), 265–280

Deakin, S., 'Labour Law as a Market Regulation: The Economic Foundations of European Social Policy', in Davies, S., Lyon-Caen, A., Sciarra, S. and Simitis, S. (eds.), *European Community Labour Law: Principles and Perspective* (Oxford: Oxford University Press, 1996), pp. 63–94

'Social Rights in a Globalized Economy', in Alston, P. (ed.), *Labour Rights as Human Rights* (Oxford: Oxford University Press, 2005), pp. 25–60

Diller, J. and Levy, D., 'Child Labor, Trade and Investment: Toward the Harmonization of International Law', *American Journal of International Labour*, (1997), 663–696

Dubin, L., *La protection des normes sociales dans les échanges internationaux* (Marseille: Presses Universitaires d'Aix-Marseille, 2003)

Erickson, C. and Kuruvilla, S., 'Labor Costs and the Social Dumping Debate in the European Union', *Industrial. Labour Relations Review* 48 (1994), 28–47

Franck, T. M., *Fairness in International Law and Institution* (Oxford: Oxford University Press), 1995

Garvey, J., 'Trade Law and Quality of Life-Dispute Resolution under the NAFTA Side Accords on Labor and the Environment', *American Journal of International Labour* (1995), 439–453

Gaston, N. and Trefler D., 'Protection, Trade and Wages: Evidence from US Manufacturing', *Industrial Labour Relations Review* 47 (1994), 574–593

Habermas, J., *Die postnationale Konstellation*, Politische Essays (Frankfurt am Main: Suhrkamp, 1998)

Hayek, F. A., *Law, Legislation and Liberty. A New Statement of the Liberal Principles of Justice and Political Economy*, vol. II, *The Mirage of Social Justice* (London: Routledge & Kegan, 1976)

Held, D., *Global Covenant. The Social Democratic Alternative to the Washington Consensus* (Cambridge: Polity Press, 2004)

Hepple, B., 'A Race to the Top? International Investment Guidelines and Corporate Codes of Conduct', *Comp. Lab. Law and Policy* 20 (1999), 361–378
   'Enforcement: the law and politics of cooperation and compliance', in B. Hepple (ed.) *Social and Labour Rights in a Global Context* (Cambridge: Cambridge University Press, 2002)

Kellerson, H., 'La Déclaration de 1998 de l'OIT sur les principes et droits fondamentaux: un défi pour l'avenir?', *Rev. int. trav.* 1999, 244–251

Lalive, P., 'Ordre public international (ou réellement international) et arbitrage international', *Rev. Arbitrage* (1986), 100–107

Leary, V., 'The WTO and the Social Clause: Post-Singapore', *EJIL* 8 (1997), 118–122

Leebron, D., 'Linkages', *American Journal of International Labour* (2002), 5–27

Lord Wedderburn, B., 'Common Law, Labour Law, Global Law', in Hepple, B. (ed), *Social Rights in a Global Context* (Cambridge: Cambridge University Press, 2002)

Lyon-Caen, A., 'Pérennité d'une interrogation', in *Bulletin de droit comparé du travail et de la sécurité sociale* (1996), 13–20
   'The Legal Efficacy and Significance of Fundamental Social Rights: Lesson From the European Experience', in Hepple, B. (ed), *Social and Labour Rights in a Global Context* (Cambridge: Cambridge University Press, 2002), 182–191

Lyon-Caen, G., 'L'infiltration du droit du travail par le droit de la concurrence', *Droit Ouvrier* (1992), 313–318

Lyon-Caen, G. and Lyon-Caen, A., *droit social international et européen* (Paris: Dalloz, 1993)

Mancini, G. F., 'Effect of EC Law on Member States' Employment Law', in Mancini,

G. F. (ed.), *Democracy and Constitutionalism in the European Union* (Oxford: Oxford University Press, 2000), 98–106

Maupain, F., 'Is the ILO Effective in Upholding Workers' Rights? Reflections on the Myanmer Experience', in Alston, P. (ed.), *Labour Rights as Human Rights* (Oxford: Oxford University Press, 2005), 85–142

McCrudden, C. and Davies, A., 'A Perspective on Trade and Labour Rights', in Francioni, F. (ed.), *Environment, Human Rights and International Trade* (Oxford: Hart, 2001), 56–64

Moreau, M. A. and Trudeau, G., 'La clause sociale dans l'accord de libre-echange nord-américain', *Revue Internationale du Droit Économique* (1995), 393–406

Moreau, M. A., 'La clause sociale dans les traités internationaux: Bilan et Perspectives', *Séminaires de la Maison des Sciences de l'homme* (Nantes: Ange Guepin, 1995)

Murray, L., 'Standard syndicaux équitables en matière de commerce international', *Monde du Travail libre* (1961), 102

Novitz, T., *The European Union and International Labour Standards: The Dynamics of Dialogue between the EU and the ILO*, in Alston, P. (ed.), *Labour Rights as Human Rights* (Oxford: Oxford University Press, 2005)

Pérez-Lopez, J., 'Conditioning Trade on Foreign Labor Law: The US Approach', *Comparative Labor Law Journal* (1988) 9, 253–260

Perulli, A., *Diritto del lavoro e globalizzazione [Labour Law and Globalization]* (Padova: Cedam, 1999)

Piore, M. J., 'Labor Standards and Business Strategies', in Herzenberg, A. and Pérez-Lopez, J. F. (eds.), *Labor Standards and Development in the Global Economy* (Washington: US Department of Labor Bureau of International Labor Affairs, 1990)

Racine, J. B., *L'arbitrage commercial international et l'ordre public* (Paris: LGDJ, 1999)

Roys, A. and Parbudyal, S., 'Early Experience with NAFTA's Labour Side Accord', *Comparative Labour Law Journal* 18 (1997), 161–170

Schmitt, C., *Der Nomos der Erde* (Berlin: Duncker & Humbolt, 1997)

Sciarra, S., 'Fundamental Labour Rights after the Lisbon Agenda', in De Burca, G. and De Witte, B. (eds.), *Social Rights in Europe* (Oxford: Oxford University Press, 2005)

  'La constitutionnalisation de l'Europe sociale, entre droits sociaux fondamentaux et soft law', in De Schutter, O. and Nihoul, P. (eds.), *Une constitution pour l'Europe. Reflexions sur les trasformations du droit de l'Union européenne* (Brussels: Bruylant, 2004)

  'Market Freedom and fundamental social rights', in Hepple, B. (ed.), *Social and Labour Rights in a Global Context* (Cambridge: Cambridge University Press, 2002)

Simitis, S. and Lyon-Caen, A., 'Community Labour Law: A Critical Introduction to its History', in Davies, P. *et al.* (eds.), *European Community Labour Law: Principles and Perspective* (Oxford: Oxford University Press, 2005)

Staelens, P., 'Les conséquences sociales de l'intégration nord-américaine sur le Mexique', *Syndicalisme et société* (1998), 97

Teubner G., 'Contracting Worlds: The Many Autonomies of Private Law', *Social and Legal Studies* (2000), 399–417

Thurow, L. C., *The Future of Capitalism* (New York: William Morrow & Co, 1996)

Trebilcock, M. J., 'The Fair Trade Debate: Protection of Labour Standards and International Economic Law', in Griller, S. (ed.), *International Economic Governance and Non-Economic Concerns: New Challenges for the International Legal Order* (New York/Vienna: Springer, 2003)

Vellano, M., 'Full Employment and Fair Labour Standards in the Framework of the WTO', in Mengozzi, P. (ed.), *International Trade Law on the 50 Anniversary of the Multilateral Trade System* (Milano: Giuffrè, 1999)

Weiss, M., 'The Politics of the EU Charter of Fundamental Rights', in B. Hepple (ed.), *Social and Labour Rights in a Global Context* (Cambridge: Cambridge University Press, 2002)

PART II

The Relevance of Human Rights for International Economic Organisations

The World Trade Organization and Human Rights

WOLFGANG BENEDEK

Introduction

The topic of 'The World Trade Organization (WTO) and Human Rights' has been the subject of much controversy as well as increasing academic interest. Anti-globalisation groups blamed the WTO for not being sensitive to the consequences of its legal rules which can result in serious human rights violations. The former United Nations High Commissioner for Human Rights (UN HCHR), Mary Robinson, basing her comments on numerous resolutions and reports adopted in UN human rights bodies, has emphasised the need to investigate the relationship between international trade liberalisation and human rights.[1] This has been responded to by the academic community in a growing number of publications.[2] Since the time of the General Agreement on Tariffs and Trade (GATT), the United States has called for recognition of 'workers' rights', i.e. social standards, in GATT and WTO rules,[3] and also the European Communities have proposed to give more attention to non-

---

[1] Globalisation and its impact on the full enjoyment of human rights, Report of the High Commissioner for Human Rights submitted in accordance with Commission on Human Rights resolution 2001/32, E/CN./2002/54 of 15 January 2002, paras. 2–10.

[2] See, for example, the works of E.-U. Petersmann referred to in this volume and T. Cottier, J. Pauwelyn and E. Bürgi Bonanomi (eds.), *Human Rights and International Trade* (Oxford/New York: Oxford University Press, 2005).

[3] See E. de Wet, 'Labour Standards in the Globalized Economy: the Inclusion of a Social Clause in the General Agreement on Tariffs and Trade/World Trade Organization', *Journal of World Trade (JWT)* 36 (2002), 883–901; see also R. M. Stern and K. Terrel, 'Labor Standards and the World Trade Organization', Ann Arbor, 2003, http://www.fordschool. umich.edu/research/rsie/workingpapers/Papers476–500/r499.pdf (accessed: 17 December 2005).

[4] Cf. the 'Communication from the Commission to the Council on 'Fair Trade' of 29 November 1999, COM(1999) 619 final, available at http://trade-info.cec.eu.int/doclib/html/113080.htm (accessed: 16 January 2006); the 'Communication from the Commission to the Council, the European Parliament and the Economic and Social Committee: Promoting core labour standards and improving social governance in the

trade issues.[4] However, the developing country members of the WTO, in particular, have largely resisted any efforts to deal with non-economic issues in the WTO and successfully requested the elimination of these issues from the agenda of the Doha Round[5] as part of the 'July package' of 2004.[6] Only the issue of 'trade facilitation' survived from the so-called 'Singapore issues', which besides investment and competition originally also covered basic workers' rights.[7]

The WTO Secretariat,[8] whose task it is to preserve the legitimacy and general acceptance of the work of the organisation, has not been able to develop a more pro-active role against the opposition of the majority of the WTO Member States. However, the relationship between the WTO and the agreements negotiated under its auspices on the one hand, and human rights obligations on the other, has increasingly become a matter of debate in non-governmental and academic fora. The aim of this chapter is to contribute to the clarification of the issues at stake in the interrelationships between WTO rules and human rights obligations. In so doing, the chapter goes back to the original consensus expressed in the UN Charter, and traces the separation of originally connected issues and their thematic reunification since the late 1990s, as exemplified by the work of the UN human rights bodies. The chapter further tries to establish the necessity of overcoming this artificial separation in order to help resolve common global problems, and argues that a strengthening of the interface between the WTO and human rights is needed to address the lack of coordinated global governance. Thus a return to the original

context of globalisation' of 18 July 2001, COM(2001) 416 final, available at http://trade-info.cec.eu.int/doclib/html/111234.htm (accessed: 16 January 2006); the 'Council Conclusions on Commission Communication on Promoting Core Labour Standards of 17 July 2003, 11555/03 WTO 81 SOC 305 DEVGEN 101 OC 495, available at http://trade-info.cec.eu.int/doclib/html/113357.htm (accessed: 16 January 2006) and the 'Communication from the Commission to the European Parliament, the Council, the Economic and Social Committee and the Committee of the Regions: the Social Dimension of Globalisation and the EU's policy contribution on extending the benefits to all' of 18 May 2004, available at http://trade-info.cec.eu.int/doclib/html/117580.htm (accessed: 16 January 2006).

5 Ministerial Declaration, adopted on 14 November 2001 at Doha, WTO Doc. WT/MIN(01)/DEC/1 of 20 November 2001.

6 See Doha Work Programme – Decision Adopted by the General Council on 1 August 2004, WTO Doc.WT/L/579 of 2 August 2004, available at http://www.wto.org/english/tratop_e/dda_e/ddadraft_31jul04_e.pdf (accessed: 16 January 2006).

7 Final Declaration of the Ministerial Meeting of the WTO in Singapore of 13 December 1996, WTO Doc. WT/MIN(96)/DEC/C/W of 18 December 1996. The issue of basic workers' rights as included in the Singapore Declaration did not make it into the agenda of the Doha Round from the outset.   8 See, generally, www.wto.org.

objectives contained in Chapter IX of the UN Charter seems essential in order to give human rights an adequate place in WTO law and activities, and thereby achieve a better balance of the economic and social dimensions of globalisation. This reflection can also help to address the legitimacy crisis of the WTO and to forge a new basic consensus between the North and the South, between the economic and social dimensions of international trade and between governments and civil society.

The comprehensive approach of the UN Charter and its limited realisation

International economic cooperation

The original approach of the UN Charter, as indicated in Articles 55 and 56, was based on an ideal of cooperation among Member States in order to achieve an improvement of the general standard of living, to promote full employment and conditions of economic and social progress and development, and to resolve international economic, social, health and related problems based on general respect for human dignity, as the basis of the implementation of human rights for all, without any discrimination. For this purpose, specialised agencies are foreseen in Article 57. The UN Conference on Trade and Employment during 1946–8 elaborated the 'Havana Charter' as the Charter of the International Trade Organisation (ITO),[9] which was to be an organisation within the UN framework to meet the objectives of Article 55. However, due to US opposition, the ITO Charter never came into force. What remained was the GATT, covering only the trade chapter of the Havana Charter that subsequently entered into force on the basis of a protocol on provisional application.[10]

It was not until 1995 that an international trade organisation in the form of the WTO was established; at that point, however, Member States decided to keep it outside the UN system. The effect of this decision was to break even the limited linkages which had existed between the GATT and the UN. The GATT formally took its international legal status from the Interim Committee for the International Trade Organisation (ICITO) of the UN. The staff members of the GATT had their diplomatic privileges and immunities under the respective UN convention, were

---

[9] U.S. Department of State Publication No. 3206, Commercial Policy Series No. 114, 1948, 19 et seq.

[10] Basic Instruments and Selected Documents (BISD), Vol. I, GATT, 1952, 77 et seq; 55 U.N.T.S., 308 et seq.

members of the UN pension fund, and were paid according to the UN salaries scheme.[11] Due to their full autonomy from the UN system, employees had hoped to gain higher salaries comparable to those paid by the International Monetary Fund (IMF) and the World Bank (WB). However, this did not materialise, which led to disappointments within the staff of the WTO Secretariat.

Therefore, even now the original comprehensive approach of the UN Charter with regard to cooperation in international trade has not been realised. The Havana Charter contained a chapter on labour and economic activity,[12] which, in Article 7 on 'fair labour standards', foresaw social standards. Chapter III dealt with economic development and reconstruction, containing articles on cooperation for economic development, and also included provisions on international competition, raw materials and dispute settlement. The Preamble of the GATT and consequently also the WTO still reflects this wider approach when it refers to the objectives of raising standards of living, ensuring full employment, economic growth and the optimal use of the world's resources. However, a reference to economic and social progress and development, as in Article 55 of the UN Charter, which was included in Article 1 of the Havana Charter of 1948, was deleted in the GATT Preamble. The underlying idea was reintegrated into the Preamble of the WTO Agreement only as a reference to sustainable development, protection and preservation of the environment and recognition of the needs and concerns of parties at different levels of economic development, though without making reference to Article 55 of the UN Charter. In the Havana Charter mention was made of the importance of mutual cooperation to resolve the problems of international trade and employment, of economic development and reconstruction.[13] Cooperation in this respect was to be undertaken by the ITO.[14] The GATT and, later, the Marrakesh Agreement establishing the WTO,[15] however, follow a more restrictive approach excluding, in particular, any reference to employment except in the Preambles.

[11] See W. Benedek, *Die Rechtsordnung des GATT aus völkerrechtlicher Sicht* [*The Legal Order of GATT from an International Law Perspective*] (Berlin/Heidelberg: Springer-Verlag, 1990), pp. 27 *et seq.*, 210 *et seq.*, 464 *et seq.*   [12] See Chapter II of the Havana Charter.
[13] Cf. Chapters II and III of the Havana Charter.   [14] Cf. Articles 77 *et seq.*
[15] General Agreement on Tariffs and Trade of 30 October 1947, 55 U.N.T.S. 194; and Marrakesh Agreement Establishing the World Trade Organization of 15 April 1994, 1867 U.N.T.S. 154; 33 I.L.M. 1144 (1994); published as World Trade Organization, *The Results of the Uruguay Round of Multilateral Trade Negotiations, The Legal Texts* (Geneva: World Trade Organization/Cambridge University Press, 1994), pp. 486 *et seq.* (GATT) and 6 *et seq.* (WTO).

The WTO might have wanted to shield itself from the political debates in the UN, but in reality it came under even more fire from anti-globalisation NGOs[16] because of its self-chosen isolation. With only very limited channels of dialogue with international civil society, the WTO became an attractive target for various grievances regarding economic globalisation, some of which were unrelated to the purposes and objectives of the WTO. The possibility of a different approach can be distilled from the examples of the IMF and the WB, with whom the WTO maintains special relations.[17] These bodies did actually become specialised agencies pursuant to Articles 57 and 63 of the UN Charter, and still managed to equate that status with maintaining a large degree of autonomy. The WB, in particular, today appears to be more open to human rights concerns, which does not mean that the two institutions do not give cause for criticism as well.[18]

The isolation of the WTO created a problem of the coherence of its work with other issues of concern to the UN; in particular, in the area of human rights. While it can be understood that the wide approach of the Havana Charter did not materialise in the conditions of the Cold War, which had started at that time, one could have hoped that after the end of the Cold War in 1989 and the reinvigoration of the UN system which followed, a more comprehensive approach should have become possible again. However, the WTO largely retained the attitudes of its predecessor, the GATT, pretending to follow only a non-political, technical approach, emphasising the contractual nature of the GATT and the WTO in general, as well as its limited organisational character as a member-driven organisation.[19] Contrary to ideas formulated in the early years of the

---

[16] See, for one example among many, the website of the NGO 'ATTAC' at http://www.attac.org/ (accessed: 16 January 2006). With regard to the WTO Ministerial Conference in Cancún the issue of WTO 'isolation' is addressed, *inter alia*, by C. Raghavan, 'WTO ignores calls for democratic, inclusive processes for Cancun', *Newsletter 179 page 7(7)*, http://www.attac.org/attacinfoen/attacnews179.pdf (accessed: 16 January 2006).

[17] See Ministerial Declaration of 15 December 1993 on the relationship of the World Trade Organization with the International Monetary Fund in WTO, *The Results of the Uruguay Round of Multilateral Trade Negotiations*, pp. 447 *et seq.*

[18] See the contribution of L. Boisson de Chazournes in this volume and S. Schlemmer-Schulte, 'Building an International Grievance System: The World Bank Inspection Panel – Selected Issues', in J. Bröhmer, R. Bieber, C. Calliess, C. Langenfeld, S. Weber and J. Wolf (eds.) *Internationale Gemeinschaft und Menschenrechte*, Festschrift für Georg Ress (Cologne/Berlin/Munich: Carl Heymanns Verlag, 2005), pp. 249–284.

[19] A humorous WTO saying underscores this point of view: 'The WTO is a table of discussion. What would you want a table to do?'

WTO, namely that, together with the IMF and the WB, it could provide more coherence in global governance, no sufficient political will did materialise to allow the WTO to go in this direction although the WTO secretariat remains aware of the need.[20]

Cooperation in the field of human rights

The first major codification of international human rights standards in the field of social standards actually took place in the framework of the International Labour Organisation (ILO), which, since 1919, has elaborated an 'International Labour Code' consisting of, so far, 185 conventions and 190 declarations and resolutions on social standards.[21] The ILO Constitution was included in the Paris Peace Treaties, and established at the same time as the League of Nations; its former headquarters in Geneva today serves as the seat of the WTO. After the Second World War, the ILO became a specialised agency of the UN.

The standards proclaimed by the Universal Declaration of Human Rights (UDHR) of 1948 are a partial concretisation of the purposes and objectives of Article 55 of the UN Charter on international economic and social cooperation. The UDHR, in the same manner as the Havana Charter, pursues a comprehensive and holistic approach, bringing together civil and political as well as economic, social and cultural rights in one human rights framework; and declaring also that 'everyone is entitled to a social and international order in which the rights and freedoms set forth in the Declaration can be fully realized' (Article 28). However, the work on binding norms based on the UDHR led to a split of this approach into two covenants, the International Covenant on Economic, Social and Cultural Rights (ICESCR) and the International Covenant on Civil and Political Rights (ICCPR), which was partly due to Cold War differences as well as North-South problems. Both covenants were adopted only in 1966 and entered into force in 1976; the control mechanisms of the two covenants are not of equal strength. It was only in 1985 that a Committee on Economic, Social and Cultural Rights (CESCR) was

---

[20] See the former Director-Generals of WTO, Sutherland and Rugiero, e.g. Renato Rugiero, 'Beyond the Multilateral Trading System', address at the *Institut des Hautes Etudes Internationales* of 12 April 1999; and on WTO cooperation with the IMF and the World Bank', in: WTO Annual Reports 1998, p. 133 *et seq.* and 1999, p. 109. See also the speech of Director-General Pascal Lamy of January 2006, at fn. 121.

[21] See ILOLEX, Database of International Labour Standards, http://www.ilo.org/ilolex/ english/index.htm (accessed: 15 December 2005).

established, which has since developed activities on a similar level to the Human Rights Committee (HRC), the body charged with supervising the ICCPR, whereas a protocol which would allow individual communications on economic, social and cultural rights, in a similar manner to the Optional Protocol to the ICCPR has still not been adopted.[22] Accordingly, a bias can be observed with regard to the enforcement mechanism for the two different groups of human rights, to the detriment of economic, social and cultural rights.

The relationship between economic cooperation and human rights

There is an inherent connection between the principles of economic cooperation and human rights. The Preamble of the GATT and the WTO refer to 'raising standards of living' and 'full employment', whilst Article 25(1) of the UDHR, provides for the right to an adequate standard of living, and Article 23 for the right to work. These rights have been further elaborated in the CESCR, which, in Article 11, includes the right of everyone to an adequate standard of living, and in Articles 6 to 8 elaborates the right to work. In addition, the conventions and declarations of the ILO have specified the details of various social standards. The Declaration on the Right to Development of 1986[23] linked the implementation of the two covenants on human rights with the objective of development, the achievement of which presupposes the realisation of all human rights. The Declaration thus overcomes the separation into two groups of rights by a holistic approach similar to that of the UDHR.

The increasing concern of UN human rights bodies with international trade issues

In the course of discussions about the effects of globalisation on human rights increased attention has been given to the role of the WTO in this

---

[22] Work on such a protocol, however, is under way. See Report of the open-ended working group to consider options regarding the elaboration of an optional protocol to the International Covenant on Economic, Social and Cultural Rights on its first session, UN Doc. E/CN.4/2004/44 of 15 March 2004.

[23] See UN GA Resolution 41/128 of 4 December 1986 on the Declaration on the Right to Development. For a topical view on the interlinkage of human rights and development, see P. Alston and M. Robinson (eds.), *Human Rights and Development: Towards Mutual Reinforcement* (New York: Oxford University Press, 2005).

context.[24] The concern of NGOs regarding the role of human rights in the WTO has grown further.[25] As will be shown below, they were not alone. UN human rights bodies, too, have incorporated the human rights dimension of issues of international trade into their portfolio.

Since 1998, the UN Sub-Commission on the Promotion and Protection of Human Rights (Sub-Commission), as well as the CESCR, have increasingly taken positions on international trade matters from a human rights perspective, in particular in the fields of trade liberalisation, of intellectual property rights, trade in services, trade and investment and responsibilities of transnational corporations, as well as, more generally, globalisation and its impact on the full enjoyment of human rights. In addition, the special procedures of the UN Commission on Human Rights (CHR) were increasingly used to address trade issues from the perspective of economic and social rights, as can be seen from the reports of the Special Rapporteurs on the right to food and the right to health.[26]

The Sub-Commission in 1998 adopted a resolution on 'human rights as the primary objective of trade, investment and financial policy',[27] which must have come as a shock to the WTO-world, where trade liberalisation is largely seen as an objective in itself, that, in a quasi-automatic way, will lead to rising living standards and economic growth as well as promoting development and employment. What followed was a series of resolutions of the Sub-Commission, such as, in particular:

> Resolution 1999/30: Trade liberalisation and its impact on human rights[28]
> Resolution 2000/7: Intellectual property rights and human rights[29]

---

[24] See R. Howse and M. Mutua, 'Protecting Human Rights in a Global Economy, Challenges for the World Trade Organization', in H. Stokke and A. Tostensen (eds.), *Human Rights in Development Yearbook 1999/2000* (The Hague: Kluwer, 2001), pp. 51–82, E.-U. Petersmann, 'Human Rights and International Economic Law in the 21st Century, The Need to Clarify their Interrelationships,' *Journal of International Economic Law (JIEL)* 4 (2001) 1, pp. 3–39 as well as T. Cottier, Trade and Human Rights: A Relationship to Discover, *JIEL* 5 (2002) 1, 111–132.

[25] See C. Dommen, 'Raising Human Rights Concerns in the World Trade Organization: Actors, Processes and Possible Strategies', *Human Rights Quarterly* 24 (2002), 1–50.

[26] See the Report of the Special Rapporteur on the Right to Food, *infra*, at note 51 and the Report of the Special Rapporteur on the Right to Health, *infra*, at note 52.

[27] Sub-Commission on Human Rights Resolution 1998/12 of 20 August 1998, UN Doc. E/CN.4/Sub.2/RES/1998/12.

[28] Sub-Commission on Human Rights Resolution 1999/30 of 26 August 1999, UN Doc. E/CN.4/Sub.2/RES/1999/30.

[29] Sub-Commission on Human Rights Resolution 2000/7 of 17 August 2000, UN Doc. E/CN.4/Sub.2/RES/2000/7.

Resolution 2001/4: Liberalisation of trade in services and human rights[30]
Resolution 2001/21: Intellectual property and human rights[31]
Resolution 2002/11: Human rights, trade and investment.[32]

In addition, the Sub-Commission in Resolution 2001/5 dealt with 'globalisation and its impact on the full enjoyment of all human rights',[33] in Resolution 2003/12 with 'responsibilities of transnational corporations regarding human rights',[34] in Resolutions 2004/105 and 2004/107 with the right to food and the right to drinking water supply and sanitation,[35] and in Resolution 2005/6 with 'the effects of the working methods and activities of transnational corporations on the enjoyment of human rights'.[36] Accordingly, the Sub-Commission has covered the main fields of the relationship between trade and human rights.

The CHR, the parent organ of the Sub-Commission, has also been increasingly concerned with the interlinking of trade and human rights. It has passed, in consecutive years, numerous Resolutions on 'Globalization and its impact on the full enjoyment of all human rights' (Resolution 2002/28, Resolution 2003/23, Resolution 2004/24 and Resolution 2005/17).[37]

Specific aspects were further elaborated in the work of other UN human rights bodies, such as the CESCR, which in 2002 adopted its

---

[30] Sub-Commission on Human Rights Resolution 2001/4 of 15 August 2001, UN Doc. E/CN.4/Sub.2/RES/2001/4.

[31] Sub-Commission on Human Rights Resolution 2001/21 of 16 August 2001, UN Doc. E/CN.4/Sub.2/RES/2001/21.

[32] Sub-Commission on Human Rights Resolution 2002/11 of 14 August 2002, UN Doc. E/CN.4/Sub.2/RES/2001/11.

[33] Sub-Commission on Human Rights Resolution 2001/5 of 15 August 2001, UN Doc.E/CN.4/Sub.2/RES/2001/5.

[34] See Sub-Commission on Human Rights Resolution 2003/12 of 13 August 2003, UN Doc. E/CN.4/Sub.2/RES/2003/12; see also UN Draft Norms on the Responsibility of the Transnational Corporations and other Business Enterprises with Regard to Human Rights, UN Doc. E/CN.4/Sub.2/2003/12/Rev. 2 of 13 August 2003, as approved by Sub-Commission on Human Rights Resolution 2003/16 of 13 August 2003, UN Doc. Sub.2/RES/2003/16.

[35] See Sub-Commission on Human Rights Resolution 2004/105 of 9 August 2004, UN Doc.E/CN.4/Sub.2/RES/2004/105 and Sub-Commission on Human Rights Resolution 2004/107 of 9 August 2004, UN Doc.E/CN.4/Sub.2/RES/2004/107.

[36] See Sub-Commission on Human Rights Resolution 2005/6 of 8 August 2005, UN Doc. E/CN.4/Sub.2/RES/2005/16.

[37] See Commission on Human Rights Resolutions 2002/28 of 22 April 2002, UN Doc. E/CN.4/RES/2002/28; Commission on Human Rights Resolutions 2003/23 of 22 April 2003, UN Doc. E/CN.4/RES/2003/23; Commission on Human Rights Resolutions 2004/24 of 16 April 2004, UN Doc. E/CN.4/RES/2004/24; Commission on Human Rights Resolutions 2005/17 of 15 April 2005, UN Doc. E/CN.4/RES/2005/17.

General Comment No. 15 on 'the Right to Water', which also touches on trade in services.[38] Already in 2000 the CESCR had adopted General Comment No. 14 on 'the right to the highest attainable standard of health'[39], in which the General Agreement on Trade in Services (GATS)[40] and the Agreement on Trade-Related Aspects of Intellectual Property Rights (TRIPS Agreement)[41] were not (yet) directly addressed, when discussing international obligations or the obligations of other actors.[42] However, the duty of states to ensure physical access to water facilities or services can be found among the obligations mentioned in para. 37(c) of General Comment No. 15. According to paras. 45 *et seq.*, legislation, strategies and policies all have to promote the implementation of the obligation to ensure that everyone can enjoy the right to water. This may conflict with obligations under the GATS if it is not applied and interpreted in a way consistent with the human rights obligations; among the obligations of actual relevance, the WTO is explicitly requested to cooperate in the realisation of the implementation of the right to water.[43] The most recent CESCR General Comment, No. 17, deals with the protection of the rights of the author pursuant to Article 15(1)(c) of the ICESCR and thus touches on the relationship between human rights and intellectual property rights. It clarifies that intellectual property rights, which are of a temporary nature, cannot be equated with the human right of the author to benefit from the protection of his/her moral and material interests, which are permanent.[44]

---

[38] See UN Doc. E/C.12/2002/11 of 26 November 2002.

[39] See CESCR, General Comment No. 14 (2000) on the Right to the Highest Attainable Standard of Health, (Article 12 of the ICESCR), E/C.12/2000/4 of 4 July 2000.

[40] General Agreement on Trade in Services (GATS) of 15 April 1994, Marrakesh Agreement Establishing the World Trade Organization, Annex 1B, 1869 U.N.T.S. 183; reprinted in WTO, *The Results of the Uruguay Round*, pp. 325–364.

[41] Agreement on Trade-Related Aspects of Intellectual Property Rights, Apr. 15, 1994, Marrakesh Agreement Establishing the World Trade Organization, Annex 1C, 1869 U.N.T.S. 299, reprinted in WTO, *The Results of the Uruguay Round*, pp. 365–403.

[42] Cf. General Comment No. 14 , paras. 38 *et seq.* and 63 *et seq.*

[43] See para. 60 of General Comment No. 15. See also E. Filmer-Wilson, 'The Human Rights-Based Approach to Development: The Right to Water', *Netherlands Quarterly of Human Rights* 23 (2005) 2, 213–242.

[44] See CESCR, General Comment No. 17, The Right of Everyone to Benefit from the Protection of the Moral and Material Interests Resulting from any Scientific, Literary or Artistic Production of which he is the Author (Article 15, para. 1(c) ICESCR), UN Doc. E/C.12/GC/17, adopted on 21 November 2005. See also CESCR, *Statement on Human Rights and Intellectual Property*, UN Doc. E/C.12/2001/15; and A. R. Chapman, 'The Human Rights Implications of Intellectual Property Protection', *JIEL* 5 (2002) 4, 861–882.

Since 1995, the special procedures of the CHR have increasingly been instrumental in clarifying the relationship between economic, social and cultural rights, and the obligations and policies under the agreements made by the WTO. For example, the Special Rapporteur on the Adverse Effects of Illicit Movement and Dumping of Toxic and Dangerous Products and Wastes on the Enjoyment of Human Rights, Okechukwu Ibeanu, also looked at illicit trading in toxic and dangerous products and wastes,[45] a matter which was of much concern to, in particular, African countries and also led to the conclusion of the so-called 'Bamako Convention on Hazardous Waste'.[46]

The Independent Expert on the Right to Development, appointed in 1998, has the task of looking into the implementation of the Declaration on the Right to Development and thus also covers matters related to raising standards of living and the needs of countries at different levels of economic development, which are also recognised in the Preamble of the WTO. Again in 1998, an Independent Expert on the Question of Human Rights and Extreme Poverty was appointed. Poverty alleviation is one of the tasks to which the WTO has committed itself, together with five other international organisations, in the 'Integrated Framework for Trade-Related Assistance to Least-Developed Countries' endorsed also by the Doha Declaration.[47]

The Special Rapporteur on the Right to Education, appointed in 1998, is charged by this mandate to look into the effects of the GATS on the right to education.[48] There is an on-going controversy whether education should be considered as a public service and therefore exempted from the GATS under the conditions provided in the agreement as 'services supplied in the exercise of governmental authority' which are supplied

---

[45] Cf. Adverse effects of the illicit movement and dumping of toxic and dangerous products and wastes on the enjoyment of human rights, Report of the Special Rapporteur, Okechukwu Ibeanu, UN Doc. E/CN.4/2005/45 of 14 December 2004.

[46] Bamako Convention on the Ban of the Import into Africa and the Control of Transboundary Movement and Management of Hazardous Waste within Africa, adopted 30 January 1991, Bamako, Mali, 30 ILM 775, 1991.

[47] See Doha Ministerial Declaration of 14 November 2001, para. 43. The other organisations are WB, IMF, UNCTAD, UNDP and International Trade Centre.

[48] Pursuant to Commission on Human Rights Resolution 1998/33 of 17 April 1998, UN Doc. E/CN.4/RES/1998/33, the Special Rapporteur's mandate includes '(i) To report on the status, throughout the world, of the progressive realization of the right to education, including access to primary education, and the difficulties encountered in the implementation of this right, taking into account information and comments received from Governments, organizations and bodies of the United Nations system, other relevant international organizations and non-governmental organizations'.

neither on a commercial basis nor in competition with one or more service suppliers (Article I:3 (b) and (c)).[49]

The Special Rapporteur on the Right to Food, appointed in 2000, has also to deal with WTO agreements, such as the Agreement on Agriculture and the Ministerial Decision of 1993 on Measures Concerning the Possible Negative Effects of the Reform Programme on Least-Developed and Net Food-Importing Developing Countries;[50] and, additionally, the consequences of ongoing further liberalisation in agricultural trade for food security.[51]

The Special Rapporteur on the Right to Health, Paul Hunt, appointed in 2002, has paid an official visit to the WTO in 2004 in order to inquire into the relationship between his mandate and WTO activities. This has been an important step towards linking human rights and WTO agreements. In the report on his mission to the WTO, in which he addresses intellectual property and access to medicines as well as, *inter alia*, GATS and health services, the Special Rapporteur underlines a number of obligations of WTO members, among them, to promote policy coherence and to undertake impact assessments on the right to health when liberalising health services and to promote access to affordable medicines. The report concluded that the WTO needs to be respectful of the human rights obligations of its members.[52]

In addition, both the UN Secretary-General, Kofi Annan,[53] in his reports on 'Globalization and its impact on the full enjoyment of all human rights', [54] and the UN HCHR, Mary Robinson, in her report on

[49] See M. Krajewski, 'Public Services and Trade Liberalization: Mapping the Legal Framework', *JIEL* 6 (2003) 2, 341–367. See also K. Tomaševski, *Education Denied, Costs and Remedies* (London/New York: Zed Books, 2003), pp. 108 *et seq.*

[50] Ministerial Decision, adopted on 15 December 1993, reprinted in WTO, *Results of the Uruguay Round*, pp. 448 *et seq.*

[51] See the Report submitted by Jean Ziegler, the Special Rapporteur on the Right to Food to the Commission on Human Rights, UN Doc. E/CN.4/2005/47 of 24 January 2005.

[52] See the Reports of the Special Rapporteur on the Right of Everyone to the Enjoyment of the Highest Attainable Standard of Physical and Mental Health, Paul Hunt, on his mission to the World Trade Organization, in Addendum to his general report, UN Docs. E/CN.4/2004/49/Add.1 of 1 March 2004 and the last report in E/CN.4/2005/51 of 11 February 2005.

[53] The General Assembly, in its Resolution 58/193, UN Doc. A/58/193 of 22 December 2003, has specifically requested the Secretary-General to seek the views of Member States and relevant United Nations agencies on globalisation and its impact on the full enjoyment of all human rights. Unfortunately only twelve states contributed to the first and second reports.

[54] See the reports entitled 'Globalization and its Impact on the Full Enjoyment of All Human Rights', contained in UN Doc. A/59/320 of 1 September 2004 and UN Doc.

'Globalization and its Impact on the Full Enjoyment of Human Rights'[55] and on the 'Fundamental Principle of Non-Discrimination in the Context of Globalization'[56] have touched on WTO matters.

Furthermore, the UN HCHR, in 2001 and 2002, presented reports on the impact of the TRIPS Agreement on human rights and on 'Liberalisation of Trade in Services and Human Rights'.[57]

Kofi Annan has also been active in mainstreaming human rights in the context of private sector issues and, especially, transnational corporations (TNCs) by introducing, in 2000, as his personal initiative, the UN Global Compact.[58] Under the Global Compact, private enterprises are committing themselves to originally nine, now ten, core principles relating to human rights, labour standards, the environment and anti-corruption. Five UN specialised agencies cooperate actively with the Secretary-General's Global Compact office: the Office of the HCHR (OHCHR), ILO, UN Environmental Programme (UNEP), UN Development Programme (UNDP) and UN Industrial Development Organization (UNIDO).

For the UN Secretary-General, the relationship between trade and the achievement of the UN Millennium Development Goals (MDGs) is of particular concern. All organisations within the UN system are under an obligation to contribute to the implementation of the MDGs, adopted by the UN General Assembly in 2000.[59] Thereby, all UN Member States

A/60/301 of 24 August 2005 with an addendum contained in UN Doc. A/60/301/Add.1 of 1 September 2005; see also the earlier preliminary report of the Secretary-General on Globalization and its impact on the full enjoyment of all human rights in accordance with General Assembly resolution 54/248, UN Doc. A/55/342 of 31 August 2000.

55 See Report of the United Nations High Commissioner for Human Rights on 'Globalization and its Impact on the Full Enjoyment of Human Rights', UN Doc. E/CN.4/2002/54 of 5 January 2002; see also the final report submitted by Special Rapporteurs J. Oloka-Onyango and D. Udagama, on 'Economic, Social and Cultural Rights: Globalization and its Impact on the Full Enjoyment of Human Rights', UN Doc. E/CN.4/Sub.2/2003/14 of 25 June 2003.

56 See Analytical Study of the High Commissioner for Human Rights on the Fundamental Principle of Non-Discrimination in the Context of Globalization, UN Doc. E/CN.4/2004/40 of 15 January 2004.

57 CHR, Sub-Commission on the Promotion and Protection of Human Rights, Report of the High Commissioner, 'The Impact of the Agreement on Trade-Related Aspects of Intellectual Property Rights on Human Rights', UN Doc. E/CN.4/Sub.2/2001/13 of 27 June 2001 and 'Liberalization of Trade in Services and Human Rights', UN Doc. E/CN.4/Sub.2/2002/9 of 25 June 2002.

58 See, for more information on the UN Global Compact, www.unglobalcompact.org (accessed: 15 December 2005), and, on holding transnational corporations accountable, the contributions of F. Francioni, and F. Marella, in this volume.

59 See UN GA Resolution A/RES/55/2 of 18 September 2000.

have pledged to eradicate extreme poverty and hunger, achieve universal primary education, promote gender equality and empower women, reduce child mortality, improve maternal health, combat HIV/AIDS, malaria and other diseases, ensure environmental sustainability, and develop a global partnership for development.

The UNDP is committed to 'human development' and for this purpose has adopted a programme on 'mainstreaming human rights'.[60] Its yearly 'Human Development Report' regularly gives attention to human rights concerns as relevant for development and its Human Development Index contains a number of criteria which actually measure human rights performances, i.e. the rights to health, to social security and to education. The WB has also opened itself to human rights concerns, i.e. by establishing its 'Inspection Panel', which can receive complaints on human rights violations through projects it has funded;[61] it also includes human rights in its Poverty Reduction Strategy.[62]

Formally, the WTO, no longer belonging to the 'family' of UN organisations, could take the position that it was not under any obligation in this respect. Practically, however, such an attitude proves rather impossible, because it would lead to further criticism of the role, responsibility and legitimacy of the WTO. In addition, the MDGs are largely consistent with the purposes and objectives of the WTO itself. Therefore, one could well expect the WTO, within a reasonable time-frame, to draw up a report on its contribution to the achievement of the MDGs, although, strictly speaking, it does not have to. It is indicative that when requested by the Special Rapporteur on the Right to Health, Paul Hunt, in 2004, the former Director-General of the WTO, Supachai Panitchpakdi affirmed the vital importance of the MDGs, but could not make any commitments without express approval by the WTO

---

[60] See UNDP, *Integrating Human Rights with Sustainable Human Development*, 1998, which provides the basis for HURIST, a joint programme of UNDP and OHCHR, http://magnet.undp.org/Docs/policy5.html (accessed: 15 December 2005).

[61] See S. Schlemmer-Schulte, 'Building an International Grievance System', pp. 249–284; see also L. Boisson de Chazournes, 'Issues of Social Development: Integrating Human Rights into the Activities of the World Bank', in International Institute of Human Rights (ed.), *World Trade and the Protection of Human Rights, Human Rights in the Face of Global Economic Exchanges* (Brussels: Bruylant, 2001), pp. 51–70 and her contribution in this volume.

[62] For this purpose the UN HCHR has elaborated Draft Guidelines on 'A Human Rights Approach to Poverty Reduction Strategies', http://www.unhchr.ch/development/povertyfinal.html (accessed: 15 December 2005).

Member States. Yet they have all agreed, as members of the UN General Assembly, to the MDGs.[63]

The office of the UN HCHR has expressed itself on human rights and trade before the failed WTO Ministerial Conference in Cancún in 2003, drawing attention, in particular, to the relationship between agricultural reform and human rights.[64] Before the WTO Ministerial Conference in Hong Kong in 2005, the current UN HCHR, Louise Arbour, issued a study on possible interpretations of general exceptions clauses in WTO agreements to protect human rights,[65] which seems to be inspired by the 'Gambling Case' just decided before by WTO dispute settlement bodies. This case had, for the first time, interpreted the concepts of 'public morals' and 'public order' contained in the general exception clauses of the GATT and GATS.[66]

Consequently, the question of whether the 'human rights approach' advocated by the UN HCHR is relevant for the WTO[67] can only be answered in the affirmative. There appears to be an 'unavoidable link' between human rights and international trade agreements. The latter cannot escape from being scrutinised for their human rights impact just as the WTO cannot avoid being held accountable, in a general way, for the results of its policies. The argument, which is usually put forward from the side of the WTO, that it is up to the Member States to take non-trade interests such as human rights into account, is not convincing in view of the structural effects of WTO rules and the wide disparities of power and capabilities among the WTO membership. It is therefore clear that the relationship between trade and human rights interests needs to be addressed on an international level, in WTO fora as well as UN fora, with a view, as formulated by Mary Robinson, former UN HCHR, to a 'mutuality of interests' which can be established between the trading community and those concerned with implementation of

---

[63] See Report on Mission to the WTO, para. 8.

[64] OHCHR, *Human Rights and Trade*, Fifth WTO Ministerial Conference, Cancún, Mexico, 10–14 September 2003. During the Conference Bertrand Ramcharan was acting High Commissioner for Human Rights.

[65] See OHCHR, 'Human Rights in World Trade Agreements, Using general exception clauses to protect human rights', UN Doc. HR/PUB/05/5 (2005).

[66] *United States – Measures Affecting the Cross-border Supply of Gambling and Betting Services*, Panel Report, WT/DS 285/R (November 2004) and Appellate Body report, WT/DS 285/ AB/R (April 2005).

[67] See E.-U. Petersmann, 'The 'Human Rights Approach' advocated by the UN High Commissioner for Human Rights and by the International Labour Organisation: Is it relevant for WTO law and policy?', *JIEL* 7 (2004) 3, 605–627.

international human rights law,[68] because of existing linkages and suggested convergences.[69]

Common interests can be found, too, in one of the main concerns of the WTO and the human rights system, i.e. protecting the rule of law, which includes also the human right to a fair trial, and is a precondition for legal security. For example, when the head of the Chinese delegation in the EU-China Dialogue on human rights was asked what he considered the most important factor for the strengthening of human rights in China, he answered, to the surprise of many, that it was the accession of China to the WTO in 2001. This had forced China to establish a judicial system based on the principles of the rule of law and fair trial,[70] which has also improved the framework conditions for implementing human rights.

Still, it is difficult to measure the impact of the new institutions and activities in the field of human rights, as presented above, on the policies of the WTO Member States and the WTO as an organisation. In practice, the division existing at the national level between the agenda of the Ministries for Foreign Affairs, which represent their States at the UN, and that of the Ministries in charge of trade affairs, is reflected also at the international level, where the latter send their representatives to the WTO and little is done to achieve more cohesion between the two agendas.[71] It can be noted, however, that the Secretariat of the WTO is showing an increasing interest in the matter and some staff members have contributed to the academic discussion.[72]

In academic circles, there has been a controversy about the proper human rights approach to be taken when analysing the relevance of human rights and other non-economic concerns for the WTO. Petersmann, who

---

[68] Cf. M. Robinson, 'Making The Global Economy Work for Human Rights', in G. P. Sampson (ed.), *The Role of the World Trade Organization in Global Governance* (Tokyo/New York: United Nations University Press, 2001), pp. 209–222.

[69] See G. Zagel, 'WTO and Human Rights: Examining Linkages and Suggesting Convergence', *IDLO Voices of Development Jurists Paper Series* 2 (2005), 2.

[70] Cf., *inter alia*, the Report and Recommendations stemming from *EU-China Human Rights Dialogue Seminar: Capacity Building of NGOs and Judicial Guarantees of Human Rights* (15–16 December 2003) dealing, *inter alia*, with judicial guarantees of human rights, Venice, 15–16 December 2003, http://www.nuigalway.ie/sites/eu-china-human-rights/seminars/ds0312r.doc (accessed: 15 December 2005).

[71] For most countries, the Permanent Representative to the United Nations in Geneva is also the Permanent Representative to the WTO.

[72] See, in particular, H. Lim, 'Trade and Human Rights – What's at Issue?', *JWT* 35 (2001) 2, 275–300, and G. Marceau, 'WTO Dispute Settlement and Human Rights', *EJIL* 13 (2002) 4, 753–813.

consistently argues in favour of a constitutional perspective on the WTO, proclaimed that the organisation is protecting human rights values,[73] which was opposed by Alston as a 'merger and acquisition of human rights by trade law'.[74] Petersmann clarified that his concern was to see civil society and human rights taken seriously by the WTO through constitutional reforms.[75] There is also a related controversy around the concept of the 'constitutionalisation' of the WTO. While there are different approaches towards this concept, basic human rights as constitutional values of the international legal system have to be considered to be relevant for WTO law, the legitimacy of which is 'thus enhanced'. This would not be in contradiction of recent suggestions that economic development through non-discriminatory trade should be a central focus of the constitutionalisation approach.[76] Indeed, the inclusion of non-economic values such as human rights could strengthen and widen the value-basis of the WTO and commit it to common public concerns, which is central to any constitutional approach.

The response of GATT/WTO to so-called 'non-trade issues'

As already indicated above, the WTO, and before that the GATT, have proven to be rather resistant to dealing with so-called non-trade issues in the past.[77] However, there is also a long history of the increasing recognition of non-trade issues in the WTO framework. In the 1960s, it was the issue of 'trade and development', which first led to the establishment of the UN Conference on Trade and Development (UNCTAD) outside the WTO, and to the amendment of GATT by Part IV on 'Trade and Development' in 1965.[78] Since that time, the issue of trade and development has become a continuous topic in the GATT and the WTO, with a Committee on Trade and Development in charge of the issue and numerous declarations and provisions dealing with special and differential

---

[73]   E.-U. Petersmann, 'The WTO Constitution and Human Rights', *JIEL* 3 (2000) 1, 19–25.
[74]   P. Alston, 'Resisting the Merger and Acquisition of Human Rights by Trade Law: A Reply to Petersmann', *EJIL* 13 (2002) 4, 815–844.
[75]   See E.-U. Petersmann, 'Taking Human Rights, Poverty and Empowerment of Individuals More Seriously: Rejoinder to Alston', *EJIL* 13 (2002) 4, 845–852.
[76]   See B. Z. Cass, *The Constitutionalization of the World Trade Organization. Legitimacy, Democracy and Community in the International Trading System* (Oxford/New York: Oxford University Press, 2005), pp. 97 *et seq.* and 243.
[77]   See S. Griller (ed.), *International Economic Governance and Non-Economic Concerns, New Challenges for the International Legal Order* (Vienna/New York: Springer, 2003).
[78]   BISD, Vol. IV, 1969; 55 U.N.T.S. 194 *et seq.*

treatment of developing countries in order to compensate existing inequalities.[79]

Another non-trade issue which made it into the WTO is the issue of the environment. Again, there was heavy opposition to the inclusion of environmental issues into the framework of the WTO, using the argument that these matters can be better dealt with by other, existing organisations. However, environmental issues were already discussed by panels in cases under Article XX of the GATT. Additionally, the environment also achieved recognition in the Preamble of the Marrakesh Agreement on the WTO, where the objectives of sustainable development and the protection and preservation of the environment are specifically mentioned. Furthermore, the Ministerial Declaration of Doha, which is the basis for the Doha Round, contains numerous provisions on sustainable development and environmental concerns, referring, for example, to national environmental assessments of trade policies and clarifying that 'under WTO rules no country should be prevented from taking measures for the protection of the environment at the level it considers appropriate'. Pursuant to para. 31 of the Doha Ministerial Declaration negotiations on 'the relationship between existing WTO rules and specific trade obligations set out in multilateral environmental agreements', were launched, 'with a view to enhancing the mutual supportiveness of trade and environment'. Para. 32 of the Doha Ministerial Declaration stresses that the outcome of the negotiations 'shall be compatible with the open and non-discriminatory nature of the multilateral trading system, shall not add to or diminish the rights and obligations of Members under existing WTO agreements . . ., nor alter the balance of these rights and obligations, and will take into account the needs of developing and least-developed countries.' Efforts are also encouraged to promote cooperation between the WTO and relevant international environmental and developmental organisations.[80] The task of substantiating the relationship between WTO law and multilateral environmental agreements has

---

[79] See, for example, Decision of GATT CONTRACTING PARTIES on Differential and More Favourable Treatment, Reciprocity and Increased Participation of Developing Countries ('enabling clause') of 28 November 1979, BISD, 26S/203 et seq.; see also W. Benedek, 'Die Entwicklungsländer in der WTO' [The Developing Countries in the WTO], Zeitschrift für Europarechtliche Studien (ZEuS) (2000) 1, 41–60 and the study 'Mainstreaming the right to development into international trade law and policy at the World Trade Organization', commissioned by OHCHR and prepared by Robert Howse, UN Doc. E/CN.4/Sub.2/ 2004/17 of 9 June 2004.

[80] See para. 6 of the Ministerial Declaration of Doha, WT/MIN (01)/DEC/W/1 of 14 November 2001.

been given to the Committee on Trade and Environment.[81] This raises a number of issues of principle which are similar to the question of the legal relationship between WTO agreements and human rights instruments. However, it needs to be noted that little progress has been made in the already numerous special sessions of this committee because of lack of political will to give priority to environmental obligations.[82]

Another issue with strong human rights connotations is the issue of 'trade and health', which has led to major disputes, such as the *'Hormones Case'*[83] between the United States and the European Communities, or the ongoing case on GMO products[84] between the United States and the European Union. Human rights issues are raised by the TRIPS Agreement, which had to be reinterpreted by the Doha Declaration on the TRIPS Agreement and Public Health of 2001[85] and subsequent WTO decisions in order to clarify what measures states can undertake and what exceptions they can make to the TRIPS Agreement, in particular when they encounter major problems of public health; an epidemic or pandemic, HIV/AIDS or malaria being the main examples used.[86] One could argue that the WTO agreements do have provisions providing for exceptions in the case of threats to human, animal or plant life or health. Yet the measures possible under these provisions were traditionally interpreted to refer only to the products which could create such a threat – such as hormones or GMO food – and which could therefore only be restricted by the importing state in these cases. Therefore, in the EC *'Asbestos Case'*, the legality of import restrictions on asbestos products, which were known to create a high risk to human health, was confirmed.[87] However, negative health effects of the production and processing methods are considered a matter to be left to the producing state. This can be seen as a

---

[81] Cf. para. 32 of the Doha Declaration, *ibid.*

[82] Cf. the Summary Reports on the Meetings of the Committee on Trade and Environment in Special Session, TN/TE/R/1 of 19 April 2002 to TN/TE/R/12 of 14 September 2005.

[83] European Communities – *Measures Concerning Meat and Meat Products (Hormones)*, Report of the Appellate Body, WT/DS26/AB/R of 18 January 1998; see W. Benedek, *Die Europäische Union im Streitbeilegungsverfahren der WTO* [*The European Union in WTO Dispute Settlement Procedures*] (Vienna/Graz: Neuer Wissenschaftlicher Verlag/ Schulthess/BWV, 2005), pp. 182 *et seq.* and pp. 201 *et seq.*

[84] European Communities – *Measures Affecting the Approval and Marketing of Biotech Products*, Complaints by the United States (WT/DS291 of 13 May 2003), Canada (WT/DS292 of 13 May 2003) and Argentina (WT/DS293 of 14 May 2003).

[85] WTO Doc. WT/MIN(01)/DEC/W/2 of 14 November 2001.

[86] See the contribution by D. Ovett in this volume.

[87] European Communities – *Measures Affecting Asbestos and Products Containing Asbestos*, Report of the Appellate Body, WT/DS135/AB/R of 5 April 2001.

variant of the international legal principle of non-interference in domestic affairs, which, from a human rights perspective, can hardly be accepted as it is agreed that the said principle can no longer be used under international law to avoid human rights concerns.

Exceptions for public health reasons under the TRIPS agreement are not linked with restrictions of imports, but rather with enabling access to drugs, which are needed at affordable prices to address a public health crisis. In this case, the WTO system has shown that it is capable of the flexibility necessary to address the human rights problems at stake, if only after widespread international criticism.[88]

As far as trade and human rights in general are concerned, the same principles should apply. Accordingly, the WTO will have to find ways and means to address human rights concerns within its framework. It will not be possible to argue that WTO law is a special, self-contained regime which shields it from the obligation to take other international law requirements, and in particular those of human rights law, into account.[89] The linkages between trade and human rights are 'a relationship to discover'.[90] By way of example, it can be pointed out that WTO law offers no express provision preventing trading in the products of forced labour. There is a provision for products from prison labour in Article XX(e) among the general exceptions from the GATT, but a general provision regarding products which have been produced in violation of basic human rights obligations does not yet exist. However, it is difficult to see how a WTO organ, such as the dispute settlement body, could argue that products of forced labour, or even slavery, which is prohibited, *inter alia*, by Article 8 of the ICCPR, could not be restricted by a WTO Member State.

Another example would be products from child labour or products which have been produced under conditions involving inhuman or degrading treatment, as prohibited in Article 7 of the ICCPR, and in the UN Convention against Torture and other Cruel, Inhuman or Degrading Treatment or Punishment (CAT) of 1984.[91] The UN Convention on the Rights of the Child (CRC) of 1989[92] has been ratified by almost all

---

[88] For more details, see, again, the contribution of D. Ovett in this volume.

[89] See Lim, 'Trade and Human Rights', 275 *et seq.* and Marceau, 'WTO Dispute Settlement' 753–813.

[90] See T. Cottier, 'Trade and Human Rights: A Relationship to Discover', *JIEL* 5 (2002) 1, pp. 111–132.

[91] Convention against Torture and Other Cruel, Inhuman or Degrading Treatment or Punishment of 10 December 1984, 1465 U.N.T.S. 85, 113.

[92] Convention on the Rights of the Child of 20 November 1989, 1577 U.N.T.S. 3.

Member States. It provides, in Article 32 *et seq.*, for the protection of the child from economic exploitation, and other employment in illicit production. Should a WTO Member State decide to ban imports produced in violation of the CRC, a dispute settlement panel could hardly declare the CRC irrelevant. Among the forms of illicit trade is drug trafficking and trafficking in humans. The latter is the subject of a Special Protocol to the Palermo Convention on Transnational Organized Crime of 2000,[93] which again might need to be taken into account by the WTO.

A controversial matter is the issue of workers' rights or social standards,[94] which have been called for by the United States since the time of the GATT. But the continuous opposition of the developing countries resulted in the exclusion of this aspect from the WTO agenda today. It has mainly been argued that social standards should be dealt with by the organisation which has been specifically created for this purpose, i.e. the ILO. But this does not explain why the WTO could not have closer relations with the ILO, which still does not even have observer status in WTO meetings. This approach is also inconsistent with TRIPS. Intellectual property rights are covered by the World Intellectual Property Organisation (WIPO), but nevertheless a specific agreement on TRIPS has also been incorporated into WTO law. The ILO has a clear human rights focus by promoting and protecting social standards, developed in its framework. The question whether labour standards are part of human rights law can today be answered largely in the affirmative.[95]

In conclusion, the main objective of the WTO is to protect the rule of law in international trade relations by providing legal security, assuring transparency and preventing discrimination. This also has important implications for the national legal systems and the protection of human rights, such as the right to a fair trial. In the GATT and the WTO issues including development, the environment, sustainable development and

---

[93] Protocol to Prevent, Suppress and Punish Trafficking in Persons, Especially Women and Children, supplementing the United Nations Convention against Transnational Organized Crime, adopted by the Millennium Assembly of the United Nations General Assembly in November 2000, UN Doc. A/55/25, Annex II, of 15 November 2000, entry into force: 25 December 2003.

[94] See C. McCrudden and A. Davies, 'A Perspective on Trade and Labour Rights', *JIEL* 3 (2000) 1, pp. 43–62 and P. Alston, "Core Labour Standards' and the Transformation of the International Labour Rights Regime', *EJIL* 15 (2004) 3, pp. 457–521, see also *supra* note 2.

[95] See also A. Perulli, in this volume, and P. Alston, 'Labour Rights as Human Rights. The Not so Happy State of the Art', in: P. Alston (ed.), *Labour Rights as Human Rights, Collected Courses of the Academy of European Law* (Florence: European University Institute, 2005), pp. 1–24, especially p. 23.

public health have become issues of discussion, whereas social standards and human rights in general are waiting to be included. The general response to non-trade issues has been predominantly hesitant. The WTO has thus not yet embraced human rights; the fact that the WTO remained outside the UN system has contributed to this omission. Still, the former UN HCHR, Mary Robinson, underlined that human rights and trade were an issue which needed to be discussed in the negotiations of the Doha Round, in particular in the context of the negotiations on agriculture.[96] This turned out to be an important stumbling block for the 2003 Ministerial Conference in Cancún, which therefore failed.[97] Independent of the WTO itself, the UN human rights bodies have, since 1998, entered into the discussion of substantive issues covered by the WTO agreements and have substantiated that human rights obligations should be taken into account in the work of the WTO, and shown how this could be done. This alone is a major new development.

Overcoming separate approaches in resolving common global problems

Generally, human rights have become a concern in international economic relations and the work of international economic organisations, and the relevancy of economic, social and cultural rights has been increasingly recognised. This development could also strengthen the accountability and – thereby – the legitimacy of international economic organisations, the former being a prerequisite for the latter.[98] Legitimacy further requires transparency of the organisation and democratic participation of its members. Furthermore legitimacy necessitates involvement of the public affected by the scope of the activities of the organisation. The GATT and the WTO have been severely criticised for their unsatisfactory levels of transparency and the lack of opportunities of participation; this has resulted in some, albeit limited, improvements. The WTO has increased the transparency of its activities by providing better access to its documents and by developing a more open information policy. It

---

[96] Cf. Report of the United Nations High Commissioner for Human Rights on 'Globalization and its Impact on the Full Enjoyment of Human Rights', UN Doc. E/CN.4/2002/54 of 5 January 2002.

[97] Cf. S. Cho, 'A Bridge Too Far: The Fall of the Fifth WTO Ministerial Conference in Cancún and the Future of Trade Constitution', *JIEL* (2004) 7, 219–244.

[98] See J.-M. Coicaud and V. Heiskanen (eds.), *The Legitimacy of International Organisations* (Tokyo/New York: United Nations University Press, 2001), pp. 355–407.

has, however, not significantly improved the opportunities for participation of non-members. The possibility of granting consultative status, foreseen in Article V, para. 2 of the WTO Agreement, to, in particular, NGOs that are concerned with matters related to the WTO, has been used only to give NGOs observer status in Ministerial Conferences. Their status is, however, not comparable to that of NGOs wishing to contribute to the work of UN bodies in the human rights field on the basis of a similar provision in the UN Charter.[99]

The calls for institutional reforms, leading towards a 'democratisation' of the WTO,[100] have become widespread and can even be found in a report prepared by the Consultative Board to the Director-General of the WTO.[101] The report stops short of supporting recommendations in academic literature to establish an advisory body with NGO participation, and/or a parliamentary body of the WTO.[102] Such reforms would allow the WTO to take human rights concerns better into account. It would allow NGOs which are specialised in the field of the WTO to better contribute to the work of the organisation,[103] and it would, additionally,

---

[99] Compare Article 71 of the UN Charter and W. Benedek, 'Developing the Constitutional Order of the WTO – The Role of NGOs', in W. Benedek, H. Isak and R. Kicker (eds.), *Development and Developing International and European Law, Essays in Honour of Konrad Ginther* (Frankfurt am Main: Peter Lang, 1999), pp. 228–250, especially 240 *et seq.*; see also E. Tuerk, 'The Role of NGOs in International Governance, NGOs and Developing Country WTO Members: Is there Potential for Alliance?', in S. Griller (ed.), *International Economic Governance and Non-Economic Concerns*, (Vienna/New York: Springer, 2003), pp. 169–210. See also P. van den Bossche and I. Alexovicová, 'Effective Global Economic Governance by the WTO', *JIEL* 8 (2005) 3, 667–690.

[100] See R. Howse, 'How to Begin to Think About the "Democratic Deficit" at the WTO', in S. Griller (ed.), *International Economic Governance and Non-Economic Concerns* (Vienna/New York: Springer, 2003), pp. 79–102.

[101] See 'The Future of the WTO. Addressing Institutional Challenges in the New Millennium', Report by the Consultative Board to the Director-General Supachai Panitchpakdi (Chairman: Peter Sutherland), World Trade Organization: Geneva 2005, pp. 41 *et seq.*

[102] See E.-U. Petersmann (ed.), *Preparing the Doha Development Round: Challenges to the Legitimacy and Efficiency of the World Trading System* (Florence: Robert Schumann Centre for Advanced Studies, European University Institute, 2003); and R. Howse, 'Legitimacy of the World Trade Organization', in: J.-M. Coicaud and V. Heiskanen (eds.), *The Legitimacy of International Organisations* (Tokyo/New York: United Nations University Press, 2001), pp. 355–407. See also W. Benedek, 'Demokratisierung Internationaler Wirtschaftsorganisationen am Beispiel der WTO' ['Democratisation of International Economic Organizations, the Example of the WTO'] in H. Kopetz, J. Marko and K. Poier (eds.), *Sozio-kultureller Wandel im Verfassungsstaat, Phänomene Politischer Transformation, Festschrift für Wolfgang Mantl [Socio-cultural Change and the Constitutional State, Phenomena of Political Transformation]* (Vienna/Graz: Böhlau, 2004), pp. 225–238.   [103] See also the contribution by D. Ovett, in this volume.

strengthen the legitimacy of the Organisation, and the public support for its work. The same outcome could be expected from a stronger human rights-based approach by the WTO to trade issues within its remit.

Another important possibility for participation are *amicus curiae* briefs in the WTO dispute settlement process. This would be an opportunity for 'friends of the court', who could be NGOs acting in the public interest, to offer their views. The Appellate Body (AB) of the WTO has confirmed that the panels are free to accept such briefs and has even adopted certain rules regarding submission of *amicus curiae* briefs. This has resulted in massive criticism, in particular from developing states members of the WTO, as they are afraid of a loss of membership control in the procedure. Although the AB has maintained its position, there have so far been no references in panel or AB reports to *amicus curiae* briefs submitted and accepted; furthermore many such briefs were refused, which has disappointed the original hopes of the NGOs. Still, the report of the Consultative Board of the Director General has recognised the usefulness of such briefs, *inter alia*, for their potential of improving the quality of panel reports.[104] Finally, Article 13 of the Dispute Settlement Understanding (DSU) enables panels and the AB to consult with other actors.

The WTO has, arguably, largely proven resistant to the human rights dynamic. It should therefore be asked, which major reasons can be identified for the difficulties expressed by the WTO in integrating human rights aspects into its work?

Among the arguments against linking trade and human rights is the fear of a 'politicisation' of the WTO bodies or an 'overload' of the already very full agenda of the WTO; for this reason, it is argued that the mandate of the WTO does not cover human rights, and that this aspect should be left to other more competent organisations. It has also been put forward that human rights obligations reside with individual Member States and not the organisation. This has resulted in a structural deficit as, consequently, the WTO has not invested in staff with specific human rights knowledge or established a unit in charge of human rights matters. On the other hand, an opening, however limited, of the WTO agenda can be identified, and activities linking trade with development, environment, and public health do exist.

As mentioned before, the UN HCHR, in the report for the 2003 Cancún Ministerial Meeting, has identified eight main linkages between

---

[104] See 'The Future of the WTO', Report by the Consultative Board (2004), 57 *et seq.*

trade and human rights, of which six are still relevant, i.e. trade and non-discrimination, the issue of gender, TRIPS and public health, a focus on 'neglected diseases' of particular concern to developing countries, agriculture negotiations, in particular focusing on the right to food, market access and human rights, service negotiations, requesting human rights impact assessments in TRIPS negotiations, and requesting particular attention to trade and the human rights of indigenous peoples.[105] Consequently, these are the linkages which need to be addressed in the international trade negotiations, whereas others might be addressed in the daily operations of the WTO, in particular in its dispute settlement system.

So far, panels established under the DSU and the AB have not been faced with a situation where they needed to solve conflicts between the law of WTO agreements and human rights norms; or they have avoided doing so. Petersmann has proclaimed that in the more than 400 dispute settlement cases under GATT and WTO over more than fifty years, 'no conflict between GATT and WTO rules and human rights has so far been identified'.[106] Whether this is proof that there are no systemic conflicts between the two fields of international law or whether this is due to a coherent interpretation of WTO law with human rights law and its application in good faith[107] is open for discussion. This pragmatic approach is in contrast to others which are diametrically opposed to each other and which either claim that international law should be taken into account in WTO dispute settlement if relevant,[108] or that WTO dispute settlement should exclusively be concerned with the agreements covered by the WTO.[109] However, as the existence of linkages, i.e. primarily between trade and poverty, but also between the environment and human rights, cannot be ignored, the proposal exists to take this dimension up in

---

[105] OHCHR, Human Rights and Trade, 5th WTO Ministerial Conference, Cancún, Mexico, 10–14 September 2003, www.unhchr.ch/html/hchr/cancunfinal.doc (accessed: 15 December 2005).

[106] E.-U. Petersmann, 'The 'Human Rights Approach' advocated by the UN High Commissioner for Human Rights', *JIEL* 7 (2004), 622. See also E.-U. Petersmann, 'Human Rights and the Law of the WTO', *JWT* 37 (2003), 241–281.

[107] See Marceau, 'WTO Dispute Settlement', 753–813.

[108] See J. Pauwelyn, 'The Role of Public International Law in the WTO: How Far Can We Go?', *American Journal of International Law (AJIL)* (2001), 535–578; and J. Pauwelyn, *Conflict of Norms in Public International Law: How WTO Law Relates to other Rules of International Law* (Cambridge: Cambridge University Press, 2003).

[109] See J. Trachtman, 'The Domain of WTO Dispute Resolution', *Harvard International Law Journal* 40 (1999), 333–377.

negotiations and create 'institutional linkages' between trade and 'non-trade' policies by defining how WTO rules interact with other rules in order to provide for coherence through horizontal coordination or even cooperation.[110]

It is unlikely that WTO dispute settlement will lend itself to the enforcement of human rights, except when the linkages to trade cannot be avoided. One reason could also be that panels might want to avoid having to interpret human rights, with which they are not familiar. A similar idea with regard to the social standards of the ILO has been refused by the WTO members, which are opposed to the use of the WTO enforcement mechanism for non-trade concerns. Still, there is a possibility that human rights obligations may be used to explain trade measures not in conformity with WTO law; consider the hypothetical case of child labour. This would first require a complaint by a WTO member, which is not likely to happen, as states will hardly insist on their rights in violation of international human rights obligations. A practical case could be the trade in equipment designed to inflict torture or inhuman or degrading treatment or punishment, which, at the request of the UN Special Rapporteur on Torture, certain states and the European Union decided to restrict or ban because of the human rights obligation to prevent torture.[111]

For the implementation of economic sanctions decided by the UN Security Council, Article XXI(c) of the GATT, or the identically worded Article XIV bis 1(c) of the GATS, provide the necessary legal basis for an exception. In particular cases, a specific waiver may be granted as in the case of public health under TRIPS or the 'Kimberley process'.[112] In this cases, the WTO has also shown its capacity to deal with global common

---

[110] See J. Trachtman, 'The Missing Link: Coherence and Poverty at the WTO', *JIEL* 8 (2005) 3, 611–622, commenting on 'The Future of the WTO', Report by the Consultative Board (2004), esp. para. 171 and J. Trachtman, 'Institutional Linkage: Transcending "Trade and . . ." ', *AJIL* 96 (2002) 1, 77–93.

[111] Cf. Study on the situation of trade in and production of equipment, which is specifically designed to inflict torture or other cruel, inhuman or degrading treatment, its origins, destination and forms, submitted by Theo van Boven, Special Rapporteur on Torture, pursuant to Resolution 2002/38 of the Commission on Human Rights, E/CN.4/2003/69 of 13 January 2003; Report of the Special Rapporteur on the question of torture, Theo van Boven, E/CN.4/2005/62 of 15 December 2004 and Council Regulation (EC) no. 1236/2005 of 27 June 2005 concerning trade in certain goods which could be used for capital punishment, torture or other cruel, inhuman or degrading treatment of punishment.

[112] See, for the Waiver on public health, D. Ovett, in this volume and for the Waiver concerning the Kimberley Process Certification Scheme for Rough Diamonds, WT/L/518 of 15 March 2003.

problems, i.e. the control of 'blood diamonds', which contribute to keeping conflicts in Africa alive, through a waiver for the 'Kimberley Process', which introduced a certification scheme for rough diamonds. Thereby, the WTO wants to contribute to international action against gross violations of human rights in conflicts fuelled by the trade in diamonds.

With regard to the question of a human rights approach to the liberalisation of trade in services, a study by the OHCHR suggests two obligations, 'choosing the right policy', i.e. undertaking a Human Rights Impact Assessment, and 'avoiding the wrong policy', i.e. avoiding commitments which would be problematic because of the effects on human rights.[113] This could relate to commitments which might create problems for states in meeting their obligations under the rights to health and to education. For example, the European Community and, later, the EU have refrained from making offers in the field of such public services in view of the opposition of parts of its population. The linkages between trade policies and human rights could also be addressed in the Trade Policy Review Mechanism of the WTO, in which trade policies of all Member States are reviewed at regular intervals. Generally, a Human Rights Impact Assessment should be done, whenever major trade policy decisions need to be taken.[114]

Conclusion: Elements of an interface between the World Trade Organization and human rights to strengthen coordinated global governance

Different possibilities exist for determining linkages between international economic law and human rights. In particular, a greater coherence of approaches, the creation of minimum standards in the social field – as has been done by the ILO – the strengthening of the 'development dimension of the WTO', and the enrichment by a social dimension of the international globalisation process, can be envisaged. In this connection

---

[113] See OHCHR, Human Rights and Trade, 5th WTO Ministerial Conference, Cancún, Mexico, 10–14 September 2003, www.unhchr.ch/html/hchr/cancunfinal.doc (accessed: 15 December 2005).

[114] An example in case is the 'Sustainable Impact Assessment of WTO Negotiations' (Doha Round), completed on behalf of the European Commission by the Impact Assessment Research Centre of the Institute for Development Policy and Management of the University of Manchester, which also covers 'social impacts', see www.sia-trade.org (accessed: 15 December 2005).

a dynamic interpretation of Article XX of the GATT on general exceptions could be of relevance; which also allows addressing the conditions
of production and process methods (PPMs) that violate human rights.
There is also a need to strengthen global governance through a better
coordination of international economic organisations, both by giving
international NGOs a larger role, and by strengthening transparency and
participation in global governance. Global governance should be based on
a process which is inclusive and involves competent international organisations, both governmental and non-governmental. It cannot be left to a
self-appointed club like the G7 (8),[115] but should instead be based on a
stronger cooperation of trading and monetary and financial organisations, i.e. the WTO, the IMF and the WB and UN bodies, in particular
those charged with human rights-related mandates. The UN framework is
still the main source of legitimacy, and more representative structures of
global governance need to be developed. The best forum would be the one
originally designed for coordination in this field, i.e. the Economic and
Social Council (ECOSOC).[116] The Report of the Secretary-General on UN
reform points in the same direction when it suggests annual high-level
assessments made on the progress towards the Millennium Development
Goals by ECOSOC in order to better coordinate the UN Development
Agenda; it also proposes giving ECOSOC a new and more flexible structure to promote its development into an 'effective, efficient and representative intergovernmental mechanism for engaging its counterparts in the
institutions dealing with trade and finance.'[117] On similar lines, the new
Director-General of WTO, Pascal Lamy, in his speech on 'Humanising
Globalisation' in Chile, addressed the 'double face of globalisation', which
needed to be humanised by greater attention to social, economic and ecological aspects of humanity in line with the Millennium Development
Goals and enhanced global governance to respond to emerging global
challenges as part of a new 'Geneva consensus'.[118]

---

[115] Cf. the documents available at the G8 Information Center's site at http://www.g7.
utoronto.ca (accessed: 15 December 2005).

[116] See W. Benedek, 'Globale Governance der Weltwirtschaft' ['Global Governance of the
World Economy'], in P. Koller (ed.), *Die globale Frage, Empirische Befunde und Ethische
Herausforderungen* [*The Global Question, Empirical Findings and Ethical Challenges*]
(Vienna: Passagen-Verlag, 2006), pp. 257–274.

[117] Report of the Secretary-General, In larger freedom: towards development, security and
human rights for all, UN Doc. A/59/2005 of 21 March 2005, paras. 171 *et seq.*, especially
para. 180.

[118] See speech of Director-General Pascal Lamy of 30 January 2006 in Santiago de Chile,
http://www.wto.org/english/news_e/sppl_e/sppl16_e.htm.

In conclusion, the international economic system in general and the WTO in particular would benefit from returning to the original objectives as contained in Article 55 of the UN Charter and from ensuring a better balance of the economic and the social dimensions of globalisation. The yearly 'Social Forum', organised since 2002 by the Sub-Commission on the Promotion and Protection of Human Rights with the authorisation of ECOSOC, is an important initiative in this respect. It has focused on the linkages between human rights and international trade, finance and economic policies and thus the relationship between globalisation and its effect on, *inter alia*, poverty, vulnerable groups and rural communities. The Social Forum brings together all stakeholders in the debate, including UN bodies and specialised agencies such as UNCTAD, UNDP, ILO, the IMF, and NGOs and community associations in the framework of the UN, although it appears that the WTO as an organisation outside the UN framework is not participating.[119]

The developments in the Doha Round, in which, after the failure of Cancún, the voice of developing countries has gained in importance, are a step towards a more balanced approach. However, there is still a lack of a more inclusive approach with regard to civil society as non-state actors pursuing public interests.[120] Here the developing countries remain an obstacle towards progress; it might still take time for them to agree that a human rights approach in the WTO would also be in their best interests. Generally, a new basic consensus between the North and the South, between the economic and social dimensions of international trade, between governments and civil society needs to be established.

As has been said by Eric Stein: 'While many accept the WTO essentially as currently constituted, others find it increasingly difficult to conceive of a multilateral trade regime confined exclusively to promoting economic efficiency through trade liberalization, in isolation from other vital values.'[121]

---

[119] Cf. Sub-Commission on the Promotion and Protection of Human Rights Resolution 2005/8, UN Doc. E/CN.4/Sub.2/2005/8 of 23 June 2005 and the Report of the Chairman-Rapporteur of the the Social Forum, José Bengoa, in accordance with Sub-Commission Resolution 2004/8, UN Doc. E/CN.4/Sub.2/2005/21 of 3 August 2005.

[120] See W. Benedek, 'The Emerging Global Civil Society: Achievements and Prospects', in M. Nettesheim and V. Rittberger (eds.), *Changing Patterns of Authority in the Global Political Economy* (Houndmills: Palgrave Macmillan Publishers, 2007), in print.

[121] See E. Stein, 'International Integration and Democracy: No Love at First Sight', *AJIL* (2001), 489–534.

Bibliography

Alston, P. (ed.), *Labour Rights as Human Rights, Collected Courses of the Academy of European Law* (Florence: European University Institute, 2005)
'Core Labour Standards' and the Transformation of the International Labour Rights Regime, *EJIL* 15 (2004) 3, 457–521
'Resisting the Merger and Acquisition of Human Rights by Trade Law: A Reply to Petersmann', *EJIL* 13 (2002) 4, 815–844
Alston, P. and Robinson, M. (eds.), *Human Rights and Development: Towards Mutual Reinforcement* (New York: Oxford University Press, 2005)
Benedek, W., 'The Emerging Global Civil Society: Achievements and Prospects', in Nettesheim, M. and Rittberger, V. (eds.), *Changing Patterns of Authority in the Global Political Economy* (2007), in print
Die Europäische Union im Streitbeilegungsverfahren der WTO [*The European Union in WTO Dispute Settlement Procedures*] (Vienna/Graz: Neuer Wissenschaftlicher Verlag/Schulthess/BWV, 2005)
'Globale Governance der Weltwirtschaft' ['Global Governance of the World Economy'], in Koller, P. (ed.), *Die globale Frage, Empirische Befunde und ethische Herausforderungen* [*The Global Question, Empirical Findings and Ethical Challenges*] (Vienna: Passagen-Verlag, 2006), pp. 257–274
'Demokratisierung Internationaler Wirtschaftsorganisationen am Beispiel der WTO' ['Democratisation of International Economic Organizations, the Example of the WTO'], in Kopetz, H., Marko, J. and Poier, K. (eds.), *Sozio-kultureller Wandel im Verfassungsstaat, Phänomene Politischer Transformation, Festschrift für Wolfgang Mantl, [Socio-cultural Change and the Constitutional State, Phenomena of Political Transformation]* (Vienna/Graz: Böhlau, 2004), pp. 225–238
'Die Entwicklungsländer in der WTO' [The Developing Countries in the WTO], *Zeitschrift für Europarechtliche Studien (ZEuS)* (2000) 1, 41–60
'Developing the Constitutional Order of the WTO – The Role of NGOs', in Benedek, W., Isak, H. and Kicker, R. (eds.), *Development and Developing International and European Law, Essays in Honour of Konrad Ginther* (Frankfurt am Main: Peter Lang, 1999), pp. 228–250
Die Rechtsordnung des GATT aus völkerrechtlicher Sicht [The Legal Order of GATT from an International Law Perspective] (Berlin/Heidelberg: Springer-Verlag, 1990)
Boisson de Chazournes, L., 'Issues of Social Development: Integrating Human Rights into the Activities of the World Bank', in International Institute of Human Rights (ed.), *World Trade and the Protection of Human Rights, Human Rights in the Face of Global Economic Exchanges* (Brussels: Bruylant, 2001), pp. 51–70

Cass, B. Z., *The Constitutionalization of the World Trade Organization. Legitimacy, Democracy and Community in the International Trading System* (Oxford/New York: Oxford University Press, 2005)

Chapman, A. R., 'The Human Rights Implications of Intellectual Property Protection', *Journal of International Economic Law (JIEL)* 5 (2002) 4, 861–882

S. Cho, 'A Bridge Too Far: The Fall of the Fifth WTO Ministerial Conference in Cancún and the Future of Trade Constitution', *JIEL* (2004) 7, 219–244

Coicaud, J.-M. and Heiskanen, V. (eds.), *The Legitimacy of International Organisations* (Tokyo/New York: United Nations University Press, 2001), pp. 355–407

Cottier, T., Pauwelyn, J. and Bürgi Bonanomi, E. (eds.), *Human Rights and International Trade* (Oxford/New York: Oxford University Press, 2005)

Cottier, T., 'Trade and Human Rights: A Relationship to Discover', *JIEL* 5 (2002) 1, 111–132

Dommen, C., 'Raising Human Rights Concerns in the World Trade Organization: Actors, Processes and Possible Strategies', *Human Rights Quarterly* 24 (2002), 1–50

Filmer-Wilson, E., 'The Human Rights Based Approach to Development: The Right to Water', *Netherlands Quarterly of Human Rights* 23 (2005) 2, 213–242

Griller, S. (ed.), *International Economic Governance and Non-Economic Concerns, New Challenges for the International Legal Order* (Vienna/New York: Springer, 2003)

Howse, R., 'How to Begin to Think About the "Democratic Deficit" at the WTO', in Griller, S. (ed.), *International Economic Governance and Non-Economic Concerns* (Vienna/New York: Springer, 2003), pp. 79–102

'Legitimacy of the World Trade Organization', in: Coicaud, J.-M. and Heiskanen, V. (eds.), *The Legitimacy of International Organisations* (Tokyo/New York: United Nations University Press, 2001), pp. 355–407

Howse, R. and Mutua, M., 'Protecting Human Rights in a Global Economy, Challenges for the World Trade Organization', in Stokke, H. and Tostensen A. (eds.), *Human Rights in Development Yearbook 1999/2000* (The Hague: Kluwer, 2001), pp. 51–82

Krajewski, M., 'Public Services and Trade Liberalization: Mapping the Legal Framework', *JIEL* 6 (2003) 2, 341–367

Lim, H., 'Trade and Human Rights – What's at Issue?', *Journal of World Trade (JWT)* 35 (2001) 2, 275–300

Marceau, G., 'WTO Dispute Settlement and Human Rights', *EJIL* 13 (2002) 4, 753–813

McCrudden, C. and Davies, A., 'A Perspective on Trade and Labour Rights', *JIEL 3* (2000) 1, 43–62

Pauwelyn, J., *Conflict of Norms in Public International Law, How WTO Law Relates to other Rules of International Law* (Cambridge: Cambridge University Press, 2003)

Pauwelyn, J., 'The Role of Public International Law in the WTO: How Far Can We Go?', *American Journal of International Law (AJIL)* (2001), 535–578

Petersmann, E.-U., 'The 'Human Rights Approach' advocated by the UN HCHR and by the International Labour Organisation: Is it relevant for WTO law and policy?', *JIEL* 7 (2004) 3, 605–627

(ed.), *Preparing the Doha Development Round: Challenges to the Legitimacy and Efficiency of the World Trading System* (Florence: Robert Schumann Centre for Advanced Studies, European University Institute, 2003)

'Human Rights and the Law of the WTO', *JWT* 37 (2003), 241–281

'Taking Human Rights, Poverty and Empowerment of Individuals More Seriously: Rejoinder to Alston', *EJIL* 13 (2002) 4, 845–852

'Human Rights and International Economic Law in the 21st Century: The Need to Clarify their Interrelationships', *JIEL* 4 (2001) 1, 3–39

'The WTO Constitution and Human Rights', *JIEL* 3 (2000) 1, 19–25

Raghavan, C., 'WTO ignores calls for democratic, inclusive processes for Cancun', *Newsletter 179 page 7*(7), http://www.attac.org/attacinfoen/attacnews179.pdf (accessed: 16 January 2005)

Robinson, M., 'Making the Global Economy Work for Human Rights', in Sampson, G. P. (ed.), *The Role of the World Trade Organization in Global Governance* (Tokyo/New York: United Nations University Press, 2001), pp. 209–222

Schlemmer-Schulte S., 'Building an International Grievance System: The World Bank Inspection Panel – Selected Issues', in Bröhmer, J., Bieber, R., Calliess, C., Langenfeld, C. Weber, S. and Wolf, J. (eds.), *Internationale Gemeinschaft und Menschenrechte*, Festschrift für Georg Ress (Cologne/Berlin/Munich: Carl Heymanns Verlag, 2005), pp. 249–284

Stein, E., 'International Integration and Democracy: No Love at First Sight', *AJIL* 2001, 489–534

Tomaševski, K., *Education Denied: Costs and Remedies* (London/New York: Zed Books, 2003)

Trachtman, J., 'The Missing Link: Coherence and Poverty at the WTO', *JIEL* 8 (2005) 3, 611–622

'Institutional Linkage: Transcending "Trade and . . ." ', *AJIL* 96 (2002) 1, 77–93

'The Domain of WTO Dispute Resolution', *HILJ* 40 (1999), 333–377

Tuerk, E., 'The Role of NGOs in International Governance, NGOs and Developing Country WTO Members: Is there Potential for Alliance?', in Griller, S. (ed.), *International Economic Governance and Non-Economic Concerns* (Vienna/New York: Springer, 2003), pp. 169–210

Van den Bossche, P. and Alexovicová, I., 'Effective Global Economic Governance by the WTO', *JIEL* 8 (2005) 3, 667–690

WTO, *The Results of the Uruguay Round of Multilateral Trade Negotiations, The Legal Texts* (Geneva: World Trade Organization/Cambridge University Press, 1994)

Zagel, G., 'WTO and Human Rights: Examining Linkages and Suggesting Convergence', *IDLO Voices of Development Jurists Paper Series* 2 (2005)

Making Trade Policies More Accountable and Human Rights-Consistent: A NGO Perspective of Using Human Rights Instruments in the Case of Access to Medicines

DAVINIA OVETT[1]

Trade is not only the driving force behind economic globalisation, but also a major influence on the extent to which States can implement economic, social and cultural policies. Indeed, trade rules, including those of the World Trade Organization (WTO), are increasingly curtailing the policy space of States. Without sufficient policy flexibility to adapt trade agreements to national circumstances and development goals, States can find themselves in a position where trade rules undermine their capacity to comply with their human rights obligations. In order to address this problem, it is necessary to understand how trade rules adversely affect the enjoyment of human rights. Moreover, it is important to assess whether international human rights rules and accountability mechanisms can provide solutions capable of reducing the negative impact of trade rules on the enjoyment of human rights.

One of the first trade-related issues to involve clearly recognised human right implications is the effect of intellectual property (IP) rules on access to affordable medicines. IP protection became an international trade issue with the adoption of the WTO Agreement on Trade-Related Aspects of Intellectual Property Rights (TRIPS Agreement) in 1994.[2] Developing countries, supported by public-interest NGOs and the international

---

[1] Davinia Ovett was (at the time of writing) Programme Officer of 3D → Trade – Human Rights – Equitable Economy (3D), a not-for-profit NGO based in Geneva, Switzerland. The views expressed in this chapter are those of the author only and do not necessarily reflect those of 3D. The author would like to thank Caroline Dommen, Judith Bueno de Mesquita and Wolfgang Benedek for their helpful comments on an earlier draft of this chapter. The chapter was written in September 2005 with final up-dates on 15 November 2005.

[2] Agreement on Trade-Related Aspects of Intellectual Property Rights, 15 April 1994, Marrakesh Agreement Establishing the World Trade Organization, Annex 1C, 1869 U.N.T.S. 299.

media, raised concerns about the public health impacts of the TRIPS Agreement very early on. These concerns resulted in an unprecedented political commitment: the WTO Doha Declaration on TRIPS and Public Health 2001 (Doha Declaration).[3] This Declaration reaffirms a State's ability to use all the flexibilities in the TRIPS Agreement to reduce the cost of medicines and fulfil public health obligations.

Despite this political commitment, a State's ability to take measures that ensure access to affordable medicines is being curtailed by IP standards. In particular, IP rules requested in bilateral and regional trade agreements are pushing the boundaries of IP law, achieving a degree of protection of Human Rights that cannot be reached at the multilateral level. This puts States in a situation where they could violate their obligations under international human rights law if they comply with their trade obligations. Also, the fact that these bilateral and regional trade agreements are often negotiated in secret and without proper consultation contravenes the States' obligation to ensure access to information and participation in public affairs of all citizens. This lack of transparency also limits independent monitoring of trade negotiations in order to ensure that trade rules are consistent with human rights.

3D → Trade – Human Rights – Equitable Economy (3D) is a public-interest NGO based in Geneva, Switzerland, working to ensure that trade rules are developed and applied in ways that promote an equitable economy.[4] 3D has consultative status with the United Nations Conference on Trade and Development (UNCTAD), *ad hoc* observer status with the World Intellectual Property Organization (WIPO) and maintains a good working relationship with the Office of the High Commissioner for Human Rights, the World Health Organization (WHO), UNAIDS and other UN institutions.

One of 3D's objectives is to promote the use of human rights rules and mechanisms in order to ensure that States refrain from adopting trade rules or policies that would undermine their compliance with human rights. 3D chose to look at the issue of IP, access to medicines and human rights because many of the public-interest NGOs active on this issue were not using human rights tools to support their work. In 2004 and early 2005, 3D used a number of international human rights mechanisms in

---

[3] WTO, Doha Ministerial Declaration on the TRIPS Agreement and Public Health, WT/MIN (01)/DEC/2, 14 November 2001.

[4] For information on 3D's work in general, or on 3D's project on the impact of trade-related intellectual property rules on access to medicines and human rights, please visit www.3dthree.org (accessed: 15 November 2005).

order to provide additional arguments to advocates and to decision-makers involved in trade negotiations. The mechanisms used include the UN human rights treaty monitoring bodies, and the special procedures of the UN Human Rights Commission. This work was conducted in close collaboration with public-interest NGOs from the North and South working to achieve fairer trade rules.

This chapter uses 3D's experience of working on the issue of IP, access to medicines and human rights as an illustration of how a policy-focused NGO can use human rights tools to support a human rights-consistent approach to trade. Part one will consider the relationship between international trade rules and human rights obligations by focusing on the case of IP and access to affordable medicines, whilst part two of the chapter will explain how 3D has used international human rights rules and mechanisms to provide tools to advocates who are working to ensure access to affordable medicines and to make trade-related IP policy more accountable and transparent.

Trade agreements and international human rights law: the case of access to medicines

The impact of trade-related IP rules, especially patents, on the ability of States to ensure access to affordable medicines serves as a good illustration of how trade rules affect the enjoyment of human rights. The following sections will explain how the WTO Agreement on Trade-Related Aspects of Intellectual Property Rights (TRIPS Agreement) and subsequent trade agreements risk limiting State policy space to such a degree that a State's ability to comply with their obligations under international human rights law will be dramatically affected.

The impact of trade-related intellectual property rules on the cost of medicines

Multilateral trade agreements: the WTO TRIPS Agreement

The United States (USA) was the first country to link IP standards with trade policy, by using trade sanctions to enforce IP standards in third countries.[5] In order to consolidate this approach internationally, the USA and Japan proposed the inclusion of IP rules in the Uruguay Round of

---

[5] J. Watal, *Intellectual Property Rules in the WTO and Developing Countries* (The Hague: Kluwer Academic Publishers, 2001), p. 18.

trade negotiations that led to the creation of the WTO.[6] Many developing countries fought against the inclusion of IP rules, but were pressurised into accepting them after threats of trade sanctions from the US and promises of trade-offs in agriculture and textiles.[7] Despite strong resistance from a group of ten developing countries – including India and Brazil[8] – the TRIPS Agreement was included in the final WTO Agreement adopted in 1994. This marked the beginning of the trend towards systematic inclusion of IP rules in trade agreements.

The TRIPS Agreement is a framework agreement that sets a minimum standard of IP protection to be implemented by all WTO Members. It has raised protection standards beyond that which previously existed in many countries. For example, the TRIPS Agreement requires States to grant patents on all processes and products, including medicines. Moreover, the TRIPS Agreement grants patent owners at least twenty years of exclusive commercial rights to make, use, offer for sale, sell or import their inventions.[9] This contrasts with the patent terms that existed in many developed and developing countries before the implementation of TRIPS, which ranged from one year in Costa Rica to fifteen years in Brazil.[10] By granting these patent periods, the TRIPS Agreement enables patent owners to keep prices of medicines artificially high for longer than previously, thereby affecting economic access to medicines ('affordability'), an inherent part of the realisation of the right to health[11] and the right to life.[12]

In order to remedy these negative effects, developing countries succeeded in including a certain number of legal flexibilities in the TRIPS Agreement, which are capable of reducing the cost of medicines. Firstly,

[6] Watal, *Intellectual Property Rules*, p. 19.   [7] *Ibid.*, p. 44.
[8] Argentina, Brazil, Cuba, Egypt, India, Nicaragua, Nigeria, Peru, Tanzania and Yugoslavia. See Watal, *Intellectual Property Rules*, p. 19.   [9] Article 33 of the TRIPS Agreement.
[10] Watal, *Intellectual Property Rules*, p. 114.
[11] Article 12 of the International Covenant on Economic, Social and Cultural Rights (ICESCR) of 16 December 1966, 993 U.N.T.S. 3; 6 I.L.M. 368 (1967) as interpreted by General Comment No. 14 (2000), The right to the highest attainable standard of health, UN Doc. E/C.12/2000/4 of. 11 August 2000; and Article 24 of the Convention on the Rights of the Child (CRC) of 20 November 1989, 1577 U.N.T.S. 3; 28 I.L.M. 1456 (1989) as interpreted by General Comment No. 3 (2003), HIV/AIDS and the rights of the children, UN Doc. CRC/GC/2003/3 of 17 March 2003 and General Comment No. 4 (2003), Adolescent health and development in the context of the Convention on the Rights of the Child, UN Doc. CRC/GC/2003/4 of 1 July 2003.
[12] Article 6 of the International Covenant on Civil and Political Rights (ICCPR) of 16 December 1966, 999 U.N.T.S. 171; 6 I.L.M. 368 (1967) as interpreted by General Comment No. 6 (1982), The right to life, UN Doc. HRI/GEN/1/Rev.7 of 12 May 2004, at 128, and Article 6 CRC, as interpreted by General Comment No. 3 (2003) on HIV/AIDS and General Comment No. 4 (2003) on Adolescent Health.

the objective and purpose of the TRIPS Agreement is defined as a balance between public and private interests, and the Agreement specifically says that Members can 'adopt measures necessary to protect public health.'[13] Furthermore, the TRIPS Agreement allows for 'use without the authorization of the right holder.'[14] This includes the ability of the State to grant compulsory licences or non-commercial government use orders to obtain cheaper generic versions of patented medicines.[15] Other crucial flexibilities include the ability to exclude from patentability 'diagnostic, therapeutic and surgical methods for the treatment of humans' – such as diagnostic kits for HIV/AIDS,[16] or the regulatory freedom to allow parallel importation of patented medicines from markets where they are sold more cheaply.[17]

Whilst developed countries were required to implement the agreement by 1 January 1995, the TRIPS Agreement granted delays to developing countries and Least Developed Countries (LDCs). Developing countries were required to implement TRIPS by 1 January 2000. Developing countries that did not patent products such as medicines – India being the main one concerned – were given until the 1 January 2005 to comply. Without patents on the final product, the Indian generic industry was able to produce about 70 per cent of bulk medicines used in India and became a leading exporter of generic versions of new medicines.[18] Since the Indian Patent Ordinance, adopted on 1 January 2005, and the subsequent Indian Patents (Amendment) Act 2005, adopted on 23 March 2005,[19] patent protection will now be granted to new medicines for which applications have been filed in India since 1995. It is feared that in the long term the implementation of this legislation will reduce access to new medicines at an affordable price, both within and outside India.[20]

---

[13] Articles 7 and 8 of the TRIPS Agreement.   [14] Article 31 of the TRIPS Agreement.

[15] These are licences granted by public authorities to make, use, offer for sale, sell or import cheaper generic versions of medicines without the consent of the patent holder, as long as he is informed and paid adequate remuneration. The requirement to inform can be waived in certain circumstances. The term 'compulsory licence' will be used to describe both compulsory licences and government use orders.

[16] Article 27.3 (a) of the TRIPS Agreement.   [17] Article 6 of the TRIPS Agreement.

[18] S. Musungu and C. Oh, *The Use of Flexibilities in TRIPS by Developing Countries: Can They Promote Access to Medicines?*, WHO Commission on Intellectual Property Rights, Innovation and Public Health, Study 4C, August 2005, http://www.who.int/intellectualproperty/studies/TRIPSFLEXI.pdf (accessed: 15 November 2005), at 9.

[19] The Patents (Amendment) Act 2005, No.15 of 2005, IP/N/1/IND/P/2, http://www.wipo.int/clea/docs_new/pdf/en/in/in018en.pdf (accessed: 1 October 2005).

[20] *Médecins Sans Frontières* (MSF), 'Prognosis: Short-Term Relief, Long-Term Pain. The Future of Generic Medicines Made In India,' Briefing Note, 21 April 2005, at 2,

LDCs have the right to delay implementation of the TRIPS Agreement into national law until 2006 at the earliest, with the option of extending this date if they submit a request to the WTO TRIPS Council.[21] Furthermore, they may delay implementation and enforcement of patent protection with respect to pharmaceutical products until 1 January 2016.[22] The vast majority of LDC Members of the WTO have already passed TRIPS-compliant IP regimes. Nevertheless, a limited number of countries are making express use of the delays for LDCs in relation to pharmaceutical patents. Cambodia incorporated the 2016 deadline into national law and Malawi has invoked the 2016 deadline to suspend IP protection on pharmaceutical products in order to supply its UNICEF antiretroviral programme.[23] The Maldives is the first country, however, to submit a formal request to the TRIPS Council to make use of this extended transition period. The TRIPS Council granted the Maldives an additional delay on 15 June 2005.[24]

Implementation of the TRIPS Agreement has been a cumbersome and costly process for developing countries, especially for those that did not previously grant patent protection on medicines.[25] Moreover, since implementing TRIPS, many developing countries have been strongly dissuaded by economic actors from making use of the flexibilities. Some instances of this are well known: the cases brought against South Africa and Brazil to prevent them from using TRIPS flexibilities to reduce the cost of medicines was front-page news all over the world during 2000 and 2001.[26] In 1997, 39 pharmaceutical companies, supported by the USA

---

http://www.msf.fr/documents/sida/2005–04–21-IndiaPatentsAnalysis.pdf (accessed: 15 November 2005).   [21] Article 66.1 of the TRIPS Agreement.

[22] WTO, *Extension of the Transition Period Under Article 66.1 of the TRIPS Agreement for Least-Developed Country Members for Certain Obligations with Respect to Pharmaceutical Products*, Decision of the Council for TRIPS of 27 June 2002, IP/C/25, 1 July 2002.

[23] Musungu and Oh, *The Use of Flexibilities*, at 8.

[24] The TRIPS Council extended the delay for the implementation of patents on pharmaceutical products from 1 January 2006 until 20 December 2007, as the Maldives are due to change from LDC status to developing country status on 21 December 2007. If the Maldives were to remain an LDC, then it could make another request to the TRIPS Council to extend the delay until 2016. See WTO, *Maldives – Extension of the Transition Period Under Article 66.1 of the TRIPS Agreement*, Decision of the Council for TRIPS of 15 June 2005, IP/C/35, 17 June 2005.

[25] UK Commission on Intellectual Property Rights, *Integrating Intellectual Property Rights and Development Policy*, February 2003, (3rd Edition), p. 37, http://www.iprcommission.org/papers/pdfs/final_report/Ch2final.pdf (accessed: 1 October 2005).

[26] G. G. Yerkey and D. Pruzin, 'United States Drops WTO Case Against Brazil Over HIV/AIDS Patent Law,' *The Bureau of National Affairs* (26 June 2001) and N. Mathiason, 'Drugs: Round One to Africa,' *The Observer*, 22 April 2001, http://observer.guardian.co.uk/business/story/0,6903,476408,00.html (accessed: 1 October 2005).

and the EU, filed a case against the South African government for passing legislation that allowed parallel imports of patented HIV/AIDS medicines. In 2000, the USA initiated a WTO Dispute Settlement case against the Brazilian government for trying to issue a compulsory licence to supply antiretroviral medicines to its national HIV/AIDS treatment programme.[27] Although both these cases were eventually withdrawn due to NGO pressure and media exposure, they demonstrated the need for greater commitment to enabling States to use the flexibilities provided in the TRIPS Agreement to limit the cost of medicines.[28]

The WTO Doha Declaration on TRIPS and Public Health

The need for a permanent solution and legal clarity in the interpretation of TRIPS flexibilities led a coalition of eighty developing countries – including the Africa Group, Brazil and India – to submit a proposal for a Declaration on TRIPS and Public Health in 2001. This proposal was supported by an access to medicines campaign coordinated by an international coalition of public-interest NGOs from the North and South.[29] These included international NGOs such as Consumers International, Health Action International (HAI), *Médecins Sans Frontières* (MSF), Oxfam International; Northern NGOs such as the Canadian HIV/AIDS Legal Network, Consumer Project on Technology (CP-Tech), Act-UP Paris, or Health Gap; and Southern NGOs such as Third World Network, and the Treatment Action Campaign (TAC), South Africa. The strength of the developing country coalition, coupled with NGO advocacy and the political climate prevalent at the time, led to the adoption of the WTO Doha Declaration on TRIPS and Public Health (Doha Declaration) on 14 November 2001. Although the Doha Declaration is a political commitment, it is also an authoritative legal interpretation of the TRIPS Agreement that can be invoked by developing countries if faced with a legal challenge.[30]

The text of the Doha Declaration says that the TRIPS Agreement 'can and should be interpreted and implemented in a manner supportive of WTO Members' right to protect public health and, in particular, access to

---

[27] F. M. Abbot, 'The Doha Declaration on the TRIPS Agreement and Public Health: Lighting a Dark Corner at the WTO', *JIEL* 5 (2002), 471.

[28] S. K. Sell, *Private Power, Public Law: The Globalisation of Intellectual Property Rights* (Cambridge: Cambridge University Press, 2003), p. 157.

[29] Sell, *Private Power*, p. 149.

[30] C. M. Correa, *Implications of the Doha Declaration on TRIPS and Public Health*, WHO, Health Economics and Drugs EDM Series No.12, June 2002, at 44.

medicines for all.'[31] Moreover, it expressly 'reaffirms the right of WTO Members to use, to the full, the provisions in the TRIPS Agreement, which provide flexibility for this purpose.'[32] The Doha Declaration then goes on to enumerate a non-exhaustive list of policy flexibilities that can be used to ensure access to affordable medicines. These include the ability to interpret the TRIPS Agreement according to the customary rules of interpretation of international law;[33] the ability to determine the regime and grounds for granting a compulsory licence in order to make, use, offer for sale, sell or import cheaper generic versions of medicines;[34] and the ability to determine the regime of parallel importation of cheaper patented medicines from other markets.[35]

The developing countries that have issued compulsory licences or government use orders since the adoption of the Doha Declaration include Zimbabwe in 2002, Malaysia in 2003, and Indonesia, Mozambique, and Zambia in 2004.[36] In March 2005 Brazil began negotiations for voluntary licences with three US pharmaceutical companies in order to manufacture four patented antiretroviral medicines that cost the Brazilian HIV/AIDS national programme three-quarters of its budget. If Brazil did not obtain a voluntary licence, the government announced that it would seek a compulsory licence. Brazil has repeatedly – and successfully – used threats of issuing compulsory licences as a tool to obtain price reductions from patent owners. However, Brazilian and international NGOs fear that voluntary licences cannot guarantee sustained access. In May 2005 Brazilian and international NGOs sent a joint declaration to the Brazilian government requesting compulsory licences.[37] The Brazilian Lower House approved a bill granting compulsory licences to local generic manufacturers, in order to allow them to make generic versions of the four patented antiretroviral medicines.[38] However, despite Parliamentary and NGO pressure, final approval of the bill was postponed in order to allow for further negotiations for voluntary licences between the Brazilian government and the pharmaceutical companies involved.[39]

---

[31] WTO, *Doha Declaration on TRIPS and Public Health*, 2001, at para. 4.   [32] *Ibid.*
[33] *Ibid.*, para 5(a).   [34] *Ibid.*, para 5(b) and 5(c).   [35] *Ibid.*, para 5(d).
[36] Musungu and Oh, *The Use of Flexibilities*, at iv.
[37] Grupo de Trabalho sobre Propriedade Intelectual – GTPI – da Rede Brasileira pela Integração dos Povos – GTPI/REBRIP, *Declaration of Civil Society regarding the Brazilian Negotiations for Voluntary Licence for Aids Drugs*, Rio de Janeiro, 5 May 2005. http://lists. essential.org/pipermail/ip-health/2005-May/007908.html (accessed: 1 October 2005).
[38] K. Cortes, 'Brazil Deputies Suspend Patents on AIDS Drugs', *Bloomberg*, 1 June 2005.
[39] As of date of writing, 1 October 2005.

The WTO General Council Decision of 30 August 2003 on the implementation of paragraph 6 of the Doha Declaration on TRIPS and Public Health

Another legal mechanism that could be used by developing countries in order to help reduce the cost of medicines is the WTO General Council Decision of 30 August 2003.[40] This text is a solution to the problem raised by paragraph 6 of the Doha Declaration concerning the 'difficulties in making effective use of compulsory licensing' faced by States with insufficient or no pharmaceutical manufacturing capacity.[41] The reason why such countries cannot make full use of compulsory licensing is due to provisions in the TRIPS Agreement requiring that compulsory licences be 'predominantly for the supply of the domestic market of the Member authorizing such use.'[42] This has the effect of restricting the quantity of generic medicines that can be exported to non-producing countries under a compulsory licence. The Decision is a 'temporary waiver' to these limitations, thereby allowing States to grant compulsory licences exclusively for export of generic versions of medicines under patent.[43]

Although it was necessary to find an expeditious solution to the paragraph 6 problem in order to ensure sustained export of new generic medicines once India implemented TRIPS patent rules, the General Council Decision is too complex to have an effective impact on price. The mechanism's requirements are burdensome for developing countries, such as the requirement of compulsory licences in both the exporting and importing countries.[44] In view of these hurdles, the mechanism has been criticised as creating a 'complex, procedural labyrinth that stands between a willing, low-cost supplier and a country desperately needing imported generics.'[45] As a result of this, only a limited number of countries – Canada,

---

[40] WTO, *Implementation of Paragraph 6 of the Doha Declaration on the TRIPS Agreement and Public Health*, Decision of the General Council of 30 August 2003, WT/L/540, 1 September 2003.

[41] WTO, Doha Ministerial Declaration on the TRIPS Agreement and Public Health, WT/MIN (01)/DEC/2, 14 November 2001, at 6.   [42] TRIPS Agreement, article 31(f).

[43] P. Vandoren and J. C. van Eeckhaute, 'The WTO Decision on Paragraph 6 of the Doha Declaration on the TRIPS Agreement and Public Health: Making it Work', *Journal of World Intellectual Property* 6 (2003) 6, 787.

[44] C. M. Correa, Implementation of the WTO General Council Decision on Paragraph 6 of the Doha Declaration on the TRIPS Agreement and Public Health, WHO Essential Drugs and Medicines Policy, April 2004

[45] B. K. Baker, *Process and Issues for Improving Access to Medicines, Willingness and Ability to Utilise TRIPS Flexibilities in Non-Producing Countries*, DFID Health Systems Resource Centre, August 2004, 31.

India and Norway – have passed implementing legislation,[46] the EU[47] and Switzerland[48] have draft implementing legislation under discussion in Parliament, and no developing country has yet made use of the mechanism to import generic medicines.

Bilateral and regional trade agreements and the dangers of TRIPS-plus rules

The emergence of TRIPS-plus rules

Although the TRIPS Agreement does not prevent countries from having higher standards, it allows them to limit themselves to the level imposed by the Agreement.[49] Nevertheless, developed countries seeking to advance the interests of their industry have begun demanding higher IP protection standards. These stricter IP rules are termed 'TRIPS-plus rules,' as they go beyond the TRIPS Agreement and are against the spirit of the Doha Declaration on TRIPS and Public Health. They are increasingly being put forward in IP technical assistance programmes; WTO accession packages, World Intellectual Property Organization (WIPO) treaties, investment agreements and bilateral and regional trade agreements. The emergence of these TRIPS-plus rules has served to legitimise the TRIPS Agreement to a certain degree, by turning it into a reference point and maximum threshold, even though it remains strongly contested by public-interest NGOs from the North and South.

TRIPS-plus rules that increase patent protection include extensions of the patent term beyond the twenty years required by the TRIPS Agreement in cases of unreasonable delays, extension of the scope of patent protection to new uses of medicines which allows for the 'ever-greening' of patents,[50] restrictions on the ability of countries to issue compulsory licences to reduce the cost of medicines, and limitations on

---

[46] By June 2005, Canada, India and Norway have informed the WTO TRIPS Council that they have passed implementing legislation.

[47] European Commission, *Proposal for a Regulation of the European Parliament and of the Council on compulsory licensing of patents relating to the manufacture of pharmaceutical products for export to countries with public health problems*, COM (2994), 29 October 2004.

[48] *Loi fédérale sur les brevets d'invention, avant-projet de révision de la loi sur les brevets 2004*, http://www.ige.ch/F/jurinfo/documents/j10013f.pdf (accessed: 1 October 2005).

[49] C. M. Correa, *Implementing the TRIPS Agreement: General Context and Implications for Developing Countries*, Third World Network, 1998, at 12.

[50] The term 'ever-greening' refers to the renewal of patent protection for a product whose patent has expired, following the discovery of a new use for the particular invention.

parallel importation of cheaper patented medicines by contractual means or by requiring regional marketing of a medicine before importation is allowed. Furthermore, the introduction of new rules granting at least five year exclusivity on pharmaceutical test data performed by patent owners will delay the introduction of generic medicines on the market, as they will not be able to use this data to obtain marketing authorisation. This is extremely problematic ethically and economically, as generic manufacturers should not have to repeat clinical trials that have already been conducted by the patent owner, just in order to sell a drug on the market.[51]

The inclusion of TRIPS-plus rules in bilateral and regional trade agreements

The types of TRIPS-plus rules outlined above are particularly promoted by the US in bilateral and regional trade agreements (known as Free Trade Agreements or FTAs).[52] The standard of protection achieved in agreements concluded by the USA, such as the US-Chile FTA, the US-Morocco FTA or the US-Dominican Republic-Central American FTA,[53] is being used as a benchmark for negotiations with other developing countries.[54] Indeed, a comparison of the IP standards achieved in each of these FTAs shows a net progression in the degree of protection imposed.[55] Therefore, even if the text under negotiation in the US-Thailand FTA, or the US-Southern African Customs Union (SACU) FTA[56] is kept confidential, patterns of previous negotiations point towards a net increase in the standard of IP protection in FTAs.

However, the USA is not the only developed country to pursue TRIPS-plus rules in trade agreements. Indeed, the Member States of the European Free Trade Association (EFTA),[57] particularly Switzerland, are

---

[51] MSF, 'Access to Medicines at Risk Across the Globe: What to Watch Out For in Free Trade Agreements with the United States', Briefing Note, May 2004, at 2. See http://www.accessmed-msf.org/documents/ftabriefingenglish.pdf (accessed: 1 October 2005).

[52] Section 2101 of the United States Trade Promotion Authority (Trade Act) 2002.

[53] An agreement between the USA on the one hand, and Costa Rica, El Salvador, Guatemala, Honduras, Nicaragua and the Dominican Republic on the other.

[54] Oxfam International, 'Undermining access to medicines: Comparison of five US FTA's. A technical note', Oxfam Briefing Note, June 2004, http://www.oxfam.org.uk/what_we_do/issues/health/undermining_access_ftas.htm (accessed: 15 November 2005), at 2.

[55] C. Fink and P. Reichenmiller, 'Tightening TRIPS: The Intellectual Property Provisions of Recent US Free Trade Agreements', World Bank Trade Note 20 (7 February 2005), at 5.

[56] SACU is composed of Botswana, Lesotho, Namibia, South Africa and Swaziland.

[57] EFTA is composed of Iceland, Liechtenstein, Norway and Switzerland.

also seeking to include TRIPS-plus rules in their FTAs with developing countries.[58] In order to ensure that TRIPS-plus rules are not included in the FTA between EFTA and SACU, NGOs from EFTA countries and from Southern Africa sent an open letter to the negotiators of EFTA Member States requesting 'no intellectual property provisions in the Free Trade Agreement between the EFTA states and the SACU states.'[59] The South African Minister of Trade replied to the NGOs saying that SACU would not accept TRIPS-plus provisions on medicines and agriculture in the FTA negotiations with EFTA countries.[60]

TRIPS-plus commitments in bilateral and regional trade agreements are particularly problematic, as they not only apply to the parties to the trade agreement, but are also applicable to all members of the WTO.[61] Indeed, the most-favoured nation (MFN) clause in the WTO Agreements requires that any IP protection standard in a regional trade agreement is applicable to all the members of the WTO.[62] Therefore, even if the European Union does not promote a TRIPS-plus strategy with regards to pharmaceuticals, the European pharmaceutical industry may still benefit from the TRIPS-plus rules applicable in the countries that have signed FTAs with the US or EFTA Member States.[63]

Although FTAs have made explicit reference to the need to respect public health, as well as uphold the Doha Declaration and the General Council Decision,[64] these assertions have limited weight if the implementation of the TRIPS-plus rules in the agreement nullifies

---

[58] J. Reinhard, 'Deprive Doha of all substance: How through bilateral agreements EFTA states impose on developing countries intellectual property rules on medicines that are beyond the WTO obligations and that restrict access to medicines', Lausanne: *Déclaration de Berne*, November 2004, at 1, http://www.evb.ch/cm_data/depriveDoha.pdf (accessed: 1 October 2005).

[59] *Déclaration de Berne* and MSF-Switzerland, 'Open letter to the trade and foreign ministers of EFTA's states', Lausanne, 4 November 2004. http://www.evb.ch/en/p25009520.html (accessed: 1 October 2005).

[60] *Déclaration de Berne* and *Liechtensteinische Gesellschaft für Umweltschutz* (LGU), 'Southern African countries have taken a firm stand against EFTA demands on Intellectual Property Rights in Free Trade Agreement', Press Release, Lausanne, 4 March 2005, http://www.evb.ch/en/p25009521.html (accessed: 1 October 2005).

[61] J. Reinhard, 'Deprive Doha', at 6.

[62] P. Roffe, 'Bilateral agreements and a TRIPS-plus world: the Chile-USA Free Trade Agreement', UNCTAD-ICTSD TRIPS Issues Papers, Ottowa: QIAP, 2004, 18.

[63] See 3D → Trade – Human Rights – Equitable Economy, *Denmark and Italy, Trade-related intellectual property rights, access to medicines and human rights*, Geneva, October 2004 http://www.3dthree.org/pdf_3D/3DCESCRDenmarkItalyBriefOct04en.pdf (accessed: 1 October 2005).

[64] The US-Morocco FTA, for example, includes a side-letter of 15 June 2004.

the flexibilities reaffirmed by the Doha Declaration. Hence, if developing countries agree to sign on to TRIPS-plus rules they may find themselves in a situation where they may no longer have the regulatory
flexibility to ensure access to affordable medicines and fulfil their
human rights obligations.

International human rights law as a benchmark and framework for trade agreements: ensuring access to affordable medicines for all

Access to affordable medicines as an obligation under international human rights law

All State parties to the TRIPS Agreement are also parties to at least one of
the core international human rights treaties, including the International
Covenant on Civil and Political Rights (ICCPR), the International
Covenant on Economic, Social and Cultural Rights (ICESCR), and the
Convention on the Rights of the Child (CRC). International human
rights law not only provides a legal basis upon which to develop legislative measures and administrative policies regulating accessibility of medicines, it also provides a framework by which to assess the trade measures
adopted by States and non-State actors in relation to IP rules and access
to affordable medicines.[65]

International human rights bodies,[66] scholars,[67] and human rights
advocates, such as the Canadian HIV/AIDS Legal Network,[68] have looked
at the relationship between the TRIPS Agreement and human rights.
Notwithstanding their clear demonstrations of the impact of strict IP
rules on the State's ability to ensure access to affordable medicines and
comply with human rights obligations, public-interest NGOs participating in the access to medicines campaign and decision-makers have only

---

[65] A.E. Yamin, 'Not Just a Tragedy: Access to Medications as a Right Under International Law', *Boston University International Law Journal* 21 (2003), 103.

[66] Sub-Commission on the Promotion and Protection of Human Rights Resolution 2000/7 and 2001/21 and High Commissioner for Human Rights, *The Impact of the Agreement on Trade-Related Aspects of Intellectual Property Rights on Human Rights*, UN Doc. E/CN.4/Sub.2/2001/13 (2001).

[67] See for instance P. Cullet, 'Patents and medicines: the relationship between TRIPS and the human right to health', *International Affairs* 79 I (2003) 139–160.

[68] See for instance R. Elliot, *TRIPS and Rights: International Human Rights Law, Access to Medicines and the Interpretation of the WTO Agreement on Trade-Related Aspects of Intellectual Property* (Toronto: Canadian HIV/ AIDS Legal Network, November 2001), http://www.aidslaw.ca/Maincontent/issues/cts/briefs/TRIPS-human-rights-briefPDF.pdf (accessed: 1 October 2005).

rarely referred to human rights[69] or used human rights mechanisms[70] to support their policy positions.

The main internationally-recognised human rights that ensure access to medicines are: the right to life and the right to health.[71] These human rights contain obligations which States must take into account in their entire policy making, including trade policy.[72] Other human rights of particular relevance are those that encourage greater transparency and accountability, notably the right to access information and the right to participate in public affairs.[73] These human rights are very important to stress as trade negotiations – particularly those that take place bilaterally – are notoriously untransparent.

The right to life

The right to life is a supreme right under international human rights law that cannot be derogated from even in times of a public emergency.[74] This is set out in Article 6 of the ICCPR as well as in other human rights treaties such as Article 6 of the CRC. The Human Rights Committee (HRC), which is the UN human rights treaty body that monitors the application of the ICCPR, provides an authoritative interpretation of the right to life in General Comment No. 6 (1982).[75] In this General

---

[69] Exceptions include HAI and Consumers International – Asia Pacific, who have used right to health arguments to support their advocacy work on IP and access to affordable medicines.

[70] Brazil is unique in having used human rights mechanisms to support its positions on IP and health issues. Brazil sponsored the Commission on Human Rights resolutions on access to medication and the resolutions on the right to health which have consistently raised concerns about the impact of trade-related IP rules on the cost of medicines.

[71] The right to life: Article 6 of the ICCPR and Article 6 of the CRC. The right to an adequate standard of physical and mental health: Article 12 of the ICESCR and Article 24 of the CRC.

[72] Even States such as the USA that have signed and not ratified the ICESCR or CRC are bound by a good faith legal obligation to refrain from acts that could defeat the object and purpose of these rights. See Article 18 of the 1969 Vienna Convention on the Law of Treaties, 1155 U.N.T.S. 331.

[73] The right to seek, receive and impart information: Article 19 ICCPR, Article 12 of the ICESCR, Articles 13(1) and 17 of the CRC. The right to participate in public affairs: Article 25 of the ICCPR. The right to respect the views of the child: Article 12 of the CRC.

[74] Cf. Human Rights Committee General Comment No. 29: States of emergency and rights derogation (Article 4), CCPR/C/21/Rev.1/Add.11 of 31 August 2001, para. 7, reprinted in Compilation of General Comments and General Recommendations Adopted by Human Rights Treaty Bodies, UN Doc. HRI/GEN/1/Rev.6 (2003) at 186.

[75] Cf. Human Rights Committee General Comment No. 6: The right to life (Article 6), Compilation of General Comments and General Recommendations Adopted by Human Rights Treaty Bodies, UN Doc. HRI/GEN/1/Rev.6 (2003) at 127.

Comment, the HRC expressly states that the right to life 'cannot be understood in a restrictive manner.'[76] Accordingly, State parties are required to 'adopt positive measures' which include 'all possible measures to reduce infant mortality and to increase life expectancy, especially in adopting measures to eliminate malnutrition and epidemics.'[77] Access to affordable medicines therefore emerges as an inherent element of the right to life.

This has been confirmed by the HRC in its consideration of State party reports. For example, in its consideration of the report of Uganda in May 2004 the HRC recommended that 'while the Committee takes note of the measures taken by the State party to deal with the widespread problem of HIV/AIDS, it remains concerned about the effectiveness of these measures and the extent to which they guarantee access to medical services, including antiretroviral treatment, to persons infected with HIV (article 6). The State party is urged to adopt comprehensive measures to allow a greater number of persons suffering from HIV/AIDS to obtain adequate antiretroviral treatment.'[78] This recommendation demonstrates that State parties have an obligation to take comprehensive legal and administrative measures to ensure access to affordable medicines in order to comply with their obligations under the right to life.

The right to health

Access to affordable medicines is also an integral part of the right to health. This right is protected by a number of international treaties, most notably Article 12 of the ICESCR and Article 24 of the CRC. The Committee on Economic, Social and Cultural Rights (CESCR), the UN body that monitors the application of the ICESCR, has provided the most detailed exposition of the right to health. This can be found in the General Comment No. 14 (2000) on the right to health.[79] The General Comment clearly explains that the normative content of the right to health includes *accessibility* of health facilities, goods, and services on a non-discriminatory basis.[80] Accessibility includes affordability for all, in a way that 'poorer households should not be disproportionately burdened with health expenses as compared to richer households.'[81] Access

---

[76] *Ibid.*, at para. 5.   [77] *Ibid.*

[78] HRC, Uganda, Concluding Observations, UN Doc. CCPR/CO/80/UGA (2004).

[79] CESCR, General Comment No. 14: The right to the highest attainable standard of health, UN Doc. E/C.12/2000/4 (11 August 2000).   [80] *Ibid.*, at 12.   [81] *Ibid.*

to affordable health goods includes 'appropriate treatment for prevalent diseases, illnesses, injuries and disabilities' and 'the provision of essential drugs.'[82] The Special Rapporteur on the right of everyone to the enjoyment of the highest attainable standard of physical and mental health, Mr Paul Hunt, has emphasised that 'whether publicly or privately provided, the essential medicine must be affordable for all, not just the well off. Clearly, the affordability of essential medicines raises crucial issues, such as drug pricing, compulsory licensing, parallel importing, and the reduction of import duties.'[83]

Although the right to health can be realised progressively over a period of time, the State has an immediate obligation to take 'deliberate, concrete and targeted' steps towards the full realisation of the right to health.[84] These include measures to *respect, protect and fulfil* their obligations.[85] The requirement to *respect* means that States should refrain from interfering with the enjoyment of the right to health. This could be interpreted as meaning that States should not sign on to TRIPS-plus rules that would limit access to affordable medicines. The obligation to *protect* requires States to adopt measures that will prevent third parties from threatening the enjoyment of the right to health. This may include the State taking measures to ensure that third parties, such as the pharmaceutical industry, do not adversely affect the cost of medicines by imposing high prices. Finally, the obligation to *fulfil* requires the State to implement national policies and legislative measures that ensures the realisation of the right to health. This could involve the implementation and use of the mechanisms such as compulsory licences or parallel imports to ensure access to affordable medicines for all.

Finally, the right to health also includes the obligation of States not to take steps that constitute retrogression from realisation of the right. The State has the burden of proving whether these measures were introduced after careful consideration.[86] This imposes an obligation on States to undertake human rights impact assessments of the TRIPS-plus rules in bilateral and regional trade agreements before they sign on to them, in order to ensure that they do not pass measures that violate the right to

---

[82] *Ibid.*, at 16.
[83] Commission on Human Rights (CHR), *The right of everyone to the enjoyment of the highest attainable standard of physical and mental health*, Report of the Special Rapporteur of the Commission on Human Rights on the right of everyone to the enjoyment of the highest attainable standard of physical and mental health, Paul Hunt, UN Doc. E/CN.4/2004/49/ Add.1 (1 March 2004), at 37 (c).   [84] *Ibid.*, at 30.
[85] CESCR, General Comment No. 14.   [86] *Ibid.*, at 32.

health. This has recently been reaffirmed by the CHR Resolution on access to medicines which 'calls upon States to conduct an impact assessment of the effects of international trade agreements with regard to public health and to the progressive realisation of the right of everyone to the highest attainable standard of health.'[87]

Children's rights

The 'best interests of the child' is one of the key underlying principles of human rights law relating to children. Article 3(1) of the CRC requires State parties to give prime consideration to the best interests of the child in all decision-making, including the conduct of 'public or private social welfare institutions, courts of law, administrative authorities or legislative bodies.' The Committee on the Rights of the Child (CRC), the UN treaty body that monitors the application of the CRC, has looked at the issue of access to medicines in the context of pandemics such as HIV/AIDS. It has expressly stated that the best interests of the child should be 'fundamental to guiding the action of States in relation to HIV/AIDS. The child should be placed at the centre of the response to the pandemic, and strategies should be adapted to children's rights and needs.'[88]

General Comment No.3 (2003) on HIV/AIDS encourages a 'holistic child rights-based approach' that includes consideration of the right to life (Article 6 of the CRC),[89] the right to health (Article 24),[90] the right to non-discrimination (Article 2),[91] the right of the child to have his/her interests as a primary consideration (Article 3)[92] and the right of the child to have his/her views heard (Article 12).[93] This interpretation of children's rights and obligations of States is particularly ground-breaking in its integrated approach. In relation to treatment and care, State parties are required to ensure that 'children have sustained and equal access to comprehensive treatment and care, including necessary HIV-related drugs, goods and services on a basis of non-discrimination.'[94] The Committee goes on to add that 'comprehensive treatment and care includes anti-retroviral and other drugs, diagnostics

---

[87] CHR Resolution 2005/23, *Access to medication in the context of pandemics such as HIV/AIDS, tuberculosis and malaria*, 51st meeting, 15 April 2005, at para. 14.

[88] CRC, General Comment No. 3: *HIV/AIDS and the rights of the child*, UN Doc. CRC/GC/2003/3 of 17 March 2003, at para. 8.   [89] *Ibid.*, e.g. para. 11

[90] *Ibid.*, e.g. paras. 5 and 6.   [91] *Ibid.*, e.g. paras. 5, 6, 7, 8 and 9.   [92] *Ibid.*, e.g. para. 10.

[93] *Ibid.*, e.g. para. 12.   [94] *Ibid.*, at 28.

and related technologies for the care of HIV/AIDS, related opportunistic infections and other conditions.'

A similar approach is taken by the CRC in General Comment No. 4 (2003) relating to adolescent health and development. In the interpretation of State obligations relating to adolescent health, the Committee requires States to 'ensure that appropriate goods, services and information for the prevention and treatment of STDs [sexually transmitted diseases], including HIV/AIDS, are available and accessible' for all and without discrimination.[95] These obligations, coupled with the obligations under the General Comment on HIV/AIDS could be interpreted as requiring States to take into account the best interests of the child and obligations under the CRC in all IP negotiations that will affect access to affordable medicines and the enjoyment of children's rights.

These obligations under the CRC are also reinforced by Article 24 of the ICCPR which requires States to ensure that every child benefits from 'measures of protection as are required by his status as a minor.' The HRC has interpreted this in General Comment No. 17 (1989) as meaning that 'every possible economic and social measure should be taken to reduce infant mortality.'[96] Therefore, the obligations under the ICCPR could be interpreted as requiring States to ensure that they grant compulsory licences for generic medicines and undertake parallel imports of patented medicines that are cheaper in other countries in order to obtain sufficient quantities of medicines capable of reducing infant mortality, at an affordable price.

International cooperation and assistance

Article 2(1) of the ICESCR, as interpreted by the Committee on Economic, Social and Cultural Rights (CESCR) in General Comment No. 3 (1990) requires State parties to take 'deliberate, concrete and targeted' steps 'through international assistance and cooperation, especially economic and technical' towards full realisation of Covenant rights.[97] This obligation is echoed by Article 4 of the CRC, as interpreted by General Comment No. 5 (2003), which states that members of international

---

[95] CRC, General Comment No. 4: *Adolescent health and development in the context of the Convention on the Rights of the Child*, UN Doc. CRC/GC/2003/4 of 1 July 2003, at para. 30.

[96] General Comment No. 17: *Rights of the child* (Article 24) of 7 April 1989, Thirty-fifth session, 1989, at para. 3.

[97] CESCR, General Comment No. 3: *The nature of State parties obligations*, UN Doc. E/1991/23 (14 December 1990), at para. 13.

organisations, including the WTO, 'should ensure that their activities related to international cooperation and economic development give primary consideration to the best interests of children and promote full implementation of the Convention.'[98] States also have an obligation to ensure that their actions as members of international organizations take due account of the right to health.[99] This can be interpreted as meaning that States should take into account the right to health when they negotiate IP rules in all trade agreements and implement these rules domestically.

International cooperation and assistance under the right to health requires States to 'respect the enjoyment of the right to health in other countries, and to prevent third parties from violating the right in other countries, if they are able to influence these third parties by way of legal or political means.'[100] This requires States to intervene politically and legally to ensure that third parties, such as the pharmaceutical industry or States that have not ratified the Covenant, do not have trade policies that violate access to affordable medicines in developing countries. In addition, States are required to refrain from imposing measures that restrict the supply of another State with adequate medicines.[101] This could include refraining from imposing TRIPS-plus rules that would restrict the supply of affordable medicines in another country.

States are also obliged, particularly if they have sufficient resources, to facilitate 'access to essential health facilities, goods and services in other countries.'[102] This can be interpreted as meaning that State parties to the ICESCR, such as the members of the European Union, Canada or Switzerland, have a legal obligation to take steps to facilitate access to affordable medicines in developing countries.

Access to information and participation in decision-making

Due to the lack of transparency in trade negotiations, especially in bilateral and regional trade negotiations, it is important to consider which State obligations could ensure greater accountability of trade decision-makers. The obligations to ensure access to information and participation in public affairs are crucial in allowing citizens and civil society groups to

---

[98] CRC, General Comment No. 5: *General measures of implementation of the Convention on the Rights of the Child*, UN Doc. CRC/GC/2003/5 (27 November 2003), at para. 64.
[99] CESCR, General Comment No. 14., at para. 39.   [100] *Ibid.*, at para. 39.
[101] *Ibid.*, at para. 41.   [102] *Ibid.*, at para 39.

monitor trade processes and ensure that IP rules being negotiated do not further undermine access to affordable medicines and the realisation of human rights.

State parties have a general obligation to ensure the freedom to seek, receive and impart information under Article 19 of the ICCPR;[103] additionally, under the right to health, there is an obligation to ensure the right to access information and ideas concerning health issues.[104] Furthermore, State parties to the CRC have an obligation to ensure the child's freedom to seek, receive and impart information under Article 13(1) of the CRC, and an obligation to ensure access of the child to information on his or her health under Article 17 of the CRC. State parties therefore have an obligation to ensure that information about trade policies and trade rules that affect the realisation of the right to health or the right to life are made public. It is particularly important that States ensure access to information relating to proposed IP rules in bilateral and regional trade agreements, in order to allow independent assessments of the effect of trade rules on human rights.

Article 25 of the ICCPR requires State parties to ensure participation in the conduct of public affairs.[105] This involves the conduct of 'all aspects of public administration, and the formulation and implementation of policy at international, national, regional and local levels.'[106] This is echoed by the right to health, which requires access to information and participation of the population in health-related decision-making at the community, national and international level.[107] Moreover, under Article 12 of the CRC, States have an obligation to respect the views of the child in 'all matters affecting the child.' This involves opening government decision-making processes to children in a way that encourages the participation of the child in the 'promotion, protection and monitoring of his or her rights.'[108] These participatory rights are crucial in ensuring greater accountability in trade decision-making processes, independence in human rights impact assessments of trade rules[109] and in ensuring that trade agreements are consistent with human rights standards.

---

[103] HRC, General Comment No. 10.   [104] CESCR, General Comment No. 14, at para. 12.

[105] HRC, General Comment No. 25: *The right to participate in public affairs, voting rights and the right to equal access to public service (Article 25)*, UN Doc. HRI/GEN/1/Rev.7 at 194 (12 July 1996).   [106] *Ibid.*, at para. 5.   [107] *Ibid.*, at para 43.

[108] CRC, General Comment No. 5, at para 12.

[109] CHR, *Analytical study of the High Commissioner for Human Rights on the fundamental principle of participation and its application in the context of globalisation*, Report of the High Commissioner, UN Doc. E/CN.4/2005/41 (23 December 2004).

Using international human rights mechanisms to make trade more accountable and human rights-consistent

In the current political climate, there is an urgent need to stall the prolifer-ation of TRIPS-plus rules and to safeguard human rights from being undermined by trade rules. Independent monitoring of trade processes, especially bilateral and regional trade negotiations is particularly import-ant. There are a number of avenues available at the national, regional and international levels to individuals and NGOs to challenge trade policy and trade rules that may be inconsistent with human rights obligations. These avenues range from national constitutional appeals, to providing submis-sions to regional mechanisms such as the African Commission on Human and Peoples' Rights, the Inter-American Commission on Human Rights, or the European Court of Human Rights, and to the international human rights mechanisms of the UN.

This section will focus on the potential of international human rights mechanisms to monitor and challenge the impact of trade rules on the realisation of human rights, and will describe the experience of one NGO in using these mechanisms. The work of 3D → Trade – Human Rights – Equitable Economy (3D) will be considered as an illustration of how a policy-focused NGO has used international human rights law and mechanisms to make trade rules more accountable and human rights-consistent. 3D believes that human rights rules and mechanisms are invaluable accountability tools for trade policy, and chose to test this conviction by raising the issue of trade-related IP rules, access to medicines and human rights with the UN human rights mechanisms. The issue of IP, access to medicines and human rights was chosen because it was familiar to human rights advocates, and because it was probably the trade issue with the most clearly-recognised human rights implications.

The overall objective of 3D's project on IP, access to medicines and human rights was to hold States accountable to their duties to ensure access to affordable medicines in a way that is human rights-consistent. The project also had several underlying objectives. First, to enhance understanding within the human rights community of how trade impacts on human rights, through publishing concise, country-focused briefing notes, which would serve to indicate how to approach analysing these issues. Second, the work aimed to contribute to strengthening exist-ing campaigns on access to medicines by demonstrating that IP rules are not only undesirable and immoral, but also incompatible with human rights law. Thirdly, the project aimed to demonstrate to developing country decision-makers that human rights standards can be used as 'shields' when faced with pressure to accept TRIPS-plus rules in trade negotiations. A final objective was to achieve greater accountability in trade policy and greater coherence between trade rules and human rights obligations.

3D is not a grass roots organisation: its method of work is to intervene on policy issues by providing targeted information to individuals and organisations that can act as multipliers in disseminating a human rights-consistent approach to trade policy. Therefore, the results of 3D's work with the UN human rights mechanisms was disseminated to policy-focused NGOs in the North and South and key decision-makers in international organisations, regional organisations and national institutions working on IP and human rights policy.

United Nations human rights treaty monitoring bodies

Rationale for raising trade-related issues in human rights treaty bodies

Treaty bodies are independent organs that monitor the application of international human rights treaties, such as the ICESCR, ICCPR and CRC. 3D chose to focus the majority of its IP and access to medicines work on these bodies, as they provide a high-profile international accountability mechanism where State policies are monitored. The fact that States are obliged to periodically report on the measures they have taken in order to implement their human rights obligations and answer questions in public on these measures – or lack thereof – is a valuable accountability mechanism.[110] This public dialogue and questioning is particularly important when there is a lack of access to information and consultation at the national level.[111] Furthermore, the fact that treaty bodies encourage NGO participation and submissions, and often ask questions and make recommendations based on these concerns, facilitated 3D's work. Most importantly, States have a legal obligation to take into account treaty body recommendations, which makes them critical tools for civil society. The treaty body process therefore emerges as a

---

[110] The obligation for State parties to submit periodic reports to the treaty bodies is enshrined in Article 16 of the ICESCR, Article 40 of the ICCPR, and Article 44 of the CRC.

[111] Leckie, S., 'The Committee on Economic, Social and Cultural Rights: Catalyst for Change in a System Needing Reform', in Alston, P. and Crawford, J., *The Future of UN Human Rights Treaty Monitoring* (Cambridge: Cambridge University Press, 2000), p. 134.

valuable mechanism to expose a human rights problem and achieve concrete recommendations that can support the ongoing efforts of advocates and decision-makers on a particular issue

Treaty bodies have been specifically requested to look at the issue of IP and human rights by other UN human rights organs. The UN Sub-Commission on the Promotion and Protection of Human Rights, in Resolution 2001/21, suggested that the CESCR and other treaty bodies 'explore, in the course of reviewing State parties' reports, the implications of the TRIPS Agreement for the realisation of economic, social and cultural rights.'[112] Moreover, a number of UN Commission on Human Rights resolutions have repeatedly invited CESCR to 'give attention to the issue of access to medication and invites States to include appropriate information thereon in the reports they submit to the Committee.'[113] However, treaty bodies and States have been slow to respond to these requests. The most notable response was the Statement on Human Rights and Intellectual Property made by CESCR in 2001.[114] Unfortunately, these UN resolutions and the CESCR Statement are little known outside specialist UN human rights circles and did not have much resonance with IP experts and decision-makers.

In order to give more exposure and relevance to the work of the UN human rights mechanisms on IP and human rights, 3D decided to encourage the treaty bodies to intervene on the issue of IP and access to medicines in such a way that their recommendations could provide useful tools to access to medicines advocates and decision-makers at the national, regional and international level.

3D's experience of using UN treaty bodies to make trade rules more accountable and human rights-consistent

In order to best achieve the objectives outlined above, 3D chose to submit briefings on countries coming up for review in front of the CESCR, the CRC, or the HRC. During 2004 and 2005, 3D made submissions on countries that were either reforming their IP laws, such as Uganda,[115] or

---

[112] Sub-Commission on the Promotion and Protection of Human Rights Resolution 2001/21.   [113] CHR Resolutions 2001/33, 2002/32, 2003/29, 2004/26 and 2005/23.

[114] CESCR, *Follow-up to the day of general discussion on article 15(1)(c), Human rights and intellectual property*, Statement by the Committee on Economic, Social and Cultural Rights, UN Doc. E/C.12/2001/15 (November 2001).

[115] 3D → Trade – Human Rights – Equitable Economy, 'Trade-related intellectual property rights, access to HIV/AIDS medicines and the fulfilment of civil and political

negotiating bilateral and regional trade agreements, such as Botswana,[116] Ecuador,[117] and El Salvador,[118] or planning to enter into bilateral trade negotiations with the USA and European countries, such as the Philippines.[119] Moreover, 3D also made a submission on two EU countries – Denmark and Italy[120] – in order to highlight the international obligations of developed countries regarding access to medicines and realisation of the right to health in developing countries. The next sections describe 3D's submissions on Ecuador, Botswana, Demark and Italy, to illustrate how an NGO can raise a trade-related issue with a treaty body.

Ecuador

3D submitted a country briefing on Ecuador to be considered at the 32nd Session of CESCR in May 2004.[121] Ecuador was selected because it began trade negotiations for a US-Ecuador Free Trade Agreement (FTA) in May 2004 and it was also participating in regional trade negotiations for a Free Trade Agreement of the Americas (FTAA).[122] These trade agreements risk putting Ecuador in a situation where TRIPS-plus rules may affect its

rights – Uganda', March 2004. See http://www.3dthree.org/pdf_3D/3DHRCUganda-Brief04en.pdf (accessed: 1 October 2005).

[116] 3D → Trade – Human Rights – Equitable Economy, 'Trade-related intellectual property rights, trade in services and the fulfilment of children's rights – Botswana', September 2004. See http://www.3dthree.org/pdf_3D/3DCRCBotswanaSept04en.pdf (accessed: 1 October 2005).

[117] 3D → Trade – Human Rights – Equitable Economy, 'Trade-related intellectual property rights, access to medicines and the right to health – Ecuador', April 2004. See http://www.3dthree.org/pdf_3D/3DCESCREcuadorBrief04en.pdf (accessed 1 October 2005) and 3D, 'International trade, health, and children's rights – Ecuador', September 2004. See http://www.3dthree.org/pdf_3D/3DCRCEcuadorBrief_Sept04.pdf (accessed: 1 October 2005).

[118] 3D → Trade – Human Rights – Equitable Economy, 'The impact of international trade agreements regulating intellectual property rights on access to medicines and the fulfilment of children's rights – El Salvador', February 2004. See http://www.3dthree.org/pdf_3D/3DCRCElSalvadorBrief04en.pdf (accessed: 1 October 2005).

[119] 3D → Trade – Human Rights – Equitable Economy, 'International trade, health and children's rights – The Philippines', December 2004. See, http://www.3dthree.org/pdf_3D/3DCRCPhilippines_Dec04.pdf (accessed: 1 October 2005).

[120] 3D → Trade – Human Rights – Equitable Economy, 'Denmark and Italy, Trade-related intellectual property rights, access to medicines and human rights', October 2004. See http://www.3dthree.org/pdf_3D/3DCESCRDenmarkItalyBriefOct04en.pdf (accessed: 1 October 2005).

[121] 3D → Trade – Human Rights – Equitable Economy, 'Trade-related intellectual property rights, access to medicines and the right to health – Ecuador', April 2004.

[122] Ecuador was still negotiating these agreements at the date of writing, October 2005.

ability to ensure access to affordable medicines and the realisation of the right to health, under Article 12 of the ICESCR.

3D's briefing explains how TRIPS-plus rules, such as patent extensions, limits on compulsory licensing and five year data exclusivity, could put Ecuador in a situation where it will no longer be able to ensure its obligation to ensure access to affordable medicines.[123] Moreover, the lack of access to information and consultation with civil society during the FTA negotiations is contrary to Ecuador's obligations under the right to health. The briefing concludes with a list of questions that the members of CESCR could ask the government of Ecuador, and recommendations they could make. These include the need to use TRIPS flexibilities, ensure access to information and participation in trade processes and to undertake an impact assessment of the effect of TRIPS-plus rules on access to affordable medicines in order to assess whether trade commitments will undermine human rights obligations.

When considering Ecuador's report,[124] three CESCR members raised the issue of IP and access to affordable medicines. The Ecuadorian representative to the WTO, who had been advised in advance that these questions were likely to come up, attended the CESCR session to answer the treaty body's questions. This was one of the few situations in which a trade representative has directly answered questions in front of a human rights treaty body. Following the public dialogue with the delegation of Ecuador, CESCR stated in its Concluding Observations that it was 'concerned about the enjoyment of the right to health by all people in the State party and particularly with regard to access to generic medicine'[125] and made the following recommendations in its Concluding Observations:

> The Committee strongly urges the State party to conduct an assessment of the effect of international trade rules on the right to health for all and to make extensive use of the flexibility clauses permitted in the WTO Agreement on Trade-related Aspects of Intellectual Property Rights (the TRIPS Agreement) in order to ensure access to generic medicine and more broadly the enjoyment of the right to health for everyone in Ecuador.
>
> The Committee strongly recommends that the State party's obligations under the Covenant should be taken into account in all aspects of its negotiations with the international financial institutions and other regional

---

[123] 3D → Trade – Human Rights – Equitable Economy, 'Trade-related intellectual property rights, access to medicines and the right to health – Ecuador', April 2004, para 4.

[124] Ecuador was considered by CESCR on 5–6 May 2004.

[125] CESCR, Ecuador, Concluding Observations, UN Doc. E/C.12/1/Add.100 (June 2004), at para. 30.

trade agreements to ensure that economic, social and cultural rights, particularly of the most disadvantaged and marginalized groups, are not undermined.[126]

3D disseminated these recommendations to networks of human rights groups, access to medicines advocates and development NGOs in Ecuador, the Andean region and internationally.[127] 3D also sent them to international organisations such as UNAIDS, UNCTAD and OHCHR as well as to the Ecuadorian trade representatives. The purpose of distributing these recommendations so widely was to provide these advocates and decision-makers with authoritative human rights arguments, which assert that the State could not agree to IP rules which would put it in a situation where it would be forced to contravene its international human rights obligations present in a number of treaties, as described above.

The CESCR recommendations on Ecuador were crucial to Ecuadorian civil society in their advocacy work. In particular, these recommendations were used in an open letter sent by a coalition of human rights and access to medicines advocates in response to a draft Presidential Decree that included TRIPS-plus rules,[128] attempting to pass them into Ecuadorian law before the end of the US-Ecuador FTA bilateral trade negotiations. This would have resulted in a situation of 'fait accompli', where it would not have been possible to argue that the FTA agreement was introducing laws that forced Ecuador to take measures that would be in violation of the right to health. The Ecuadorian chief trade negotiator at the time sent a written response to the *Centro de Derechos Economicos y Sociales* (CDES)-Ecuador, the NGO which coordinated the letter.[129] In his response the chief trade negotiator admitted that the proposed TRIPS-plus rules in the draft decree risked violating the Ecuadorian constitution, especially the right to health. The draft decree was not adopted and this letter was used by NGOs to lobby against possible TRIPS-plus rules

---

[126] *Ibid.*, at paras. 55 and 56.

[127] 3D → Trade – Human Rights – Equitable Economy, 'Access to Affordable Drugs: A Right no FTA can Ignore. UN Committee Warns Ecuador that US-Andean FTA Must Not Undermine Human Rights', Press Release, 18 May 2004. See http://www.3dthree.org/pdf_3D/EcuadorPress18May04_en.pdf (accessed: 1 October 2005).

[128] *Centro de Derechos Económicos y sociales* (CDES), *Cuanto cuesta el derecho a la salud en Ecuador? Carta abierta al Presidente de la Republica de Ecuador*, [What is the Cost of Health in Ecuador? Open letter to the President of the Republic of Ecuador] 9 July 2004 (on file with author).

[129] CDES, *Medicamentos Genéricos y Derechos Humanos, DESC Para la Acción*, Boletín 1, September 2004. [Generic Medicines and Human Rights], see http://www.cdes.org.ec/biblioteca/biblioteca.html (accessed: 1 October 2005).

in the US-Ecuador FTA.[130] This outcome was used as a precedent for other NGOs from the region and disseminated in regional campaign documents against bilateral and regional FTAs.[131]

Botswana

3D submitted a country briefing on Botswana to the 37th Session of the CRC in September 2004. 3D chose to focus on Botswana as it was negotiating a bilateral trade agreement with the USA, as part of the Southern African Customs Union.[132] 3D's briefing outlines how Botswana risks undermining its ability to provide access to affordable medicines, of which antiretroviral treatment for its national HIV/AIDS treatment programme, if it agrees to include TRIPS-plus rules in the US-SACU FTA.[133] Adhering to these rules could put Botswana in a position where it will no longer be able to take all the measures necessary to respect, protect and fulfill the child's right to health and the child's right to life. The report also emphasises the need to take into account the best interests of the child in all aspects of trade policy and to ensure access to information on trade negotiations that will affect children's rights. The briefing proposes questions and outlines recommendations that the CRC could make to the government of Botswana in order to ensure that the rights of the child are given prime consideration in trade negotiations.

During the consideration of the report on Botswana,[134] the Chair of the CRC explicitly said that the outcome of the US-SACU FTA negotiations should not impede Botswana from producing or acquiring cheap medicines to treat HIV/AIDS. The Chair also wanted to know whether Botswana was considering providing itself with generic versions of antiretroviral medicines and whether South Africa was developing them.

---

[130] CDES, *Ecuador: Jefe de equipo negociador TLC contrario al Decreto Ejecutivo. Genéricos son esenciales 'para el derechos a la salud' y están por sobre intereses privados y específicos*, Press Release, 16 August 2004. [Ecuador: The Chief negotiator of FTA team is against the Executive Decree. Generic medicines are essential 'for the right to health' and should be above private interests], see http://www.cdes.org.ec/biblioteca/biblioteca.html (accessed: 1 October 2005).

[131] Centro Pro Juarez, Unfulfilled Obligations, Human Rights and Free Trade Agreements in the Americas', 9 July 2004, at 22. See http://www.centroprodh.org.mx/english/publications/publications/2004/alca_english_web.pdf (accessed. 1 October 2005).

[132] The SACU Member States were still negotiating an FTA with the USA at the date of writing, 1 October 2005.

[133] See 3D → Trade – Human Rights – Equitable Economy, 'Trade-related intellectual property rights, trade in services and the fulfilment of children's rights – Botswana'.

[134] Botswana was considered by the CRC on 16 September 2004.

Although the delegation of Botswana did not reply to this question or to the Chair's remark on the US-SACU FTA negotiations, it is important that such questions are on record in order to warn other governments that the Committee may question them on IP rules in trade agreements, and particularly FTAs.

In view of this dialogue with the Botswana delegation, the CRC made the following recommendation:

> [T]he Committee also recommends that the State party ensure that regional and other free trade agreements do not have a negative impact on the implementation of children's rights and, more specifically, that these will not affect the possibility of providing children and other victims of HIV/AIDS with effective medicines for free or at the lowest price possible.[135]

3D disseminated the recommendation to human rights groups, access to medicines advocates and development groups in Botswana, Southern Africa and internationally.[136] It was also sent to international organisations working on HIV/AIDS in Botswana, such as UNAIDS, WHO and the OHCHR.

The recommendations of the CRC on Botswana were useful for access to medicines advocates working against the inclusion of TRIPS-plus rules at the regional level, and especially in the US-SACU FTA negotiations. South African civil society groups; TAC and the National Labour and Economic Development Institute (NALEDI), disseminated the CRC recommendations to their networks and welcomed them as a 'pro-poor' approach to trade.[137] Although the recommendations have not been explicitly used in advocacy campaigns so far, they were welcomed by the Aids Law Project, South Africa,[138] as complementary to the South African constitutional requirements and the UN international guidelines on HIV/AIDS and Human Rights.[139] Moreover, according to the Trade Law

---

[135] CRC, Concluding Observations, Botswana, UN Doc. CRC/C/15/Add.242 (3 November 2004), para. 20.

[136] 3D → Trade – Human Rights – Equitable Economy, 'Access to Affordable Drugs: Victims of HIV/AIDS Should Not Suffer From Trade Rules, UN Committee Warns Botswana that US-SACU FTA Should Not Undermine Access to HIV/AIDS Treatment', 4 October 2004. See http://www.3dthree.org/pdf_3D/BotswanaCOPressRelease_en.pdf (accessed: 1 October 2005).

[137] Emails from TAC and NALEDI, South Africa, October 2004, on file with the author.

[138] Email from the AIDS Law Project, South Africa, May 2005, on file with the author.

[139] UNAIDS, HIV/AIDS and Human Rights International Guidelines, Revised Guideline 6, UN Doc. UNAIDS/02.49E, March 2003.

Centre for Southern Africa (TRALAC), the CRC recommendations played a role in supporting Southern African trade negotiators in maintaining a negotiating position against TRIPS-plus provisions in the US-SACU FTA negotiations and supported the decision not to include TRIPS-plus rules in the FTA between SACU and EFTA countries.[140]

Denmark and Italy

3D submitted a briefing on Denmark and Italy to the 33rd Session of CESCR in November 2004.[141] The purpose of the briefing was to highlight the human rights obligations of EU Member States in relation to trade policy, and especially trade-related IP policy. The relevant obligations highlighted in the briefing include the obligation to ensure 'individually or through international assistance and cooperation' access to affordable medicines in developing countries, prevent third parties from violating the right to health in other countries, and ensuring that the actions of EU members in international organisations take due account of the right to health.[142] The briefing focuses on the need to ensure that EU trade policy promotes TRIPS flexibilities and access to affordable medicines in developing countries and that the implementation of the WTO General Council Decision is done in a human rights-consistent manner.

Although the then EU Trade Commissioner, Mr Pascal Lamy, publicly committed not to make demands for TRIPS-plus rules relating to medicines in its bilateral and regional trade agreements,[143] the EU is promoting an IP enforcement strategy that requires states to achieve the 'highest international standards in this area.'[144] 3D's briefing stresses that the EU enforcement strategy should not undermine access to affordable medicines. The briefing also emphasises that technical assistance, provided by individual EU Members and the EU as a whole, must promote the full use of TRIPS flexibilities to ensure access to affordable medicines for all. The

---

[140] Email from TRALAC, May 2005, on file with the author.
[141] 3D, 'Denmark and Italy, Trade-related intellectual property rights, access to medicines and human rights, October 2004.
[142] Articles 2(1) of the ICESCR, as interpreted by General Comment No. 3 (1990) and Article 12 of the ICESCR, as interpreted by General Comment No. 14 (2000).
[143] P. Lamy, 'Speech of the European Commissioner for Trade at the International Conference on the 10th Anniversary of the WTO TRIPS Agreement', 23 June 2004.
[144] European Commission, *Strategy for the Enforcement of Intellectual Property Rights in Third Countries*, 2005/C 129/03, 23 June 2004.

briefing ends with an outline of possible questions and recommendations that the CESCR could make to Denmark and Italy, as individual States and as Member States of the EU, including the need for access to information and increased participation in the EU trade decision-making processes, which lack transparency.[145]

During the consideration of the reports of Denmark and Italy,[146] the members of CESCR asked the delegation what they were doing to ensure that developing countries can use all the flexibilities under the TRIPS Agreement to ensure access to affordable medicines. The Committee members also wanted to know what the positions of the governments of Denmark and Italy were in relation to the EU's proposed regulation aimed at implementing the compulsory licensing mechanism of the WTO General Council Decision.[147] The Danish and Italian delegations replied by confirming their commitment to the WTO Doha Declaration on TRIPS and Public Health and the General Council Decision. In a written reply to the Committee, Denmark explicitly confirmed its commitment to 'gaining maximum flexibility within the existing framework for developing countries and the least developed.'[148] Moreover, the Danish delegation said that the 'WTO decision would be integrated swiftly into Danish national legislation. Every effort would be made to ensure that developing countries were in a position to take full advantage of the Doha Declaration.'[149]

In view of the encouraging statements of the Danish and Italian delegations, the Committee did not make any recommendations on the issue of access to affordable medicines. This is problematic, because a recommendation emphasising the human rights obligations of developed countries regarding access to affordable medicines would have been a valuable tool for advocates working to ensure that developed countries do not impose TRIPS-plus rules on developing countries. Without a

[145] In particular the 133 Committee, which elaborates EU trade policy.e.g.: Written Question E-4036/00, Bart Staes (Verts/ALE) to the Council, (3 January 2001), 2001/C 261 E/020 *Official Journal of the European Communities*, 18/09/2001, http://europa.eu.int/eur-lex/pri/en/oj/dat/2001/ce261/ce26120010918en00210021.pdf (accessed: 1 October 2005).

[146] Denmark was considered by CESCR on the 10–11 November 2004, and Italy was considered on 15–16 November 2004.

[147] European Commission, *Proposal for a Regulation of the European Parliament and of the Council on Compulsory Licensing of Patents Relating to the Manufacture of Pharmaceutical Products for Export to Countries with Public Health Problems*, COM (04) 737, 29 October 2004.

[148] CESCR, Denmark, Written Replies, 15 November 2004, on file with author.

[149] CESCR, Denmark, Summary Record, UN Doc. E/C.12/2004/SR.37, 16 November 2004.

written recommendation it was difficult to encourage national NGOs to take up the issue with their governments and parliamentarians. The only NGOs that expressed strong interest in the outcome of the CRC dialogue were the national offices of *Médecins Sans Frontières*, Denmark and Italy. The outcome of this joint submission on Denmark and Italy therefore demonstrates that further work is needed to encourage treaty bodies to make recommendations on the human rights obligations of developed countries vis-à-vis developing countries.

United Nations Commission on Human Rights mechanisms

Special procedures: the Special Rapporteur on the right to health

The UN Commission on Human Rights has special procedures in order to investigate, monitor and report on thematic or country-specific human rights issues. One of the main mechanisms relevant to the issue of IP and access to affordable medicines is the establishment of a Special Rapporteur on the right of everyone to the enjoyment of the highest attainable standard of physical and mental health (Special Rapporteur on the right to health), currently Mr. Paul Hunt. The mandate of this Special Rapporteur includes making recommendations on appropriate measures to promote and protect the right to health, which includes access to affordable medicines.[150] The Special Rapporteur on the right to health chose to consider the impact of trade-related IP rules on the enjoyment of the right to health.[151] During 2004 and 2005, 3D worked in close collaboration with the Special Rapporteur, providing him with information on the human rights impacts of the TRIPS Agreement and TRIPS-plus rules in FTA agreements.

The Special Rapporteur chose to visit the WTO for his first mission to highlight the impact of trade rules on the right to health, and to enter into dialogue with WTO Members.[152] In his report, the Special Rapporteur recommends that 'States be cautious about enacting 'TRIPS-plus' legislation without first understanding the impact of such legislation on the

---

[150] CHR Resolution, 'The right of everyone to the enjoyment of the highest attainable standard of physical and mental health', UN Doc. E/CN.4/RES/2002/32 of 22 April 2002.

[151] P. Hunt, 'The UN Special Rapporteur on the Right to Health: Key Objectives, Themes, and Interventions', *Health and Human Rights: An International Journal* 7 (2003) 1, 18.

[152] CHR, *The right of everyone to the enjoyment of the highest attainable standard of physical and mental health, Report of the Special Rapporteur of the Commission on Human Rights on the right of everyone to the enjoyment of the highest attainable standard of physical and mental health*, Paul Hunt, UN Doc. E/CN.4/2004/49/Add.1 (1 March 2004).

protection of human rights, including the right to health.' He goes on to add that 'wealthy countries should not pressure a developing country to implement 'TRIPS-plus' legislation, unless reliable evidence confirms that such legislation will enhance enjoyment of the right to health in the developing country.'[153] The Special Rapporteur raised similar concerns in a subsequent country mission, to Peru, in 2004, in that instance regarding the on-going US-Peru FTA negotiations. In a Press Release dated 5 July 2004 he expressly stated that 'the US-Peru trade agreement must not restrict Peru's ability to use the public health safeguards enshrined in the TRIPS and the Doha Declaration.'[154] Furthermore, in his report on Peru, he affirmed that:

> The Special Rapporteur urges Peru to take its human rights obligations into account when negotiating bilateral trade agreements. He suggests that before any trade agreement is finalized assessments identify the likely impact of the agreement on the enjoyment of the right to health, including access to essential medicines and health care, especially of those living in poverty. All stages of the negotiations must be open, transparent and subject to public scrutiny.
>
> In accordance with its human rights responsibility of international cooperation, the United States should not apply pressure on Peru to enter into commitments that either are inconsistent with Peru's constitutional and international human rights obligations, or by their nature are WTO-plus.[155]

By focusing on the risks relating to TRIPS-plus rules in the Andean FTAs, and the human rights obligations of the USA vis-à-vis third countries, the Special Rapporteur has provided invaluable tools to advocates working on access to affordable medicines in Peru and the Andean region.[156]

In addition to missions, the Special Rapporteur's mandate includes the ability to accept individual complaints of violations of the right to health.

---

[153] *Ibid.*, at para. 82.
[154] UN Press Release, 'US-Peru Trade Negotiations: Special Rapporteur on Right to Health Reminds Parties of Human Rights Obligations', 5 July 2004.
[155] The Special Rapporteur refers to 'WTO-plus' as including 'TRIPS-plus' rules Commission on Human Rights (CHR), The right of everyone to the enjoyment of the highest attainable standard of physical and mental health, Report of the Special Rapporteur, Paul Hunt, Mission to Peru, E/CN.4/2005/51/Add.3 (4 February 2005), paragraphs 50 and 51.
[156] R. Lopez Linares, '*La Salud Pública en riesgo, Los medicamentos en el TLC*', [Public Health at Risk, Medicines in FTAs] *Observatorio del Derecho a la Salud* 10, 2005, p. 10. See http://www.aislac.org/pdf/otras_publicaciones/4_saludenriesgo_tlc.pdf (accessed: 1 October 2005).

If the Special Rapporteur accepts a complaint he may send an urgent action communication to the State concerned, reminding them of their human rights obligations. These communications can be invaluable tools for human rights advocates, even if they are confidential until their publication at the CHR.

One of 3D's activities is to work with partners to encourage them to bring concrete examples, such as complaints relating to trade rules, to the attention of the different human rights mechanisms. 3D collaborated with a coalition of Thai NGOs and NGOs from EFTA countries in the submission of two requests to the Special Rapporteur on the Right to Health, in June 2005.[157] These requests urge the Special Rapporteur to send an urgent appeal communication to the governments of Thailand and the EFTA Member States reminding them of their obligations to ensure that IP rules in FTA negotiations do not undermine access to affordable medicines for all in Thailand. Also, the letters urge the Special Rapporteur to remind the Thai government and the EFTA Member States of their obligation to ensure access to information and participation in public affairs, including FTA negotiations.[158] Such an initiative can provide additional support and legitimacy to advocates and campaigners at the national level, as well as draw media and public attention to the risks involved in FTAs.[159]

The resolutions of the United Nations Commission on Human Rights

Resolutions of the UN Commission on Human Rights can also be used to ensure that States are held accountable to their duties to ensure access to affordable medicines when negotiating and implementing trade agreements into national law. Moreover, these resolutions can provide

---

[157] FTA Watch, 'Request for an urgent appeal on the impact of strict intellectual property rules in free trade agreement (FTA) on access to affordable medicines in Thailand', June 2005, http://www.ftawatch.org/autopage1/show_page.php?t=22&s_id=3&d_id=3 (accessed: 1 October 2005) and *Déclaration de Berne* and *Liechtensteinische Gesellschaft für Umweltschutz* (LGU), 'Request for an urgent appeal to stop EFTA Member States (Switzerland, Norway, Iceland and Liechtenstein), from imposing TRIPS-plus rules in free trade agreements (FTAs) with Thailand', June 2005. http://www.evb.ch/en/p25009762.html (accessed: 1 October 2005).

[158] FTA Watch, 'Request for an urgent appeal on the impact of strict intellectual property rules in free trade agreement (FTA) on access to affordable medicines in Thailand', Press Release, 15 June 2005. http://www.ftawatch.org/autopage1/show_page.php?t=22&s_id=3&d_id=3 (accessed: 15 November 2005).

[159] At the time of writing the Special Rapporteur had not yet informed the NGOs from Thailand and EFTA countries of his response to their request, September 2005.

tools to access to medicines advocates and developing country decision-makers in support of human rights-consistent trade policies. 3D participated in the 2005 Commission on Human Rights[160] in order to ensure that the resolution on access to medicines provided greater support to advocates and decision-makers. The final text of the resolution includes language that is more explicit than in previous years and requires States to undertake impact assessments of trade rules on human rights.[161] The text explicitly refers to trade agreements and makes the following recommendations:

> Urges States to consider, whenever necessary, enacting appropriate national legislation in order to use to the fullest extent the flexibilities contained in the TRIPS Agreement and encourages States to take into account such flexibilities when entering into international trade agreements that may affect public health;
>
> Calls upon States to conduct an impact assessment of the effects of international trade agreements with regard to public health and to the progressive realisation of the right of everyone to the highest attainable standard of health.[162]

3D contributed informally to the drafting of the resolution, and disseminated information on its trade-related aspects to advocates and decisionmakers working on IP and access to affordable medicines. This contributed towards giving greater exposure to the work of human rights mechanisms for a trade-orientated audience by emphasising the fact that trade-related recommendations are also being negotiated in human rights fora.[163]

Conclusion

The impact of the WTO TRIPS Agreement on access to affordable medicines is one of the first trade issues to be recognised as having clear human rights implications. It is also one of the first WTO issues to have been challenged by developing country governments backed by an unprecedented coalition of public-interest NGOs from the North and

---

[160] The 61st Session of the UN Commission on Human Rights took place from 14 March – 22 April 2005.
[161] CHR Resolutions UN Doc. E/CN.4/RES/2001/33, UN Doc E/CN.4/RES/2002/32, UN Doc E/CN.4/RES/2003/29, and UN Doc E/CN.4/RES/2004/26.
[162] CHR Resolution UN Doc. E/CN.4/RES/2005/23.
[163] ICTSD, 'Human Rights Commission Calls on States to Use TRIPS Flexibilities', *Bridges' Weekly Trade News Digest* 9 (13) (20 April 2005).

South. Since the adoption of the WTO Doha Declaration on TRIPS and Public Health and subsequent mechanisms, the TRIPS Agreement has become a reference point despite its numerous failings. This has been exacerbated by the appearance of even stricter IP rules in other trade agreements. Bilateral and regional trade agreements in particular have emerged as the main trade threats to access to affordable medicines and the enjoyment of human rights, making TRIPS appear to be the lesser evil.

The emergence of TRIPS-plus rules raises a number of questions about the ability of States to comply with their human rights obligations. This is particularly urgent and problematic, as TRIPS-plus rules restrict a State's ability to procure its most vulnerable groups with medicines at a sufficiently low cost in order to comply with the right to life and the right to health obligations. This is a question of life or death in the case of pandemics such as HIV/AIDS, tuberculosis or malaria. Moreover, the proliferation of bilateral and regional trade agreements that are negotiated in secret, without any proper consultation with civil society, raise strong concerns regarding access to information, consultation and participation of citizens in public affairs.

In the light of these political and legal developments, the NGO 3D → Trade – Human Rights – Equitable Economy tried to move the issue forward by seeking additional human rights tools that could help access to medicines advocates and developing country decision-makers in their efforts to quell TRIPS-plus rules. 3D's submissions to the UN human rights mechanisms, particularly the treaty bodies, were attempts to ensure greater accountability and transparency in the negotiation of IP rules. The submissions were also aimed at encouraging the treaty bodies to begin systematically looking at the issue of IP and access to affordable medicines. The treaty bodies began to take up the issue regularly and have made recommendations that were instrumental in helping access to medicines advocates and decision-makers to fight against the inclusion of TRIPS-plus rules in FTAs.

3D's work on IP, access to medicines and human rights emerges as an illustration of how human rights rules and mechanisms can support a more human rights-consistent approach to trade policy. It has also confirmed that in order for policy work such as this to be effective, it has to be complemented by advocacy work at the national, regional and international level. One example of a regional initiative is the NGO submission to the Inter-American Commission on Human Rights on regional economic integration in the Americas which raised concerns about IP and access to medicines amongst other issues.[164] However, if anything is to change, these NGO initiatives must be accompanied by State political action, such as human rights impact assessment of trade rules before making any trade commitments. Human rights law and mechanisms can help to ensure greater accountability in trade processes, but in order for trade rules to be more human rights consistent, political action at all levels is fundamental.

Bibliography

3D → Trade – Human Rights – Equitable Economy, 'Denmark and Italy, Trade-related intellectual property rights, access to medicines and human rights', Geneva, October 2004, http://www.3dthree.org/pdf_3D/3DCESCR-DenmarkItalyBriefOct04en.pdf (accessed: 1 October 2005)

'Access to Affordable Drugs: Victims of HIV/AIDS Should Not Suffer From Trade Rules, UN Committee Warns Botswana that US-SACU FTA Should Not Undermine Access to HIV/AIDS Treatment', Geneva, 4 October 2004, http://www.3dthree.org/ pdf_3D/BotswanaCOPressRelease_en.pdf (accessed: 1 October 2005)

'Trade-related intellectual property rights, trade in services and the fulfilment of children's rights – Botswana', Geneva, September 2004, http://www.3dthree.org/pdf_3D/ 3DCRCBotswanaSept04en.pdf (accessed: 1 October 2005)

'Access to Affordable Drugs: A Right no FTA can ignore. UN Committee Warns Ecuador that US-Andean FTA Must Not Undermine Human Rights', Press Release, 18 May 2004, http://www.3dthree.org/pdf_3D/EcuadorPress18May 04_en.pdf (accessed: 1 October 2005)

'Trade-related intellectual property rights, access to medicines and the right to health – Ecuador', April 2004, http://www.3dthree.org/pdf_3D/ 3DCESCREcuadorBrief04en. pdf (accessed: 1 October 2005)

Abbot, F.M., 'The Doha Declaration on the TRIPS Agreement and Public Health: Lighting a Dark Corner at the WTO', *JIEL* 5 (2002), 469–505

Baker, B. K., 'Process and Issues for Improving Access to Medicines, Willingness and Ability to Utilise TRIPS Flexibilities in Non-Producing Countries', *DFID Health Systems Resource Centre*, August 2004, http://www.dfidhealthrc.org/shared/publications/Issues_papers/ATM/Baker.pdf (accessed: 1 October 2005)

---

[164] *Centro de Derechos Humanos 'Miguel Agustin Pro Juarez' (Centro Pro Juarez), Los Derechos Humanos en los Procesos de Integración Económica en las Americas*, Statement for the CIDH, October 2004. See http://www.choike.org/documentos/tlc_cidh_ddhh.pdf (accessed: 1 October 2005).

Centro de Derechos Económicos y Sociales, 'Medicamentos Genéricos y Derechos Humanos', DESC Para la Acción, Boletín 1, September 2004, http://www.cdes.org.ec/biblioteca/biblioteca.html (accessed: 1 October 2005)

'Ecuador: Jefe de equipo negociador TLC contrario al Decreto Ejecutivo. Genéricos son esenciales "para el derechos a la salud" y están por sobre intereses privados y específicos', Press Release, 16 August 2004, http://www.cdes.org.ec/biblioteca/biblioteca.html (accessed: 1 October 2005)

Cuanto cuesta el derecho a la salud en Ecuador? Carta abierta al Presidente de la Republica de Ecuador, 9 July 2004 (on file with author)

Centro Pro Juarez, 'Unfulfilled Obligations, Human Rights and Free Trade Agreements in the Americas', 9 July 2004, http://www.centroprodh.org.mx/english/publications/publications/2004/alca_english_web.pdf (accessed: 1 October 2005)

'Los Derechos Humanos en los Procesos de Integración Económica en las Americas', Statement for the CIDH, October 2004 http://www.choike.org/documentos/tlc_cidh_ddhh.pdf (accessed: 1 October 2005)

Correa, C.M., 'Implementation of the WTO General Council Decision on Paragraph 6 of the Doha Declaration on the TRIPS Agreement and Public Health', WHO Essential Drugs and Medicines Policy, April 2004, http://www.who.int/medicines/areas/policy/WTO_DOHA_DecisionPara6final.pdf (accessed: 1 October 2005)

'Implications of the Doha Declaration on TRIPS and Public Health', WHO, Health Economics and Drugs EDM Series No.12, June 2002

'Implementing the TRIPS Agreement: General Context and Implications for Developing Countries', Third World Network (1998)

Cortes, K. 'Brazil Deputies Suspend Patents on AIDS Drugs', Bloomberg, 1 June 2005

Cullet, P., 'Patents and medicines: the relationship between TRIPS and the human right to health', International Affairs 79 I (2003) 139–160

Déclaration de Berne and MSF-Switzerland, 'Open letter to the trade and foreign ministers of EFTA's states', Lausanne, 2 November 2004, http://www.evb.ch/en/p25009520.html (accessed: 1 October 2005)

Déclaration de Berne and Liechtensteinische Gesellschaft für Umweltschutz, 'Southern African Countries have taken a firm stand against EFTA demands on Intellectual Property Rights in Free Trade Agreement', Press Release, Lausanne, 4 March 2005. http://www.evb.ch/en/p25009521.html (accessed: 1 October 2005)

Déclaration de Berne and Liechtensteinische Gesellschaft für Umweltschutz (LGU), 'Request for an urgent appeal to stop EFTA Member States (Switzerland, Norway, Iceland and Liechtenstein), from imposing TRIPS-plus rules in free trade agreements (FTAs) with Thailand', Lausanne, 20 June

2005, http://www.evb.ch/en/p25009762.html (accessed: 1 October 2005)

Elliot, R., *TRIPS and Rights: International Human Rights Law, Access to Medicines and the Interpretation of the WTO Agreement on Trade-Related Aspects of Intellectual Property* (Toronto: Canadian HIV/AIDS Legal Network, November 2001), http://www.aidslaw.ca/Maincontent/issues/cts/briefs/TRIPS-human-rights-briefPDF.pdf (accessed: 1 October 2005)

European Commission, Proposal for a Regulation of the European Parliament and of the Council on Compulsory Licensing of Patents Relating to the Manufacture of Pharmaceutical Products for Export to Countries with Public Health Problems, COM (04) 737, 29 October 2004

Strategy for the Enforcement of Intellectual Property Rights in Third Countries, 2005/C 129/03, 23 June 2004

Proposal for a Regulation of the European Parliament and of the Council on compulsory licensing of patents relating to the manufacture of pharmaceutical products for export to countries with public health problems, COM (2994), 29 October 2004

Fink, C. and Reichenmiller, P., 'Tightening TRIPS: The Intellectual Property Provisions of Recent US Free Trade Agreements', *World Bank Trade Note* 20 (7 February 2005)

FTA Watch, 'FTA Watch and allies sent an appeal to the Special Rapporteur, urging for monitoring of the Thai government's violation of right to access to medicines of Thai people through FTAs Thailand-the US', Press Release, 15 June 2005, http://www.ftawatch.org/autopage1/show_page.php?t=22&s_id=3&d_id=3 (accessed: 1 October 2005)

'Request for an urgent appeal on the impact of strict intellectual property rules in free trade agreement (FTA) on access to affordable medicines in Thailand', June 2005, http://www.ftawatch.org/autopage1/show_page.php?t=22&s_id=3&d_id=3 (accessed: 1 October 2005)

Hunt, P., 'The UN Special Rapporteur on the Right to Health: Key Objectives, Themes, and Interventions', *Health and Human Rights: An International Journal* 7 (2003) 1, 1–27.

International Centre for Trade and Sustainable Development, 'Human Rights Commission Calls on States to Use TRIPS Flexibilities', *Bridges' Weekly Trade News Digest* 9 (13) (20 April 2005)

Lamy, P., 'Speech of the European Commissioner for Trade at the International Conference on the 10th Anniversary of the WTO TRIPS Agreement', 23 June 2004

Leckie, S., 'The Committee on Economic, Social and Cultural Rights: Catalyst for Change in a System Needing Reform', in Alston, P. and Crawford, J., *The Future of UN Human Rights Treaty Monitoring* (Cambridge: Cambridge University Press, 2000), pp. 129–144

Lopez Linares, R., 'La Salud Pública en riesgo, Los medicamentos en el TLC',

Observatorio del Derecho a la Salud 10 (2005) http://www.aislac.org/pdf/
    otras_publicaciones/4_saludenriesgo_tlc.pdf (accessed: 1 October 2005)
Mathiason, N., 'Drugs: Round One to Africa,' *The Observer*, 22 April 2001,
    http://observer.guardian.co.uk/business/story/0,6903,476408,00.html
    (accessed: 1 October 2005)
Médecins sans Frontières, Prognosis: 'Short-Term Relief, Long-Term Pain. The
    Future of Generic Medicines Made In India', Briefing Note, 21 April 2005,
    http://www.msf.fr/documents/sida/2005–04–21-IndiaPatentsAnalysis.pdf
    (accessed: 1 October 2005)
'Access to Medicines at Risk Across the Globe: What to Watch Out For in Free
    Trade Agreements with the United States', Briefing Note, May 2004,
    http://www.accessmed-msf.org/documents/ftabriefingenglish.pdf
    (accessed: 1 October 2005)
Musungu, S. and Oh, C., *The Use of Flexibilities in TRIPS by Developing Countries:
    Can They Promote Access to Medicines?*, WHO Commission on Intellectual
    Property Rights, Innovation and Public Health, Study 4C, August 2005,
    http://www.who.int/intellectualproperty/studies/TRIPSFLEXI.pdf
    (accessed: 1 October 2005)
Oxfam International, Undermining access to medicines: Comparison of five US
    FTA's, A technical note, Oxfam Briefing Note, June 2004, http://www.oxfam.
    org.uk/what_we_do/issues/health/undermining_access_ftas.htm (accessed:
    1 October 2005).
REBRIP, Declaration of Civil Society regarding the Brazilian Negotiations for
    Voluntary Licence for Aids Drugs, Rio de Janeiro, 5 May 2005, http://lists.
    essential.org/pipermail/ip-health/2005-May/007908.html (accessed: 1 October
    2005)
Reinhard, J., 'Deprive Doha of all Substance, How through Bilateral Agreements
    EFTA States impose to Developing Countries Intellectual Property Rules on
    Medicines that are beyond the WTO Obligations and that restrict Access to
    Medicines', Lausanne: *Déclaration de Berne*, November 2004, http://www.
    evb.ch/cm_data/depriveDoha.pdf (accessed: 1 October 2005)
Roffe, P., 'Bilateral agreements and a TRIPS-plus world: the Chile-USA Free Trade
    Agreement', UNCTAD-ICTSD TRIPS Issues Papers, Ottowa: QIAP, 2004
Sell, S. K., Private Power, Public Law: The Globalisation of Intellectual Property
    Rights (Cambridge: Cambridge University Press, 2003)
UK Commission on Intellectual Property Rights, Integrating Intellectual
    Property Rights and Development Policy, February 2003, 3rd edition, http://
    www.iprcommission.org/papers/pdfs/final_report/Ch2final.pdf (accessed: 1
    October 2005)
Vandoren, P. and Van Eeckhaute, J. C., 'The WTO Decision on Paragraph 6 of the
    Doha Declaration on the TRIPS Agreement and Public Health: Making it
    Work', *Journal of World Intellectual Property* 6 (2003) 6, 779–793

Watal J., *Intellectual Property Rules in the WTO and Developing Countries* (The Hague: Kluwer Academic Publishers, 2001)

Yamin, A. E., 'Not Just a Tragedy: Access to Medications as a Right Under International Law', *Boston University International Law Journal* 21 (2003), 101–145

Yerkey, G. G. and Pruzin, D., 'United States Drops WTO Case Against Brazil Over HIV/AIDS Patent Law,' *The Bureau of National Affairs* (26 June 2001)

The Bretton Woods Institutions and Human Rights: Converging Tendencies

LAURENCE BOISSON DE CHAZOURNES

Introduction

In the early 1940s, planning for the creation of post-war institutions began, with a vision for the creation of three different international economic and financial organisations; the United States was particularly adamant in its belief that the international economy should be at the center of the new world order. At the time, these future institutions were supposed to be the International Monetary Fund (IMF), the International Bank for Reconstruction and Development (IBRD), and the International Trade Organization (ITO). This last one was never created, although the few foundations which were laid gradually evolved with the progressive institutionalisation of the GATT and, ultimately, the creation of the World Trade Organization (WTO) in 1994.[1] The IMF and the IBRD, known as the 'Bretton Woods' institutions (named after the resort at which the constitutive agreements were negotiated), officially began functioning in 1946.[2]

Parallel to the creation of these institutions, the adoption of the UN Charter in 1945, and of the Universal Declaration of Human Rights (UDHR) in 1948 by the UN General Assembly, were instrumental in bringing about another change in international relations.[3] Human rights became a matter of international concern, and they constituted one of the

---

[1] Marrakech Agreement Establishing the World Trade Organization, 15 April 1994, 33 *ILM* 1144, (1994).

[2] Articles of Agreement of the International Monetary Fund, 22 July 1944, as amended on November 11, 1992, 2 UNTS 39; Articles of Agreement of the International Bank for Reconstruction and Development, 27 December 1945, as amended on 16 February 1989, 2 UNTS 134.

[3] UDHR, adopted by the UN General Assembly, resolution 217 A (III), 10 December 1948, U.N. Doc A/810.

four purposes of the UN;[4] specific bodies and mechanisms were set up within the UN aiming at their promotion. Since then, human rights have developed tremendously, making these issues, once thought to be part of a state's *domaine reserve*, to be one of the most important concerns of the UN system, as well as of the international legal order.

Over the years, alongside these international developments, the effects of economic liberalisation on human rights issues has raised questions, initiating the relationship of the Bretton Woods institutions with human rights, a relationship which began reluctantly but has become, progressively, an alliance.[5] Although human rights have not yet become an issue in their own right on the agenda of the Bretton Woods institutions, they have nonetheless started to find a place.[6]

When dealing with the relationship of Bretton Woods institutions and human rights, one has to bear in mind that the former are international organisations, i.e. subjects of international law with a specific legal standing in the international legal order.[7] In order to ascertain the place and the role of human rights within the framework of the activities of these institutions, this issue will first be assessed in the context of the mandates of these institutions as laid down in their constitutive instruments and developed through subsequent practice. Second, an analysis of the operational and policy means which are at their disposal will be made.

---

[4] Art. 1 of the UN Charter: 'The Purposes of the United Nations are: . . . (3) To achieve international co-operation in solving international problems of an economic, social, cultural, or humanitarian character, and in promoting and encouraging respect for human rights and for fundamental freedoms for all without distinction as to race, sex, language, or religion'.

[5] See R. Dañino, 'The Legal Aspects of the World Bank's Work on Human Rights: Some Preliminary Thoughts', in P. Alston and M. Robinson (eds.), *Human Rights and Development. Towards Mutual Reinforcement* (Oxford: Oxford University Press, 2005), p. 509.

[6] For an assessment, see: *Development and Human Rights: The Role of the World Bank*, 1998. The interview with the Senior Advisor to World Bank Managing Director Mamphela Ramphele in the occasion of the Human Rights Day of 2003, is available at http://www. un.org/esa/coordination/ecosoc/hl2002/wb.pdf (accessed: 9 February 2006). With regard to the IMF, see: S. Pereira Leite, 'Human Rights and the IMF', *Finance and Development. A Quarterly Magazine of the IMF* 38 (2001), available at http://www.imf.org/external/pubs/ ft/fandd/2001/12/leite.htm (accessed: 9 February 2006).

[7] A recent judgment of the European Court of First Instance illustrates the controversy which raises the topic of the capacities of international institutions and their relations to international law. Judgment of the Court of First Instance, *Yassin Abdullah Kadi v. Council of the European Union and Commission of the European Communities*, Case T-315/01, 21 September 2005, available at http://europa.eu.int/eur-lex/lex/LexUriServ/LexUriServ. do?uri=CELEX:62001A0315:EN:HTML (accessed: 9 February 2006).

The mandate of the Bretton Woods institutions and the promotion of human rights

The purposes and the capacities of international organisations such as the World Bank[8] and the IMF, are defined by their constitutive agreements. Apart from concerns related to fair conditions of work and full employment, the constitutive agreements of these institutions give almost no place to issues other than economics. The objectives of the IBRD encompass the promotion of 'long-range balanced growth of international trade and the maintenance of equilibrium in balances of payments by encouraging international investment for the development of the productive resources of members, thereby assisting in raising productivity, the standard of living and conditions of labour in their territories'.[9] The objectives of the IMF include 'to facilitate the expansion and balanced growth of international trade, and to contribute thereby to the promotion and maintenance of high levels of employment and real income and to the development of the productive resources of all members as primary objectives of economic policy'.[10]

The IMF was to achieve its objectives by providing financial assistance to its members in order to enable them to correct disequilibriums in their balance of payments, while the IBRD was to promote reconstruction and development. Issues of human rights could, therefore, at the time of their creation, readily have been perceived as falling within their mandate and activities.[11] Reconstruction of the European economies was the foremost objective, whilst development started to become an objective of its own in

---

[8] The 'World Bank group' is made of five institutions: the International Bank for Reconstruction and Development (IBRD), established in 1944; the International Finance Corporation (IFC) and the International Development Association (IDA), respectively established in 1956 (IFC Articles of Agreement entered into force on 20 July 1956 as amended on 28 April 1993, 264 UNTS 117), and in 1960 (IDA Articles of Agreement entered into force on 24 September 1960, 6333 UNTS 439); the International Center for the Settlement of Investment-related Disputes (ICSID) set up in 1965 by the Convention on the Settlement of Investment Disputes between States and Nationals of Other States (the 'Washington Convention') entered into force on 14 October 1966, 575 UNTS 159 and the Multilateral Investment Guarantee Agency (MIGA), set up by the 1985 Convention Establishing the Multilateral Investment Guarantee Agency ('Seoul Convention') entered into force on 12 April 1988, 1508 UNTS 99 respectively. In the context of this chapter, the reference to the World Bank covers the IBRD and IDA since its creation in 1960.

[9] Art. 1(iii) of the Articles of Agreement of the IBRD.

[10] Art. 1(ii) of the Articles of Agreement of the IMF.

[11] See fn. 4 for the UN Charter's perspective in its Art. 1(3); it was negotiated during the same period.

the early 1950s. In the years which followed the establishment of the Bretton Woods institutions, the Cold War ideology dominated their functioning. The IMF and the World Bank became beacons for the 'free world' within the bipolar international politics of the Cold War, and this ideological divide was to persist for the next forty years. The history of these institutions is indelibly marked by this ideology, as free trade and the market economy came to be used by the Western countries as symbols,[12] an identity reflected by the Bretton Woods institutions, which operated in isolation from the majority of the Eastern bloc countries[13] until the fall of the Berlin Wall in 1989. Communist countries were not to become members of these organisations, although the notable exception to this rule was the People's Republic of China, which was welcomed into the fold of the Bretton Woods club with great ceremony in the early 1980s.

As previously said, during the first decades of its existence, the activities of the World Bank focused on specific projects, the purpose of which was the reconstruction of the infrastructures that suffered damage in World War II; it then turned to developmental activities, again with a similar focus on infrastructures, such as hydroelectric works.[14] This development-oriented approach was intended to achieve economic success, and other considerations were marginalised. Over time, the failure of some of the initiatives undertaken by the Bretton Woods institutions, the lessons learnt as well as the political change which occurred in the early 1990s, opened the window for a broader vision of development, and their activities consequently became more multidimensional and more centred on the individual.

Predominance of economic considerations in the decision-making process: limitations and evolution

The founders of the IBRD included a clause within the Bank's Articles of Agreement stating that only economic considerations were to be relevant

---

[12] For some Western states, liberalism was to become the predominant societal value. See J. G. Ruggie, 'International Regimes, Transactions and Change: Embedded Liberalism in the Postwar Economic Order', *International Organization* 36 (1982) 2, 379–415.

[13] While the USSR did participate at the Bretton Woods Conference, it did not ratify the agreements that were subsequently adopted. Poland left the IMF in 1950 and Czechoslovakia was excluded from the organisation in 1954. Of the former Eastern Bloc, the only country which has enjoyed uninterrupted membership of the IMF and the World Bank since their foundation in 1945 is the Former Republic of Yugoslavia, followed by Romania which became a member in 1972.

[14] See A. Rigo Sureda, 'The Law Applicable to the Activities of International Development Banks', *Recueil des Cours* 308 (2004), 29–31.

to its decision-making.[15] Whilst the Articles of Agreement of the IMF do not contain any similar provision, the organisation also excluded any questions not of an economic or financial nature from its decision-making processes;[16] this requirement of not taking into account non-economic considerations has often raised ambiguities as to its interpretation.

The attempt of the Bretton Woods institutions to take political issues outside their mandate was motivated by several preoccupations, including the fear that their assistance could be used as a political means against member States, instead of using assistance for reconstruction and development purposes. In this manner, the assistance given by the World Bank and IMF could become a tool for furthering the political interests of some member States or group of States. Moreover, giving place to political considerations was seen as putting at risk flows of capital, both private and public investments. These considerations showed their limitations over time: by the 1960s, the belief that a clear separation could be made among political, social and economic considerations started to show its limits in practice.

Whereas the dilemma of isolating economic considerations from the political ones has characterised the Bretton Woods institutions' history until recent times, this has not impeded these institutions in dealing with human rights-related issues in the context of their activities. The difficulty of keeping political considerations outside their mandate was particularly glaring in the context of the apartheid regime established in South Africa, and in the Portuguese colonial practice; several resolutions of the UN General Assembly severely condemned these countries during the 1960s. A number of these resolutions also requested 'all States and international institutions, including the specialised agencies of the UN, to withhold assistance of any kind to the Governments of

---

[15] Art. IV, Section 10 of IBRD's Articles of Agreement states under the heading 'Political Activity Prohibited' that: 'The Bank and its officers shall not interfere in the political affairs of any member; nor shall they be influenced in their decisions by the political character of the member or members concerned. Only economic considerations shall be relevant to their decisions, and these considerations shall be weighed impartially in order to achieve the purposes stated in Article 1'.

[16] See for example J. Gold, 'Interpretation: the IMF and International Law', (Kluwer Law International, London) 1996, pp. 434 et seq.; F. Gianviti, 'Economic, Social and Cultural Rights and the International Monetary Fund', IMF Conference – Washington, D.C., May 7–17, 2002, p. 5, available at http://www.imf.org/external/np/leg/sem/2002/cdmfl/eng/gianv3.pdf (accessed: 9 February 2006).

Portugal and South Africa until they renounce their policy of colonial domination and racial discrimination'.[17] For the Bretton Woods institutions these UN resolutions revealed the dilemma arising from the separation to be made between economic and political considerations; the fear of being considered as 'judges' of political regimes and the preoccupation with being used for achieving political rather than economic purposes played a significant role in creating this dilemma. In 1967, the IBRD eventually interrupted its relationships with both countries, invoking economic justifications.[18] It was considered that the political regime established in South Africa and the colonial practice of Portugal negatively affected the economic purposes of the development assistance provided by IBRD. The IMF suspended its assistance to South Africa in 1968, invoking macro-economic effects caused by the apartheid regime.[19]

Over the years, the interpretation made by the Bretton Woods institutions of the requirement of not taking into account the political situation prevailing in a country resulted in contradictory practice. Many of their clients, such as Mobutu's Zaïre, were concerned neither with the protection of human rights nor with integration into the global market economy or even with economic efficiency.[20] In contrast, when other States, such as Iran, argued that their good economic conduct meant that they should qualify for assistance, the major lenders did not hesitate to cite the internal political situations in these countries as the reason for refusing financial aid.[21]

On a few occasions, the limitations attached to the distinction between economic and political considerations – the latter being understood as including human rights considerations – were stressed.[22] The situation

---

[17] Resolution 2105 (XX), 20 December 1965. See also Resolution 2184 (XXI), 12 December 1966. See P. Pierson-Mathy, 'L'action des Nations Unies contre l'apartheid', *Revue belge de droit international* (1973), 160–177.

[18] See S.I. Skogly, *The Human Rights Obligations of the World Bank and the International Monetary Fund* (London: Cavendish, 2001), p. 9.

[19] See M. Darrow, *Between Light and Shadow: The World Bank, the International Monetary Fund and International Human Rights Law* (Oxford: Hart, 2003), p. 172.

[20] See L. Boisson de Chazournes, 'Issues of Social Development: Integrating Human Rights into the Activities of the World Bank', in Institut international des droits de l'homme, *Commerce mondial et protection des droits de l'homme, les droits de l'homme à l'épreuve de la globalisation des échanges économiques* (Brussels: Bruylant, 2001), pp. 50 *et seq.*

[21] *Ibid.*

[22] Examples include Pakistan (regarding 1998 nuclear bombing testing and 1999 military coup); Russia (regarding human rights violations in Chechnya); Indonesia (regarding East Timor referendum). See Darrow, *Between Light*, pp. 190–191.

prevailing in Myanmar enabled the World Bank to state explicitly that a country's human rights situation may create conditions that are not conducive to economic investment and that in such cases the World Bank was entitled to demand that the State in question take remedial measures. The example of Myanmar is instructive, even if it is an 'exceptional' case given the gravity and volume of the human rights violations being committed.[23] After having conducted an 'economic and social assessment' of the country in 1999, the Bank's report on Myanmar emphasised the linkages that exist between poverty, human rights violations and poor economic performance.[24] The recommendations of the World Bank's assessment stressed the need to address the connection between 'bad economic development', poverty, and threats to social cohesion these comments were taken up by the UN Secretary-General, Kofi Annan, in his report to the General Assembly in 1999.[25]

Another example is the *Chad-Cameroon Petroleum Development and Pipeline Project*,[26] which gave rise to a request brought before the World

---

[23] See *Forced Labour in Myanmar (Burma) – Report of the Commission of Inquiry appointed under Article 26 of the Constitution of the International Labor Organization to examine the observance by Myanmar of the Forced Labour Convention, 1930 (No. 29)*, ILO, Geneva, 2 July 1998, Official Bulletin *International Labor Organization*, Series B, Reports of the Committee on Freedom of Association Special Supplement, 1998, pp. 5 *et seq.*

[24] Myanmar: An Economic and Social Assessment, World Bank Poverty Reduction and Economic Management Unit, East Asia and Pacific Region. Report No 19628-BA. September, 1999. See, in particular, the section entitled 'Civil Society' (paras. 3.39 – 3.42, pp. 36–37) which begins with the following declaration:

> 'A description of the background of poverty and human development in Myanmar would be incomplete without a discussion of the human rights problems and civil conflicts that have plagued the country for many years and impeded its development. (. . .) More generally, civil society has not been able to fulfil its potential in Myanmar over the past four decades, up to today'.

The authors highlight the particular practices that aroused the indignation of the international community and led to the above-mentioned ILO Commission of Inquiry:

> 'Two major human rights issues, which are well known to the international community, are the failure of the regime to accept the results of a multi-party election held in 1992, and forced labor practices. Progress in both respects will be key to progress in human development in Myanmar [. . .]'.

[25] UN Doc. A/54/499 of 27 October 1999.

[26] World Bank Inspection Panel Report, *Chad-Cameroon Petroleum and Pipeline Project* (Loan No. 4558-CD); *Petroleum Sector Management Capacity Building Project* (Credit No. 3373-CD); and *Management of the Petroleum Economy* (Credit No. 3316-CD), 17 September 2002, pp. 60–63, available at http://wbln0018.worldbank.org/ipn/ipnweb.nsf/ 8442778ba27b386185256878000a5e6a/66acde37a016f16685256c37006465d6/$FILE/Cha d%20Investigation%20Final%20Report.pdf, (accessed: 9 February 2006).

Bank Inspection Panel,[27] in the context of which, the Bank's management stated that human rights issues are of relevance to the Bank only if 'they may have a significant direct economic effect on the project'[28] and the Inspection Panel considered that '(it) felt obliged to examine whether the issues of proper governance or human rights violations in Chad were such as to impede the implementation of the Project in a manner compatible with the Bank's policies'.[29]

As can be noted, the requirement to only take into account economic considerations has shown its limitations over time, and its interpretation has evolved. The entanglement of economic and human rights considerations clearly emerged in the 1990s; the World Bank now admits that certain patterns of violations of human rights in a country may have so-called 'direct economic effects' on a project, and this requires the institution to reconsider its financing activities with a country.

The early 1990s also saw a revamping of Chapter VII of the UN Charter with the resort by the Security Council to binding decisions imposing trade and financial sanctions; political considerations and human rights violations could constitute reasons for the imposition of UN sanctions. In this context, the position taken by the World Bank is interesting as it once more highlights the limitations of the requirement of not taking into account non-economic considerations. The then General Counsel, Ibrahim Shihata, stated that 'if the UN Security Council decides, as it did in 1992 with respect to the Federal Republic of Yugoslavia, that it members must not make available any funds to a

---

[27] On this mechanism, see below, Part II B.

[28] In particular, the Management stated in its Response to the Panel that:

> 'The Bank is concerned about violations of human rights in Chad as elsewhere while respecting the Bank's Articles of Agreement which require the Bank to focus on economic considerations and not on political or other non-economic influences as the basis for its decisions. In evaluating the economic aspects of any project, human rights issues may be relevant to the Bank's work if they may have a significant direct economic effect on the project. Having carefully considered all aspects of this issue, Management's conclusion is that the Project can achieve its developmental objectives'.

> Bank Management Response to Request for Inspection Panel Review of the Chad-Cameroon Petroleum Development and Pipeline Project, Chad Petroleum Sector Management Capacity Building Project, and Chad Management of the Petroleum Economy Project, 10 May 2001, p. 47, para.151, available at http://siteresources.worldbank.org/EXTINSPECTIONPANEL/Resources/ManagementResponse051001.pdf (accessed: 9 February 2006).

[29] World Bank Inspection Panel Report, *Chad-Cameroon Petroleum and Pipeline Project*, see fn. 26, pp. 62–63, para. 215.

member country and calls on international organisations to do the same, the Bank will not be in position to ignore this decision in reliance on its Articles'.[30] The IMF has not so far stated in explicit terms its position with respect to taking into account sanctions imposed by the Security Council.

The evolution of the concept of development in the post-Cold War period: towards a comprehensive and participative development

The taking into account of human rights considerations should also be assessed within the context of the evolution of the World Bank and IMF development activities. During the first decades of their functioning, development was conceived by the Bretton Woods institutions in purely macro-economic terms. In the 1960s, however, the World Bank started to include health, education and housing projects in its portfolio. These projects took flight in the context of the theory of 'essential needs' elaborated in alternative development circles and taken up by Robert MacNamara, the then President of the World Bank; a broader vision of development started to emerge.

The first example of social programming by the World Bank was a project focusing on education set up with the Philippines in 1961,[31] and it was at this time that the Bank first began to read its mandate from a multidimensional perspective and to redefine its activities accordingly. The establishment of the International Development Association (IDA) in 1960 provided confirmation of the expansion of the World Bank's activities. The IDA was specifically mandated to provide favourable terms of credit for social development projects in the least developed countries. The IMF also viewed an enlargement of the reading of its mandate; during the second revision of the Fund's Articles of Agreement in 1976,[32] following debate over the adoption of provisions relating to supervision

---

[30] See also: I. F. I. Shihata, 'The Relationships between the United Nations and the World Bank', in I. F. I. Shihata, *The World Bank Legal Papers* (The Hague/Boston/London: Kluwer Law International, 2000), pp. 808–810. See Guidelines on Procurement under IBRD Loans and IDA Credits, May 2004, 1.13, p. 8, available at http://siteresources.worldbank.org/INTPROCUREMENT/Resources/Procurement-May-2004.pdf (accessed: 9 February 2006), which contain a provision reflecting the above-mentioned statement. As a reminder, Art. 103 of the United Nations Charter reads as follows: 'In the event of a conflict between the obligations of the Members of the United Nations under the present Charter and their obligations under any other international agreement, their obligations under the present Charter shall prevail.'

[31] Rigo Sureda, 'The Law Applicable', pp. 192–205.

[32] These modifications to the Articles of Agreement of the IMF were approved by the Board of Governors in its resolution no. 31–4 of 30 April 1976 and came into effect on 1 April 1978.

of exchange arrangements, a reference to the social policies of the organisation's Member States was inserted.[33]

During the 1980s, the World Bank began to approach questions of judicial reform, the promotion of the rule of law, popular participation and the issue of good governance, and the issue of environmental protection also became increasingly prominent. Officially, however, the Bank's focus remained economic efficiency and effective financial management; nevertheless, it did not oppose the movement towards an enlargement of its operations to incorporate issues of social and sustainable development. This trend was reinforced by the far-reaching changes occurring in Eastern Europe that culminated in the eventual disintegration of the USSR. At the end of the 1990s, the financial crisis that erupted in Asia, Russia and Mexico highlighted the serious and negative impact of volatile

---

[33] According to the Second Amendment of the Articles in 1978, the IMF is endowed with the responsibility of overseeing the exchange rate policies of member States. Art. IV, Section III reads as follows:

> 'a) The Fund shall oversee the international monetary system in order to ensure its effective operation, and shall oversee the compliance of each member with its obligations under Section 1 of this Article.
>
> b) In order to fulfil its functions under (*a*) above the Fund shall exercise firm surveillance over the exchange rate policies of members, and shall adopt specific principles for the guidance of all members with respect to those policies. Each member shall provide the Fund with the information necessary for such surveillance, and, when requested by the Fund, shall consult with it on the member's exchange rate policies. The principles adopted by the Fund shall be consistent with cooperative arrangements by which members maintain the value of their currencies in relation to the value of the currency or currencies of other members, as well as with other exchange arrangements of a member's choice consistent with the purposes of the Fund and Section 1 of this Article. These principles shall respect the domestic social and political policies of members, and in applying these principles the Fund shall pay due regard to the circumstances of members'.

The Executive Board decision of 1977 (Decision No. 5392, as amended), which took effect when the Second Amendment entered into force in 1978, clarifies the principles underlying this surveillance responsibility:

> 'The Fund's appraisal of a member's exchange rate policies (. . .) shall be made within the framework of a comprehensive analysis of the general economic situation and economic policy strategy of the member, and shall recognise that domestic as well as external policies can contribute to timely adjustment of the balance of payments. The appraisal shall take into account the extent to which the policies of the member, including its exchange rate policies, serve the objectives of the continuing development of the orderly underlying conditions that are necessary for financial stability, the promotion of sustained sound economic growth, and reasonable levels of employment'.

capital movements in societies lacking regulatory or institutional safe-guards. Attention thus eventually focused on the rules, institutions and mechanisms in place in those countries and their inability to respond to the vagaries of international capital markets.

The reforms undertaken by the Bretton Woods institutions at the end of the 1990s have further opened the institutions to a more inclusive nature of the concept of development. As an example, the 'Comprehensive Development Framework' (CDF)[34] presented in 1999 by the then President of the World Bank, James Wolfensohn, placed economic and financial concerns on the same footing as social justice, culture and respect for the rule of law, thereby advocating a more holistic approach to development than that which has been previously taken by the Bank. The comprehensive character of development is also reflected in the proclaimed objectives of the World Bank, in which the fight against poverty plays a central role. For the Bank, poverty is 'more than inadequate income or human development – it is also vulnerability and lack of voice, power and representation.'[35] The significance of social equity for attaining long-term development is stressed in the context of the Bank's 2006 Development Report.[36] The changed paradigm of development also includes a social participation process encompassing issues of openness and transparency. Development goals and strategies should be 'owned' by countries and their design should make room for public involvement.[37]

---

[34] This document was elaborated by the former President of the World Bank, James Wolfensohn, and subsequently approved by the Bank's administrators in 1999. Information on the CDF is available at: http://web.worldbank.org/WBSITE/EXTER-NAL/PROJECTS/STRATEGIES/CDF/0,pagePK:60447~theSitePK:140576,00.html (accessed: 9 February 2006).

[35] World Bank, World Development Report 2000/2001, *Attacking Poverty*, p. 12. The extensive nature of the World Bank's activities is illustrated by some data on the lending activities of the Bank. For example during the 2005 fiscal year, the World Bank lending for governance, public sector reform and promotion of the rule of law totalled $ 2.9 billion. This represents approximately 13% of the Bank's total new lending. Lending Data, *The World Bank Annual Report*, 1 July 2004 to 30 June 2005. Information available at http://web.worldbank.org/WBSITE/EXTERNAL/EXTABOUTUS/EXTANNREP/EXTAN NREP2K5/0,contentMDK:20639643~menuPK:1578490~pagePK:64168445~piPK:6416 8309~theSitePK:1397343,00.html (accessed: 9 February 2006).

[36] World Bank, World Development Report 2006, *Equity and Development*. See Dañino, 'The Legal Aspects', p. 514, see fn. 5.

[37] World Bank, *Toward Country-led Development A Multi-Partner Evaluation of the Comprehensive Development Framework*, Synthesis Report, 2003, available at http://lnweb18.worldbank.org/oed/oeddoclib.nsf/DocUNIDViewForJavaSearch/8746BD3C3A 06832285256DAC005872C0/$file/synthesis_report.pdf (accessed: 9 February 2006).

The IMF gradually moved towards an approach favouring a multidimensional and participative understanding of development.[38] Whilst remaining focused on monetary, fiscal and exchange rate policy issues, the organisation shares with the World Bank a comprehensive understanding of the notion of development.[39] The Mexican crisis of 1994–95 and the 1990s Asian crisis underscored the fact that economic and financial policies of one country may affect many other countries, and also illustrated the need to strengthen the monitoring of economic and financial national strategies in order to prevent financial crisis. In this context the mechanisms dealing with international financial cooperation are essential and the IMF, with its nearly universal membership of 184 countries, can help in this task. In particular, through a consultation process carried out under Art. IV of its Articles of Agreement, the IMF can exercise surveillance over the exchange rate policies of its member countries.[40] Whereas the objectives of its surveillance activity remain the same as those foreseen by its constitutive agreement, its framework has evolved significantly, now covering a wide range of institutional and structural policies.[41]

In the 1980s, with the establishment of a concessional facility designed for countries having protracted balance of payments problems, the IMF started to deal with poverty alleviation, and its involvement in this area has been strengthened by the creation of the Poverty Reduction and Growth Facility (PRGF) in 1999. In the design of the Poverty Reduction Strategy Papers (PRSPs) which serve as a framework for requesting loans to the Facility, considerations concerning human rights issues can be included.[42] Whilst the IMF is increasingly placing emphasis on good

---

[38] S. Pereira Leite, 'Human Rights and the IMF', see fn. 6. In this regard, the then IMF General Counsel and Director of the Legal Department François Gianviti stated however, that: 'The Fund is a monetary agency, not a development agency. While its mandate and policies have evolved over time, it remains a monetary agency, charged with the responsibility to maintain orderly exchange rates and a multilateral systems of payments free of restriction on current payments'. F. Gianviti, 'Economic, Social and Cultural Rights and the International Monetary Fund', see fn. 16, p. 42.

[39] See the joint statement made by the two presidents in 2000. *The IMF and the World Bank Group: an enhanced partnership for sustainable growth and poverty reduction*, Joint Statement by Horst Köhler and James Wolfensohn, 5 September 2000, available at http://www.imf.org/external/np/omd/2000/part.htm (accessed: 9 February 2006).

[40] Art. IV, Section III, see fn. 29.

[41] There are calls for also including social issues during the consultation process. See *Independent Evaluation Office – Evaluation of Fiscal Adjustment in IMF-Supported Programs*, September 2003, available at http://www.imf.org/External/NP/ieo/2003/fis/pdf/all.pdf (accessed: 9 February 2006).   [42] *Ibid.*

governance issues in its policy advice, financial and technical assistance to member States,[43] its understanding of good governance is still being centred on economic aspects of governance that could have a significant macroeconomic impact.

Calls for having the World Bank and the IMF involved in the realisation of the Millennium Development Goals (MDGs) were strong at the Monterrey Conference held in 2002.[44] The endorsement of the MDGs by the Bretton Woods institutions contributed to further the multidimensional character of development. In order to achieve the MDGs, the World Bank is targeting investments towards education, health as well as the expansion of the borrower capacity to provide basic services such as water supply and sanitation services.[45] The IMF is also involved in the realisation of the MDGs through the poverty reduction strategies that it has put in place. Poverty Reduction Strategy Papers may introduce

---

[43] In this regard in 1996, the Board of Governors of the IMF adopted a declaration to 'promote good governance in all its aspects, including by ensuring the rule of law, improving the efficiency and accountability of the public sector, and tackling corruption, as essential elements of a framework within which economies can prosper'. *Partnership for Sustainable Global Growth*, Interim Committee Declaration Washington, D.C. 29 September 1996 http://www.imf.org/external/np/sec/pr/1996/pr9649.htm#partner. See also *The Role of the IMF in Governance Issues: Guidance Note*, approved by the IMF Executive Board on 25 July 1997 (http://www.imf.org/external/pubs/ft/exrp/govern/govindex.htm) and *Executive Board Reviews IMF's Experience in Governance Issues*, 28 March 2001, available at http://www.imf.org/external/np/gov/2001/eng/report.htm (accessed: 9 February 2006).

[44] UN, *Monterrey Consensus of the International Conference on Financing for Development*, Monterrey, 1 March 2002, A/ CONF/198, paras. 63 and 71. See Dañino, 'The Legal Aspects', see fn.5, p. 521. On the relation between human rights and the MDGs see the Sachs Report affirming that: 'Human rights are both a central practical objective of good governance and a normative standard agreed to by all signatories to the UN Millennium Declaration. The declaration reaffirmed the commitment of all signatory nations to respect and uphold the principles identified in the Universal Declaration of Human Rights and to fully protect social, cultural, economic, and political rights for all, including the right to development'. Millenium Project, *Investing in Development, A Practical Plan to Achieve the Millenium Development Goals*, Earthscan (2005), p. 118, available at http://www.unmillenniumproject.org/documents/MainReportComplete-lowres.   pdf (accessed: 9 February 2006).

[45] IDA, Report from the Executive Directors of the International Development Association to the Board of Governors, Additions to IDA Resources: Fourteenth Replenishment, *Working Together to Achieve the Millennium Development Goals*, approved by the Executive Directors of IDA on 10 March 2005, http://siteresources.worldbank.org/IDA/Resources/14th_Replenishment_Final.pdf (accessed: 9 February 2006). See also the World Bank, Global Monitoring Report *Millennium Development Goals: from consensus to momentum*, 2005. http://siteresources.worldbank.org/GLOBALMONITORINGEXT/Resources/complete.pdf (accessed: 9 February 2006).

structural and social policies that are needed to improve health and education, safeguard the environment, and combat diseases.[46]

Over time the Bretton Woods institutions have increasingly paid attention to a broader range of matters such as governance, health, education and housing,[47] and the proportion of social projects has consequently vastly increased. The World Bank's projects in 2005 regarding public sector governance, environmental protection, and social and human development represent more than half of the IBRD/IDA lending activities[48] and this evolution, which has paved the way for the promotion of human rights, was made possible through the use of various modes of intervention.

The promotion and protection of human rights in the activities of the Bretton Woods institutions: on linkages

The wide range of possibilities of interventions along with the development of several normative and institutional instruments adopted by the Bretton Woods institutions have favoured an evolving interpretation of their mandates, and an analysis of those mandates promotes understanding of the increasing role played by these institutions in the human rights field. Given its rather technical objectives and its less operational nature, the IMF has developed fewer instruments which allow it to play a role in the human rights field; however, the fact that it has been progressively involved in poverty reduction activities – for example, through the establishment of the above-mentioned Poverty Reduction Facility – has made room for human rights issues. Moreover, the 2002 Monterrey Consensus highlighted the role of the World Bank and the IMF in meeting the MDGs and gave an opportunity for the inclusion of social policy considerations in their activities.[49]

Financing activities and the promotion of human rights

The broad interpretation of their mandate, together with a far-reaching concept of development, have empowered the Bretton Woods institutions

---

[46] See *The IMF and the Millennium Development Goals*, 2005, available at http://www.imf.org/external/np/exr/facts/mdg.htm (accessed: 9 February 2006).

[47] See the interview with the Senior Advisor to World Bank Managing Director Mamphela Ramphele in the occasion of the Human Rights Day of 2003, see fn. 6.

[48] See *Lending Data*, *The World Bank Annual Report*, 1 July 2004 to 30 June 2005, see fn. 35.

[49] UN, *Monterrey Consensus of the International Conference on Financing for Development*, see fn. 44.

in the development of means for legitimising their activities, to increase public participation and to create mechanisms of accountability.[50] These institutions have also extended their modes of intervention and developed normative instruments. In the first decades of their activities, each financial institution had a role to play; on the one hand, the World Bank provided loans for projects in various countries in order to promote development and reconstruction, whilst on the other hand, the IMF supported countries with problems in their balance of payments. However, over time this distinction has become blurred. Since the 1980s, the World Bank has been financing structural adjustment programs, an activity also pursued by the IMF. Whilst pursuing funding mechanisms to helping low-income countries, the IMF began to run activities similar to those of the World Bank in the area of governance, rule of law and organised crime.

Originally, the World Bank's primary means of intervention was meant to be the granting of loans for specific projects. The World Bank's Articles of Agreement allow the institution to lend money for non-specific projects and activities only in exceptional cases; over the years, however, the exception has become a principle of action together with the financing of specific projects. During the 1980s, the World Bank began to provide loans for the purpose of structural adjustment.

The oil crises and the ensuing increase in the price of 'black gold' on the global market, as well as some of the economic policies implemented by the recipient States, were used by the Bretton Woods institutions as justification for the promotion of structural adjustment programs. Loans were therefore granted to recipient States to allow them to undertake the reforms necessary in order to attain the goal of balancing their external trade. These loans imposed conditions on the countries regarding fiscal policy, free trade, or public affairs management. The social consequences of these programmes (including layoffs, reductions in public spending, and overall increased vulnerability for certain segments of the population) were criticised by UN specialised agencies, such as the UNDP and UNICEF, and were equally criticised by civil society, which had begun to organise itself both at the national and international levels.[51]

---

[50] Rigo Sureda, 'The Law Applicable', p. 247.
[51] See P. Klein, 'Les institutions financières internationales et les droits de la personne', *Revue belge de droit international* (1999), 97–114.

During the 1990s, as a result of the failures of previous initiatives and confronted with the task of integrating the needs of the newly arrived Eastern bloc countries, the Bretton Woods institutions engaged themselves in a process of reshaping their structural adjustment programmes, which allowed for an increased focus on human rights considerations. Social safety nets were put in place. The notion of social safety covers actions to diminish the consequences of economic redress measures and to promote better social protection.[52] These remedial actions were conceived for those who may suffer damages due to the implementation of a programme supported by the World Bank and the IMF.[53] Social safety nets can take many forms; they can integrate subsidies or cash compensation directed at the most disadvantaged segments of the population, and may also take into account improved distribution of essential commodities, such as medicines, as well as temporary price controls on some essential commodities. These remedial actions help States protect the most vulnerable segments of their population during the adjustment period. In most cases, the IMF largely relies on the World Bank to take the lead in the design of social safety nets, which are then incorporated into IMF-supported programs.[54] Projects which lead to the closure of factories and large-scale layoffs may include the allocation of funds for financial compensation or to facilitate professional reintegration.

Social safety nets can also take the form of social funds.[55] Whilst at the beginning these funds were conceived as short-term instruments dealing with emergency situations, in recent times they have been used for local development purposes with a focus on the participation of local communities. For instance, social funds may finance small projects ranging from infrastructure and social services to training and micro-enterprise

[52] See 'Managing the Social Consequences of Economic Crises', *Workshop on Social Policy Principles and The Social Development Agenda* (Carnegie Council on Ethics and International Affairs), 3–5 December 1999. This document is an extract from 'Managing the Social Dimensions of Crises: Good Practices in Social Policy' (presented at the Fall 1999 meetings of the Development Committee), available at http://www.worldbank.org/poverty/library/index.htm (accessed: 9 February 2006).

[53] See T. Lane, A. Ghosh, J. Hamann, S. Phillips, M. Schulze-Ghattas, and T. Tsikata, 'IMF-Supported Programs in Indonesia, Korea, and Thailand: A Preliminary Assessment', *IMF Occasional Paper* 178 (1999).

[54] S. Gupta, L. Dicks-Mireaux, R. Khemani, C. McDonald, and M. Verhoeven, 'Social Issues in IMF-Supported Programs', *IMF Occasional Paper* 191 (2000).

[55] In 1986, the first social fund, the Bolivian Emergency Social Fund, was created. See *The World Bank Participation Sourcebook*, 1996, available at http://www.worldbank.org/wbi/sourcebook/sb0405t.htm#E2 (accessed: 9 February 2006).

development projects that have been identified by the communities, and they may be managed by a wide range of actors, including local governments, NGOs, community groups and local project committees.[56]

Following the Mexican economic crisis of 1994–1995 and that of 1997, the shockwaves from which were felt in Asia and then in Russia, as well as in Latin America, the Bretton Woods institutions intervened in order to assist the affected countries. Through the granting of stabilisation loans, the World Bank supported (with a loan of several billion dollars) South Korea, which at that time was unable to cope with the simultaneous withdrawal of a large amount of private capital from its financial markets. This financial crisis brought to the fore the role of the IMF and the World Bank (to a lesser extent) as the financiers of globalisation. The question remains whether the public funds being lent by these institutions should be used, as they have been, to repay the debts incurred by political and economic elites in developing countries to the credit of private investors (the majority of which are European or North American), attracted by the idea of investing in developing markets but very quick to withdraw their funds at the smallest sign of instability. This uncontrolled capital movement has rocked the economic systems of the countries concerned to the extent that they have collapsed, to the great detriment of local populations who have suffered in return large-scale retrenchments, programs of austerity and other drastic measures.[57]

These problems lie at the heart of considerations on the future role of the IMF and its relationship with the World Bank in what should become a new financial system.[58] The move from a 'real economy' of production to a 'symbolic economy' of finance, forces the role of these financial institutions, which were created in a period of real economy, to be questioned. In particular, their role with regard to the beneficiaries of development activities – that is, the populations of recipient countries rather than the creditors, investors or other speculators on the international stock market – should be considered with a view to ascertaining whether the symbolic economy is beneficial to the populations in recipient countries.

---

[56] M. Bhatia, 'Social Funds: A Review of Public Sector Management and Institutional Issues, Social Protection', Social Protection Unit, Human Development Network, World Bank, Discussion Paper Series, No. 0508 (2005).

[57] L. Boisson de Chazournes, 'Issues of Social Development'.

[58] See A. Swoboda, 'Reforming the International Financial Architecture', Finance and Development. A Quarterly Magazine of the IMF 36 (1999), available at http://www.imf.org/external/pubs/ft/fandd/1999/09/swoboda.htm (accessed: 9 February 2006).

Other considerations relate to the role that the Bretton Woods institutions may play in the context of national policies. As lenders, these institutions have a dominant position in their dialogue with recipient States and they may use this position to take social considerations into account. The World Bank's power is even greater if one keeps in mind the fact that it frequently presides over groups of lenders and is therefore able to direct decision-making in the area of public financing. The institution also plays the role of mediator (or facilitator) in the context of financial operations involving a number of different public and private partners and, as a result, it is able to affect the choices and decision-making of States in areas such as social or environmental protection.[59]

Debt reduction strategies have recently included a social dimension which allows human rights considerations to play a role. Those adopted in the 1980s were essentially financial in nature, aiming at rescheduling private loans, negotiating new loans, or repurchasing. By contrast, those implemented in the 1990s are more concerned with public debts and with the incorporation of a social dimension into the debt reduction programs. In 1996 the World Bank and IMF established a programme to alleviate the servicing of multilateral debts to Heavily Indebted Poor Countries (HIPC) under the condition that a portion of the unused amount be used for social development activities.[60] The 1999 enhancements of the HIPC Programme along with the calls made by the 2002 Monterrey Conference in 2002[61] have strengthened the links between debt relief and social policies such as poverty reduction and the achievement of the MDGs.

The G-8 Summit held at Gleneagles in 2005 favoured an agreement on the cancellation of the debts owed by eligible HIPCs to IDA, the IMF and the African Development Fund.[62] Following the statement made by the G-8, the IMF Executive Board discussed the G-8 proposal, saying that they 'reiterated their commitment to further debt relief by the IMF as

---

[59] On the importance of this role, see *Review of Aid Coordination in an Era of Poverty Reduction Strategies* (IDA Review 2001), 1 May 2001.

[60] Resolution on the Establishment of the Heavily Indebted Poor Countries (HIPC) Debt Initiative Trust Fund, 36 *ILM* 990 (1997). See also Modifications to the Heavily Indebted Poor Countries (HIPC) Initiative, 23 July 1999, available at http://www.imf.org/external/np/hipc/modify/hipc.htm (accessed: 9 February 2006).

[61] On the occasion of the 2002 Monterrey Conference, the role of the HIPC for achieving the MDGs was highlighted. UN, *Monterrey Consensus of the International Conference on Financing for Development*, see fn. 44, para. 49.

[62] G-8, Chair's Summary, Gleneagles Summit, 8 July 2005, available at http://www.g8.gov.uk/servlet/Front?pagename=OpenMarket/Xcelerate/ShowPage&c=Page&cid=1119518698846 (accessed: 9 February 2006).

part of the international support for low-income countries.'[63] The HIPC might be a privileged framework for developing new forms of interactions between social and economic considerations, even though it should not be understood as a panacea.

Due to the increased attention being given to the social dimensions of its operations, the World Bank has developed some normative and institutional instruments over time, which play an important role in operationalising human rights. The most important ones are the Operational Policies and Procedures (hereinafter: 'operational policies')[64] designed to guide World Bank staff in the preparation, assessment and implementation of the projects it finances. Originally, these instruments were conceived as aspirational targets drawn from practice and enshrined in policy documents to provide the Bank staff with guidance when designing or implementing operational activities. These policies have increasingly become considered to be indispensable means in assessing the quality of Bank-financed activities,[65] including as vehicles for promoting the implementation of human rights. Such is the case with the operational policies dealing with the conduct of environmental impact studies, compensation of people displaced as a result of a project, the protection of indigenous peoples, and the fight against poverty.[66]

---

[63] IMF, Statement by the IMF Managing Director Following Executive Board Discussion on the G-8 Proposal for Further Debt Relief, Press Release No. 05/183, 3 August 2005, available http://www.imf.org/external/np/sec/pr/2005/pr05183.htm (accessed: 9 February 2006). With respect to the World Bank, at the UN High-level Dialogue on Financing for Development in New York (New York, 27–28 June 2005, UN Doc. A/60/219), the World Bank's Chief Economist, François Bourguignon, welcomed the G-8 proposal to cancel the debt of the poorest countries and the agreement to fully cover the costs of the debt relief. World Bank, News, G-8 Gleneagles Summit and Development, 1 July 2005, available at http://web.worldbank.org/WBSITE/EXTERNAL/NEWS/0,contentMDK:20567463~pagePK:64257043~piPK:437376~theSitePK:4607,00.html (accessed: 9 February 2006).

[64] L. Boisson de Chazournes, 'Policy Guidance and Compliance: The World Bank Operational Standards' in Shelton, D. (ed.), Commitment and Compliance (Oxford: Oxford University Press, 2000), pp. 281–303.

[65] Various events in the early 1990s contributed to this change of perception, especially the release of two reports commissioned by the Bank: the Morse Report, an independent review of highly-criticised projects known as the 'Narmada Projects', and the Wapenhans Report, an internal review of Bank operations commissioned by its President in the wake of the Morse Report to assess the implications of Bank-financed projects and to draw some lessons and recommendations on how to improve their effectiveness. B. Morse and T.R. Berger, Sardor Sarovar: The Report of the Independent Review Resource Futures International Inc., Ottawa. (1992) and World Bank, Effective Implementation: Key to Development Impact (R92–125), 3 November 1992.

[66] See OP/BP 4.01 on Environmental Assessment OP/BP 4.12 on Involuntary Resettlement; OP/BP 4.10 on Indigenous Peoples, OP. 1.0 on Poverty Reduction. All World Bank

Environmental and social policies are geared towards an elaborated consideration of international good practices as reflected in international agreements and instruments adopted in the UN arenas and other fora. In the design and implementation of its policies, the World Bank does not operate in isolation and its operational policies reflect many concerns expressed in various international fora. The relationship between these policies and international law standards highlight their mutually reinforcing contribution to the promotion of human rights and the rule of law.

Operational policies also expressly refer to international principles and rules as a means of identifying the good and best practices to be followed. They provide guidance and help identify the minimum standards to be complied with in a Bank project. The operational policy on 'management of cultural property in Bank-financed projects', for example, makes explicit reference to country obligations under international treaties concerning cultural property, such as the 1972 Convention Concerning the Protection of the World Cultural and Natural Heritage.[67] Although some operational policies make precise reference to various international instruments,[68] they do not exclude the possibility of taking into account other instruments not explicitly mentioned, such as human rights instruments. International treaties or instruments of a programmatic nature may provide guidance in the context of the application of the World Bank operational policies.

operational policies and procedures are available at http://wbln0018.worldbank.org/institutional/manuals/opmanual.nsf/284229c803270fad8525705a00112597/4f259df5b66ff0e e8525705c0022f931?OpenDocument (accessed: 9 February 2006). In particular, paragraph 1 of the operational policy on indigenous peoples explicitly states that: 'This policy contributes to the Bank's mission of poverty reduction and sustainable development by ensuring that the development process fully respects the dignity, human rights, economies, and cultures of Indigenous Peoples'.

[67] The 1972 Convention Concerning the Protection of the World Cultural and Natural Heritage is given as a reference for defining the notion of cultural property (See OP 4.11, para. 2(a)). OP 4.11 is under preparation; until it is issued, the Bank staff is guided by the provisions of Operational Policy Note (OPN) 11.03. See fn. 66.

[68] For instance the OP 4.09 on Pest Management Minimum Standards employs definitions with reference to the FAO's Guidelines for Packaging and Storage of Pesticides (1985), Guidelines on Good Labeling Practice for Pesticides (1985) and Guidelines for the Disposal of Waste Pesticide and Pesticide Containers on the Farm (1985). See also the policy on application of Environmental Assessment to projects involving pest management (BP 4.01-Annex C), which refers to the WHO Classification of Pesticides by Hazard and Guidelines to Classification (1994–1995) and to the UN Consolidated List of Products Whose Consumption and/or Sale have been Banned, Withdrawn, Severely Restricted or not Approved by Governments (1994). See the OP 4.09 on Pest Management Minimum Standards and OP/BP 4.01 on Environmental Assessment, see fn. 66.

The policies on environmental assessment, indigenous populations and involuntary resettlement require that projects financed by the Bank take into account the domestic legal order of the borrowing country, and that the Bank should exercise due diligence and good faith in assessing the legal situation prevailing in a borrowing country, including the international commitments the country has undertaken. Clearly, various means exist for the integration of international commitments into domestic legal orders, be it through enabling legislation, direct incorporation or by other means that make international requirements part of the domestic legal order of the borrower. Such requirements may then be taken into consideration when implementing the relevant operational policies. Normally the Bank's policies will correspond to the domestic legal order, but in some cases these policies may override the relevant national requirements and call for the application of higher standards.

The interactions between international law instruments and operational policies underline the pragmatic nature of these policies, which aim to identify and implement the best practices to promote compliance with international law requirements. The fact that the international instruments to which a borrowing country has committed itself should be taken into consideration, or should be considered as reflecting agreed international good and best practices, shows the close relationship of the operational standards with international law principles and standards in areas covered by them. It also demonstrates the virtues of operational policies and procedures in promoting the implementation of international law instruments. Operational policies constitute a means by which new patterns of behaviour are encouraged in borrowing countries; as such, they favour the emergence or consolidation of international practices which may acquire the status of customary norms.

As a general requirement, first stated in a policy adopted in 1984,[69] the Bank has committed itself not to finance projects that contravene

---

[69] See OMS 2.36 on Environmental Aspects of Bank Work (1984). The provision reads: 'The Bank will not finance projects that contravene any international environmental agreement to which the member country concerned is a party'. See also Operational Policy (OP 4.36 on Forestry and Operational Policy (OP) 4.01 on Environment Assessment. The provision of the OP 4.36 reads: 'Governments must also commit to adhere to their obligations as set forth in relevant international instruments to which they are a party'. The relevant part of the policy on Environment Assessment reads: '[E]A . . . takes into account the obligations of the country, pertaining to project activities, under relevant international environmental treaties and agreements. The Bank does not finance project activities that would contravene such country obligations, as identified during the EA'. See fn. 56.

international environmental agreements to which the concerned member country is a party. This requirement not only shapes the conduct of the Bank with respect to international environmental agreements, but also increases the awareness of borrowing countries to the significance of international law standards and the importance of implementing them, and, as has been observed, this requirement not to contravene international law should find application in other areas than international environmental law:

> 'The IBRD is rightly concerned with its borrowers respecting the treaties that bind them in the course of its operations. In its work, there should not be any question that the IBRD is bound to respect them. Itself should not be instrumental in creating opportunities for the violation of human rights.'[70]

The relationship between operational policies and human rights was highlighted in the context of the request brought before the World Bank Inspection Panel in the *Chad-Cameroon Petroleum Development and Pipeline Project*.[71] The Inspection Panel considered whether the situation of human rights in Chad was such 'to impede the implementation of the Project in a manner compatible with the Bank's policies' and it concluded 'the Panel observes that the situation is far from ideal. It raises questions about compliance with Bank policies, in particular those that relate to informed and open consultation'.[72] The report of the World Bank Inspection Panel illustrates the links between compliance with operational policies and the protection of human rights, and it also confirms the importance of the involvement of public participation in the design and implementation of projects. Human rights give body to the interpretation of this principle.

Public participation and accountability, with special emphasis on the World Bank Inspection Panel

Public participation has gained an important status in the context of the World Bank operations. It is an operative and interactive notion which includes the concepts of transparency and access to justice. It reveals the growing importance of individuals and local groups in decision-making processes at the local, national and international levels. Resolutions of the

---

[70] Rigo Sureda, 'The Law Applicable', p. 218.   [71] See fn. 26.
[72] *Ibid.*, p. 63, para. 217.

UN Commission on Human Rights[73] and of the UN General Assembly[74] have highlighted the links between human rights and public participation as well as democracy.

The various facets of the notions of public participation and accountability

Since the end of the 1980s the concept of public participation has become increasingly prominent with regard to the preparation and implementation of projects financed by the World Bank. The calls are many for public participation in the operational policies and procedures of the Bank. They include consultation of concerned populations and local NGOs about a project's environmental aspects within the context of an Environmental Assessment (EA),[75] community participation and consultations with people affected by a resettlement as a result of a project financed by the Bank,[76] and informed participation of indigenous populations in projects in which they have interests at stake.[77] Public participation practices also involve local groups in the planning, designing and monitoring of projects related to the protection of natural habitats[78] as well as in forestry and conservation management activities.[79]

In the case of the Bank's EA policy, meaningful consultations with project-affected groups and local NGOs must be held during the environmental assessment process and should be initiated as early as possible.

[73] For example, the Commission on Human Rights in its Res. 2005/29 on 'Strengthening of popular participation, equity, social justice and non-discrimination as essential foundations of democracy' stated that 'the right to development is a crucial area of public affairs in every country and requires free, active and meaningful popular participation'. UN Doc. E/CN.4/RES/2005/29, 20 March 2005, para. 5.

[74] In its Res. 55/96 on 'Promoting and consolidating democracy' adopted in 2001 the General Assembly called States to promote and consolidate democracy, *inter alia*, by 'promoting pluralism, the protection of all human rights and fundamental freedoms, maximizing the participation of individuals in decision-making and the development of effective public institutions', UN Doc. A/RES/55/96, 28 February 2001, para.1. See also the *Agenda for Development* adopted by the General Assembly in 1997, which proclaims that: 'Democracy, respect for all human rights and fundamental freedoms, including the right to development, transparent and accountable governance and administration in all sectors of society, and effective participation by civil society are also an essential part of the necessary foundations for the realization of social and people centred sustainable development', UN Doc. A/RES/51/240, 20 June 1997, para. 1.

[75] See OP 4.01 on Environmental Assessment, para. 15. See fn. 66.

[76] See OP 4.12 on Involuntary Resettlement, paras. 7–12. See fn. 66.

[77] See OP 4.10 on Indigenous Peoples, paras. 10–11. See fn. 66.

[78] See OP 4.04 on Natural Habitats, para. 10. See fn. 66.

[79] See OP 4.36 on Forestry, paras. 11–12. See fn. 66.

Dam and reservoir projects receive special treatment in the Bank's environmental assessment procedures in order to avoid, minimise or compensate for adverse environmental impacts wherever possible, using design features and other measures implemented as part of the project. Potential project impacts are identified at an early stage with the advice of environmental specialists, and the Bank must ensure that the borrower selects independent, recognised experts to carry out environmental reconnaissance to identify the project impacts, ascertain the scope of the EA, assess the borrower's capacity to manage an EA process, and advise on the need for an independent advisory panel, which would normally be set up for large dam projects.

The purpose of the policy for indigenous peoples is to ensure that these groups benefit from development projects and that potentially adverse effects of Bank projects on indigenous populations are avoided or mitigated. The policy requires the 'informed participation' of indigenous peoples in projects and programs that affect them. To this effect, the borrowing country must prepare an indigenous peoples' development plan to provide the framework for their participation in project activities and to ensure that they receive socially and culturally appropriate benefits.

Like the policy on indigenous peoples, the policy on resettlement requires informed participation and consultation with the affected people during the preparation of the resettlement plan, and community participation in planning and implementing resettlement should be encouraged as well. The policy on resettlement stresses the need to pay particular attention to the needs of the poorest and to give appropriate attention to indigenous peoples, ethnic minorities and 'pastoralists' who may have customary rights to the land or other resources taken for the project.

The policies and procedures on environmental impact assessment, indigenous peoples and involuntary resettlement also contain specific provisions requiring the involvement of NGOs. A policy on disclosure of operational information sets out procedures to be followed for making copies of environmental assessments and environmental action plans accessible to affected groups and local NGOs in borrowing countries.[80]

---

[80] A policy on disclosure of operational information was formally adopted in 1993. See 'The World Bank and Non-Governmental Organizations', in I. F. I. Shihata, *The World Bank in a Changing World. Selected Essays and Lectures*, vol. II (The Hague/London/Boston: Martinus Nijhoff, 1995), pp. 265–266.

Legally, these operational policy requirements are important vehicles for 'operationalising' or implementing broader international standards on access to information, public awareness and participation in decision-making. As such they acknowledge the role of the beneficiaries of development assistance activities in ensuring the sustainability of such activities

There is no doubt that these policy prescriptions, which are operationalised in the Bank's activities, contribute to a large extent to the development of international rules and standards in development assistance activities. Furthermore, the measures that have been taken to strengthen information disclosure have contributed to the promotion of transparency and access to information. In doing so, the policy prescriptions have contributed to the empowerment of non-state actors, and more especially local populations, by giving them the opportunity to be more effectively involved in the decision-making process. By favouring the participation of non-state actors in the Bank's activities, these policies make them the 'guardians' of respect for the norms and procedures contained therein.

A further step was the establishment of the World Bank Inspection Panel. The Inspection Panel is a subsidiary body of the World Bank's Board of Executive Directors (the Board),[81] and has been established to ensure better quality in the projects financed by the organisation, by means of an investigation mechanism. It has jurisdiction over the operational activities of two of its affiliates, the International Bank for Reconstruction and Development (IBRD) and the International Development Association (IDA).[82]

At the time of its adoption, the Panel procedure constituted a first in providing a remedy against actions of an international organisation.

---

[81] See para. 12 of the Resolution establishing the Inspection Panel, Resolution No. IBRD 93–10, resolution No IDA 93–6; 34 *International Legal Materials* 503 (1995). On the basis of para. 27 of the Resolution, two Board Reviews of the Inspection Panel have been conducted. They have clarified and in some respects amended the Resolution; see Clarifications of Certain Aspects of the Resolution Establishing the Inspection Panel (R96–204) dated September 30, 1996 and approved by the Board of Executive Directors on October 17, 1996, The Inspection Panel, *Annual Report*, August 1, 1996 to July 31, 1997, pp. 29–30. The second set of Clarifications, also entitled 'Conclusions of the Board's Second Review of the Inspection Panel' was approved on 20 April 1999. See L. Boisson de Chazournes, 'The World Bank Inspection Panel: About Public Participation and Dispute Settlement', in T. Treves *et al.* (eds.), *Civil Society, International Courts and Compliance Bodies*, (The Hague: TMC Asser Press, 2005) pp. 187–203.

[82] On the World Bank Inspection Panel, see below.

Similar types of procedures subsequently have been put into place by other financial institutions.[83] Two other affiliates of the World Bank group, the International Finance Corporation (IFC) and the Multilateral Investment Guarantee Agency (MIGA) have created another mechanism in 1999, i.e. the Compliance Advisor Ombudsman (CAO).[84] The significant difference when compared to other models is that this mechanism only deals with private sectors projects. The CAO has three functions, the first being its Ombudsman's role, using mediation and other dispute settlement techniques to address complaints by people who feel that they are or will be affected by MIGA- or IFC-supported projects; the second is as a compliance auditor to verify selected projects; and finally the CAO provides independent advice to senior management, either with regard to specific projects or more generally on the application and effectiveness of policies. Whilst functionally independent, the CAO nonetheless reports to the President of the Bank.

The IMF on its side set up in 2000 an Independent Evaluation Office (IEO) evaluating IMF's general policies as well as completed country operations.[85] The establishment of this body follows the calls for independent reviews of the programmes undertaken by the IMF, in particular after the 1990s financial crisis, and some of its features suggest a possible involvement of the public in the IMF activities. According to its terms of reference, 'in carrying out its mandate, including in the preparation of its Work Program, IEO will be free to consult with whomever and whichever groups it deemed necessary, both within and outside the Fund.'[86] The work programme performed by this body during the first years of its activities illustrates a growing concern of the IMF in the fields of openness and transparency. Some of the most sensitive issues for the organisation were dealt with by this body; in particular, it tackled issues such as the IMF role in the recent Indonesian, Brazilian and Korean financial crises, and in the year of writing, 2006, it will complete the work on IMF structural conditionality.[87]

---

[83] For further developments on the World Bank Inspection Panel, see Boisson de Chazournes, 'The World Bank Inspection Panel', pp. 200–202.

[84] See *Operational Guidelines for the Office of the IFC/MIGA Compliance Advisor/ Ombudsman*, 1999, available at http://www.cao-ombudsman.org/pdfs/FINAL% 20CAO%20GUIDELINES%20%20IN%20ENGLISH%20(09–20–00).doc (accessed: 9 February 2006).

[85] See IMF, *Executive Board Report to the IMFC on the Establishment of the Independent Evaluation Office (IEO) and its Terms of Reference*, 12 September 2000. [86] *Ibid.*

[87] Work programme for fiscal year 2006, 24 June 2005, available at http://www.imf.org/ External/NP/ieo/2005/wp/eng/index.htm (accessed: 9 February 2006).

In some of the IMF activities, there is an emerging trend for involving the public in the programmes that it finances, for example national governments and civil society are asked to cooperate closely in order to formulate the objectives of national strategies against poverty. Moreover, the IMF encourages States to adopt policies which meet a broader support from the public.[88] In this context, the IMF has developed a certain number of codes of good practice and standards related to transparency in national decision-making processes.[89] At the national level access to information is promoted, thus allowing local communities to participate effectively in the design and implementation of IMF-supported programs; it also contributes to better transparency of the national decision-making processes.

The procedure of the World Bank Inspection Panel

The establishment of the Inspection Panel constitutes a pioneering endeavour in the field of international organisations. Under the procedure put in place, private persons are given direct access to the World Bank if they believe they are directly and adversely affected by a Bank-financed project. With this mechanism, the Bank has created a new vehicle for public participation and has provided access to administrative proceedings, including remedies.

One of the main objectives behind the creation of the Inspection Panel was the improvement of quality control in project preparation and in the supervision of the implementation of projects financed by the Bank. In this context, the Inspection Panel was established as an independent and permanent organ within the Bank's structure. It is composed of three members of nationalities of Bank member countries who are nominated by the Bank's President and appointed by the Board. The Panel was granted the competence to receive and, subject to the approval of the Bank's Board, to investigate complaints from groups of individuals whose rights or interests have been, or are likely to be, directly and

---

[88] On 25 September 2002, the Executive Board approved a new set of guidelines on conditionality, replacing guidelines that had been in effect since 1979. *Guidelines on Conditionality*, 25 September 2002 http://www.imf.org/External/np/pdr/cond/2002/eng/guid/092302.pdf, and *Operational Guidance on the New Conditionality Guidelines*, 8 May 2003, available at: http://www.imf.org/External/np/pdr/cond/2003/eng/050803.htm (accessed: 9 February 2006).

[89] See IMF, *Code of Good Practices in Fiscal Transparency* approved by the Executive Board of Directors of the IMF on 23 March 2001 http://www.imf.org/external/np/fad/trans/code.htm#code (accessed: 9 February 2006).

adversely affected by the Bank's failure to follow its operational policies with respect to the design, appraisal, and/or implementation of a project financed by the World Bank. An individual Executive Director of the Bank, and the Bank's Board, may also instruct the Panel to conduct an investigation.

Upon receiving a complaint, the Inspection Panel assesses whether the complaint meets the eligibility criteria described below relating to the person of the complainant, to the subject-matter of the complaint and to the timing of the complaint.[90] However, as a preliminary condition for triggering the procedure, the Management of the Bank is asked to provide the Inspection Panel with evidence that it has already received the allegations raised in the request. The management is also asked to provide information on whether it complies with the Bank policies and procedures targeted by a complaint.[91] The Panel may recommend to the Executive Directors that an investigation be carried out; if the Board authorises an investigation, the Panel conducts it, and submits its report to the Board. The Management has the possibility to comment on the findings, and the Bank then informs the affected parties of the results of the investigation and of the action taken, if any, by the Board.

Any affected group of people who share common concerns or interests in the country where the project is located may submit a request under the condition that it is possible to demonstrate that 'its rights or interests have been or are likely to be directly affected by an action or an omission of the Bank'. In defining a group of individuals who can bring a complaint, the Resolution provides in a non-restrictive manner that 'the Panel shall receive requests for inspection presented to it by an affected party in the territory of the borrower which is not a single individual (i.e., a community of persons such as an organisation, association, society or other grouping of individuals).' A group of individuals alleging to be

---

[90] The Resolution states as a principle that no requests will be declared eligible regarding a project after the project's loan closing data or after 95 per cent or more of the loan proceeds have been disbursed. For the interpretation of this requirement, see 'Time-Limits on the Eligibility of Complaints Submitted to the Inspection Panel', Legal Opinion of the Senior Vice President and General Counsel, July 28, 1997. More generally, on eligibility issues, see Memorandum of the Senior Vice President and General Counsel, Role of the Inspection Panel in the Preliminary Assessment of whether to recommend Inspection (SecM95–11), 3 January 1995, 34 *ILM* 525 (1995).

[91] Also, as a matter of principle, complaints brought for borrowing countries' misconducts do not fall within the mandate of the Inspection Panel. In addition, it should be noted that no procurement action is subject to inspection by the Panel, whether taken by the Bank or a borrower.

affected should be understood as meaning 'any two or more individuals with common interests or concerns.'[92]

Parties may present their requests directly or through local representatives acting as the agent of adversely affected people; NGOs based in the country can take on this representation role, and international NGOs may play this role in exceptional cases where the party submitting the request contends that appropriate representation is not locally available. In such circumstances, the Executive Directors have to agree to such representation when they consider the request for inspection. It should also be noted that during the investigation, any individual or group may provide the Panel with additional information if they believe it is relevant to their request. The Operating Procedures of the Inspection Panel allow for submission by representatives of the public at large of supplemental information that they believe is relevant to evaluating the request.[93]

In practice, most of the requests so far made to the Inspection Panel allege that the Bank has not followed its environmental and social policies and procedures. Among the most quoted are the EA policy, the indigenous peoples policy and the involuntary resettlement policy, as well as the policies dealing with the involvement of NGOs in Bank-supported activities and disclosure of operational information.[94] In addition to alleging a violation of operational policies and procedures, the complainants must demonstrate that the violation is due to an omission or action of the Bank with respect to the design, appraisal and implementation phases of a project financed by the Bank.[95]

The request for inspection may relate either to a project under consideration by Bank Management, i.e. a project in the design, preparation, pre-appraisal or appraisal stage, or to a project already approved by the

---

[92] See Clarifications of Certain Aspects of the Resolution Establishing the Inspection Panel (R96–204) dated 30 September 1996 and approved by the Board of Executive Directors on October 17, 1996, see fn. 81.

[93] On this basis, NGOs in Switzerland and in the United States submitted memoranda in the *Indian NTPC Power Generation Project*. See, R.E. Bissel, 'Recent Practice of the World Bank Inspection Panel', *American Journal of International Law* (1997), 743.

[94] See The World Bank Inspection Panel, *Accountability at the World Bank, The Inspection Panel 10 Years On* (World Bank: IMF, 2003).

[95] The Resolution refers to the 'failure of the Bank to follow its operational policies and procedures with respect to the design, appraisal and/or implementation of a project financed by the Bank (including situations where the Bank is alleged to have failed in its follow-up on the borrower's obligations under loan agreements with respect to such policies and procedures (. . .)' para. 12, see fn. 81.

Board and financed by the Bank. More particularly, with respect to the implementation phase, the Resolution specifies that a complaint can be lodged for 'situations where the Bank is alleged to have failed in its follow up on the borrower's obligations under loan agreements' with respect to operational policies and procedures. The Panel has the mandate to investigate whether the Bank has properly followed up on the carrying out by the borrower of its obligations under a loan agreement. A number of legal techniques have been developed for ensuring that policy requirements are reflected in loan agreements; they pertain to what is generally known as the notion of 'green conditionality'.[96] Techniques, such as the attachment of an implementation programme or plan of action as a schedule to the loan agreement, are used for specifying the actions to be taken by the borrower. Within the framework of its responsibilities, the Bank should exercise all due diligence required to ensure that the borrower's obligations are fully complied with in a timely fashion, i.e. that the borrowing country does abide by all its contractual obligations.

The Inspection Panel procedure is important in many respects. It contributes to the strengthening of access to justice for individuals before an international organisation and provides for preventive and remedial action for their benefit; as such, individuals are entitled to ensure that the organisation complies with its operational policies in its financial activities. The Inspection Panel in fact provides a new venue for dialogue on compliance issues between a lending institution and the direct beneficiaries of its developmental activities. The implementation of this Panel procedure has also contributed to improve the quality of Bank-financed operations. The financial institution has decided to withhold the implementation of certain projects, if not to renounce them, and has also enforced corrective measures, premised largely on the contribution of local populations. In addition, it has established within the organisation a series of mechanisms and procedures to ensure the supervision of the quality of the operations during the preparation and implementation of projects.[97]

---

[96] See M. A. Bechechi, 'Some Observations Regarding Environmental Covenants and Conditionalities in World Bank Lending Activities', *Max Planck Yearbook of UN Law*, 3 (1999), pp. 289–314.

[97] L. Boisson de Chazournes, 'Policy Guidance'; D. Freestone, 'The Environmental and Social Safeguard Policies of the World Bank and the Evolving Role of the Inspection Panel' in A. Kiss, D. Shelton, K. Ishibashi (eds.), *Economic Globalization and Compliance with International Environmental Agreements* (London: Kluwer Law International, 2003), pp. 139–156.

Conclusion

The wide range of modes of intervention developed by the Bretton Woods institutions over the years has opened the doors to the inclusion of non-economic considerations and, among them, human rights. On the one hand, the consideration of the latter has prevented the pursuance of financing activities in some cases. On the other hand, social activities have become increasingly prominent, allowing for the promotion of human rights considerations. Debt relief strategies and the adherence to the Monterrey Consensus are important pathways towards this end.

Operational policies have been important means for operationalising human rights within the World Bank. Originally designed to provide guidance to the staff of the Bank in its operational work, these policies have been increasingly perceived as quality assessment tools in Bank operations. These instruments create normative expectations between the World Bank and the borrowing countries, and they pave the way for the consolidation of patterns of behaviour favouring the promotion of human rights. In addition, the establishment of the Inspection Panel has institutionalised the concern for quality improvement of the Bank's activities. It has provided for the possibility of remedial action taken by the Bank in the case of a violation of operational policies and procedures which has impaired the rights or interests of a group of people. As a means for promoting the right of access to justice, the Inspection Panel is an important contribution to the human rights field as individuals are granted the right to bring complaints if they believe that their interests have been impaired. More generally, it demonstrates the growing importance of the individual as a rights-holder in areas of international concern such as the environment, and development issues.

The increasingly acknowledged role of public participation, openness and transparency, alongside the establishment of accountability mechanisms, bring their contribution to strengthen the place of human rights within the activities of the Bretton Woods institutions. These diverse trends taken together emphasise the fact that there are more and more converging tendencies between the Bretton Woods institutions and the promotion of human rights.

Bibliography

Bechechi, M. A., 'Some Observations Regarding Environmental Covenants and Conditionalities in World Bank Lending Activities', *Max Planck Yearbook of UN Law* 3 (1999), pp. 289–314

Bhatia, M., 'Social Funds: A Review of Public Sector Management and Institutional Issues, Social Protection', Social Protection Unit, Human Development Network, World Bank, *Discussion Paper Series*, No. 0508 (2005)

Bissel, R. E., 'Recent Practice of the World Bank Inspection Panel', *American Journal of International Law* (1997), 741–744

Boisson de Chazournes, L., 'The World Bank Inspection Panel: About Public Participation and Dispute Settlement', in Treves, T. *et al.* (eds.), *Civil Society, International Courts and Compliance Bodies* (The Hague: TMC Asser Press, 2005), pp. 187–203

'Issues of Social Development: Integrating Human Rights into the Activities of the World Bank', in Institut international des droits de l'homme, *Commerce mondial et protection des droits de l'homme, les droits de l'homme à l'épreuve de la globalisation des échanges économiques* (Brussels: Bruylant, 2001), pp. 47–70

'Policy Guidance and Compliance: The World Bank Operational Standards' in Shelton, D. (ed.), *Commitment and Compliance* (Oxford: Oxford University Press, 2000), pp. 281–303

Dañino, R., 'The Legal Aspects of the World Bank's Work on Human Rights: Some Preliminary Thoughts', in Alston, P., and Robinson, M. (eds.), *Human Rights and Development. Towards Mutual Reinforcement* (Oxford: Oxford University Press, 2005), pp. 509–524

Darrow, M., *Between Light and Shadow: The World Bank, the International Monetary Fund and International Human Rights Law* (Oxford: Hart, 2003)

Freestone, D., 'The Environmental and Social Safeguard Policies of the World Bank and the Evolving Role of the Inspection Panel' in Kiss, A., Shelton, D., and Ishibashi, K. (eds.), *Economic Globalization and Compliance with International Environmental Agreements* (London: Kluwer Law International, 2003), pp. 139–156

Gianviti, F., 'Economic, Social and Cultural Rights and the International Monetary Fund', IMF Conference, Washington, D.C., May 7–17, 2002, available at http://www.imf.org/external/np/leg/sem/2002/cdmfl/eng/gianv3.pdf (accessed: 9 February 2006)

Gupta, S., Dicks-Mireaux, L., Khemani, R., McDonald, C. and Verhoeven, M., 'Social Issues in IMF-Supported Programs', *IMF Occasional Paper* 191 (2000)

Klein, P., 'Les institutions financières internationales et les droits de la personne', *Revue belge de droit international* (1999), 97–114

Lane, T., Ghosh, A., Hamann, J., Phillips, S., Schulze-Ghattas, M. and Tsikata, T., 'IMF-Supported Programs in Indonesia, Korea, and Thailand: A Preliminary Assessment', *IMF Occasional Paper* 178 (1999)

Pereira Leite, S., 'Human Rights and the IMF', *Finance and Development. A Quarterly Magazine of the IMF* 38 (2001), available at http://www.imf.org/external/pubs/ft/fandd/2001/12/leite.htm (accessed: 9 February 2006)

Pierson-Mathy, P., 'L'action des Nations Unies contre l'apartheid', *Revue belge de droit international* (1973), 160–177

Rigo Sureda, A., 'The Law Applicable to the Activities of International Development Banks', *Recueil des cours*, The Hague Academy of International Law, 308 (2004), 13–251

Ruggie, J. G., 'International Regimes, Transactions and Change: Embedded Liberalism in the Postwar Economic Order', *International Organization* 36 (1982) 2, 379–415

Shihata, I.F.I., 'The World Bank and Non-Governmental Organizations', in Shihata, I. F. I., *The World Bank in a Changing World. Selected Essays and Lectures*, vol. II (The Hague/London/Boston: Martinus Nijhoff, 1995), pp. 265–266

'La Banque mondiale et les droits de l'homme', *Revue belge de droit international*, 1999, 86–96

The World Legal Papers (The Hague/Boston/London: Kluwer Law International, 2000)

'The relationships between the United Nations and the World Bank', in I.F.I Shihata, *The World Bank Legal Papers* (The Hague/Boston/London: Kluwer Law International, 2000) pp. 808–810

Skogly, S. I., *The Human Rights Obligations of the World Bank and the International Monetary Fund* (London: Cavendish, 2001)

Swoboda, A., 'Reforming the International Financial Architecture', *Finance and Development. A Quarterly magazine of the IMF* 36 (1999), available at http://www.imf.org/external/pubs/ft/fandd/1999/09/swoboda.htm (accessed: 9 February 2006)

World Bank Inspection Panel, *Accountability at the World Bank: The Inspection Panel 10 Years On* (Washington, D.C: IMF, 2003)

PART III

International Corporate Accountability

Alternative Perspectives on International Responsibility for Human Rights Violations by Multinational Corporations

FRANCESCO FRANCIONI

Introduction

When in 1945 the United Nations Charter laid the foundation for the development of the modern law of human rights, the intent of the drafters was to protect and promote the dignity and equal rights of individuals from the arbitrary use of governmental powers. International human rights were conceived in a vertical dimension as claims against the state, as instruments to safeguard the dignity and autonomy of human beings against the hitherto unlimited authority of the state in respect of its subjects. In the second part of the last century, international standard-setting in the field of human rights, both at a universal and at a regional level, developed along much the same vertical dimension and states remained the typical addressees of the international obligation to respect, protect and fulfil human rights.

Today, the attention of international lawyers is gradually shifting from state to non-state actors, especially large business enterprises, as a possible cause of human rights violations. This is not because states have ceased to commit human rights abuses: it is sufficient to see the chaos in many developing countries, the violent oppression by dictatorial regimes, the discrimination produced by religious and ideological fundamentalism, and the persistence of war, including the 'War on Terror', to realise that the power of the state is still at the origin of most human rights abuses. The reasons for this shift of focus are related, to some extent, to the process that, with a ubiquitous term, we call globalisation. The changing structure of the international economy, the opening of national markets and the removal of traditional barriers to the circulation of goods, services and capital, has weakened the traditional shield of

245

national sovereignty. States are less able than in the past to exercise effective control over human activities carried out in their territory or abroad. New centres of power have emerged. Of particular importance, because of their transnational reach, are the centres of technological, financial and industrial power that today are represented by large corporate enterprises operating at a multinational level.

The focus on these economic subjects is not new. In the 1960s and 1970s the operations of large business enterprises had already become the object of international attention and the need for their governance had emerged as a priority within the program for the establishment of the so-called 'New International Economic Order' (NIEO).[1] Codes of conduct were negotiated, without success, at the United Nations level, and with some success at a regional level.[2] However, these early attempts at regulating the operations of multinational corporations (MNCs) occurred in an historical and political context totally different from the one we are facing today. In the 1970s the issue of the international responsibility of MNCs was raised in the context of decolonisation[3] and the main preoccupation was to ensure effective independence of the young countries from the centres of economic powers established within their territory during the period of colonial domination. Further, the Cold War placed the issue of MNCs squarely within the context of the ideological opposition between

---

[1] In 1974 the UN General Assembly adopted a Declaration on the Establishment of a New International Economic Order (A/RES/3201 (S-VI)) and a Charter of Economic Rights and Duties of States (A/RES/3281 (XXIX)).

[2] The Draft Code of Conduct for Transnational Enterprises elaborated within the *ad hoc* Commission of the UN Economic and Social Council (ECOSOC) was never approved; whilst at the Organisation for Economic Co-operation and Development (OECD) level, Guidelines for Multinational Enterprises were adopted in 1976 as an Annex to the Declaration on International Investment and Multinational Enterprises (see 15 ILM 967 (1976)). A revised version is available at http://www.olis.oecd.org/olis/2000doc.nsf/ LinkTo/daffe-ime(2000)20.

[3] A typical example from this period was the imposition on business enterprises of specific obligations to cooperate in the effective implementation of UN sanctions against Southern Rhodesia, following the unilateral proclamation of independence by the white minority regime in 1965; also, the resolutions aimed at preventing, in the 1970s, the cooperation of multinational corporations with the apartheid regime of South Africa, especially in respect of the exploitation of natural resources of Namibia. The famous Namibia Decree no. 1, adopted on 27 September 1974 by the UN Council for South West Africa, a subsidiary organ of the General Assembly (G.A.O.R., twenty-ninth session, Suppl. 24 A, pp. 27 *et seq.*), established a general prohibition of exploration and exploitation of the natural resources of Namibia, at the time still unlawfully occupied by South Africa, and such prohibition was meant to be binding upon states and private persons, including commercial enterprises.

the Western view of a market economy, and the socialist view of a NIEO to be realised by heavy-handed governmental intervention in the pursuit of a far-reaching redistributive agenda. Today, the scenario is radically different. First, decolonisation is a distant memory and the Cold War has ended, giving way to concerns about a unipolar world dominated by a hegemonic power and by the threat of terrorism. Second, the triumphant march of liberal ideology has led to a formidable increase of international investments, de-localisation of many economic activities and the rise of China as a new economic power, one in which human rights problems persist. Third, non-governmental organisations have become very active in the monitoring and disclosure of human rights abuses by states and economic actors alike, and their contribution to the rise of an international civil society is recognised world-wide. Fourth, a by-product of the rise of an international civil society is the elaboration and refinement, at an academic and operational level, of the new concept of 'corporate social responsibility'. This concept tends to look at the activities of the economic enterprises beyond the horizon of strict legal regulation, taking into account the broader social context in which the enterprise operates and developing a bottom-up approach to the identification of the ethical and legal standards that a good and responsible corporation should follow in the pursuit of its economic mission. Finally, in this contemporary scenario the concept of individual criminal responsibility for serious violations of human rights has gained nearly universal acceptance and is now buttressed by the constitutive instruments and the case law of the existing international criminal tribunals and the ICC.[4]

As compared to the period of the NIEO, these developments provide a broader analytical framework and a wider range of policy options in the evaluation of the possible alternative forms of international responsibility for violations of human rights resulting from operations of multinational

[4] We are referring especially to the Statutes of the International Criminal Tribunals for Yugoslavia and Rwanda (Statute of the International Tribunal for the Prosecution of Persons Responsible for Serious Violations of International Humanitarian Law Committed in the Territory of the Former Yugoslavia Since 1991, UN Doc. S/25704, annex (1993) reprinted in 32 *ILM* 1192 (1993) and Statute of the International Criminal Tribunal for the Prosecution of Persons Responsible for Genocide and Other Serious Violations of International Humanitarian Law Committed in the Territory of Rwanda and Other Such Violations Committed in the Territory of Neighbouring States, Between 1 January 1994 and 31 December 1994, SC Res. 955, annex, UN Doc. S/INF/50 (1994), reprinted in 33 *ILM* 1602 (1994)) and to the Rome Statute of the International Criminal Court, which entered into effect in 2002. (UN DOC. A/CONF.183/9 (1998) reprinted in 37 *ILM* 999 (1998).

corporations. In this chapter I shall examine four different options, which are based on a varying degree of progressive development of international law on this subject.

The first, and most traditional, assumes that the responsibility to prevent and suppress human rights violations by multinational corporations falls upon the host state on whose territory the MNC's activities take place; the second is based on the imposition of individual criminal responsibility on the corporate managers who have ordered or have negligently failed to prevent some particularly serious breaches of human rights; the third is the construction of a theory of legal liability of the corporation as such under public international law; the fourth postulates the attribution of the responsibility for human rights violations to the state of origin of the MNC on the basis of a theory of effective control over the transnational network of corporate activities.

Sovereignty and the responsibility of the territorial state

Under customary international law, every state has the sovereign right to grant access to its territory to foreign companies that seek investment and trading opportunities abroad. The establishment of a foreign corporation in the national territory must occur in accordance with local laws and, in most cases, in accordance with investment treaties that provide guarantees for the security and eventual protection of the investment.[5] From this perspective, the legality of the conduct of foreign companies operating within the national territory depends upon local laws. To the extent that such conduct entails violations of human rights protected under international law – such as discrimination, breaches of economic or social rights, or even graver breaches such as torture or deprivation of life – it will be up to the territorial state to take action to enforce the law. In this sense, the 'responsibility' to enforce human rights belongs to the host state, both in terms of 'primary rules', i.e. obligation to ensure respect for human rights in its territory, and of 'secondary obligations' to provide remedies and reparation to the victims. This approach is certainly reassuring for those who maintain a conception of international law as a purely inter-state system and who continue to conceive human rights purely in terms of legal obligations that states undertake one toward another. Further, this approach is consistent also with the contemporary trend toward the expansion in international

---

[5] For the practice in this area, see M. R. Mauro, *Gli accordi bilaterali sulla promozione e la protezione degli investimenti* (Torino: Giappichelli, 2003).

law of the notion of 'positive obligations', i.e. obligations not only to refrain from using state powers to afflict individuals, but also to take positive steps and concrete action to prevent private persons from violating other individuals' human rights. International human rights law and the jurisprudence of human rights courts[6] have developed this notion considerably in fields such as racial discrimination,[7] discrimination against women,[8] and torture;[9] and even outside the field of human rights in areas such as the prevention of bribery and corruption in international business.[10]

But, in spite of its ability to fit the classical paradigm of international law as a system designed to regulate the interaction between different spheres of sovereignty, such an approach presents serious shortcomings. First of all, reducing the human rights obligation of the MNC to the pure and simple respect of local law, it introduces an element of relativism that is hardly compatible with the universal value of human rights. A company may operate in a foreign state where racial or gender discrimination is not only tolerated but actually prescribed by local law and policy. Another company may establish its foreign subsidiary in a country where forced labour is practiced in open or disguised form, or where core labour rights are totally disregarded and even suppressed by violence. It would be absurd to hold that in these circumstances the company may well go along with, and profit from, the violations of human rights

---

[6] For the case law of the European Court of Human Rights see B. Conforti, 'Reflections on State Responsibility for the Breach of Positive Obligations in the Case Law of the European Court of Human Rights', *Italian YIL* 13(2003), 3 *et seq.*

[7] See, in particular, Article 2(1)(d) of the International Convention on the Elimination of All Forms of Racial Discrimination, (CERD), which requires the elimination of racial discrimination in all its forms and requires that each State Party '. . . shall prohibit and bring to an end, by all appropriate means, including legislation as required by circumstances, racial discrimination by any person, group or organization'. It is evident that racial discrimination practised by a MNC would follow within this last clause. CERD, GA Res. 2106 (XX), UN Doc. A/6014 (1966), 660 UNTS 195, entered into force on 4 January 1969.

[8] See, in particular, Articles 2, 3, 5, 6, 10, 11, 12, 13, 14 of the Convention on the Elimination of All Forms of Discrimination against Women (CEDAW), adopted 18 December 1979 and entered into force on 3 September 1981, 19 *ILM* 33 (1980).

[9] See Article 2 of the Convention against Torture and Other Cruel, Inhuman, or Degrading Treatment of Punishment (CAT), adopted on 10 December 1984 and entered into force on 26 June 1987, 24 *ILM* 535 (1985).

[10] See the 1997 OECD Convention on Combating Bribery of Foreign Public Officials in International Business Transactions, entered into force on 15 February 1999, 37 *ILM* 1 (1998). For a comment and comparative analysis with similar anti-bribery instruments in Europe and Latin America and other parts of the world, see G. Sacerdoti, 'The 1997 Convention on Combating Bribery of Foreign Public Officials in International Business Transactions', *Italian YIL* 9 (1999), 27 *et seq.*

permitted or required under the local law. The need to maintain an international standard of protection of basic human rights has dramatically emerged in relation to recent cases involving claims brought before the courts of the state of origin of the parent company, by groups of individuals injured in their state of residence by the foreign activities of a subsidiary. Many such cases concern grave violations of human rights committed against the local population, by way of forced deportation, compulsory labour end even torture, in the course of the realisation of a large project in the extractive industry.[11] One important case concerns the class action brought in the United Kingdom courts by victims of asbestos' mineral extraction during the period of apartheid in South Africa, where legal and judicial protection would have been clearly inadequate because of the limited resources of the local subsidiary, a legally separate entity, and because of the possible application of the principle *tempus regit actum*, which might have resulted in the adoption of compensatory standards in accordance with racially discriminatory parameters. These considerations seem to have played a relevant role in the decision of the House of Lords to decline to allow the exception of *forum non conveniens* raised by the respondent company.[12]

But even if we leave aside the extreme case of grave breaches of universally recognised human rights, at a substantive level the exclusive reliance on the law of the host state may provide only illusory guarantees of human rights against corporate conduct. The reasons for this conclusion are in the process of globalisation itself. Globalisation creates acute competition among different states in the attraction of finance capital and technology to support growth and development. The more acute the need for foreign capital and investments becomes, the more illusory is the expectation that the host state may be the guardian of human rights standards. Poverty and a low level of technological, scientific and social development may render as totally unrealistic the expectation that the local authority will exercise effective supervision and human rights monitoring over the activities of MNCs on their territory. With a situation of foreign debt weighing heavily on the future of many least developed countries, and with international financial institutions such as the World Bank and the International Monetary Fund still not legally bound by

[11] See cases cited below, notes 12, 36 and 43.
[12] For the series of judicial decisions relating to this case, see *Lubbe et al. v. Cape plc* (CA 30 July 1998) *C.L.C.* 1559; *Rachel Lubbe et al. v. Cape plc* (CA 29 Nov. 1999, 1 *Lloyd's Rep.* 139); and *Lubbe at al. v. Cape plc.*, House of Lords, Judgment of 20 July 2000, [2000] 1 WLR 1545.

human rights considerations in the their lending and financing decisions,[13] it is difficult to avoid the conclusion that the role of the host
state in ensuring corporate compliance with human rights is a starting
point, at best, but certainly not the final solution of the problem we are
discussing.

Individual responsibility of corporate officials

Contemporary international law has developed the idea that besides the
responsibility of the State for breaches of their international obligations,
individual liability may arise under international law for violations of
certain obligations, although it must be noted that this form of responsibility was not included in the work of the International Law Commission
on State Responsibility.[14] The idea of international criminal responsibility
of the individual for acts contrary to international law is not new; it goes
back to the twentieth century, namely the Nuremberg Charter,[15] and the
following trials by the International Military Tribunal of those charged
with crimes of war, crimes against peace and crimes against humanity.
Today, this idea has become firmly rooted in international law through the
constitution of the *ad hoc* international tribunals (ICTY and ICTR)[16] and
the establishment of the International Criminal Court.[17] So, if individuals
affiliated with the armed forces, police, national liberation movements or
other organised military or para-military groups may incur international
responsibility for violations of certain basic human rights, what would
prevent extending this notion of individual responsibility to the officers of
a corporation who have planned, decided and conducted corporate activities involving human rights violations? In principle there is no obstacle to
extending the doctrine of individual responsibility to activities of corporate officials. From the point of view of primary rules, the requisite is that

---

[13] Of course we are aware of the attention given by the World Bank to the issue of the social
and human rights impact of its activities, especially by way of establishing the Inspection
Panel, a body of independent experts, which may be called to express an opinion on the
social, environmental and cultural impact of projects. However, from a strictly legal point
of view, the Bank remains bound by its own statute to operate in accordance with economic criteria and not with human rights criteria. On this issue, see Ovett in this volume.

[14] See Articles 4–8 and discussion in J. Crawford, *The International Law Commission's
Articles on State Responsibility, Introduction, Text and Commentaries* (Cambridge,
Cambridge University Press, 2002)

[15] See Agreement for the Prosecution and Punishment of the Major War Criminals of the
European Axis, Aug. 8, 1945, 59 Stat. 1544, 82 UNTS 279.   [16] *Supra* note 4.

[17] *Ibid.*

the conduct complained of amounts to an international crime. Indeed, in several trials conducted under the Allied Forces' Control Council Law No. 10,[18] officials of some German corporations were prosecuted for international crimes connected to their active participation in the Nazi regime and, in particular in the manufacturing and supply of Zyklon B gas used for the extermination of innocent civilians,[19] in the enslavement and forced labour of populations deported from occupied territories,[20] and in the destruction or voluntary appropriation of property in violation of the Hague Conventions on the conduct of warfare.[21] These precedents are important in so far as they indicate a legal basis for construing a theory of individual liability of corporate administrators. Their validity is confirmed by the adoption of Article 25(3)(d) of the Statute of the ICC, which establishes individual criminal responsibility of a natural person who '. . . contributes to the commission or attempted commission of [a] crime by *a group of persons acting with a common purpose*',[22] as is certainly typical of corporate enterprises. However, in spite of this promising language the transferability of the theory of individual criminal responsibility to the contemporary context of MNCs is intrinsically limited. First, these precedents relate to serious violations of human rights committed by representatives of industrial enterprises in connection with belligerent activities or with military occupation of foreign territory. The individual violations in these cases remain contiguous or collateral to criminal acts of their state of nationality, which, standing alone, would have already entailed international responsibility. Second, the 'individual criminal liability approach' supported by this practice offers a limited basis for effective enforcement of MNCs' human rights obligations, because the scope of 'international crimes' is much narrower than the general category of 'human rights violations' under international law. Individual criminal liability arises in connection with particularly grave breaches of human rights, notably, genocide, crimes against humanity, such as torture, and crimes of war. So, at the level of primary rules there is a considerable

---

[18] Control Council Law No. 10, Punishment of War Crimes, Crimes Against Peace and Against Humanity, 20 December 1945, *Official Gazette of the Control Council for Germany*, No. 3, 31 January 1946, pp. 50–55.

[19] *Trials of Bruno Tesch and Two Others*, 1 Law Reports of Trials of War Criminals, British Military Court, 1946, reprinted in 1997, 93.

[20] *United States v. Carl Krauch et al.*, Vol. VIII, Trials of War Criminals before the Nuremberg Military Tribunals under Control Council Law No. 10, 1140 (1948).

[21] *United States v. Krauch et al., ibid.*, and *United States v. Krupp et al.*, Vol. IX Trials of War Criminals before the Nuremberg Military Tribunals under Control Council Law No. 10, 1327 (1948).   [22] Emphasis added.

mismatch between the norms contemplating international crimes and the very broad category of international human rights norms. The consequence of this is that only a fraction of all possible human rights violations committed by a MNC could be prosecuted through the individual criminal liability of the responsible officers. Further, this approach also raises some difficulty at the level of secondary rules regulating the origin and content of the responsibility. How are we to establish which individuals acted on behalf of the offending corporation? Arguably this is a matter to be regulated by national company law. But which law? The law of the host state where the violation occurred, or the law of the home country of the MNC? Would the theory of 'command responsibility' apply to the corporate chain of management? And what role would the defence of 'superior orders' play in the context of the company's hierarchical structure? An international law solution to these problems is not provided by the current ILC work on the progressive development and codification of international responsibility. The 2001 Articles adopted by the ILC are concerned only with acts of the state and even the provisions concerning 'de facto organs' or the attribution to the state of acts exceeding the authority of the agent or contravening to instructions[23] cannot easily be transplanted to the very different context of corporate operations.

In conclusion, the 'individual criminal liability approach', although well grounded in international law, offers a limited scope for the enforcement of human rights standards in relation to transnational activities of MNCs. The threshold of the violation remains too high and limited to international crimes, such as genocide, torture, slavery, and gross and systematic violations of human rights, while the activities of MNCs may have a much wider impact on human rights and the corresponding violations – such as discrimination, breach of private life, breaches of environmental or labour rights – would not reach the level of international crimes. Besides, at a policy level, this approach may not be the most satisfactory for the victims of human rights abuses by a MNC. As the Bhopal precedent shows,[24] in the event of corporate activities that affect the life and health of thousands of people, the most pressing need is a timely response to the damage caused, and the

---

[23] See, in particular, Articles 5, 7, 8, 9 and 11 of the 'Articles' reprinted, with comment, in J. Crawford, *The International Law Commission's Articles on State Responsibility*.

[24] For a detailed analysis of the Bhopal gas leak disaster, see T. Scovazzi, 'Industrial Accidents and the Veil of Transnational Corporations", in F. Francioni and T. Scovazzi (eds.), *International Responsibility for Environmental Harm* (London: Graham & Trotman, 1991), pp. 403 *et seq.*

provision of adequate resources to provide remedial action to the victims, including compensation. This brings us to the third model of responsibility, the one where the MNC itself is accountable for human rights violations committed in the course of its activities.

The direct liability of the corporation

Under the orthodox view of international law, commercial corporations do not possess international legal personality and therefore may neither be the direct addressees of international human rights norms nor the direct bearers of international responsibility for their breach. Although this view may largely reflect the reality of an international legal system still modelled on sovereign states, empirical observation of the practice shows that more and more corporations participate in international life besides and together with states and that today they can assert rights and bear duties directly under international law.

As far as rights are concerned, even before we started speaking of globalisation a web of investment treaties and arbitration agreements had already permitted corporations to establish substantive rights vis-à-vis sovereign states, and to assert such rights by means of direct access to international adjudication procedures, without resorting to the diplomatic protection of their national state. Today, this system has become a permanent feature of international law, both at a global level, with the preponderant majority of states being parties to the World Bank Convention establishing the International Centre for the Settlement of Investment Disputes (ICSID),[25] and at the regional level with the acceptance of direct access of investors to international remedies in trade agreements such as the North American Free Trade Agreement (NAFTA).[26] The position of corporations in international law also has been reinforced by the internationalisation of investment insurance[27] and of intellectual property rights (IPRs) through their linkage to the WTO, so as to enable MNCs to obtain world-wide

---

[25] 1965 ICSID Convention, 575 *UNTS* 159.
[26] See North American Free Trade Agreement, Dec 17, 1992, US-Can.-Mex., 32 ILM 289.
[27] See the Multilateral Investment Guarantee Agency (MIGA), established as an offshoot of the World Bank in 1988 to provide investment insurance in developing countries against non-commercial risks. On this agency see I. Shihata, *MIGA and Foreign Investment: Origins, Operations, Policies and Basic Documents of the Multilateral Investment Guarantee Agency* (Dordrecht/Boston/Lancaster: Kluwer Law International, 1988).

protection of a type of intangible asset that is the wellspring of their power and the driving force of their technological and industrial development.[28]

But the international status of corporations is not limited to the recognition of their rights at a substantive and procedural level. Consistent with the concern about the increasing powers of corporations that has been indicated in the introduction to this chapter, international law has increasingly focused on corporations as duty bearers toward the goal of securing human rights. Leaving aside the well known cases of UN economic sanctions directly applied to commercial companies in the cases of South Africa and of Southern Rhodesia, a quick sampling of recent practice can illustrate this development:

Security Council Resolution 1499,[29] in addressing the situation in the Democratic Republic of the Congo established a group of experts whose report recognises that multinational companies operating in the area, especially in the development and exploitation of natural resources, have an unavoidable impact on the ongoing conflict because of the long term economic and trade relations established with the relevant political organisations controlling the territory, and demanded that multinational enterprises operate in accordance with the same corporate norms that they would follow in their home countries.

Concerns about the role of diamond companies in fuelling conflicts in Africa, especially in Sierra Leone and Angola, have led to the adoption of Security Council Resolution 1306,[30] and to the condemnation of the association of diamond traders with those committing atrocities. This has paved the way for cooperation between diamond trading associations in establishing a system of labelling of diamonds of legitimate provenance, and to corresponding official trade restriction within the WTO.[31]

In the 2000 Global Compact, the programme launched by UN Secretary-General Kofi Annan to develop an ethical dimension of globalisation, out of the proclaimed ten fundamental principles, five concern the responsibility of business toward securing human rights, including

---

[28] Such protection is granted by the *Agreement on Trade-Related Aspects of Intellectual Property Rights* (TRIPS Agreement), available at http://www.wto.org (last accessed: 7 November 2005).   [29] S/RES/1499 (2003), 13 August 2003.

[30] UN SCOR, 55th Session, 4168th mtg., UN Doc. S/RES/1306 (2000).

[31] See Waiver concerning Kimberley Process Certification Scheme for Rough Diamonds, WTO doc. G/C/W/432/Rev.1 of 24 February 2003.

labour rights, abolition of forced labour and child labour as well as the elimination of discrimination.[32]

In 2003 the UN Sub-Commission on the Promotion and Protection of Human Rights adopted a set of *Norms on the Responsibilities of Transnational Corporations and Other Business Enterprises With Regard to Human Rights*.[33] The Norms include the following statement: '(w)ithin their respective spheres of activity and influence, transnational corporations and other business enterprises have the obligation to promote, secure the fulfilment of, respect, ensure respect of and protect human rights recognized in international law as well as national law, including the rights and interests of indigenous peoples and other vulnerable groups'.[34]

In judicial practice multinational companies have become the target of claims brought by people whose lives were severely affected by corporate activities involving alleged violations of human rights. In the United States this type of claim has been made possible by the operation of the Alien Tort Claims Act,[35] which gives jurisdiction to federal courts to hear tort claims arising from alleged violations of international law. In *Doe v. Unocal*,[36] citizens of Myanmar sued a US multinational company under this statute to obtain redress for a variety of human rights abuses allegedly committed by the defendant in Myanmar in the course of the realisation of an oil and gas project and involving forced relocation of people, compulsory labour and torture. Expanding the earlier jurisprudence that had began with the landmark decision in *Filartiga v. Pena Irala*,[37] the Court upheld its own jurisdiction on the basis of the principle that multinational corporations, with their foreign operations, are also capable of violating norms of customary international law, including human rights norms, and thus of becoming liable under the terms of the Alien Tort Statute.[38]

---

[32] For the ten principles see http://www.unglobalcompact.org/AboutTheGC/TheTen-Principles/index.html (last accessed: 29 May 2006).

[33] Adopted on 26 August 2003, UN Doc. E/CN.4/Sub.2/2003/12/Rev.2.

[34] A.1, *ibid.*, page 4.   [35] 28 U.S.C. § 1350 (2000).

[36] *Doe v. Unocal*, 963 F. Supp. 880 U.S.; 110 F. Supp. 2d 1294 (C.D. Cal. 2000), *Aff'd*. 248 F.3d 915 (9th Cir. 2001).

[37] *Filartiga v. Pena-Irada*, United States Court of Appeals, Second Circuit, 1980, 630 F.2d 876.

[38] Although the plaintiff failed to substantiate their claim in the merits and eventually the claim was settled by Unocal in 2004, the decision on jurisdiction is important since case law had recognised the liability only of public officials and of individuals for violations of international law and not of corporations.

These various manifestations of international practice cannot, of course, be taken as evidence that multinational corporations have to be treated as full subjects of international law on a par with states. Clearly, the full range of international human rights obligations still remains applicable only to states. Many human rights, such as equality before the law, fair trial, asylum, to mention just a few, can be guaranteed only by the state and in a system where the rule of law applies. So, the role of private corporations in securing compliance with human rights is limited and subsidiary at best. At the same time, we must remain aware that even when a corporation is implicated in the violation of human rights and the conditions exist for invoking its responsibility under international law, direct recourse to international legal remedies may not be possible, simply because no such remedies exist. Thus, resort to national remedies is unavoidable and the role of the state in securing human rights is re-established. Even in the sophisticated and advanced system of human rights protection under the European Convention, the Court can entertain claims only against states, and the failure by private corporations to secure human rights may be relevant only to the extent that a state failed to exercise due diligence or take positive measures to prevent the corporation from causing harm.[39]

But even with these limits and obstacles, the perspective of a direct corporate responsibility to secure international human rights is the promising starting point for the progressive development of a more balanced system of allocation of rights and responsibilities of multinational corporations under international law. This development is already underway. In the traditional top-down approach to regulation, the 2000 Organisation for Economic Co-operation and Development (OECD) Guidelines for Multinational Enterprises set out the general principle that enterprises are under a duty to respect '. . . the human rights of those affected by their activities consistent with the host government's international obligations and commitments'.[40] This concept is elaborated in the commentary to this general principle where it is stated:

> While promoting and upholding human rights is primarily the responsi-
> bility of governments, where corporate conduct and human rights inter-
> sect enterprises do play a role, and thus MNEs are encouraged to respect

---

[39] On the issue of positive obligations under the European Convention, see Conforti, 'Reflections on State Responsibility'.

[40] 40 ILM 237 (2001), II.2. Also available at http://www.oecd.org/dataoecd/56/36/1922428.pdf (last accessed: 20 May 2006).

human rights, not only in their dealings with employees, but also with respect to others affected by their activities, in a manner that is consistent with host governments' international obligations and commitments. The Universal Declaration of Human Rights and other human rights obligations of the government concerned are of particular relevance in this regard'.[41]

This is a very cautious language quite far from introducing the revolutionary concept that corporations are fully independent subjects of international law and autonomously bound by the whole international body of human rights law. Yet, it recognises that MNCs have a duty and must play a role as partners with governments in securing human rights in the area of influence of their conduct abroad. This duty goes beyond a strict compliance with the host states' laws and policy, and involves a commitment to respect 'the human rights of those affected by their activities'. This last sentence provides a useful indication of the appropriate criterion for determining the scope of responsibility of the MNC to ensure respect and protection of human rights. The criterion is neither 'territorial' nor 'personal', since corporations are not territorial entities with physical boundaries, nor entities endowed with precise jurisdictional powers over a population of 'citizens' or 'subjects'; it is rather 'functional' in the sense that it relates to the actual functions performed by the corporation and to the impact that the activities conducted in the performance of such functions will have on the sphere of human rights of the peoples exposed to them. From this perspective, the intersection between corporate conduct and human rights can be evaluated along a scale of varying degrees of involvement of the MNC in the commission of human rights abuses. At the top of the scale is the conduct of the corporation vis-à-vis the persons who come in direct contact with it, primarily workers and employees whose fundamental labour and social rights should be secured even in the absence of host state's legal requirements, but also ordinary people who may be enrolled by the MNC in specific programmes for the experimentation of new products, such as trials of new drugs in developing countries. At a second level we can place the impact of the corporate activities on the local communities where operations, plants or mining activities are located. Industrial accidents like Bhopal[42] or international

---

[41] *Ibid.*, para. 4 of the commentary.
[42] The Bophal gas leak resulted in thousands of victims as the plant was located, in a densely populated area, and there were inadequate contingency plans, and action in response to the disaster; especially because of lack of knowledge by the people affected by the toxic spill of the nature of the risk and of the danger involved. For example, lack of information

controversies such as the one concerning uranium mining at Kakadu[43] in Australia or the Ogoni in Nigeria,[44] indicate that the operation of hazardous industrial plants or the development of large extraction projects may have a direct impact on the life, health or living culture of the local population or indigenous peoples. Adherence to international human rights norms by the MNC in such situations is not only consistent with the overall goal of securing human rights, but may be in the best interest of the corporation, in order to avoid international scandal and costly suits to fend off liability claims. At a third and lowest level of the scale we can place the activities of the MNC that are likely to affect human rights of the general public in the host country. This is the most problematic level at which we can construe specific obligations of the MNC with regard to human rights. It is clear that the mere fact of doing business in a country that does not respect human rights does not make the company responsible under international law. Sometimes the investment in a country that violates human rights is not an option but a necessity, for example when the natural resources to be developed are localised in that country. However, even at this level, MNCs have a duty to abstain from the direct participation in the host country's policies that involve violations of international human rights. In many of the current litigations involving claims of corporate abuses of human rights, the typical situation is that of companies that benefit from human rights abuses committed by military or security forces of the host government or from local laws that ignore human rights standards for the benefit of investment maximisation and economic growth. In these situations international legal doctrine has already analysed the varying degrees of participation, complicity or acquiescence of corporations with host governments.[45] They vary from the mere passive enjoyment of the benefits deriving from the host

---

about the hazard posed by the gas leak led to the attempt to extinguish the fire caused by the accident by water rather than other appropriate chemicals, thus causing the deadly fog that led to the aggravation of casualties and health problems. See C. Zilioli, 'Il caso Bhopal e il controllo sulle attività pericolose svolte da società multinazionali', *Riv. Giur. dell'ambiente* 11 (1987), 99–251; Scovazzi, 'Industrial Accidents', 395 *et seq.*

[43] On the case of the Kakadu National Park see *Report on the mission to Kakadu National Park, Australia, 26 October to 1 November 1998*, UNESCO Doc. WHC-98/CONF.203/INF.18 of 29 November 1998.

[44] See African Commission on Human and Peoples' Rights, Communication No. 155/96, *The Social and Economic Rights Action Center and the Center for Economic and Social Rights/Nigeria*, decided in October 2001, OAU doc. ACHPR/COMM/A044/1 of 27 May 2002.

[45] For a thorough analysis of this subject, see S. Ratner, 'Corporations and Human Rights: A Theory of Legal Responsibility', 111 *Yale L J* (2001), 443.

country's disregard for international human rights, to active complicity, instigation and even deliberately engaging in human rights breaches. A theory of direct responsibility of corporations to secure international human rights would help to discourage this type of complicity between corporate conduct and the host state's human rights abuses. In the long term it may help to redress the normative imbalance that today exists in international law, on the one hand a strong and far-reaching protection of the rights of MNCs under investment and arbitration treaties, and on the other hand a weak and very soft system of obligations on the MNC to comply with fundamental human rights and other norms of international law.[46]

The international responsibility of the home state

After having examined the role of the host state, of individual criminal responsibility and of the MNCs as such, what remains to be examined is the home state's role in securing the compliance with human rights standards of the MNC's foreign activities. Even if the recent work of the ILC hardly shows any opening to the consideration of this issue,[47] its relevance to the present discussion becomes apparent in the light of three basic considerations.

First, as we have elaborated in the introduction to this chapter, the salient characteristic of globalisation is the rise, alongside the growth of MNCs, of transnational centres of technological and economic power which spread in a plurality of states, through the network of branches and subsidiaries, but still remain responsive to a global strategy and direction localised in the state of origin. It is therefore in the state of origin that the overall control, with respect to the planning and execution of the activities of the MNC, is located; and it is the state of origin that is in the best position to effectively oversee this centre of control through the exercise of its territorial jurisdiction.[48]

---

[46] For this observation and the suggestion that bilateral investment treaties should evolve toward including investors' obligations to respect human rights, see V. Lowe, 'Corporations as International Actors and Law Makers', *Italian YIL* 14 (2004), 23 *et seq.*

[47] For a critique of the work of the ILC in the field of state responsibility from the point of view of the inadequate attention given to the issue of responsibility for violations of human rights, see R. Pisillo Mazzeschi, 'The Marginal Role of the Individual in the ILC's Articles on State Responsibility", *Italian YIL* 14 (2004), 39 *et seq.*

[48] For an early and more extensive elaboration of this concept, see F. Francioni, *Imprese multinazionali, protezione diplomatica e responsabilità internazionale* (Milano: Giuffé, 1979).

The second consideration relates to the vast practice of actual exercise by home states of extraterritorial regulatory and adjudicatory powers over foreign activities of corporations, when the exercise of such powers is deemed to be necessary to fulfil certain societal interests or policy objectives, such as antitrust enforcement, national security, export controls, securities regulation, investment insurance, and other similar national interests. This practice is widespread, it has been widely discussed in the literature, and there is no need here for further elaboration.[49] What is important to note is that if capital-exporting countries, especially European countries and the United States, are willing to assert extra-territorial regulatory powers over foreign corporate activities through the effective control they have over the parent companies in the above-mentioned contexts, it is hard to understand what would prevent them from exercising the same powers and the same degree of extraterritorial 'curiosity' with regard to the internationally shared objective of securing and promoting human rights.

The third consideration concerns the symmetry between the just-indicated powers of extra-territorial regulation and the extra-territorial scope of every state's obligation to respect and protect human rights. While it is true that the scope of this obligation is primarily territorial, at the same time it is undisputable that under human rights treaties the responsibility to respect and protect human rights extends also to activities outside the territory, provided that the state has jurisdiction over the actor or the conduct. This is the principle accepted in Article 1 of the European Convention on Human Rights (ECHR)[50] and Article 1 of the American Convention on Human Rights (ACHR),[51] as well as in Article 2 of the International Covenant on Civil and Political Rights (ICCPR).[52]

---

[49] For a detailed examination of international practice, see *ibid.*, pp. 95–137 and the literature cited therein.

[50] Article 1 of the ECHR provides that 'The High Contracting Parties shall secure to everyone within their jurisdiction the rights and freedoms defined in Section I of this Convention.'

[51] Article 1, para. 1 of the ACHR provides that 'The States Parties to this Convention undertake to respect the rights and freedoms recognized herein and to ensure to all persons subject to their jurisdiction the free and full exercise of those rights and freedoms, without any discrimination for reasons of race, color, sex, language, religion, political or other opinion, national or social origin, economic status, birth, or any other social condition.'

[52] Article 2, para. 1 of the ICCPR provides that 'Each State Party to the present Covenant undertakes to respect and to ensure to all individuals within its territory and subject to its jurisdiction the rights recognized in the present Covenant, without distinction of any kind, such as race, colour, sex, language, religion, political or other opinion, national or social origin, property, birth or other status.' For a detailed analysis of the respective

The European Court of Human Rights (ECtHR) and the Human Rights Committee (HRC, established under the ICCPR) have confirmed in their jurisprudence that, under certain conditions, State Parties are responsible for human rights violations occurring abroad.[53]

The above considerations can sustain the argument that today a legal and rational basis exists for the development of a theory of responsibility of the state of origin of a MNC. In general terms such a theory can be formulated in the following manner: a state is responsible for its failure to exercise due diligence in regard of a MNC's conduct in its own territory when that conduct is causing or is likely to cause human rights violations in the foreign state where the MNC is doing business through its subsidiary, and when the state of origin has sufficient knowledge that such conduct may cause a violation of international human rights abroad, and has the legal and technical means to take positive action to prevent harm.

The codification and progressive development of the law of state responsibility has shown so far a lack of political imagination in conceiving a theory of the home-state responsibility for violations of human rights committed abroad by a MNC. However, it is our view that in the current process of transformation of international law under the forces of globalisation, it will become increasingly difficult to elude this form of responsibility. States of origin are closely linked by their own system of regulations, licences and administrative oversight to the MNCs based in their territory. They benefit from their world-wide operations by way of tax revenues and the increase in wealth of their citizens. They finance and control much of the research which is the engine of technological innovation and economic growth. Thus, they are in the best position also to assess and manage the risk connected to the conduct of foreign activities that, because of their inherent danger

articles in the ECHR, ACHR and ICCPR, and of implementing practice, see P. De Sena, *La nozione di giurisdizione statale nei trattati sui diritti dell'uomo* (Torino: Giappichelli, 2002).

[53] For the HRC see *Lilian Celiberti de Casariego v. Uruguay*,,Communication No. 56/1979, UN Doc. CCPR/C/OP/1 at 92 (1984), para. 10.3, where it is stated that 'it would be unconscionable to so interpret the responsibility under article 2 of the Covenant as to permit a State party to perpetrate violations of the Covenant in the territory of another State, which violations it could not perpetrate on its own territory". For the ECtHR, see, among others, the well known *Loizidou* case (jurisdictional phase, 1995) where Turkey was found to be under an obligation to ensure human rights in the area of the Turkish-occupied Northern Cyprus on the basis of the effective control exercised by Turkey over the territorial authorities on Northern Cyprus (see *Loizidou v. Turkey (Preliminary Objections)*, 15318/89, 1995 *ECHR* 10 (23 March 1995)).

or because of the modalities of their execution, are susceptible of causing harm to people abroad.

Of course, the opponents of this theory will invoke the separation of legal personality of the parent company and of the foreign subsidiary to insulate the former and, *a fortiori*, the home country from the activities of the latter. But this objection cannot really hold. In recent practice tort claims arising from damage caused by foreign operations of MNCs have systematically entailed the 'piercing of the veil' of the individual corporate entity, to focus on the controlling parent company or on the economic unity of the whole group in order to provide effective remedies to the victims. This has happened in the tragedy of *Bhopal*, where the parent company, Union Carbide, a United States corporation, agreed to pay compensation to the victims of the gas leak which occurred at the site of its Indian subsidiary, and in the *Seveso* toxic spill involving the subsidiary of a Swiss multinational operating in Italy;[54] as well as in more recent practice, including the already mentioned *Lubbe et al. v. Cape*.[55] Further, the piercing of the corporate veil has been accepted as an ordinary technique to permit the protection of the parent company's interest in international claims relating to investment disputes.[56] If piercing of the veil is permissible to provide effective protection to the controlling economic interests of the investor, we see no reason why it cannot work the other way around to link a human rights abuse by a foreign subsidiary to the controlling parent company and, through it, to the territorial control of the home state.

In a more general perspective, the engagement of home states in the legal discourse over the responsibility of MNCs for violation of human rights is supported by a robust affirmation of the fundamental principle of equal rights and non-discrimination, as proclaimed in the UN Charter, and by the principle of indivisibility of human rights and human dignity as proclaimed in the 1993 Vienna Declaration[57] on human rights. These principles are incompatible with a conception of international human rights *à géometrie variable*, where States would be allowed to permit corporations subject to their jurisdiction or control to commit abroad human rights abuses that are both impermissible and subject to

---

[54] For detailed analysis of these cases, see Scovazzi, 'Industrial Accidents', 395 *et seq.*

[55] *Supra* note 12.

[56] See *United States of America v. Italy – Case Concerning Elettronica Sicula S.p.A. (ELSI)* [1989] ICJ Rep. 15 (20 July 1989).

[57] See World Conference on Human Rights, Vienna, 14–25 June 1993, *Vienna Declaration and Programme of Action*, UN doc. A/CONF.157/23 of 12 July 1993.

sanctions at home. To think otherwise is to perpetuate a double standard based on the old notion of territorial sovereignty that today is easily circumvented by the ubiquitous structure of the MNC. Non-discrimination requires that people are not discriminated against in the enjoyment of their international human rights simply because of their nationality, or their place of residence at a given time. Today, this fundamental principle has been stretched to the point of explicitly recognising the 'responsibility to protect',[58] that is, the responsibility to take action, including military action, to prevent or redress particularly grave violations of human rights occurring in a foreign country that is unwilling or unable to prevent attacks upon the life or liberty of its people. It would be cynical and contradictory to accept the state's 'responsibility to protect' by direct coercive intervention abroad, and at the same time to oppose a theory of responsibility to protect by simple enforcement of human right standards within the national territory of a State where the operations of a MNC are planned and deliberated.

Conclusion

The purpose of this chapter was to show the various intellectual approaches to the development of a theory of international responsibility for breaches of human rights committed by MNCs. The point I have tried to make is that in dealing with this issue, besides the fashionable theories of corporate social responsibility, several avenues remain open for enforcing human rights standards with regard to transnational activities of corporations. The examination of the four approaches to this problem can lead to the following conclusions: firstly, that the four approaches are not mutually exclusive, on the contrary they can be in a relation of mutual support to the extent that, for example, civil liability of the corporation can be established in addition to the individual criminal liability of the MNC's directors. Secondly, the MNC cannot be seen, any longer, as a simple sum of fragmented legal entities subject to the law and jurisdiction of the different states where they operate, but must be seen rather as a unitary economic entity which, although not endowed with full legal personality as a state or an international organisation, can act as a partner with states and must therefore assume its own share of direct responsibility in securing human rights in the conduct of its business abroad.

---

[58] See the Report of the International Commission on Intervention and State Sovereignty available at http://www.iciss.ca/report-en.asp.

Finally, this chapter has argued that, far from requiring a radical reconceptualisation of the role of states in the present process of globalisation, what is needed is the simple extension to the MNC of the old principle that States have the responsibility to ensure that activities within their jurisdiction or control do not cause harm in the territory of other states, including harm to human beings and violation of international human rights.

Bibliography

Conforti, B., 'Reflections on State Responsibility for the Breach of Positive Obligations in the Case Law of the European Court of Human Rights', *Italian YIL* 13 (2003), 3–10

Crawford, J., *The International Law Commission's Articles on State Responsibility, Introduction, Text and Commentaries* (Cambridge: Cambridge University Press, 2002)

De Sena, P., *La nozione di giurisdizione statale nei trattati sui diritti dell'uomo* (Torino: Giappichelli, 2002)

De Schutter, O., 'The Liability of Multinational Enterprises in European Law' in P. Alston (ed.) *Non-State Actors and Human Rights* (Oxford: OUP, 2005)

Francioni, F., *Imprese multinazionali, protezione diplomatica e responsabilità internazionale* (Milano: Giuffé, 1979)

Lowe, V., 'Corporations as International Actors and Law Makers', *Italian YIL* 14 (2004), 23–38

Mauro, M. R., *Gli accordi bilaterali sulla promozione e la protezione degli investimenti* (Torino: Giappichelli, 2003)

Pisillo Mazzeschi, R., 'The Marginal Role of the Individual in the ILC's Articles on State Responsibility', *Italian YIL* 14 (2004), 39–51

Ratner, S., 'Corporations and Human Rights: A Theory of Legal Responsibility', *Yale Law Journal* 111 (2001), 443–545

Sacerdoti, G., 'The 1997 Convention on Combating Bribery of Foreign Public Officials in International Business Transactions', *Italian YIL* 9 (1999), 26–50

Scovazzi, T., 'Industrial Accidents and the Veil of Transnational Corporations', in F. Francioni and T. Scovazzi (eds.), *International Responsibility for Environmental Harm* (London: Graham & Trotman, 1991)

Shihata, I.F.I., *MIGA and Foreign Investment: Origins, Operations, Policies and Basic Documents of the Multilateral Investment Guarantee Agency* (Dordrecht: Kluwer Law International, 1988)

Zilioli, C., 'Il caso Bhopal e il controllo sulle attività pericolose svolte da società multinazionali', *Riv. Giur. dell'ambiente* 11 (1987), 99–251

Human Rights, Arbitration, and Corporate Social Responsibility in the Law of International Trade

FABRIZIO MARRELLA[1]

Introduction

In the traditional legal discourse, the responsibility for ensuring that Transnational Corporations (hereinafter TNCs) respect human rights, as should any other business entity, is a matter for territorial State action at the domestic level and under international law. Today, economic globalisation regulation demands a multi-faceted and multi-layered network of rules that tend to be increasingly complex and sophisticated. Two extreme approaches dominate the literature on the matter: *le droit de l'hommisme*[2] and total self-regulation of markets. The purpose of this chapter is to focus on the relationships between human rights, arbitration, and corporate social responsibility. The discussion centres on international commercial contracts, and not labour law issues, or the World Trade Organization (WTO), as they are addressed elsewhere in this book;[3] instead, the chapter engages with models of international responsibility for human rights violations by TNCs, which are also identified in this volume.[4] Beyond models of international responsibility of the territorial State – be it the host or the home State of a TNC, of international liability of corporate directors and of TNCs, there are also emerging issues of responsibility for violations of

---

[1] The author wishes to express his gratitude to Prof. John Ruggie of Harvard University, Special Representative of the United Nations Secretary-General on the issue of human rights and business, for his comments on an earlier draft of this chapter.

[2] See A. Pellet, 'La mise en oeuvre des normes relatives aux droits de l'homme', in CEDIN (H. Thierry and E. Decaux), *Droit international et droits de l'homme. La pratique juridique française dans le domaine de la protection internationale des droits de l'homme* (Paris: Montchrestien, 1990) p. 126, as well as by the same author 'Droits de l'hommisme et droit international', in http://www.droits-fondamentaux.org/article.php3?id_article=27 (accessed: 18 April 2006).

[3] See contributions by Benedek and Perulli in this volume.

[4] See contribution by Francioni in this volume.

human rights in the transnational arbitral process and, last but not least, in the field of corporate social responsibility.

An invisible red line seems to connect human rights protection, international arbitration and corporate social responsibility. Human rights issues are more and more important in arbitration, and they are the driving force underlying corporate social responsibility. In the law of international trade, it is not domestic courts but arbitration tribunals which are the most common *fora* for dispute resolution. Hence, first of all, the question of relevance of human rights issues in the transnational arbitration process must be addressed.

The second level of analysis concerns the assumption of human rights concerns directly by TNCs through self-regulation. At a global level, human rights protection is not uniform, due to the different ratifications of the main human rights conventions, and to the different obligations or enforcement mechanisms provided by each intergovernmental legal instrument. Furthermore, the most important actors in economic globalisation are TNCs, and therefore it becomes crucial to analyse human rights issues at the TNC level. Under the auspices of many Governments and inter-governmental organisations, TNCs have developed Codes of Conduct regulating corporate social responsibility, which are intended, *inter alia*, as a response to public opinion criticism vis-à-vis TNCs, especially after recent scandals.[5] Introducing rules of corporate social responsibility has become, for certain firms, a moral need; for others, a marketing tool, providing better performance in sales, better access to financing and better corporate identity for workers. However, the same considerations lead to another conclusion. Since arbitration is the 'ordinary' means of dispute resolution in international trade, businesses may start litigation *inter se* for alleged human rights violations. They may even ask the arbitration tribunal to apply Codes of Conduct, including those of corporate social responsibility, to decide a case.

In conclusion, there is a potential development of human rights issues in international arbitration. As a result, and unexpectedly, arbitration may turn out to be a new and unusual forum for human rights litigation. Arbitral case law, in its turn, may contribute to shaping the scope of corporate social responsibility and, finally, to the application of human rights standards in the law of international trade.

---

[5] See C. K. Prahalad, Allen Hammond, Michael E. Porter, Harvey C. Fruehauf (eds.), *Harvard Business Review on Corporate Responsibility* (Boston: Harvard Business School Publishing, 2003), pp. 66 *et seq.*

The development of human rights issues in international commercial arbitration

It appears that human rights and international commercial arbitration are far distant from each other; international human rights conventions do not specifically contemplate commercial arbitration and, conversely, relevant treaties for international commercial arbitration do not mention human rights. They have historically evolved in isolation from each other. However, on examining them more closely, what is seen is rather, the progressive 'clash of two transnational juridical phenomena'.[6] International human rights treaties bind Governments to secure to everyone within their jurisdiction fundamental rights and freedoms. According to one author:

> The arrival of human rights on the international scene is, indeed, a remarkable event because it is a subversive theory . . . Today the human rights doctrine forces States to give account of how they treat their nationals, administer justice, run prisons and so on. Potentially, therefore, it can subvert their domestic order and, consequently, the traditional configuration of the international community as well.[7]

Arbitration is the main dispute resolution method practiced in international business transactions. It may take place in any country, in any language and with arbitrators of any nationality. With this flexibility, it is generally perceived by TNCs as a neutral kind of 'a-national' justice offering no undue advantage to any party. It is commonly estimated that about eighty per cent of arbitral awards are spontaneously enforced by businesses, a result radically different from the outcome of multi-State litigation in domestic courts and international circulation of foreign judgments. In this sense, it may be said that transnational arbitration is a legal process that *per se* does not pertain *in toto* to any domestic legal system.[8] It has even been suggested by courts in

---

[6] See A. Jaksic, *Arbitration and Human Rights* (Frankfurt am Main: Lang, 2002), pp. 17 *et seq.*

[7] A. Cassese, *International Law*, 2nd ed. (Oxford: Oxford University Press, 2005), p. 349.

[8] See, amongst many other works, A. Redfern and M. Hunter, *Law and Practice of International Commercial Arbitration*, 4th ed. (London: Sweet & Maxwell, 2004); J. D. Lew, L. A. Mistelis, and S. M. Kroll, *Comparative International Commercial Arbitration* (The Hague: Kluwer Law International, 2003); E. Gaillard and J. Savage (eds.), *Fouchard, Gaillard, Goldman on International Commercial Arbitration* (The Hague: Kluwer Law International, 2004). Reference here is to be made to the debate on the modern *lex mercatoria*, on which see F. Marrella, *La nuova lex mercatoria. Principi Unidroit ed usi dei contratti del commercio internazionale* (Padova: CEDAM, 2003).

France[9] and the USA[10] that it would be helpful to remove judicial control from the seat of the arbitration in order to concentrate them (and only if need be) in the country of enforcement.[11]

Further, in contrast with State judicial systems, arbitration offers the parties the unique opportunity to designate persons of their choice as private judges; and finally, in case of non-compliance, arbitral awards enjoy much greater international recognition than judgments of national courts. Presently, 137 countries[12] have ratified the 1958 United Nations Convention on the Recognition and Enforcement of Foreign Arbitral Awards, known as the 'New York Convention',[13] which greatly facilitates enforcement of arbitral awards by domestic courts in all States which are party to the treaty.[14]

States that recognise international commercial arbitration as a good method for resolving disputes are, in general, prepared to give their assistance to the arbitral process. Indeed, in many cases they are bound to

---

[9] Cour de Cassation, 10 July 1997, *Omnium de Traitement et de Valorisation v. Hilrnarton*, reported in *Yearbook of Commercial Arbitration* 22 (1997), 696–701, approving enforcement of an award that had been set aside in Switzerland.

[10] US District Court, District of Columbia, 31 July 1996, *Chromalloy Aeroservices Inc. v. The Arab Republic of Egypt* reported in *Yearbook of Commercial Arbitration* 22 (1997), pp. 1001–1012, declaring enforceable in the United States an award that had been set aside in Egypt.

[11] See, e.g., P. Fouchard, 'La portée internationale de l'annulation de la sentence arbitrale dans son pays d'origine', *Revue de l'arbitrage* (1997), 329, particularly at 351–352.

[12] As of 18 September 2006.

[13] United Nations Convention on Recognition and Enforcement of Foreign Arbitral Awards, (New York, 10 June 1958) (1959) 4739 UNTS 330.

[14] In addition to the NYC which is the main international treaty and to which reference shall be made throughout this essay, there are a number of established multilateral treaties which provide for enforcement of awards. The principal global multilateral treaties are: the Geneva Protocol on Arbitration Clauses, 1923 (27 LNTS 157); the Geneva Convention on the Enforcement of Foreign Awards, 1927 (92 LNTS 301); the Washington Convention on the Settlement of Investment Disputes between States and Nationals of Other States, 1965 (575 U.N.T.S. 159, available at http://www.worldbank.org/icsid/basicdoc-archive/9.htm (accessed: 18 April 2006)). Regional multilateral conventions are: the European Convention on International Commercial Arbitration, 1961 (484 U.N.T.S. 364); the Panama Inter-American Convention on International Commercial Arbitration, 1975 (available at http://www.sice.oas.org/dispute/comarb/iacac/iacac2e.asp, accessed: 18 April 2006); The Amman Arab Convention on Commercial Arbitration, 1987 (http://www.jurisint.org/pub/01/en/155.htm, accessed: 18 April 2006); the OHADA Treaty on Harmonisation of Business Law in Africa, 1993 (available at http://www.jurisint.org/pub/ohada/text/text.01.en.html, accessed: 18 April 2006). Bilateral treaties, may also be appropriate instruments for the recognition and enforcement of arbitral awards. They have been frequently used for such a purpose in the past. At the present time however, these matters are primarily governed by the NYC.

do so by international treaties to which they are parties; however, it is generally recognised that, in return, each national state is entitled to exercise a degree of control over the arbitral process. Such a control is usually exercised on a territorial basis, both over arbitration conducted in the territory of the State concerned and over awards brought into the territory for the purpose of recognition and enforcement.

When crossing international commercial arbitration with human rights regulation, reference should also be made to international judicial bodies capable of deciding contentious cases by way of binding decisions. Despite an extensive framework of international legal instruments and bodies, international judicial mechanisms for human rights enforcement can be found only at the regional level with reference to the 1950 European Convention for the Protection of Human Rights and Fundamental Freedoms (European Convention on Human Rights, hereinafter ECHR)[15] or, to a lesser extent, the 1969 American Convention on Human Rights[16] as well as the 1981 African Charter on Human and People's Rights.[17]

With reference to ECHR case law two legal principles can be drawn.[18] First of all, the ECHR only creates obligations for Governments who are Contracting Parties to it, and for *their* courts. Since an arbitral tribunal is not recognised as a 'court' it follows that if the operation of an arbitral tribunal contravenes the ECHR or the 1966 International Covenant on Civil

---

[15] European Convention for the Protection of Human Rights and Fundamental Freedoms of 4 November 1950, Rome, (1955); ETS no. 5, 213 UNTS 221, as subsequently amended.

[16] American Convention on Human Rights of 22 November 1969, S. José, (1979) 1144 UNTS 144. Despite its inter-American vocation, this treaty has only been signed but not ratified by the USA.

[17] African Charter on Human Rights and the People's Rights of 27 June 1981, Nairobi, (1988) 1520 UNTS 217, (1982) 21 ILM 58. The Asian continent remains without an international regional system of human rights protection.

[18] Of course, the European Commission of Human Rights no longer exists since the entry into force of Protocol No.11, European Convention of Human Rights on Procedural Reform. However, the decisions rendered by the Commission may still have persuasive authority. See generally R. Blackburn and J. Polakiewicz, *Fundamental Rights in Europe: the European Convention on Human Rights and its Member States, 1950–2000* (New York: Oxford University Press, 2001); O. Jacot-Guillarmod, 'La nouvelle cour européenne des droits de l'homme dans la perspective du juge national', in C. Zanghì, *La Convenzione europea dei diritti dell'uomo: 50 anni d'esperienza gli attori e i protagonisti della convenzione: il passato e* l'avvenire (Torino: Giappichelli, 2002), pp. 283–326; C. Ovey and R. A. White, *Jacobs and White, The European Convention of Human Rights*, 3rd ed. (Oxford: OUP, 2002); F. Sudre, *Droit européen et international des droits de l'homme*, 6th ed. (Paris: PUF, 2003), pp. 88 *et seq.*

and Political Rights (hereinafter ICCPR),[19] no Government can be held *per se* directly responsible.[20] However, and this constitutes the second maxim of law, when hearing cases connected with an arbitration (whether in assisting the arbitration, or reviewing or enforcing an award), domestic courts of Contracting States must comply with the Convention's fundamental guarantees. In other words, whenever arbitration establishes *a contact* with domestic courts they will certainly be bound to enforce applicable international human rights law.[21] A different solution would lead to international responsibility of the forum State. Human rights, then, in such a context, become paradoxically a factor of re-territorialisation of arbitration.

It is possible, therefore, to expand upon human rights issues concerning arbitration in the following contexts: (1) the arbitration agreement; (2) arbitral proceedings including determination of applicable law to the merits of disputes; (3) mandatory rules and public policy.

Human rights and arbitration agreements

When one of the parties contests the validity of an arbitration agreement, and wishes to initiate proceedings before a given domestic court, it will often seize a court that has jurisdiction on the merits under its domestic

[19] GA Resolution 2200 A (XXI), 21 UN GAOR Supp. (Mo.16) at 52, UN Doc. A/6316 (1966), 999 UNTS 171.

[20] On the domestic level this conclusion has been confirmed, (although outside the jurisdiction of ECHR discussed above) by the US Second Circuit in the case of *National Broadcasting Company, Inc. v. Bear Stearns & Co., Inc.*, No. 98–7468 (26 January 1999). The Court held that 28 USC sect. 1782, which authorises US courts to provide judicial assistance to foreign courts and tribunals by ordering testimony or the production of evidence does not apply to private commercial arbitration because such a panel does not constitute a 'foreign or international tribunal' under sect. 1782. In interpreting the statute, the Court stated that the term 'foreign or international tribunal' did not clearly include or exclude private commercial arbitrations. The Court noted that a broader reading of section 1782, permitting discovery of evidence from third parties, would conflict with sect. 7 of the Federal Arbitration Act which reflects the traditional contractual limitations on discovery in arbitration. 'The popularity of arbitration rests in considerable part on its asserted efficiency and cost-effectiveness-characteristics said to be at odds with full-scale litigation in the courts, and especially at odds with the broad-ranging discovery made possible by the Federal Rules of Civil Procedure . . . Opening the door to the type of discovery sought by NBC in this case likely would undermine one of the significant advantages of arbitration, and thus arguably conflict with the strong federal policy favouring arbitration as an alternative means of dispute resolution.'

[21] See generally: H. Yu, 'Total Separation of International Commercial Arbitration and National Court Regime', *Journal of International Arbitration* 2 (1998), 145–66; M. Storme and F. de Ly (eds.), *The Place of Arbitration* (Gent: Mys & Breesch Uitgevers, 1992).

rules or according to any applicable conventions. Article II of the New York Convention provides in this respect that 'the court of a Contracting State, when seized of an action in a matter in respect of which the parties have made an agreement within the meaning of this article, at the request of one of the parties, refer the parties to arbitration, unless it finds that the said agreement is null and void, inoperative or incapable of being performed'.[22] Human rights issues may arise at this level in the same way as any other question involving validity of the arbitration agreement. Within the Council of Europe's territorial jurisdiction, the ECHR may be invoked.

It seems clear that, as long as parties have freely agreed to arbitrate, the European Court of Human Rights (hereinafter ECtHR) will 'stay out of the fight'. The argument is that if the parties have *freely* consented to arbitration, they have, ipso facto, waived their rights before domestic courts according to Article 6(1) of the ECHR, which provides that:

> In the determination of his civil rights and obligations or of any criminal charge against him, everyone is entitled to a fair and public hearing within a reasonable time by an independent and impartial tribunal established by law. Judgement shall be pronounced publicly but the press and public may be excluded from all or part of the trial in the interests of morals, public order or national security in a democratic society, where the interests of juveniles or the protection of the private life of the parties so require, or to the extent strictly necessary in the opinion of the court in special circumstances where publicity would prejudice the interests of justice.

The history of the Convention shows that it was intended to introduce international State responsibility for the operation of its court system; it was not meant to apply to private justice.[23] The wording of Article 6 makes reference to a 'tribunal established by law'. It does not refer to an arbitral tribunal even though it is established by agreement between the parties and derives its binding force from law.[24]

The doctrine of contractual waiver has been established by the European Commission of Human Rights (hereinafter EComHR) since its first decision touching arbitration matters, *X v. Federal Republic of*

---

[22] Above, fn. 13.

[23] C. Jarrosson, 'L'arbitrage et la Convention européenne des droits de l'homme', *Revue de l'arbitrage* (1989), 577 *et seq.*

[24] O. Jacot-Guillarmod, 'L'arbitrage privé face à l'article 6 §1 de la Convention européenne des droits de l'homme', in F. Matscher and H. Petzold (eds.), *Protecting Human Rights: the European Dimension: Studies in Honour of Gérard J. Wiarda* (Cologne: Heymanns, 1988), p. 291.

Germany,[25] and has been developed by the Strasbourg Court, ECtHR, in *Deweer v. Belgium*, where it clearly stated that:

> In the Contracting States' domestic legal system, a waiver of this kind is frequently encountered both in civil matters, notably in the shape of arbitration clauses in contracts. . .the waiver which has undeniable advantages for the individual concerned as well as for the administration of justice, does not in principle offend against the Convention.[26]

The same point was made in *Axelsson v. Sweden* where the EComHR 'notes that insofar as arbitration is based on agreement between the parties to the dispute, it is a natural consequence of their right to regulate their mutual relations as they see fit. From a more general perspective, arbitration procedures can also be said to pursue the legitimate aim of encouraging non-judicial settlement and of relieving the courts of excessive burden of cases'.[27] Consequently, in this respect, no violation of Article 6 of the ECHR, was found.

But in a subsequent case, *Bramelid and Malmström v. Sweden*, some corporation rules of Swedish law were challenged.[28] In this case, minority shareholders of a Swedish company asked the EComHR to evaluate the compatibility with the ECHR of Swedish rules imposing arbitration to

---

[25] *Yearbook HR* 5 (1962), 88.

[26] 2 *EurHR Rep* (1980), 439, at 460. The European Commission, in *Nördstrom-Janzon and Nördstrom-Lehtinen v. the Netherlands* (Application 28101/95 (1996) 87 A EurCommHR, Dec. & Rep. 112) dismissing the application, noted: '. . .in the first place that the proceedings of which the applicants complain are arbitration proceedings. In the present case the arbitration was based on a joint-venture agreement and a subsequent Deed of Settlement concluded between the parties concerned. The arbitration was thus based on a voluntary agreement according to which disputes between the parties should not be settled by the ordinary courts but under a special arbitration system. Consequently, there was a renunciation by the parties of a procedure before the ordinary courts satisfying all the guarantees of Article 6 of the Convention . . . the Commission notes that in the present case it has not been alleged that the arbitration was concluded under duress'. Confirming the Article 6 (1) waiver doctrine are other European Commission cases: *R. v. Switzerland*, 51 Eur. Comm. H.R. Dec. & Rep. 85, 93 (1987); *Jakob Boss Söhne KG v. Federal Republic of Germany*, 2 December 1991, Appl. No. 18479/91, Decision of 2 December 1991, Ref. 1060; *Hedland v. Sweden*, Appl. No. 24118/94, Decision of 9 April 1997, 94 Eur. Comm. H. R. Dec. & Rep. (1997); and the European Court case, *Suovaniemi et al. v. Finland*, 23 February 1999, Appl. N.31376/96, Ref. 5131. See also for a partial critique of this approach, D. Wedam-Lukic, 'Arbitration and Article 6 of the European Convention on Human Rights', *Arbitration* 64 (1998) 516.

[27] App. N. 12213/86, (1990) 86 Eur. Comm. HR, Dec. & Rep. 99.

[28] App. N. 8588–8589/79 (1982) 29 Eur. Comm. HR, Dec. & Rep. 64. Compare the decision by the ECtHR in *Lithgow and others v. United Kingdom*, 8 July 1986, A102 8 Eur. Comm. HR, Dec. & Rep. 329.

evaluate minority shares in case of total acquisition. According to Swedish law, whenever a company owned ninety percent of shares of another company, then it could purchase the remaining ten percent for a value that in case of dispute should be decided by arbitration. In this case, the EComHR upheld the case by correctly distinguishing between *voluntary* and *mandatory* arbitration.

If the only dispute resolution system available in a country for certain matters defined by statute law is arbitration, there is no true agreement to arbitrate and then, being mandatory arbitration, it must follow all requirements set out in human rights treaties.[29] That also means the resulting award may be challenged before the ECtHR. Mandatory arbitration may in fact turn into an instrument of oppression or reduction of the freedoms that the ECHR seeks to endow and protect; hence, full transfer of judicial function to arbitrators by a nation State amounts to transfer to arbitral bodies of the obligation to respect international human rights law.

Conversely, under the 'waiver doctrine', human rights bodies have often upheld *voluntary* international commercial arbitration clauses and proceedings.

In 1994, the ECtHR decided a case in which a corporation, Stran Greek Refineries, challenged the Greek Government. The latter claimed that it had terminated by statute both a construction contract of a refinery together with the arbitration clause contained in it, despite an award having already been made on the basis of the arbitration clause.[30] The Strasbourg Court held that the unilateral termination of a contract does not pre-empt effect or validity of certain essential clauses of the contract, such as the arbitration clause, thus making a contribution to the recognition of the principle of the autonomy of an arbitration agreement from a human rights perspective. Finally, the same Court concluded that there was an interference even with the applicants' right of property as guaranteed by Article 1 of Protocol No. 1.[31] This led to the conclusion that:

---

[29] But no clear-cut distinction has so far been made between voluntary and mandatory arbitration: see S. Adam, 'Arbitration, Alternative Dispute Resolution Generally and the European Convention on Human Rights: An Anglo-Centric View', *Journal of International Arbitration* 21 (2004), 413–438.

[30] *Stran Greek Refineries et al. v. Greece*, Dec. 9, 1994, A 301-B, 19 Eur. Comm. HR, Dec. & Rep. 293. See also the commentary by Ali Bencheneb, in *Revue de l'Arbitrage* (1996), 181; as well as observations by P. Tavernier, *Journal de Droit International* 122 (1995), 796.

[31] Protocol to the Convention for the Protection of Human Rights and Fundamental Freedoms, Paris 20 March 1952, ETS No. 9, available at ⟨http://www.hrni.org/EN/issues.php?language=en&cat_ID=0&target_ID=121, accessed: 18 April 2006⟩.

. . . it was impossible for the applicants to secure enforcement of an arbitration award having final effect and under which the State was required to pay them specified sums in respect of expenditure that they had incurred in seeking to fulfil their contractual obligations or even for them to take further action to recover the sums in question through the courts. In conclusion, there was an interference with the applicants' property right.

Thus, the European Court of Human Rights ruled against the Greek Government, upholding the validity and enforcement of the arbitral award.

Human rights and arbitration proceedings

The ECHR and, to a lesser extent, the ICCPR are often relied upon by parties contesting the conduct of certain arbitrations. Although relevant guarantees may be found in most contemporary arbitration laws, it is nevertheless useful for them to be formally set out in the ECHR. Under the most rigorous view, since arbitrators are *not* State courts and human rights instruments are binding on those States (and their apparatus) having accepted to be bound by them, it follows that, *per se*, those rules are not directly applicable to arbitration proceedings. Along the same lines, in the well known *Cubic* case, the French *Cour de Cassation* dismissed an Article 6(1) ECHR plea in relation to an arbitration proceeding considering that '. . .*la Convention (CEDH) qui ne concerne que les Etats et les jurisdictions étatiques est sans application en matière [d'arbitrage]*.' [32]

In truth, if an arbitration is concluded without soliciting the intervention of a State court – which is what happens in the great majority of cases – then human rights conventions are, *per se*, inapplicable, save in a case in which arbitrators recognise a violation of transnational public policy. However, in those cases in which domestic courts, be that of the seat of the arbitration or that of *exequatur* country (or countries), are asked to step into the arbitration process, then the scenario changes. It would be unreasonable to argue that the territorial State where arbitration is conducted will lend its support to arbitral tribunals operating within its jurisdiction without claiming some degree of control over the conduct of those arbitral tribunals to ensure that certain minimum

---

[32] Cour de Cassation, Civ. (1ʳᵉ ch.), *Cubic Defense Systems v. Chambre de Commerce Internationale*, 20 February 2001, *Revue Critique de Droit International Privé* 91 (2002), 124; *Revue de l'Arbitrage*, (2001), 511 with obs. by T. Clay.

standards of justice are met, particularly in procedural matters.[33] A fortiori, all States bound by the ECHR are obliged to guarantee everyone's
fundamental right to a fair trial, regardless of the legal nature of proceedings.[34] As a result, arbitrators and arbitral institutions should take the
greatest care in treating such issues because the destiny of their award is
at stake.

Sensitive areas of arbitration proceedings include a right to due
process, a right to independent and impartial arbitrators, a right to help
with translation and legal costs, a right to have the case brought speedily,
and without undue delay, and a right to an effective remedy. These issues
will now be considered in turn.

Due process

The right of a party to due process is not only a right protected by human
rights instruments such as Article 6(1) of the ECHR, Article 8(1) of the
ACHR and Article 14 of the ICCPR, but it is also protected by most
domestic arbitration laws[35] and by Article V(1)(b) of the New York
Convention. Although the courts are not allowed to interfere ex officio in
arbitrations, the arbitrators are not given carte blanche for the conduct of
the proceedings; they have to respect the agreement of the parties on procedure and the principle of due process. States called upon to recognise
and enforce the award will refuse to do it because certain basic standards
have not been observed in the making of the award.[36]

---

[33] See M. Kerr, 'Arbitration and the Courts: the UNCITRAL Model Law', ICLQ 34 (1984),
1–24.

[34] R. Briner and F. von Schlabrendoff, 'Article 6 of the European Convention on Human
Rights and its Bearing upon International Arbitration', in R. Briner, L. Y. Fortier, K. P.
Berger and J. Bredow (eds.), Law of International Business and Dispute Settlement in the
21st Century: Liber Amicorum Karl-Heinz Böckstiegel (Cologne: Heymanns, 2001), pp. 89
et seq. See also ALI/UNIDROIT Principles of Transnational Civil Procedure (Cambridge:
Cambridge University Press, 2006).

[35] See for example Article 18 of the United Nations Commission on International Trade
Law (UNCITRAL) Model Law on International Commercial Arbitration (1985) (for an
updated list of countries following the Model Law see http://www.uncitral.org (accessed:
1 March 2006); the English Arbitration Act of 1996, sect. 33(1)(a); Swiss Code on Private
International Law, Article 182(3).

[36] For a list of such standards, see, e.g., R. de Gouttes, 'L'enchevêtrement des normes internationales relatives au procès équitable: comment les concilier?', in Université Robert
Schumann de Strasbourg/Cour De Cassation (eds.), Les nouveaux développements du
procès équitable au sens de la Convention européenne des droits de l'homme (Brussels:
Bruylant, 1996), pp. 141–144. Cf. Jarrosson, 'L'arbitrage et la Convention européenne
des droits de l'homme', 573; J.-H. Moitry, 'Right to a Fair Trial and the European

In a decision rendered in 1991, the EComHR went further, holding that a State which recognises an award as a basis for enforcement proceedings must institute a control mechanism to ensure that the arbitration proceedings have been carried out in conformity with fundamental rights and in particular with the right to be heard.[37] Therefore, even if Article 6 of the ECHR has no direct impact on the proceedings before the arbitral tribunal, it does exercise a certain influence, since the courts deciding on enforcement of awards must ascertain compliance with fundamental rights.[38] The right to a fair hearing is an expression of the very values which are protected by due process and similar concepts in arbitration. The implementation of the right to a fair hearing, with the necessary adjustments, may thus offer valuable guidance to arbitrators.

The application of the principle of equality to the constitution of the arbitral tribunal was examined by French Courts in the complex *Dutco* case, where three parties were involved. A consortium agreement between three companies – BKMI, Siemens and Dutco – for the construction of a cement factory included an arbitration clause, stipulating that disputes arising out of the agreement would be submitted to an arbitral tribunal comprising three arbitrators appointed in accordance with the International Chamber of Commerce (ICC) Arbitration Rules. Dutco commenced proceedings against its two partners and nominated an arbitrator. The ICC Court of Arbitration ordered BKMI and Siemens to jointly nominate one arbitrator, and it appointed the third arbitrator itself. However, BKMI and Siemens had differing interests at stake and they therefore challenged the Court's order. The arbitral tribunal nevertheless considered itself to be validly constituted and, consequently, an application to set aside its award was brought before the Paris Court of Appeals. The two defendants argued, *inter alia*, that as a result of the principle of equality they could not be deprived of their right to each appoint one trusted arbitrator and thus to participate equally in the constitution of the arbitral tribunal. The Court of Appeals rejected their claim, holding that

Convention on Human Rights – Some Remarks on the *République de Guinée* Case', *Journal of International Arbitration* (1989), 115. See also the decisions of the EComHR, 4 March 1987, *ASA Bulletin* (1990), 251, and 11 July 1989, *ASA Bulletin* (1990), 262, which examine the position of the Swiss courts in their review of the duration of the arbitral proceedings. See *Société X v. Société O*, ATF 128 III 50 (2001).

[37] *Association Jacob Boss Söhne KG v. Germany*, No. 18479/91.

[38] The courts may also have to review the enforceability of the arbitration agreement, i.e., the validity of the waiver: *X v. The Federal Republic of Germany* n. 1197/61, *Yearbook of the ECtHR* 5 (1962), 88 at 96.

there had been no violation of the principle of equality in the constitution of the arbitral tribunal as the arbitration clause could have been construed as requiring two of the parties to choose a single arbitrator between them. The *Cour de Cassation* reversed such a decision and annulled the award, holding that 'the principle of the equality of the parties in the designation of the arbitrators is a matter which concerns public policy',[39] an approach consistent with due process requirements imposed by ECHR.

Another area of operation of Article 6 of the ECHR has been identified in the *Stran Refineries* case by the ECtHR where it stated that '[t]he principle of the rule of law and the notion of fair trial enshrined in Article 6 [of the ECHR] preclude any interference by the *legislature* with the administration of justice designed to influence the judicial determination of the dispute'.[40] This principle offers further possibilities of application in mixed arbitration proceedings. The State, State-owned entity, and even intergovernmental organisation's agreement to submit disputes to arbitration would be meaningless if it could be circumvented by that party simply refusing to participate in the constitution of the arbitral tribunal and then relying on its immunity from jurisdiction to ensure that such refusal could not be overcome by action before the appropriate court. This was the solution reached by the Paris Tribunal of First Instance, and later by the Paris Court of Appeals, in a case concerning the United Nations Educational, Scientific and Cultural Organisation (UNESCO). Faced with UNESCO's refusal to participate in the constitution of an arbitral tribunal despite a valid arbitration agreement, the President of the Paris Tribunal of First Instance held that 'in entering into an arbitration clause, UNESCO waived its immunity from jurisdiction and necessarily agreed to allow the implementation of the method of dispute resolution set forth in the contract.'[41] This decision was upheld by the Paris Court of Appeals, stating in very clear terms that:

> [T]he immunity from jurisdiction on which UNESCO seeks to rely does not allow it to free itself from the *pacta sunt servanda* principle by refusing to nominate an arbitrator in compliance with the arbitration in the contract between it [and the claimant in the arbitration] on the grounds of the absence of a dispute as to the performance of the contract at issue, a

---

[39] Cour de Cassation, 7 January 1992, *Siemens AG/BKMI Industrieanlagen GmbH v. Dutco Construction Company, Yearbook of Commercial Arbitration* 17 (1993), 140.
[40] *Stran Greek Refineries and Stratis Andreadis v. Greece*, above, fn. 30, para. 49 (emphasis added).
[41] TGI, Paris, 20 October 1997, *Boulois v. UNESCO, Revue de l'Arbitrage*, (1997), 575, and C. Jarrosson's note at pp. 577–582.

question which is to be decided by the arbitrators alone; in addition, to allow [UNESCO's] objection would inevitably prevent [the claimant] from submitting the dispute to a judicial authority. This would be contrary to public policy in that it constitutes a denial of justice and a violation of the provisions of Article 6–1 of the European Convention for the Protection of Human Rights and Fundamental Freedoms, and should therefore lead the court – which is involved in this case only in support of the arbitration – to accept the claimant's request [to have the arbitral tribunal constituted with the assistance of the courts].[42]

It should however be pointed out that the Swiss Federal Tribunal did not reach the same conclusion with regard to the European Organisation for Nuclear Research (CERN); the court denied a party access to the Swiss courts where that party sought to bring an action against an award made in an arbitration against CERN.[43]

Right to independent and impartial arbitration

Most domestic arbitration statutory rules in the world provide some measures by which arbitrators shall act fairly, independently and impartially, so that each of the parties can present its case. There are mechanisms for recourse to State courts to prevent arbitrators from acting unfairly or with bias or even committing serious procedural irregularities. An award may thus be challenged before the courts of the *situs arbitri* (site of the arbitration) or of the *exequatur* State (or, possibly, States) and each one of them will apply due process requirements of the *lex fori*.[44] The requirement of independence and impartiality recalls the language used in various human rights instruments such as Article 10 of the Universal Declaration of Human Rights (UDHR),[45] Article 6(1) of the ECHR, Article 14(1) of the ICCPR, or Article 47 of the Charter of Fundamental Rights of the European Union.[46]

---

[42] *Cour d'Appel*, 19 June 1998, *UNESCO v. Boulois*, No. 97/26549, *Revue de l'Arbitrage* (1999), 343 with a note by C. Jarrosson at 345–349.

[43] Swiss Fed. Trib., 21 December 1992, *Groupement Fougerolle v. CERN*, *Revue de l'Arbitrage* (1994), 175, and P. Glavinis' note at p. 180.

[44] J.-F. Poudret and S. Besson, *Droit comparé de l'arbitrage international* (Zurich: Schulthess/Paris: L.G.D.J./ Brussels: Bruylant, 2002), p. 509.

[45] UDHR, adopted on 10 December 1948, GA res. 217A (III), UN Doc. A/810 at 71 (1948).

[46] Charter of Fundamental Rights of the European Union, *Official Journal of the European Communities*, No. C 364/1, 18 December 2000.

Arbitration regulations also reflect those concepts albeit with some adaptation.[47] Once again it is important to state the maxim of law according to which arbitrators do not have a forum and are not at all the clone of domestic courts. Thus, 'legal transplants' of human rights rules (and case law applying those rules) in different instruments does not mean coincidence of application. It only means *convergence* of rules applicable to State courts and transnational arbitration towards human rights values. However, since each set of rules maintains its own sphere of application, the 'convergence factor' may have some impact only on the interpretation of law.

The typical sanction for violation of arbitration institutional regulations rules on impartiality or independence is the removal of arbitrators. This is an important factor of the globalisation of procedural human rights rules, since arbitral regulations are applied throughout the world, in a space much wider than, for example, the territorial jurisdiction of the ECHR. Article 15 of the ICC Arbitration Rules requires that the arbitrator must act 'fairly and impartially and ensure that each party has a reasonable opportunity to present its case'.[48] The arbitrator should also be independent, i.e. not have had a personal, social or financial relationship with one of the parties which is reasonably liable to lead to bias or creates a reasonable apprehension of bias. Thus the existence of a prior relationship with one of the parties is a ground for challenge and removal of an arbitrator when it gives rise to reasonable doubts about his impartiality. By impartiality is generally meant a state of mind of the arbitrator, whilst partiality is a predisposition towards one of the parties as to the outcome of the disputed issue.[49] On the other hand, it is perfectly legitimate, even from a human rights perspective, that a party-appointed arbitrator ensures that the evidence and the arguments advanced by the appointing party are fully considered by the arbitral tribunal; this is simply a matter of fully implementing the fair hearing principle.

---

[47] See, for example, Article 15(1) UNCITRAL Regulations; 16(1) American Arbitration Association International Arbitration regulations; 14(1). Vienna International Arbitration Rules. Conversely, the 'mirror effect' makes the same arbitration rules difficult to amend by parties. See P. Fouchard, 'Rapport final sur le statut de l'arbitre : un rapport de la Commission de l'arbitrage international de la CCI', *ICC International Court of Arbitration Bulletin* 7 (1996), 28 *et seq.*; Lew, Mistelis and Kröll, *Comparative International Commercial Arbitration*, p. 258.

[48] Y. Derains, E. A. Schwartz, *A Guide to the New ICC Rules of Arbitration* (The Hague: Kluwer Law International, 1998), pp. 214 *et seq.*

[49] G. Petrochilos, *Procedural law in international arbitration* (Oxford: OUP, 2004), pp. 131 *et seq.*

If the legal nature of the independence, impartiality and neutrality requirements of arbitrators is structurally different from rules binding on domestic courts but closer to those of international tribunals,[50] nonetheless these requirements may be seen as vague. In the absence of a worldwide intergovernmental convention on arbitrators' duties, it seems that private codifications of such duties might play a significant role in this regard. Here we are confronted, in the procedural sphere, with a phenomenon of the generation of Codes of Conduct taking place side by side with those of corporate social responsibility in transnational businesses.[51] In this respect the *International Bar Association Guidelines on Conflict of Interest in International Arbitration* (2004)[52] as well as the *American Arbitration Association's Code of Ethics for Arbitrators in Commercial Disputes* (2004)[53] may provide objective and well accepted standards to ascertain concretely whether or not an arbitrator has failed to be impartial, independent or neutral.

The same reasoning leads to another important issue. If requirements of fairness and impartiality of arbitrators includes necessarily disclosure of all relevant facts, they may also include the inclination of the arbitrator towards specific human rights NGOs or political circles which may be involved in the case at stake. One example of this, perhaps at the far edge and controversial, was an ICC case[54] where a challenge was raised against the chairman of an arbitral tribunal during the course of an arbitration, on the basis that the chairman had been an active critic of the human rights situation under the former *régime* in the country of the challenging party. In the event, the ICC International Court of Arbitration rejected the challenge. But it may well have been preferable for the arbitrator to have disclosed these facts before confirmation so that any comments could have been received and considered prior to the commencement of the arbitration. Such is exactly the purpose of having the prospective arbitrator examine the situation through 'the eyes of the

50 G. Guillaume, 'De l'indépendance des membres de la Cour internationale de Justice', in *B. Boutros-Ghali amicorum discipulorumque liber: paix, développement, démocratie* (Brussels: Bruylant, 1998), vol. I, pp. 475–487. See in this respect Article 167 of EC Treaty; Article 21.3 of ECHR et 4 of ECHR Statute.
51 See below, the section on 'Corporate social responsibility 'from above' and 'from below': towards contractualised human rights?'
52 The publication can be found at: http://www.ibanet.org/images/downloads/International ArbitrationGuidelines.pdf (accessed: 18 April 2006).
53 http://www.adr.org/sp.asp?id=21958 (accessed: 18 April 2006).
54 Reported by S. Bond, 'The Selection of ICC Arbitrators and the Requirement of Independence', *Arbitration International* 4 (1988), 300–310.

parties', the applicable code of ethics and in the light of human rights principles.

Such issues have been partially addressed by human rights bodies, on a regional scale, in *Nördstrom-Janzon and Nördstrom-Lethinen v. the Netherlands*.[55] In this case, originating from a private arbitration between a Finnish party and a Dutch company, the former claimed a violation of due process based on the allegation that one of the three arbitrators appointed by the Netherlands Arbitrage Instituut was not independent and impartial. However, the EComHR, recalling the waiver doctrine, dismissed the application since both Dutch arbitration law and the courts' decisions were consistent with Article 6 general requirements.[56]

Language and procedural costs

Even the language of arbitration proceedings, with possible consequent translation costs, may become a crucial factor when evaluating a violation of due process. If, before the domestic courts, *lingua fori* is the dominant rule, in transnational arbitration the language used is one of the procedural variables. The point is illustrated by a case decided by the Austrian Supreme Court on 4 December 1994. In an arbitration taking place in Vienna, a disagreement arose between the parties regarding the language in which the proceedings would be carried out. The defendant obtained an injunction regarding the language in which the proceedings would be conducted, obtaining a finding that they be conducted in German (mainly) or in English. The arbitral tribunal appealed against the injunction, and the Vienna Court of Appeal (*Oberlandesgericht Wien*) set aside the injunction on the grounds that the provisions on arbitration of the Code of Civil Procedure (CCP) did not provide for such intervention. This decision was in turn appealed to the Austrian Supreme Court, which established that the instances in which the courts may interfere in arbitral proceedings should be strictly limited to those provided in the provisions on arbitration in the Code of Civil Procedure. It added that:

> An injunction may be issued in case of an imminent breach of a right guaranteed by the European Convention on Human Rights, provided that the conditions enumerated in Article 381 at 2 of the Implementing Act (*Exekutionsordnung*) are met: the injunction must appear to be necessary

---

[55] Above, fn. 26.
[56] Similar conclusions have been reached by the ECtHR, 23 February 1999, *Suovaniemi et al. v. Finland*, quoted above fn. 26.

for the prevention of imminent acts of violence or the avoidance of an imminent irreversible damage. It has not even been alleged by the claimant that such dangers were imminent.[57]

This decision must be read in light of the 'pro-arbitration policy', leaving the arbitrators to decide procedural issues, including language, within the limits of exceptional situations of a manifest violation of fundamental rights, and is a balanced solution which respects both the nature of arbitration, and the need for human rights protection by domestic courts. In essence and from a Law &Economics perspective, it can be said that procedural choices by arbitrators must be cost-effective. The due process principle, then, may be seen as security given to each one of the parties vis-à-vis procedural decisions creating an imbalance in costs for one of the parties.

Speed of arbitration, 'reasonable delay' and effective remedy

Arbitrators must complete their functions within the legal or contractual deadlines that they have been given. This rule is universally accepted, but is now rarely expressed in the form of an explicit obligation imposed upon the arbitrators. In any case, by accepting their functions the arbitrators also undertake to perform them diligently. Again, this rule is universally recognised, although it is seldom expressed as such. It mirrors the 'reasonable time' requirement found in international conventions and declarations concerning the protection of human rights in court proceedings;[58] in a 1987 decision, the EComHR confirmed this reading.[59]

A party in a Swiss arbitration, having exhausted all national remedies, filed a complaint before the Commission alleging that the arbitrators had failed to render an award 'within a reasonable time'. The Commission held that parties could validly waive the guarantees of Article 6 of the ECHR by agreeing to arbitration, and that a State could not be charged with the actions of arbitrators, 'unless and to the extent' that its courts had become involved.[60] In the case at hand, the courts had performed

---

[57] Austrian Supreme Court, 4 December 1994, 4 Ob 1542/94, in *Yearbook of Commercial Arbitration* 22 (1997), 263–265.
[58] See the *IBA Rules of Ethics for International Arbitrators.* See also Article 6(1) of the EHRC.
[59] *R. v. Switzerland*, No. 10881/84, 51 DR 83 (1987).
[60] Strangely enough, after having held, in this case, that Article 6 did not apply to arbitration (Supreme Court decision *R v. A* of 22 July 1986, ATF 112 Ia 166), the Swiss Supreme Court in later cases held to the contrary (decision *X v. Y AG* of 30 April 1991, ATF 117 Ia 166; decision *Hitachi Ltd v. SMS Schloemann Siemag AG* of 30 June 1994, *ASA Bulletin*,

their control function within a proper time period. Consequently, whatever the duration of the arbitration, the complaint was ill-founded. But the principle stays and should be considered as a *caveat* for arbitrators. The same reasoning leads one to conclude that domestic courts should provide the parties with an 'effective remedy' in the light of Article 13 of the ECHR; that is, the possibility of referring a case to the national courts before making an application to the ECtHR on the basis of Article 34 of the Convention.[61] Hence a statutory rule (and even a contractual clause) of domestic arbitration law blocking any recourse against arbitration awards would be against Article 34 ECHR.

Human rights and *lex contractus*

The principle of 'party autonomy' is the cornerstone of the modern movement towards the liberalisation and globalisation of international trade and investment.[62] In international contracts it is a reasonable expectation of the parties – and that expectation is generally protected by applicable arbitration law – that their intentions reflected in their contract (including the choice of the applicable law) should, in principle, be respected by arbitrators. In the global market place the parties' legitimate intentions should be determinative, otherwise international trade and commerce may not prosper. One writer has noted that '[t]he zenith of party freedom is arbitration'.[63] Party freedom with regard to arbitration extends to all its various aspects: choice of arbitration, arbitral forum, applicable substantive law, *lex arbitri*, etc. The parties can choose the applicable law either expressly or implicitly.[64]

(1997), 99 and *Revue Suisse de Droit International* (1997), 587; *Société X v. Société O*, ATF 128 III 50 (2001). See also the decisions of the EComHR, 4 March 1987, *ASA Bulletin* (1990), 251, and 11 July 1989, *ASA Bulletin*, (1990), 262, which examine the position of the Swiss courts in their review of the duration of the arbitral proceedings.).

[61] Article 34 states 'The Court may receive applications from any person, non-governmental organisation or group of individuals claiming to be the victim of a violation by one of the High Contracting Parties of the rights set forth in the Convention or the protocols thereto. The High Contracting Parties undertake not to hinder in any way the effective exercise of this right.'

[62] See, for example, L. Brilmayer, 'Rights, Fairness, and Choice of Law', 98 *Yale LJ* (1989), 1277–1319; E. Jayme, 'Identité culturelle et intégration: le droit international privé post-moderne', 251 *Recueil des Cours* (1995-I) 9, 147 *et seq.*

[63] P. J. Borchers, 'The Internationalization of Contractual Conflicts Law', 28 *Vanderbilt Journal of Transnational Law* (1995), 421, at 439.

[64] See P. Nygh, *Autonomy in International Contracts* (Oxford: Clarendon Press, 1999).

It is clear that human rights rules are part of the *lex contractus* and therefore human rights are part of the law applicable to the merits of the dispute; if then the applicable law is Swiss, Italian or English, it will certainly include the human rights rules in force in each legal system. Moreover, if the applicable law is *lex mercatoria* (and/or the Unidroit Principles of International Commercial Contracts[65]) it will be subject to the limitation of truly international or transnational public policy. Further, the arbitrator may have to take into account the mandatory rules or public policies of the *situs arbitri* or of the place of enforcement of the award.[66]

Human rights in the selection of international mandatory rules and in public policy

It may also be argued that Article 7(1) of the EC Convention on the Law Applicable to Contractual Obligations (the Rome Convention of 1980)[67] can be interpreted in light of the human rights justification of certain governmental measures. In fact, according to that Article:

> When applying under this Convention the law of a country, effect may be given to the mandatory rules of the law of another country with which the situation has a close connection, if and in so far as, under the law of the latter country, those rules must be applied whatever the law applicable to the contract. In considering whether to give effect to these mandatory rules, regard shall be had to their nature and purpose and to the consequences of their application or non-application.[68]

Thus, the reference to the consequences of application or non-application of mandatory rules should be weighed by a social engineer

---

[65] See http://www.unidroit.org/english/principles/contracts/principles2004/blackletter2004. pdf (accessed: 18 April 2006).

[66] See P. Mayer, 'Mandatory Rules of Law in International Arbitration', 2 *Arbitration International* (1986), 75; N. Voser, 'Mandatory rules of law as a limitation on the law applicable in international commercial arbitration', *The American Review of International Arbitration* 7 (1996), 319–357; M. Blessing, 'Mandatory rules of law versus party autonomy in international arbitration', *Journal of International Arbitration* 14 (1997), 23–40; Lew, Mistelis and Kröll, *Comparative International Commercial Arbitration*, paras. 17–27 *et seq.*

[67] Available at http://europa.eu.int/eur-lex/lex/LexUriServ/site/en/oj/2005/c_334/c_ 33420051230en00010027.pdf and see also the Proposal for a Regulation of the European Parliament on the law applicable to contractual obligations Com (2005) 650 final of 15 December 2005, available at http://europa.eu.int/eur-lex/lex/LexUriServ/site/en/com/ 2005/com2005_0650en01.pdf (both accessed: 18 April 2006). [68] *Ibid.*, Article 7(1).

such as the arbitrator, *inter alia*, in light of human rights considerations.[69]

Legislation and executive regulation imposing certain economic sanctions on particular countries because of human rights abuses (such as
apartheid regimes) would limit discretional choices to arbitrators (and
courts[70]). Hence, in the famous case of *Regazzoni v. K.C. Sethia Ltd.*,[71] the
House of Lords applied the Indian boycott of the Republic of South
Africa to a contract governed by English law, acknowledging the foundation of the Indian overriding statute, *inter alia*, on human rights concerns. Conversely, unilateral sanctions such as boycotting for racial or
religious reasons may not be applied on the basis of Article 7(1) because
this would contravene fundamental human rights principles.[72]

Last but not least, it should be underlined that domestic courts are
entitled to check that the award does not offend public policy. In the
transnational arbitral process several 'public policies' are at stake, firstly,
that of the State in which the seat of the arbitration is located, then the
public policy of the State or the States in which recognition and/or
enforcement are sought. Undoubtedly, human rights pertain both to
international[73] and to transnational public policy and they operate both
for substantive and procedural issues.[74]

---

[69] B. Goldman, 'Les conflits de lois dans l'arbitrage international de droit privé', *Recueil des Cour* 109 (1968/II), 347 *et seq.*; P. Kahn, 'Les réactions des milieux économiques', in P. Kahn and C. Kessedjian (eds.), *L'illicite dans le commerce international* (Paris: Litec, 1996), pp. 477 *et seq.* (p. 493); J. Dolinger, 'World Public Policy: Real International Public policy in the Conflict of Laws', *Texas ILJ* 17 (1982), 167 *et seq.* at pp. 175–176.

[70] See L. Picchio Forlati, 'Critères de rattachement et règles d'applicabilité. A' l'heure de la protection des Droits de l'homme en Europe', *Rivista di diritto internazionale privato e processuale* 4 (2005), 32 *et seq.*

[71] Court of Appeal, 26 April 1956 [1956] 2 All ER 487; House of Lords, 21 October 1957 [1957] 3 All ER 286.

[72] See ICC Awards Nos. 2977, 2978 and 3033 (1978), in *Yearbook of Commercial Arbitration* (1981), 133 *et seq*; ICC Award No. 3881 (1984), *Journal de Droit International* (1986), 1096.

[73] Here, reference should be made to international-domestic public policy: Italian *Corte di Cassazione*, 8 January 1981, n.189, in *Rivista di diritto internazionale privato e processuale*, (1981), 787 *et seq.*, defines international public policy as 'a body of universal principles shared by nations of similar civilisations, aiming at the protection of fundamental human rights, often embodied in international declarations or conventions'. Later see *Corte di Appello* of Milan, 4 December 1992, *Allsop Automatic Inc. v. Tecnoski s.n.c.*, *Yearbook of Commercial Arbitration* 22 (1997), 725, para. 4.

[74] Amongst a vast literature see B. Goldman, 'La protection internationale des droits de l'homme et l'ordre public international dans le fonctionnement de la règle de conflits de lois', in *Mélanges René Cassin*, (Paris : Pedone, 1969) vol. I, pp. 449 *et seq.*; P. Hammje, 'Droits fondamentaux et ordre public', *Revue critique de Droit International Privé* (1997),

After thorough study by its International Commercial Arbitration Committee, the International Law Association (ILA) adopted, in April 2002, a *Resolution on Public Policy as a Bar to Enforcement of International Arbitral Awards*, including recommendations to domestic courts.[75] In Recommendation 1(d) it is noted that:

> 'The international public policy of any State includes: i) fundamental principles, pertaining to justice and morality, that the State wishes to protect even when it is not directly concerned; ii) rules designed to serve the essential political, social or economic interest of the State, these being known as '*lois de police*' or 'public policy rules'; and iii) the duty of the State to respect its obligations towards other States or international organisations'.

Examples of a substantive 'fundamental principle' have been identified in the principle of good faith,[76] and in the prohibition of abuse of rights (especially in civil law countries).[77] Other quoted examples include the prohibition of uncompensated expropriation[78] and the prohibition against discrimination[79]. Further activities to be considered as against public policy (*ordre public*) are piracy, terrorism, genocide, slavery, smuggling, drug trafficking and paedophilia.[80] The arms trade is not considered *per se* against human rights or public policy, since most of the trade is run through State-controlled agencies. Other examples may include trade in human body parts, and contracts which may not adequately observe environmental protection rules[81].

As to procedural public policy – a notion partially overlapping with the requirements prescribed in Article V.1(b) of the 1958 New York Convention – suffice it to say that the due process requirement is so fundamental and pervasive that it has been considered to be part of both international and transnational public policy.[82] Though there is a

---

1 *et seq.;* F. Galgano and F. Marrella, *Diritto del commercio internazionale* (Padua: CEDAM, 2004), p. 563 *et seq.* ; J. Beguin and M. Menjuq, *Traité de droit du commerce international* (Paris: Litec, 2005), p. 738.

[75] Res. 2/2002, adopted at the 70th ILA Conference held in New Delhi, India, 2–6 April 2002.

[76] See the Interim Report of the ILA International Commercial Arbitration Committee on the topic of public policy as a ground for refusing recognition and enforcement of international arbitral awards at p. 20, available at http://www.ila-hq.org/pdf/Int%20Commercial%20Arbitration/ComArbitration.pdf (accessed: 18 April 2006).

[77] *Ibid.*   [78] *Ibid.*   [79] *Ibid.*   [80] *Ibid.* at p. 22.   [81]*Ibid.* at p. 17.

[82] P. Lalive, 'Transnational (or Truly International) Public Policy and International Arbitration', in P. Sanders (ed.), *Comparative Arbitration Practice and Public Policy in Arbitration*, ICCA Congress Series (The Hague: Kluwer Law International, 1986), pp. 299 *et seq.*; B. Oppetit, 'Le refus d'exécution d'une sentence arbitrale étrangère dans le cadre de la Convention de New York', *Revue de l'arbitrage* (1971), 104; other authors

consensus on the core principles, the exact confines of due process may fluctuate from one legal system to the other. Examples of breaches of procedural public policy have been identified, for instance where the making of the award was induced or affected by fraud or corruption;[83] and where there was a breach of the rules of natural justice, and the parties were on an unequal footing in the appointment of the tribunal.[84] It may also be a breach of procedural public policy to enforce an award that is inconsistent with a court decision or arbitral award that has *res judicata* effect in the enforcement forum.[85]

A consensus as to what constitutes a fundamental principle of procedural or substantive public policy might be evidenced by international instruments, for example UDHR.[86] Hence, it has been suggested that such a fundamental principle should be of universal application, albeit of very restricted scope, comprising: fundamental rules of natural law; principles of universal justice; *jus cogens* in public international law.[87] There appears to be little support amongst State courts at the present time for the application of this concept since the *lex fori* characterisation of public policy remains the common and most rooted approach. Nonetheless, the ECHR may influence deeply the way in which domestic courts control arbitration through public policy. As stated by the Strasbourg Court in the *Loizidou v. Turkey* case,[88] a concept of European public policy (*ordre public européen*) has emerged, which means that no enforcement of a foreign judgment is possible if such a judgment violates Article 6; a conclusion that might easily be applied also to arbitral awards.[89]

---

speak of principles fundamental to all systems of justice, universally recognised principles and the like (see in particular Redfern and Hunter, *Law and practice of international commercial arbitration*, pp. 541 *et seq.*).

[83] See the Interim Report of the ILA International Commercial Arbitration Committee on the topic of public policy as a ground for refusing recognition and enforcement of international arbitral awards at p. 24, available at http://www.ila-hq.org/pdf/Int%20Commercial%20Arbitration/ComArbitration.pdf (accessed: 18 April 2006).

[84] *Ibid.* at pp. 25–26.　　[85] *Ibid.* at p. 29.

[86] See T. Treves, *Diritto internazionale. Problemi fondamentali* (Milano: Giuffré, 2005), p. 193.　　[87] ILA, *Final report on public policy*, above, fn. 75.

[88] 20 Eur. Comm. HR, Dec. & Rep. 99.

[89] See on this respect *Pellegrini v. Italy*, Revue Trimestrielle de Droits de l'Homme, 2002, 463. See also, on the European Community level, ECJ, 28 March 2000, *Krombach et Bamberski*, C-7/98, Rec., 200-I, 1435, with reference to the notion of public policy ex Article 27.1 of the Brussels Convention of 27 September 1968.

Corporate social responsibility 'from above' and 'from below': towards contractualised human rights?

So far, the role of human rights in a typical transnational business dispute resolution environment, such as that of arbitration, has been highlighted; now it is time to take into consideration a peculiar form of transnational and non-governmental rule-making process: the case of Codes of Conduct embodying corporate social responsibility on human rights. The most important actors of economic globalisation are not Governments but corporations. Annual budgets of TNCs indicate that they represent almost half of the top one hundred world economic powers. Recent corporate scandals,[90] have shown that TNCs are borderless: each TNC is a single economic unity operating simultaneously in all countries where its branches are located. In the aftermath of those corporate scandals there has been concern inside the business community of systemic failures that would threaten the very essence of the free enterprise philosophy. Corporate social responsibility is at the core of these issues and it is sometimes referred to as 'responsible business conduct' and 'corporate citizenship', or more generally 'business ethics'. Corporate social responsibility thus ultimately adds a new dimension to human rights protection since it applies to activities carried out in each State where TNCs operate.

According to the 2001 European Commission Green Paper, corporate social responsibility is 'a concept whereby companies integrate social and environmental concerns in their business operations and in their interaction with their stakeholders on a voluntary basis'.[91] This broad concept, however, should be broken down into two very different sets of instruments: a) Codes of Conduct produced at the inter-governmental or even governmental level (that which I call 'corporate social responsibility from above') and b) Codes of Conduct produced directly by the business community or single TNC (i.e. 'corporate social responsibility from below').

---

[90] L. E. Mitchell, *Corporate Irresponsibility. America's Newest Export* (New Haven: Yale University Press, 2001), pp. 19 *et seq.*

[91] COM(2001) 366 final. Compare the report by the International Council on Human Rights Policy, *Beyond Voluntarism: Human rights and the developing international legal obligations of companies*, Geneva, 2004, available at http://www.cleanclothes.org/ftp/beyond_voluntarism.pdf (accessed: 1 February 2006).

Corporate social responsibility 'from above': Codes of Conduct of inter-governmental or governmental origin

Global level

There have been many attempts to regulate TNC activities via Codes of Conduct issued by intergovernmental organisations (IGOs) and Governments. Stronger forms of regulation have been frequently advocated in specialised literature, especially during the 1970s, with a reborn impetus nowadays, in the age of economic globalisation.[92] Significantly enough, the UN Conference on Trade and Development (UNCTAD) had charged a group of eminent persons with the task of studying the role (and possible form of regulation) of multinational corporations in world trade.[93] Accordingly, a UN Commission and a UN Centre on Transnational Corporations were set up in New York in 1974. As a result a Draft Code of Conduct for Transnational Corporations[94] was produced, covering many different issues such as labour, consumers, women, the environment, corruption, and restrictive business practices. The first generation of Codes of Conduct culminated in the 1977 International Labour Organisation (ILO) *Tripartite Declaration of Principles concerning Multinational Enterprises and Social Policy.*[95] Although its rules were conceived in the light of political claims coming from developing countries for a *New International Economic Order* (NIEO),[96] it nonetheless touched

---

[92] See: M. Virally, 'Les codes de conduite, pour quoi faire ?', in J. Touscoz (ed.), *Transferts de technologie, sociétés transnationales et nouvel ordre international* (Paris: PUF, 1978); H. W. Baade, 'The legal effect of Codes of Conduct for multinational enterprises', in N. Horn (ed.), *Legal Problems of Codes of Conduct for Multinational Enterprises* (Antwerp/Boston: Kluwer-Deventer, 1980), p. 390 ; P. Sanders, 'Codes of Conduct and sources of law', in P. Fouchard, A. Lyon-Caen and P. Kahn (eds.), *Le droit des rélations économiques internationals: Etudes offertes à Berthold Goldman* (Paris: Litec, 1982), p. 281; S.A. Metaxas, *Entreprises transnationales et codes de conduite* (Zurich: Schultless Verlag, 1988); A. Fatouros, 'Les principes directeurs de l'OCDE à l'intention des entreprises multinationales: perspectives actuelles et possibilités futures', in C. Dominicé, R. Patry and C. Reymond, *Etudes de droit international en l'honneur de Pierre Lalive* (Basel: Helbing & Lichtenhahn, 1993), p. 231. See also R. Mares, *Business and Human Rights: A Compilation of Documents* (Boston: Martinus Nijhoff, 2004).

[93] J. Braithwaite, P. Drahos, *Global Business Regulation* (Cambridge: CUP, 2000), p. 192.

[94] U.N. Code of Conduct on Transnational Corporations, 23 I.L.M. 626 (1984). See also A. Giardina and G. L. Tosato, *Diritto del commercio internazionale: Testi di base e note introduttive* (Milan: Giuffré, 1995), pp. 427 *et seq.*, and comments of A. Di Blase.

[95] ILO, *Tripartite Declaration of Principles concerning Multinational Enterprises and Social Policy*, 17 ILM (1978) 422.

[96] See in particular the Declaration and Programme of Action on the Establishment of a New International Economic Order proclaimed by the General Assembly in its resolutions

on some human rights of workers: employment promotion; freedom of association; collective bargaining; equality of opportunities and of treatment; security of employment; and safety and health issues. Implementation of this instrument has, however, been voluntary and, in practice, it is hard to find recorded cases of full implementation by businesses or even by courts. On 26 August 2003 and along the same 'soft law' line, the Norms on the Responsibilities of Transnational Corporations and Other Business Enterprises with Regard to Human Rights have been adopted.[97] Their effectiveness in application, as well as that of the 1998 ILO Declaration on Fundamental Principles and Rights at Work,[98] will be verified in the years to come.

A new philosophy of governance has been advanced by the UN Secretary-General in Davos in January 1999. Kofi Annan has directly addressed the transnational business community in order to identify a set of universally agreed values and principles in the areas of human rights, labour standards and environmental protection called the 'Global Compact for the 21st Century'.[99] Relevant (business) NGOs such as the International Chamber of Commerce have welcomed Annan's challenge, and various initiatives are underway between the UN, ICC, and other business organisations. Similarly, the UN Conference on Environment and Development (UNCED), which was held in Rio de Janeiro in June 1992, developed twenty-seven 'Rio Principles', the Rio Declaration on Environment and Development,[100] in which sustainable development is linked to environmental protection and a new global partnership involving 'new levels of cooperation among States, key sectors of societies and people'.[101] Those principles have been re-affirmed in the Johannesburg Summit.[102]

3201 (S-VI) and 3202 (S-VI) of 1 May 1974, UN Doc. A/9548 (1974), reprinted in 13 I.L.M. 715 (1974); the Charter of Economic Rights and Duties of States adopted by the General Assembly in its resolution 3281 (XXIX) of 12 December 1974, 29 U.N. GAOR Supp. (No. 31) at 51, UN Doc. A/9946 (1974), reprinted in 14 I.L.M. 251 (1975).

[97] E/CN.4/Sub.2/2003/12/Rev.2. Approved 13 August 2003, by the UN Sub-Commission on the Promotion and Protection of Human Rights resolution 2003/16, UN Doc. E/CN.4/Sub.2/2003/L.11 at 52 (2003).

[98] http://www.ilo.org/public/english/standards/decl/declaration/text/index.html (accessed: 26 December 2005).

[99] See http://www.unglobalcompact.org (accessed: 18 April 2006).

[100] See http://www.unep.org/Documents.multilingual/Default.asp?DocumentID=78& ArticleID=1163 (accessed: 18 April 2006).

[101] *Ibid.*, Principle http://www.unep.org/Documents.Multilingual/Default.asp? DocumentID=78&ArticleID=1163 (accessed: 26 December 2005). See I. Bantekas, 'Corporate Social Responsibility in International Law', *Boston University International Law Journal* 22 (2004), 309 at 318. [102] http://www.johannesburgsummit.org (accessed: 18 April 2006).

Regional level

At a regional level, the Organisation for Economic Co-operation and Development (OECD) Guidelines for Multinational Enterprises[103] have been developed and reviewed as an Annex to the Declaration on International Investment and Multinational Enterprises (2000).[104] However, its rules, recalling the UDHR, are recommendations to comply with local laws, safeguarding consumer interests, abolition of child labour, fighting bribery, environmental protection. Its implementation mechanism is based on national contact points charged with promoting the Guidelines and handling enquiries, as is general in OECD practice.

On the European Union level, after the European Business Declaration against Social Exclusion[105] and the 2000 Lisbon European Council Summit,[106] extensive consultation has led to the 2001 Corporate Social Responsibility Green Paper to which reference has already been made.[107] Once again, it is *recommended* to TNC's to adopt a Code of Conduct embodying corporate social responsibility, and taking into account international instruments such as ILO conventions, OECD guidelines, the UN 'Global Compact', etc., and to adopt compliance mechanisms. In practice, no 'hard law' rules have been created, and the issue of corporate social responsibility enforcement is left to TNCs' discretion, or to voluntary mechanisms.

Concluding remarks: codes 'from above' as benchmarks

The common feature of the international instruments recalled above, is that they are created by intergovernmental organisations and they are directed at business entities. In my view, these codes, embodying 'corporate social responsibility from above', have no direct binding legal effect on corporations and are similar to academic exercises. It is extremely hard to find any legal basis for allowing IGOs to regulate the activity of TNCs outside specific empowerment by member States. IGOs' Codes of Conduct are merely recommendations addressed to corporations which – paradoxically – are neither members of the IGOs nor are generally recognised as subjects of (public) international law.

---

[103] 40 ILM 237 (2001).   [104] DAFFE/IME/WPG(2000)9.
[105] http://www.csreurope.org/aboutus/socialexclusion_page393.aspx (accessed: 18 April 2006).
[106] http://www.csreurope.org/whatwedo/printpage/CSREuropeandtheEU_page410.aspx, (accessed: 18 April 2006).   [107] Above, fn. 92.

The real question then becomes the following: are codes elaborated by IGOs completely useless? My answer is no. I believe that such IGO-generated Codes of Conduct have a unique and very important value as external *benchmarks* for business-generated codes. Once the adoption of a Code of Conduct embodying corporate social responsibility becomes a need for a business it is necessary to know what the content of such a code should be. It is for an individual company or industry sector to decide what the most useful benchmark codes are and to develop their own understanding of how business principles relate to external codes/guidelines, the framework of UN values and societal expectations. However, IGO-generated Codes of Conduct identify concretely generally accepted uniform human rights rules in the international arena to which any business should adapt. For the same reason, it can even be argued that if during transnational litigation a TNC proves that a certain action has been taken in conformity with a given IGO's code of conduct, it may be presumed that such an act is lawful; a result which runs in parallel with the one reached when evaluating State acts in conformity with a recommendation by an IGO.[108] From this perspective, one should recall the importance that Model Laws prepared by IGOs have for States.[109] Model Laws are not treaties and they are not binding international unilateral acts of IGOs. Rather they are generated at IGO level to pinpoint a set of rules of universal acceptance. For this very reason some Model Laws have been quite successful in addressing issues that, probably, would have had a different destiny if left to diplomatic negotiations.[110] Therefore, it is not hard to see a similar role for IGOs: that of drafting model rules of corporate social responsibility, which are commended to responsible businesses and their NGOs.

Corporate social responsibility 'from below': generated at business community level

Corporate social responsibility 'from below' consists of all Codes of Conduct generated directly at business community level. There are two

---

[108] See in this respect B. Conforti, *International Law and the Role of Domestic Legal Systems* (Dordrecht: Martinus Nijhoff, 1993), pp. 108–109, as well as B. Conforti, 'Le rôle de l'accord dans le système des Nations Unies', *Recueil des cours* 142 (1974/II), 262–265.

[109] 'Model Laws' are generally considered as another example of 'soft law'.

[110] See, e.g., UNCITRAL Model Law on International Commercial Arbitration, (1985), 24 *ILM* 1302, 1314 (1985); at http://www.uncitral.org/pdf/english/texts/arbitration/ml-arb/ml-arb-e.pdf (accessed: 16 February 2005).

aspects of this phenomenon: unilateral and collective codes of conduct. Perhaps the starting point of the development of unilateral business Codes of Conduct may be traced back to the so-called 'Sullivan Principles'. In 1977, the Reverend Leon Sullivan launched a set of basic principles designed to persuade US companies with investments in South Africa to adopt voluntary Codes of Conduct designed to bypass the apartheid regime and, therefore, going beyond the normative standard provided by local law. The principles included non-segregation of races, providing equal and fair employment practices, and affirmative action. These rules were restated as the 'Global Sullivan Principles for Corporate Social Responsibility' in 1999 in order to 'encourage companies to support economic, social and political justice wherever they do business'.[111] A company wishing to be associated with these Principles is expected to provide information, support for universal human rights, equal opportunities, respect for freedom of association, given levels of employee compensation, training, health and safety, sustainable development, fair competition and to work in partnership to improve quality of life. Compliance has to be assessed by independent auditors, demonstrating corporate commitment to such rules. The Principles aim to be applicable to companies of any size, operating in any part of the world, and have been endorsed and implemented by a number of business councils, campaigning NGOs, local authorities, companies, and representative organisations. To date, 189 companies have signed up to them.[112]

Unilateral codes of conduct

In the 1990s, after various scandals,[113] a new wave of Codes of Conduct was instituted, leading some important TNCs to formulate their own unilateral codes, on their own initiative. An interesting analysis of the content of such codes has been offered by OECD and the World Bank Group and, whilst it cannot be examined in detail here,[114] what emerges

---

[111] See http://www.thesullivanfoundation.org/gsp/default.asp, (accessed: 18 April 2006).
[112] See however critical view by D. Pink, 'The Valdez Principles: Is What's Good for America Good for General Motors?', *Yale Law & Policy Review* (1990), 180 at 189.
[113] See for an overview L. E. Mitchell, *Corporate Irresponsibility. America's Newest Export* (New Haven:Yale University Press, 2001), pp. 19 *et seq.*
[114] OECD, *Making Corporate Codes of Conduct Work: Management Control Systems and Corporate Responsibility*, Paris, no. 2001/3; OECD, *Codes of Corporate Conduct: expanded review of their contents*, Working Papers on International Investment, no.6, Paris, 2001 (http://www.oecd.org/dataoecd/45/29/1922806.pdf); World Bank Group, *Company Codes of Conduct and International Standards: An Analytical Comparison*,

from such a study is that, at the very least, TNCs offer a basic statement – which is a signal to the market – about the company and what it does in the form of a top-level statement from the CEO or equivalent. Then, one may find some commentary about the policies and values of the business, a review of the company's stakeholder engagement, and an analysis of what are the key environmental and social issues for the company, with a commentary on how the company is responding, typically including data showing performance in each of these areas. Topics commonly treated are employment and labour relations; human rights, the environment; consumer protection and fighting corruption.

Levi Strauss, for example, indicated that it will favour business partners sharing their commitment 'to contribute to improving community conditions' and added significantly that it 'may withdraw production from [any factory that violates these standards] or require that a contractor implement a corrective action plan within a specified time period'.[115]

Moreover, some corporations (i.e. Unilever, Danone and Nestlé) are developing websites where they publish updated information on how they comply with corporate social responsibility obligations.[116]

Collective codes of conduct

Apart from individual corporations unilaterally developing their own Codes of Conduct, business organisations have become more and more active in producing what I have called 'collective codes of conduct'[117]. In this case the compilation of rules of corporate social responsibility is done directly by the business associations, of which companies are members. Examples of such codes are, from the ICC, its Business Charter for Sustainable Development;[118] Rules of Conduct on Extortion and Bribery in International Business Transactions,[119] and various marketing and

---

Washington, 2003 (http://info.worldbank.org/etools/docs/library/114195/Company%20Codes%20of%20Conduct%20and%20International%20Standards%20-%20Part%20I% 20-%202003. pdf (last accessed: 18 April 2006).

[115] Reported by R. Steinhardt, 'Corporate Responsibility and the International Law of Human Rights: The New *Lex mercatoria*', in P. Alston (ed.), *Non-State Actors and Human Rights* (Oxford: OUP, 2005), p. 183.

[116] See, for example, http://www.unilever.com/environmentsociety/socialreporting/ overview (last accessed: 26 December 2005). [117] Marrella, *La nuova lex mercatoria*, 783.

[118] See http://www.iccwbo.org/home/environment/charter.asp (last accessed: 18 April 2006).

[119] See http://www.iccwbo.org/id904/index.html?cookies=no (last accessed: 18 April 2006).

advertising codes;[120] and, from elsewhere, for example, the 'Responsible Care' programme of the chemical industry.[121]

Typical clauses address issues such as child labour, forced labour, health and safety, freedom of association, freedom from discrimination, disciplinary practices, work hours, and compensation. These rules are derived from principles expressed in the UDHR, and the UN Convention on the Rights of the Child,[122] and in relevant ILO Conventions, such as Nos. 29 and 105 on forced labour;[123] No. 87 on freedom of association;[124] No. 100 on equal remuneration;[125] No. 111 on employment discrimination;[126] No. 138 on workers'minimum age.[127]

The fact that such Codes of Conduct are directly framed by business associations (the 'business NGOs'), and then recommended to their own corporate members, endows such instruments with peculiar legal meaning. First, codes may become binding if adopted by competent governing bodies of each association and imposed on all its business members, including any new member asking for accession. Corporate social responsibility codes, then, not only become new 'rules of the game' for the market, they acquire legal strength similar to the one observed in advertising codes.[128] Secondly, since these kind of corporate social responsibility codes are drafted directly by business associations, new forms of cross-fertilisation become possible with NGOs active in the human rights field, and with intergovernmental organisations.[129]

---

[120] See, for example, the ICC international advertising code (1997) (http://www.iccwbo.org/policy/marketing/id905/index.html) as well as the ICC International Code of Sales Promotion; ICC International Code of Practice on Direct Marketing; ICC Code on Environmental Advertising; ICC Code on Sponsorship; ICC/ESOMAR International Code of Marketing and Social Research Practice, all available at http://www.iccwbo.org/policy/marketing/ (last accessed: 18 April 2006).

[121] See http://www.icca-chem.org/. (last accessed: 18 April 2006).

[122] See http://www.unhchr.ch/html/menu3/b/k2crc.htm (last accessed: 18 April 2006).

[123] Forced Labour Convention, 10 June 1930, 39 UNTS 55; Abolition of Forced Labour Convention, 25 June 1957, 320 UNTS 291.

[124] Freedom of Association and Protection of the Right to Organize Convention, 9 July 1948, 68 UNTS 17.

[125] Equal Remuneration Convention, 29 June 1951, 165 UNTS 304.

[126] Discrimination (Employment and Occupation) Convention, 25 June 1958, 363 UNTS 31.

[127] Minimum Age Convention, 26 June 1973. See the text in http://www.ilo.org/ilolex/english/convdisp1.htm (last accessed: 26 December 2005).

[128] Self-regulation codes for the advertising industry in certain countries, e.g. Italy, have typically also included compulsory arbitral dispute resolution mechanisms.

[129] For an example see the Global Reporting Initiative at http://www.globalreporting.org (last accessed: 26 December 2005).

At the very minimum, codes embodying 'corporate social responsibility from above' will provide a widely accepted benchmark for codes realising 'corporate social responsibility from below'. It is in the interest of TNCs, and their business NGOs to follow principles and rules having wide international acceptance.

Taking corporate social responsibility seriously: market-based enforcement

The issue of the applicability and concrete application of TNCs' Codes of Conduct has been the subject of wide debate since the creation of 'first generation' codes in the 1970s.[130] For most authors, the term 'corporate social responsibility' corresponds to vague statements with no legal value. The common denominator in these approaches is an assumption that most, if not all, entrepreneurs (and TNCs) are potential criminals and/or responsible for most human rights abuses occurring in the world. As a result they see liabilities of TNCs everywhere, and wonder why no specific repressive action is taken by Governments or even international courts. The debate on this point reflects the one between liberal and Marxist approaches to political economy. According to the majority view of human rights academics, the idea that corporations voluntarily give up to profitable opportunities in order to respect human rights without some governmental constraints simply seems absurd.[131] On the opposite side, there are other authors inspired by Milton Friedman and the 'Chicago School' of economics, according to whom the social responsibility of business entities is only to maximize profits for the benefit of their stakeholders.[132] On balance, I think that a good reading of Adam Smith is most enlightening for the debate on corporate social responsibility. According to Smith,

---

[130] See the contribution by F. Francioni, in this volume.

[131] For an account of such a debate see, *inter multos*, M. Addo (ed.), *Human Rights Standards and the Responsibility of Transnational Corporations* (The Hague: Kluwer, 1999); P. Spiro, 'Globalization, International Law and the Academy', 32 *New York University Journal of International Law & Politics* 567 (2000); C. Mc Crudden, 'Human Rights Codes for Trasnational Corporations: the Sullivan and Mac Bride Principles', in D. Shelton, *Commitment and Compliance* (Oxford: OUP, 2000), pp. 418–448; J. Dine, *Companies, International Trade and Human Rights* (Cambridge: CUP, 2005) and especially R. Mullerat, D. Brennan (eds.), *Corporate Social Responsibility: The Corporate Governance of the 21st Century*, (The Hague: Kluwer, 2005).

[132] See M. Friedman, 'The Social Responsibility of Business is to Increase its Profits', *The New York Times Magazine*, 13 September 1970. His view on corporate social responsibility had been expressed in M. Friedman, *Capitalism and Democracy*, (Chicago: Chicago

every individual necessarily labours to render the annual revenue of the society as great as he can. He generally, indeed, neither intends to promote the public interest, nor knows how much he is promoting it. By preferring the support of domestic to that of foreign industry, he intends only his own security; and by directing that industry in such a manner as its produce may be of the greatest value, he intends only his own gain, and he is in this, as in many other cases, led by an invisible hand to promote an end which was no part of his intention. Nor is it always the worse for the society that it was no part of it. By pursuing his own interest he frequently promotes that of the society more effectually than when he really intends to promote it. I have never known much good done by those who affected to trade for the public good. It is not from the benevolence of the butcher, the brewer, or the baker, that we expect our dinner, but from their regard to their own interest. We address ourselves, not to their humanity but to their self-love, and never talk to them of our necessities but of their advantages.[133]

Thus, in order to identify the degree of 'voluntary compliance' by TNCs to Codes of Conduct, it is crucial to recognise the driving market forces behind corporate social responsibility, which can be sketched out as the following:

a) Corporate social responsibility contributes to creating and maintaining a competitive advantage.[134]
b) Consumers will pay an extra price for goods produced under 'fair trade' standards.
c) Corporate social responsibility protects from boycott actions (mainly by consumers).
d) Corporate social responsibility guarantees strong relationships with stakeholders.
e) Corporate social responsibility creates a better, safer and more stimulating work environment.
f) Corporate social responsibility improves business management motivation.

University Press, 1962). See also David Henderson, *Misguided Virtue. False Notions of Corporate Social Responsibility* (London: Institute of Economic Affairs, 2001), pp. 17–18; C. Crook (ed.), 'The Good Company: A Sceptical Look at Corporate Social Responsibility', *The Economist*, 20 January 2005 (374) 8410.

[133] Adam Smith, *An Inquiry Into the Nature and Causes of the Wealth of Nations* (London, 1776).

[134] See Ghauri and Cateora, *International Marketing*, 2nd ed. (London: McGraw-Hill Professional, 2006), 463–481.

g) Corporate social responsibility makes access to funding easier ('socially responsible investment').

h) Corporate social responsibility allows companies to benefit from fiscal advantages and administrative facilitation.

i) Corporate social responsibility contributes to increasing shareholder value in the markets where ethical indexes are adopted. Major stock markets have developed specific indicators such as the Dow Jones Sustainability Indexes,[135] Domini 400 Social Index,[136] etc.

All in all, corporate social responsibility reduces 'enterprise global risk'.[137] This is the crucial factor in the mind of business entrepreneurs. Market sanction mechanisms, after all, are a particular kind of legal sanctions, although one should properly speak of non-governmental sanctions of variable intensity operating 'in the shadow of law'.

In order to increase external communication of compliance with corporate social responsibility codes of conduct, certification programmes have been established by independent auditors. The Worldwide Responsible Apparel Production Certification Program (WRAP),[138] the SA8000[139] and ISO 14000[140] Certification Schemes, and the Kimberley Process Certification Scheme[141] are examples of non-governmental human rights implementation control mechanisms through external auditing.

Finally, one should not underestimate the pressure from above, that is by regulators at governmental and intergovernmental level. Without a serious turn on enforcing corporate social responsibility rules by business operators themselves, there will certainly be tougher sanctions 'from above', both by increasing civil and criminal liabilities, and by strengthening the

---

135 http://www.sustainability-index.com (last accessed: 18 April 2006).
136 http://www.domini.com/Social-Screening/creation_maintenance.doc_cvt.htm (last accessed: 18 April 2006).
137 See *Harvard Business Review on Corporate Responsibility* (Boston: Harvard Business School Publishing, 2003), ICC Business in Society: making a positive and responsible contribution (7 May 2002) accessible at http://www.iccwbo.org/policy/society/id1188/index.html, as well as the vast literature on 'cause related' marketing. See also S. Melkko, *Marketing Human Rights*, European Master's Degree in Human Rights and Democratisation published dissertations (Venice: Marsilio, 2005), pp. 444 *et seq.*; and.generally R. Liubicic, 'Corporate Codes of Conduct and Product Labelling Schemes: The Limits and Possibilities of Promoting International Labor Rights Standards through Private Initiatives', *Law and Policy in International Business*, 30 (1998), 111.
138 http://www.wrapapparel.org (last accessed: 18 April 2006).
139 See http://www.sa-intl.org (last accessed: 26 December 2005).
140 See http://www.iso.ch (last accessed: 26 December 2005).
141 http://www.kimberleyprocess.com:8080/site/?name=kpcs (last accessed: 18 April 2006).

courts' inquisitorial powers. For instance, in July 2003, in the aftermath of the Enron and Worldcom scandals, the UK Government has announced changes in company law. Among these changes, all large companies must publish every year an Operating and Financial Review including sections on 'policies and performance on environmental, community, societal, ethical and reputational issues, including compliance with relevant laws and regulations'.[142] In this context, the Companies Audit Investigation and Community Enterprise Bill has been passed in the House of Commons with the aim of restoring confidence in companies and financial markets, as well as promoting social enterprise.[143]

In conclusion, there are a number of relevant factors contributing to giving 'teeth' to corporate social responsibility rules in the interest of many stakeholders, including business operators. Hence, when evaluating economic behaviour in complex areas such as corporate social responsibility, the analysis should devolve from common discussions on the 'good heart' of corporate executives which is, *per se*, legally irrelevant. Rather, all of the factors evidenced above lead one to foresee a development of corporate social responsibility business-to-business litigation in international commercial arbitration in the near future.

The 'spin-off' from corporate social responsibility into arbitration

The fact that corporate social responsibility Codes of Conduct are 'voluntary' does not necessary mean that they are deprived of legal effects,[144]

---

[142] See http://www.dti.gov.uk (last accessed: 26 December 2005). Similar rules may also be found in the French *Nouvelle régulations économiques* of 15 May 2001 (Article 116); in the Italian *Codice di Autodisciplina* (July 2003) of the Italian Stock Market; in the German *Regierungskommission Deutscher Corporate Governance Kodex*, Berlin, 21 May 2003 and in the USA, the Sarbanes-Oxley Act of 2002 (http://www.sarbanes-oxley.com, last accessed 26 December 2005). Here it should be remarked that the debate on corporate social responsibility links with the one on corporate governance.

[143] See http://www.dti.gov.uk/cld/companies_audit_etc_bill (last accessed: 26 December 2005).

[144] See in this respect G. Farjat, 'Réflexions sur les codes de conduites privés', in Fouchard, Lyon-Caen and Kahn (eds.), *Le droit des rélations économiques internationales, Etudes offertes à B. Goldman*, p. 47, observing that (61 *et seq.*) Codes of Conduct may be the source of trade usages so that progressive transformation into private customary rules eventually enrich the bulk of transnational public policy; R. B. Ferguson, 'The legal status of non statutory codes of practice', *Journal of Business Law* (1988), 12 *et seq.*; F. Osman, 'Avis, directives, codes de bonne conduite, recommendation, éthique, etc. : réflexions sur la dégradation des sources privées du droit', *Revue Trimestrielle de Droit Civil* 1995, 509 *et seq.*; G. Farjat, 'Nouvelles réflexions sur les codes de conduite privés', in J. Clam and Gilles Martin (eds.), *Les transformations de la régulation juridique*, (Paris: LGDJ, 1998), p. 151. And

which may derive, *inter alia*, from applicable contract law. Freedom of action is a fundamental liberty. However, it is a freedom subject to limits: two of them being 'good faith', and 'good morals'. Let us consider two basic situations: one in which a Code of Conduct is only mentioned during the formation of a contract, without specific reference in the final contract; and another one in which the code is part of the agreement.

In most legal systems, good faith requirements must be generally present in the formation of the contract, in its interpretation, and in the performance stage. There is an immense literature,[145] as well as case law,[146] on good faith (and fair dealing) requirements in contract law but, in essence, it amounts to re-balancing individual interests with the 'rules of the game'. In this sense, reference is made not to the state of mind of single contractors (the concept of *subjective* good faith) but to *objective* rules of behaviour.[147]

Good faith must be present in the course of negotiation of a contract, meaning that each party must act honestly and sincerely when making, rejecting, or accepting offers. Hence, individual Codes of Conduct may be analysed as unilateral statements by TNCs directed at present or potential contractors. The *voluntary* nature of such statements does not mean that Codes of Conduct are always without legal force, as is often believed, under the general label of 'soft law'. Such a conclusion amounts only to finding

---

especially P. Kahn, 'Les réactions de milieux économiques' in P. Kahn and C. Kessedjian (eds.), *L'illicite dans le commerce international*, (Litec: Paris, 1996), pp. 477 *et seq.* (esp. 491).

[145] See, amongst a huge literature, P. Atiyah, *The Rise and Fall of Freedom of Contract* (Oxford: OUP, 1985) as well as Nygh, *Autonomy in International Contracts*; R. Zimmermann and S. Whittaker, *Good Faith in European Contract Law*, available at http://assets.cambridge.org/052177/1900/sample/0521771900wsc00.pdf (last accessed: 26 December 2005); U. Magnus, 'Remarks on Good Faith: The United Nations Convention on Contracts for the International Sale of Goods and the International Institute for the Unification of Private Law, Principles of International Commercial Contracts', *Pace International Law Review* 10 (1998), 89–95.

[146] See e.g. M. Hesselink, 'The Concept of Good Faith', in Hartkamp et al., *Towards a European Civil Code*, 3rd ed. (The Hague: Kluwer, 2004), pp. 471–498.

[147] Examples of these requirements may be found in national law; *ex multis* in Articles 1175, 1337, 1338, 1366, and 1375 of the Italian Civil Code, and in those codes which have followed the model of § 242 BGB (in full) [in force up to 31 December 1999], that is *Leistung nach Treu und Glauben*, i.e. performance according to good faith, according to which: 'Der Schuldner ist verpflichtet, die Leistung so zu bewirken, wie Treu und Glauben mit Rücksicht auf die Verkehrssitte es erfordern.' ['The debtor is bound to effect performance according to the requirements of good faith, giving consideration to common usage']. Similar requirements are included in the Unidroit Principles for international commercial contracts (2004). See in particular Article 1(7): 'Each party must act in accordance with good faith and fair dealing in international trade. The parties may not exclude or limit this duty.' (http://www.unidroit.org/english/principles/contracts/principles2004/blackletter2004.pdf, last accessed: 18 April 2006).

that individual Codes of Conduct are statements not supported by the will of its author to make them binding. However, it is equally clear that the same conclusion may be discarded by the doctrine of legitimate expectations which is particularly important in international business law.[148] According to this doctrine, a unilateral statement becomes binding if and insofar as it has determined a legitimate expectation (or expectation interest) on the other contractor that it is a *serious* statement. In other words, individual codes of conduct, as any other unilateral statement, become legally binding if the other party proves that without fault he or she has considered such declaration as serious. Thus an expectation that the code will be applied may be formed and protected under the applicable law. As a consequence, one of the parties may terminate a contract and even claim damages if it proves that the information on the enforcement of the Code of Conduct was considered essential to determine its consent to be bound.

Business parties may go further and declare that a specific Code of Conduct is incorporated into their contract. In this case, there can be no doubt that 'soft law' provisions of the code are transformed into legally enforceable contract clauses. Thus, gross violations of the corporate social responsibility Code of Conduct may lead to termination of the contract. An example of such a situation may be found in the 1998 Code of Labour Practices for the Apparel Industry including Sportswear,[149] where it is stated that:

> [C]ontractors, subcontractors and suppliers must as part of their agreement with the company agree to terminate any contract or agreement for the supply or production of goods by any contractor, subcontractor or supplier that they engage not fully observing the code or they must seek and receive approval from the company to institute a procedure with fixed time limits to rectify a situation where the code is not being fully observed.
>
> Where there is repeated failure to observe or to ensure observance of the code by a particular contractor, subcontractor, supplier or licensee, the agreement should be terminated.[150]

---

[148] See E. Gaillard, 'L'interdiction de se contredire au détriment d'autrui comme principe géneral de droit du commerce international', *Revue de l'arbitrage* (1985), 241. This doctrine is today embodied in the 2004 Unidroit Principles of international commercial contracts, Article 1(8), on 'Inconsistent behaviour' according to which: 'A party cannot act inconsistently with an understanding it has caused the other party to have and upon which that other party reasonably has acted in reliance to its detriment'.

[149] Clean Clothes Campaign, Code of Labour Practices for the Apparel Industry including Sportswear, February 1998, reproduced in R. Mares, *Business and Human Rights: A Compilation of Documents* (Boston: Martinus Nijhoff, 2004), pp. 167–178.

[150] *Ibid.* at 174.

Then, since human rights thereby acquire a contractual dimension, they become binding for TNCs in all countries where they operate, even in the territory of nation States which are not parties to specific Human Rights treaties.

Further, two corporations may enter into litigation because one of them has cancelled a transnational contract arguing that non-performance of corporate social responsibility Code of Conduct rules is a breach of the contract. Since the most important method for transnational business dispute resolution is arbitration, the door for B2B human rights litigation before arbitration tribunals is then opened.[151] Moreover, the same argument holds even whether the law applicable to the merits is *lex mercatoria* and/or the Unidroit Principles of international commercial contracts. Specialised literature has ascertained that business (collective) Codes of Conduct pertain to *lex mercatoria*.[152] Hence, a choice of *lex mercatoria* as the law applicable to the merits of a dispute brings with itself a legal basis to provide for the application of relevant collective Codes of Conduct.

Also on the matter of interpretation of contracts, Codes of Conduct may be taken into account within the meaning of Article 8(1) of the 1980 UN Convention on the International Sale of Goods (CISG),[153] which states that: 'For the purposes of this Convention statements made by and other conduct of a party are to be interpreted according to his intent where the other party knew or could not have been unaware what that intent was'.[154]

---

[151] Two remarkable (although controversial) cases evidencing such a trend may be found in ICC award No. 5617 (1989), *Journal de droit international*, 1994 at 1041 (contract of sales of human glands obtained from cadavers for production of drugs); ICC award No. 3493 (1983) in 23 ILM 1048 (1984) ('Pyramids Arbitration': International Construction Contract in the Area of Egyptian Pyramids).

[152] See Farjat, 'Réflexions sur les codes de conduite privés'; P. Sanders, 'Codes of Conduct and Sources of Law'; and Marrella, *La nuova lex mercatoria. Principi Unidroit ed usi dei contratti del commercio internazionale*, p. 915.

[153] http://www.uncitral.org/pdf/english/texts/sales/cisg/CISG.pdf (last accessed: 18 April 2006).

[154] Article 8 of the CISG offers, further, the following rules: 'If the preceding paragraph is not applicable, statements made by and other conduct of a party are to be interpreted according to the understanding that a reasonable person of the same kind as the other party would have had in the same circumstances. (3) In determining the intent of a party or the understanding a reasonable person would have had, due consideration is to be given to all relevant circumstances of the case including the negotiations, any practices which the parties have established between themselves, usages and any subsequent conduct of the parties'. See the comment by A. Junge in P. Schlechtriem (ed.), *Commentary on the UN Convention on the International Sale of Goods (CISG)* (Oxford: OUP, 1998), pp. 69–80.

Conversely no reference to human rights issues or corporate social responsibility can be found in the 2004 revised version of the Unidroit Principles of International Commercial Contracts. However, when the Unidroit Principles are applicable, they contain rules on contract interpretation such as Article 4(2), on interpretation of statements and other conduct, providing a solution converging with the one offered by the CISG:

> The statements and other conduct of a party shall be interpreted according to that party's intention if the other party knew or could not have been unaware of that intention.
>
> If the preceding paragraph is not applicable, such statements and other conduct shall be interpreted according to the meaning that a reasonable person of the same kind as the other party would give to it in the same circumstances.

Another argument for legal effectiveness of corporate social responsibility is that a violation of human rights rules embodied in a code may amount to unfair competition or deceptive advertising under the applicable law. An example can be found in the litigation against *Nike* in the USA, where the California Supreme Court rejected claims by Nike's lawyers that the First Amendment immunised the company from being sued for an allegedly deceptive public relations campaign. As a result, Nike agreed to pay US$ 1.5 million to settle the case as quickly as possible.[155]

Last but not least, collective Codes of Conduct may serve as a test used by arbitrators to detect a violation of transnational public policy.

The downside of this approach is that the victim (or victims) of human rights abuses is typically not a party to the kind of disputes we are discussing. Privity of contract and arbitrators' jurisdiction in such cases do not involve third parties such as victims or NGOs. However, victims of human rights abuses may be heard as witnesses in arbitral proceedings since the breach of the contract is caused by an allegation of such abuses by one of the TNCs parties to the business dispute.[156] Also, relevant NGOs' reports may be used to prove widespread and gross human rights violations by one of the parties to the contract whose performance is challenged. Here, we face a potential area of development of *amicus*

---

[155] *Kasky v. Nike Inc.*, 119 Cal. Rptr. 2d 296 (Cal. 2002), cert. granted, 123 S.Ct. 817 (2003), cert. dismissed, 123 S.Ct. 2554 (2003), 539 U.S. 2003. See http://reclaimdemocracy.org/nike/index.html (last accessed: 25 December 2005).

[156] This perspective leaves room open for future discussion on specific matters of international investment arbitration.

curiae briefs, similarly to what has already happened in the field of international investment arbitration.[157]

Conclusion

Since arbitration proceedings deal ultimately with civil rights, from the standpoint of domestic courts awards shall conform with the requirements of fair trial, reasonable time, and independent/impartial tribunal standards, according to applicable human rights treaties. Challenges to awards before domestic courts, on the same grounds, are possible, irrespective of rules to the contrary (be they of international, national, or contractual origin) since they would trigger the international responsibility of the territorial State for human rights violations.

The present trend in corporate social responsibility involves translating certain human rights rules and principles into Codes of Conduct, and making these codes binding by contract. We are faced, then, with a new phenomenon: the 'contractualisation' of human rights. In a world divided into States having different levels of human rights protection given by different treaties and applicable laws, human rights 'contractualisation' may have the effect of promoting uniformity. In fact, highly globalised TNCs may establish, via their transnational contracts, a network of 'contractualised' human rights that may set even higher standards than those provided by the local law of a given country. And since corporate social responsibility translates into a system of contractual clauses whose violation may lead to termination of a transnational contract, it follows that arbitration may become a new and unexpected forum for litigating human rights issues in a business–to-business context. Of course one should not expect too much from contractualised human rights protection since any contract may or may not be terminated for reasons of commercial convenience, which may not coincide with human rights values. Also the means to resolve transnational business disputes (i.e. mediation and other ADR techniques, also including awards by consent in arbitration) are not specifically conceived to serve human rights purposes, but rather to end potential or actual disputes quickly and concretely: time is money, and litigation is expensive in terms of both time and money!

[157] See, for example, ICSID case No. ARB/03/19, *Aguas Argentinas S.A., Suez, Sociedad General de Aguas de Barcelona, S.A., and Vivendi S.A. v. The Argentine Republic*, Order in response to a petition for transparency and participation as *amicus curiae* of 19 May 2005. See, as well, the new rule 37 of ICSID Arbitration Rules, as amended and effective April 10, 2006.

Nonetheless, since both Governments and intergovernmental organisations have so far failed altogether to produce a worldwide binding treaty 'with teeth' for global human rights protection, corporate social responsibility initiatives should be welcomed, for the time being. Summing up all legal instruments existing at inter-governmental and governmental level aimed at protecting human rights with corporate social responsibility, it is indisputable that the total result is an increase in the global level of protection of such rights.

Bibliography

Adam, S., 'Arbitration, Alternative Dispute Resolution generally and the European Convention on Human Rights: An Anglo-centric view', *Journal of International Arbitration* 21 (2004), 413–438

Atiyah, P., *The Rise and Fall of Freedom of Contract* (Oxford: OUP, 1985)

Baade, H.W., 'The Legal Effect of Codes of Conduct for Multinational Enterprises', in Horn, N. (ed.), *Legal Problems of Codes of Conduct for Multinational Enterprises* (Antwerp/Boston: Kluwer-Deventer, 1980), pp. 390–430, also in *German Yearbook of International Law* 22 (1979), 11–52

Bantekas, I., 'Corporate Social Responsibility in International Law', *Boston University International Law Journal* 22 (2004), 309–347

Beguin, J. and Menjuq, M., *Traité de droit du commerce international* (Paris: Litec, 2005)

Blackburn, R. and Polakiewicz, J., *Fundamental Rights in Europe: The European Convention on Human Rights and its Member States, 1950–2000* (New York: Oxford University Press, 2001)

Blessing, M., 'Mandatory Rules of Law Versus Party Autonomy in International Arbitration', *Journal of International Arbitration* 14 (1997), 23–40

Bond, S., 'The Selection of ICC Arbitrators and the Requirement of Independence', *Arbitration International* 4 (1988), 300–310

Borchers, P. J., 'The Internationalization of Contractual Conflicts Law', *Vanderbilt Journal of Transnational Law* 28 (1995), 421–443

Braithwaite, J., Drahos, P., *Global Business Regulation* (Cambridge: CUP, 2000)

Brilmayer, L., 'Rights, Fairness, and Choice of Law', *Yale Law Journal* 98 (1989), 1277–1319

Briner, R. and von Schlabrendoff, F., 'Article 6 of the European Convention on Human Rights and its Bearing upon International Arbitration', in Briner, R., Fortier, L. Y., Berger, K. P. and Bredow, J. (eds.), *Law of International Business and Dispute Settlement in the 21st Century: Liber Amicorum Karl-Heinz Böckstiegel* (Cologne: Heymanns, 2001), pp. 89–100

Cassese, A., *International Law*, 2nd ed. (Oxford: Oxford University Press, 2005)

Conforti, B., 'Le rôle de l'accord dans le système des Nations Unies', *Recueil des cours*, vol. 142, 1974/II, 203–288

International Law and the Role of Domestic Legal Systems (Dordrecht: Martinus Nijhoff, 1993)

Crook, C. (ed.), 'The Good Company. A Sceptical Look at Corporate Social Responsibility', *The Economist*, vol. 374 nr. 8410, 22 January 2005

De Gouttes, Régis, 'L'enchevêtrement des normes internationales relatives au procès équitable: comment les concilier?', in Université Robert Schumann de Strasbourg and Cour De Cassation (eds.), *Les nouveaux développements du procès équitable au sens de la Convention européenne des droits de l'homme* (Brussels: Bruylant, 1996), pp. 141–185

Derains, Y. and Schwartz E. A., *A Guide to the New ICC Rules of Arbitration* (The Hague: Kluwer Law International, 1998)

Dolinger, J., 'World Public Policy: Real International Public Policy in the Conflict of Laws', *Texas International Law Journal* 17 (1982), 167–193

Farjat, G., 'Réflexions sur les codes de conduites privés', in Fouchard, P., Lyon-Caen, A. and Kahn, P. (eds.), *Le droit des rélations économiques internationales. Etudes offertes à Berthold Goldman* (Paris: Litec, 1982), pp. 47–67

'Nouvelles réflexions sur les codes de conduite privés', in Clam, J., and Martin, G. (eds.), *Les transformations de la régulation juridique* (Paris: LGDJ, 1998), pp. 151–178

Fatouros, A., 'Les principes directeurs de l'OCDE à l'intention des entreprises multinationales: perspectives actuelles et possibilités futures', in Dominicé, C., Patry, R. and Reymond, C., *Etudes de droit international en l'honneur de Pierre Lalive* (Basel: Helbing & Lichtenhahn, 1993), pp. 231–260

Ferguson, R. B., 'The Legal Status of Non-statutory Codes of Practice', in *Journal of Business Law* (1988), 12–19

Fouchard, P., 'Rapport final sur le statut de l'arbitre. Un rapport de la Commission de l'arbitrage international de la CCI', *ICC International Court of Arbitration Bulletin* 7 (1996), 28–38

'La portée internationale de l'annulation de la sentence arbitrale dans son pays d'origine', *Revue de l'Arbitrage* (1997), 329–352

Friedman, M., *Capitalism and Democracy* (Chicago: Chicago University Press, 1962)

'The Social Responsibility of Business is to Increase its Profits', in *The New York Times Magazine*, 13 September 1970

Gaillard, E., 'L'interdiction de se contredire au détriment d'autrui comme principe général de droit du commerce international', *Revue de l'Arbitrage* (1985), 241–274

Gaillard, E. and Savage, J. (eds.), *Fouchard, Gaillard, Goldman on International Commercial Arbitration* (The Hague: Kluwer Law International, 2004)

Galgano, F. and Marrella, F., *Diritto del commercio internazionale* (Padua: CEDAM, 2004)

Ghauri, P. and Cateora, P., *International Marketing*, 2nd ed. (London: McGraw-Hill Professional, 2006)

Giardina, A. and Tosato, G. L., *Diritto del commercio internazionale. Testi di base e note introduttive* (Milan: Giuffré, 1995)

Gilbert, G., 'De l'indépendance des membres de la Cour internationale de Justice', in *Boutros Boutros-Ghali amicorum discipulorumque liber: paix, développement, démocratie* (Bruxelles: Bruylant, 1998), vol. I, pp. 475–487

Goldman, B., 'Les conflits de lois dans l'arbitrage international de droit privé', *Recueil des Cours* 109 (1968/II), 347–485

'La protection internationale des droits de l'homme et l'ordre public international dans le fonctionnement de la règle de conflits de lois', in K. Vasak (ed.), *Mélanges René Cassin*, vol. I, (Paris: Pedone 1969), pp. 449–482

Hammje, P., 'Droits fondamentaux et ordre public', *Revue Critique de Droit International Privé* (1997), 1–31

Hartkamp, Hesselink, Hondius, Du Perron, Veldman, *Towards a European Civil Code*, 3rd ed. (The Hague: Kluwer, 2004).

Henderson, D., *Misguided Virtue: False Notions of Corporate Social Responsibility* (London: Institute of Economic Affairs, 2001)

Jacot-Guillarmod, O., 'L'arbitrage privé face à l'article 6 §1 de la Convention européenne des droits de l'homme', in Matscher, F., and Petzold, H. (eds.), *Protecting Human Rights: the European Dimension: Studies in Honour of Gérard J. Wiarda* (Cologne: Heymanns, 1988), pp. 100–130

'La nouvelle Cour européenne des droits de l'homme dans la perspective du juge national', in Zanghì, C., *La Convenzione europea dei diritti dell'uomo: 50 anni d'esperienza gli attori e i protagonisti della Convenzione : il passato e l'avvenire* (Torino: Giappichelli, 2002), pp. 283–326

Jaksic, A., *Arbitration and Human Rights* (Frankfurt am Main: Lang, 2002)

Jarrosson, C., 'L'arbitrage et la Convention européenne des droits de l'homme', *Revue de l'Arbitrage* (1989), 573–607

Jayme, E., 'Identité culturelle et intégration: le droit international privé postmoderne', *Recueil des Cours* 251 (1995-I), 9–267

Junge, A., in Schlechtriem, P. (ed.), *Commentary on the UN Convention on the International Sale of Goods (CISG)* (Oxford: OUP, 1998), pp. 69–80

Kahn, P., 'Les réactions des milieux économiques', in Kahn, P. and Kessedjian, C. (eds.), *L'illicite dans le commerce international* (Paris: Litec, 1996), pp. 477–494

Kerr, M., 'Arbitration and the Courts: the UNCITRAL Model Law', *ICLQ* 34 (1984), 1–24

Lalive, P., 'Transnational (or Truly International) Public Policy and International Arbitration', in P. Sanders (ed.), *Comparative Arbitration Practice and Public Policy in Arbitration*, ICCA Congress Series (The Hague: Kluwer, 1986), pp. 258–318

Lew, J. D., Mistelis, L. A. and Kröll, S. M., *Comparative International Commercial Arbitration* (The Hague: Kluwer Law International, 2003)

Liubicic, R., 'Corporate Codes of Conduct and Product Labelling Schemes: The Limits and Possibilities of Promoting International Labor Rights Standards through Private Initiatives', in *Law & Policy of International Business* 30 (1998), 111–158

Magnus, U., 'Remarks on Good Faith: The United Nations Convention on Contracts for the International Sale of Goods and the International Institute for the Unification of Private Law, Principles of International Commercial Contracts', *Pace International Law Review*, 10 (1998), 89–95

Mares, R., *Business and Human Rights. A Compilation of Documents* (Boston: Martinus Nijhoff, 2004)

Marrella, F., *La nuova lex mercatoria. Principi Unidroit ed usi dei contratti del commercio internazionale* (Padova: CEDAM, 2003)

'Autonomia privata e contratti internazionali', in G. Sicchiero (ed.), *Autonomia privata e Diritto europeo* (Padova: CEDAM, 2005), pp. 217–264

Mayer, P., 'Mandatory Rules of Law in International Arbitration', *Arbitration International* (1986) 2, 274–293

Melkko, S., 'Marketing Human Rights' in EIUC, *European Master's Degree in Human Rights and Democratisation published dissertations* (Venice: Marsilio, 2005)

Metaxas, Spyro A., *Entreprises transnationales et codes de conduite* (Zurich: Schultheiss Verlag, 1988)

Mitchell L. E., *Corporate Irresponsibility: America's Newest Export*, (New Haven: Yale University Press, 2001)

Moitry J.-H., 'Right to a Fair Trial and the European Convention on Human Rights – Some Remarks on the *République de Guinée* Case', *Journal of International Arbitration* (1989), 115–122

Nygh, P., *Autonomy in International Contracts* (Oxford: Clarendon Press, 1999)

Oppetit, B., 'Le refus d'exécution d'une sentence arbitrale étrangère dans le cadre de la Convention de New York', *Revue de l'arbitrage* (1971), 97–107

Osman, F., 'Avis, directives, codes de bonne conduite, recommandation, éthique, etc.: réflexions sur la dégradation des sources privées du droit', *Revue Trimestrielle de Droit Civil*, 1995, 509–539

Ovey, C. and White, R. A., *Jacobs and White, The European Convention of Human Rights*, 3rd ed. (Oxford: OUP, 2002)

Petrochilos, G., *Procedural Law in International Arbitration* (Oxford: OUP, 2004)

Picchio Forlati, L., 'Critères de rattachement et règles d'applicabilité. A' l'heure de la protection des Droits de l'homme en Europe', *Rivista di diritto internazionale privato e processuale*, 4 (2005), 1–32

Pink, D., 'The Valdez Principles: Is What's Good for America Good for General Motors?', *Yale Law & Policy Review* (1990), 180–190

Poudret J.-F. and Besson, S., *Droit Comparé de l'Arbitrage International* (Zürich: Schulthess/Paris: L.G.D.J./Bruxelles: Bruylant, 2002)

Prahalad, C. K., Hammond, A., Porter, M. E. and Fruehauf, H. C. (eds.), *Harvard Business Review on Corporate Responsibility* (Boston: Harvard Business School Publishing, 2003)

Redfern, A. and Hunter, M., *Law and Practice of International Commercial Arbitration*, 4th ed. (London: Sweet & Maxwell, 2004)

Sanders, P., 'Codes of Conduct and Sources of Law', in P. Fouchard, A. Lyon-Caen and P. Kahn (eds.) *Le droit des relations économiques internationales: Etudes offertes à Berthold Goldman*, (Paris: Litec, 1982), pp. 281–295

Smith, A., *An Inquiry Into the Nature and Causes of the Wealth of Nations* (London, 1776)

Steinhardt, R., 'Corporate Responsibility and the International Law of Human Rights: The New *lex mercatoria*', in Alston, P. (ed.), *Non-State Actors and Human Rights*, (Oxford: OUP, 2005), pp.177–226

Storme, M. and De Ly, P. (eds.), *The Place of Arbitration* (Gent: Mys & Breesch Uitgevers, 1992)

Sudre, F., *Droit européen et international des droits de l'homme*, 6th ed. (Paris: PUF, 2003)

Treves, T., *Diritto internazionale. Problemi fondamentali* (Milano: Giuffré, 2005)

Virally, M., 'Les codes de conduite, pour quoi faire ?' in Touscoz, J. (ed.), *Transferts de technologie, sociétés transnationales et nouvel ordre international* (Paris: PUF, 1978)

Voser, N., 'Mandatory Rules of Law as a Limitation on the Law Applicable in International Commercial Arbitration', *The American Review of International Arbitration* 7 (1996), 319–357

Yu, H., 'Total Separation of International Commercial Arbitration and National Court Regimes', *Journal of International Arbitration* 2 (1998), 145–166

Zimmermann, R. and Whittaker, S. 'Good Faith in European Contract Law', available at http://assets.cambridge.org/052177/1900/sample/0521771900-wsc00.pdf

General Conclusions

WOLFGANG BENEDEK AND FABRIZIO MARRELLA

Human rights and the new economic realities

The phenomenon of economic globalisation, which is complemented by other forms of globalisation (e.g. cultural globalisation or legal globalisation), has created new opportunities for international economic affairs, but also new challenges for human rights. While the world has become smaller and more integrated since the end of World War II,[1] the acceleration of the movement of people, capital and information and the decreasing costs of transportation and communication have not, in most cases, resulted in a reduction of the inequality of living conditions. They have, nonetheless, generated a broader sense of economic, political and moral interdependence at all levels of governance and in civil society. Today, more than ever, the systems of human rights protection need to deal with new international realities characterised by, *inter alia*, the reduction of borders, the facilitation of trade and investment, increased international interconnectedness and interdependence, the growing importance of non-state actors (transnational corporations, NGOs), but also intergovernmental organisations (IGOs) like WTO and International Financial Institutions (IFIs), and – foremost – the changing role of the State.

The developments described in the contributions of this volume, summarised under the multifaceted term 'economic globalisation', have contributed to a global interdependence that is enhanced by and is responsible for a re-definition of the functions of the State. While there is

[1] Today, with reference to the classical axis of international economic analysis (East-West; North-South), we face a new wave of economic globalisation from the South. China and India are the new 'globalisers' on the scene. After China's entry into the WTO in December 2001, economic entities located mainly in South East Asia (Japan, Korea and Taiwan), in the EU and Latin America have been amongst the beneficiaries of the booming of Chinese economic activity. On the other hand, countries like Argentina and Brazil, whose mining and agri-business companies are world cost leaders have been the main sellers of copper, oil, iron and soy beans.

no need to go as far as *Jürgen Habermas*, who has diagnosed a 'post-national constellation',[2] a very real challenge to the primary role of the state as the fundamental paradigm of political philosophy can be ascertained.[3]

Up to now the systems of human rights protection are firmly wedded to the territorial State. The challenges of economic globalisation, however, have called for a new wider approach, which is attempted in this volume. In the introduction the focus of this book has already been described as the relationship between economic globalisation and human rights. Accordingly, one focus of this book lies on the negative effects of economic globalisation on human rights and how to counter them. Two questions were proposed as a scope through which the articles in this volume could be seen and understood. Firstly, how human dignity can be protected and enhanced by human rights whenever economic globalisation has an adverse impact on local living conditions. Secondly, how human rights themselves need to evolve in response to a global economy that is no longer dominated by States.

One response to the progressive development of economic globalisation has been a more holistic approach to the concept of human rights in order to ensure human dignity vis-à-vis new threats, which economic globalisation has brought with it. Hence the increasing emphasis on economic, social and cultural rights since the mid 1980s which can also be seen in the significant growth of monitoring mechanisms in the field of these rights. Consequently, an increasing concern can be ascertained with making economic, social and cultural rights more relevant and operational in order to respond to the new social challenges resulting from economic globalisation. This requires also the full realisation of civil and political rights, for example to assure the participation of individuals and groups affected by globalisation in decision-making processes. Possible conflicts between obligations from international economic agreements and from human rights need to be resolved with regard to the wider purposes and objectives of international economic cooperation, which requires a reaffirmation of the consensus on these purposes and objectives.

The increase of the number of state and non-state actors concerned with the governance of economic globalisation raises issues of legitimacy

---

[2] J. Habermas, *The Postnational Constellation: Political Essays* (Cambridge: MIT Press, 2001).

[3] O. Höffe, 'Globalität statt Globalismus. Über eine subsidiäre und föderale Weltrepublik', in M. Lutz-Bachmann and J. Bohman (eds.), *Weltstaat oder Staatenwelt. Für und wider die Idee einer Weltrepublik* (Frankfurt: Suhrkamp, 2002), p. 11.

and of more inclusive approaches to global governance. These actors include intergovernmental organisations as well as private non-state actors as, in particular, non-governmental organisations representing public interests of a globalising civil society and transnational corporations representing private interests and operating at a global scale. Clearly, the State while being accepted as the 'natural person' of international law has not remained the only one.[4] Sharing its role on the international plane with other actors does not necessarily lead to the erosion of the state, but rather calls for more participative decision-making structures leaving room for the participation of non-statal and inter-statal actors. This approach can alleviate concerns in relation to the much criticised 'democratic deficit' in intergovernmental organisations whose regulations progressively impact national policies.

Against the background of a growing number of people being affected by the new economic realities in their daily lives, increasing concerns for human rights as instruments of the protection against new threats caused by economic globalisation have been voiced. This has also led to a challenge of existing governance structures in intergovernmental economic organisations by civil society organisations that are increasingly active at the global level.[5] An 'international community' is evolving, which includes state and non-state actors, although not at the same level. Civil society organisations demand accountability of international economic organisations and social responsibility of transnational corporations. The critique of and reactions by these organisations have been described and analysed in this volume in conceptual and practical ways. In response to the new challenges alternative human rights implementation and enforcement mechanisms have been requested and developed. They include the UN special procedures, which were extended to economic, social and cultural concerns, the World Bank Inspection Panel, the *amicus curiae* briefs in WTO disputes and the opening of arbitration procedures to human rights concerns. While human rights were historically perceived relevant only for the relationship between the State and the

---

[4] See, among the vast literature, O. Schachter, 'The Decline of the Nation-State and its Implications for International Law', *Columbia Journal of Transnational Law* (1998), 7–23; G. Arangio-Ruiz, 'Dualism Revisited: International Law and Interindividual Law', *Rivista di diritto internazionale* (2003), 909–999 as well as D. Carreau, *Droit international*, 8th ed. (Paris: Pedone, 2004).

[5] See W. Benedek, 'The Emerging Global Civil Society: Achievements and Prospects', in V. Rittberger and M. Nettesheim (eds.), *Changing Patterns of Authority in the Global Political Economy* (Houndmills: Palgrave Macmillan Publishers, 2006), in print.

individual, the contributions have shown that intergovernmental organisations and the 'new' non-State actors have human rights obligations as well.

In this light human rights should play a more essential role in economic globalisation. This development leads back to the original approach of the UN after World War II where a balance between the economic and the social dimension in international cooperation had been envisaged. This balance, however, did not materialise. The renewed focus on the interdependence of rights presents us with a new opportunity to revive the original consensus at a time when the UN reform tries to respond to the changing circumstances of the political and economic as well as the social realities in the world, characterised by greatly diverging levels of development.

The methodology employed in this volume on Economic Globalisation and Human Rights is conceived differently from other publications in its field. The authors approach their topics from different disciplinary perspectives, in particular before the background of philosophy, political science and law. They explore the relevance of human rights in the process of economic globalisation by way of discussing a number of crucial issues like the role of the State, the need for global ethics, the localisation of human rights to counter negative effects of globalisation, the neglected dimension of social rights in economic globalisation, the place of human rights in WTO and in the Bretton Woods institutions and the efforts of NGOs to use international human rights law to make international economic organisations more accountable as well as (alternative) ways of holding multinational corporations legally accountable and to increase their social responsibility.

The relationship between economic globalisation and human rights

Identifying and responding to major challenges

Jernej Pikalo finds that the rhetoric about the demise of the State as a result of globalisation is exaggerated. There is no 'withering away' of the state as a result of globalisation because states retain substantial capacities of action. The continuing role of the State in international economic relations, however, requires certain adjustments to respond to challenges for human life, exemplified as threats to human rights resulting from the globalisation process. Pikalo refutes the orthodox globalist discourse about the inevitability of negative consequences of a benign process of globalisation, which comes as an unintentional result of an objective development and thus needs to be accepted. Arguing a wider, contextual approach of the globalist discourse he concludes that it is part of the role of the state to counter this limited approach and to use its sovereignty to address the challenges of globalisation, e.g. by regulating the operation of transnational corporations or to assure the redistribution of benefits of economic globalisation to balance its often asymmetrical costs.

Global institutions need to be capable of supplying global public goods such as basic human rights through inclusive ways of global governance, taking into account that there is no automaticity that economic developments leads to more respect for or fulfilment of human rights. Human rights are seen as a framework for national and global policy choices and as a process, enriched by local and regional experiences. Thus, human rights are found to have a role for global governance as they can provide a 'universal moral code' for institutions, agencies and networks to regulate economic globalisation.

This point is reiterated by *George Ulrich* who reflects on a theory of global ethics in support of human rights. He maintains that in the global context the main function of human rights is not to provide legal norms but to operate as moral rules. He also emphasises the role of human rights as 'tools to advance social justice on a global scale'. Furthermore, human rights also serve as reference points for relations between individuals and for private actors in relation to states and international organisations and provide the necessary normative framework for what Mary Robinson called an 'ethical globalisation'. Accordingly, human rights respond to the need of 'ethical responsibility' and also the need for globally shared values. The problem of applicability of these ethical norms in a world of normative pluralism is approached through the identification of basic norms, which are essential for human dignity in any society.

Ulrich also responds to the observed apathy and a lack of actors in realising the vision of ethical globalisation by underlining the need to define responsibilities for all actors in economic globalisation. In a postscript, the contribution addresses the discussion on the cartoons of prophet Mohammed first published in a Danish Newspaper, which raises the question of the freedom of expression in view of a global ethics, i.e. the respect of the values of others in order not to offend them and thus is taken as proof for the importance of forging global ethical standards.

While basic human rights can serve to develop an ethical standard at the global level, there is a need to investigate also the role of human rights at the corollary local level. For human rights to be relevant to all they need to be relevant for people at the local level, which have to be included through appropriate modes of participation, sometimes called popular participation. Taking the Universal Declaration of Human Rights as a starting point, *Koen De Feyter* draws attention to the fact that for human rights to be relevant in a globalising world economy they need to be localised, i.e. adjusted to specific situations. The efficacy of human rights mechanisms, too, needs to be tested at the local level. This requires a more active role of communities facing human rights abuses, in particular through community-based organisations that should be assisted by local NGOs and given access to adequate instruments for the protection of human rights concerns. Grounding human rights in local experiences or pursuing a bottom-up approach to human rights should be followed by transnational advocacy networks, which are thus able to link local struggles with international campaigns supported by different actors including governments and inter-governmental institutions as well as businesses.

The localisation of human rights calls for an increased presence of UN Human Rights institutions in the field to offer 'protection and empowerment' (Louise Arbour) and it forces inter-governmental organisations such as the WTO to take into account human rights consequences of their international decisions at the local level.

Economic globalisation has created new wealth and optimism but has left populations at the bottom of the economic and social ladder vulnerable to exploitation and to human rights abuses. Mobility of production factors across frontiers generates new tensions between capital and labour markets, for which the experience of the European Union can be considered as an important benchmark. Capital is increasingly free to cross national borders due to the proliferation of international investment law instruments. Yet the same is not true for labour and its regulation as *Adalberto Perulli* shows in his contribution. While it is clear that economic globalisation exerts a significant influence on labour law, the impact of labour law on economic globalisation is very small. Labour law is mainly part of domestic law and since each state is sovereign to regulate its own politico-economic system as it wishes, labour law thus falls within the sphere of national economic choices. Labour law has a traditional role in the containment of delocalisation trends and in promoting human dignity and a traditional function of mediation between commercial values and extra-economic values of solidarity.

But the world knows different legal systems and various labour regulations. As a result and paradoxically, the 'weakness of social protection systems' becomes, in the age of economic globalisation, a competitive factor. Ultimately, the competition of social systems may generate a 'race to the bottom' to the detriment of fundamental labour standards and social rights. Then, in order to reduce the pernicious effects of this development it is necessary to adopt fundamental social standards capable to respond adequately to the challenge of globalisation. No state can impose its own labour law on other sovereign states, therefore any regulation at the global level needs to be grounded on international law. It goes without saying that adoption and enforcement of social standards should be re-launched by intergovernmental organisations such as, *inter alia*, ILO, within the scope of their competences.

On the international level, the issue is well known and concerns the controversial topic of the refusal to accept social clauses in WTO-agreements. A better result has so far been reached in international regional trade agreements such as NAFTA or in the EU and also on the unilateral level under the form of social conditionality of trade concessions. Codes of conduct on corporate social responsibility should also be taken into consideration as soft law instruments.

Institutionalising and operationalising human rights

In light of its role and importance in the many processes that constitute economic globalisation the WTO is a prime example for the concerns raised in this volume. This is exemplified by the contributions of *Wolfgang Benedek* and *Davinia Ovett*. While the WTO's predecessor, the GATT, had not aroused much controversy until the 1990s, the human rights consequences of economic globalisation supported by WTO rules have become a major issue of concern for non-governmental human rights organisations in general and the human rights system of the United Nations in particular. The fact that the WTO has not been able or willing to include 'non-trade issues' (such as human rights) in its agenda and rules has only multiplied the concerns of UN human rights bodies and civil society organisations with the organisation and the underlying principles of international trade it promotes and defends.

Benedek concludes that this is due to the lack of realisation of the 'original consensus' contained in the UN Charter of 1945, which provided for a comprehensive and balanced approach to the economic and social dimensions of global cooperation. However, in the present system of the WTO, the social dimension of globalisation rests with the national level. Thus, in cases where states are not capable of balancing negative effects of economic globalisation, human rights violations may ensue.

This approach together with the lack of a more inclusive or participatory attitude of the WTO towards NGOs has contributed to a legitimacy crises of the WTO.[6] This requires a return to the basic consensus of the early United Nations or the forging of a new basic consensus aimed at a better balance between the economic and social concerns and an institutionalised dialogue between the governments of WTO member states and civil society organisations, which so far only exists in an *ad hoc* manner.

Some developments in WTO case law and practice already point in the right direction. They include the increasing recognition of the relevance of international law in WTO dispute settlement and of global concerns such as the Millennium Development Goals in statements by the WTO Director-General. The recognition of the 'unavoidable link' between trade and human rights is perceived as an issue of WTO accountability. By the creation of advisory bodies, which include civil society, more cooperation with UN agencies and a better use of *amicus curiae* briefs, the organisation's accountability could be strengthened.

Already today, NGOs, some of which are highly professional, play an important role in the international debate on the consequences of WTO law on human rights, such as the right to health. Taking the case of access to medicines, the contribution of Ovett presents cases and other practice in order to show how international trade rules enforcing intellectual property standards limit the political space of states to ensure the right to health and even the right to life in the case of certain pandemics and thus undermine their capacity to comply with their human rights obligations.

Ovett demonstrates how specialised public interests NGOs through their advocacy role have become stakeholders in the process and use human rights tools to achieve a more human rights-consistent approach to international trade. In this way they complement the activities of UN human rights bodies which they advise at the same time. Developing countries are given assistance on how to make best use of the flexibilities contained, e.g., in the TRIPS agreement and how to avoid that these are limited again in bilateral or regional trade agreements containing so-called TRIPS-plus rules which are often signed under political pressure. Ovett explains how access to affordable medicines has become an obligation under international human rights law and demonstrates on the basis

---

[6] Cf. R. O. Keohane and J. S. Nye, 'The Club Model of Multilateral Cooperation and the WTO: Problems of Democratic Legitimacy', Harvard University Center for Business and Government, available at: www.ksg.harvard.edu/visions/publication/keohane_nye.pdf (last accessed: 1 July 2006).

of the examples from Ecuador and Botswana, Denmark and Italy, how international human rights mechanisms can be used in practice to strengthen the accountability with regard to trade rules. For a more systematic approach a human rights impact assessment of trade rules is suggested which has been requested as well by the UN High Commissioner for Human Rights.

Ovett's contribution convincingly argues that specialised NGOs can have a significant impact on the law and practice of international trade. This impact is channelled mainly through UN human rights bodies as long as the WTO is not ready to offer NGO participation through new advisory bodies. The contributions by Benedek and Ovett, both point to the fact that the renewed academic and political focus on the issue of WTO and human rights is conducive to the convergence of the trade and human rights agendas.

Converging tendencies are also observed by *Laurence Boisson de Chazournes*, who analyses the Bretton Woods institutions with regard to human rights and focuses particularly on the World Bank. While the original mandates of the IMF and the World Bank, like the GATT, have a strong focus on economic objectives, they also include raising standards of living, ensuring fair conditions of work and promoting full employment. In addition, the predominance of economic considerations in isolation of political ones could not be maintained in the face of major human rights issues the Bank was confronted with. In cases such as Myanmar a World Bank report expressly recognised the linkages between poverty, human rights violations and poor economic performance. Already since the 1960s the Bank included health, education and housing in its approach to development and started with 'social programming' which gradually evolved to include human rights in a multidimensional and participative understanding of development encompassing notably the endorsement of the UN's Millennium Development Goals.

The 'operational policies' for projects of the Bank play an important role in operationalising human rights. They have also played a major role in the context of the Chad-Cameroon Petroleum Development and Pipeline Project, which has been brought before the World Bank Inspection Panel. The Inspection Panel, which was established in an effort to increase public participation and accountability, remains the only mechanism providing remedies against actions of an international organisation. Its procedure provides the opportunity to challenge the compliance of the Bank with its operational policies. Decisions of the Inspection Panel have in a few cases resulted in concrete consequences.

According to Boisson de Chazournes, the experience of the policies of the Bank has shown that development and human rights cannot be dealt with separately and economic concerns need to be approached together with their social aspects. That human rights serve the interest of sustainable development and therefore need to be taken seriously by an institution in charge of promoting development is increasingly accepted and translated into practice.

Towards a more responsible world economy

In his contribution *Francesco Francioni* shows four different 'legal avenues' to examine issues of international responsibility of transnational coporations (TNCs). He points out that since TNCs are inevitably operating within the territory of nation-states, 'hard law' remedies should be the primary tools to punish human rights abuses. Further patterns of liability may be found considering individual liabilities of corporate officials, direct international liability of corporations and international responsibility of a TNC's home state. Individual liability of corporate directors and officers is based on the imposition of individual international criminal responsibility on those managers for having ordered or committed or failed to prevent gross human rights abuses. This approach may become fruitful only in exceptional cases since it assumes, as a necessary pre-condition, that an 'international crime' has been committed. In this respect, the newly established International Criminal Court may in the future offer interesting developments of these issues through its case law.

ICSID (International Center for Settlement of Investment Disputes) arbitration has certainly contributed to re-assess the power of TNCs and their standing in international litigation. Moreover, contemporary international law has increasingly regulated certain activities of TNCs in the context of UN-imposed economic sanctions. Thus, the theory of liability of a TNC under public international law today seems stronger than ever. From this perspective, the UN Global Compact confirms the trend of integrating TNCs into international law. But it also follows that the door to making TNCs duty bearers of human rights protection has been opened. The final approach examined by Francioni consists of highlighting the home state's role in securing compliance with human rights by TNC's activities abroad. From this perspective new forms of international responsibility may be developed based on the theory of effective control over the decision-making of multinational groups. The theory implies extra-territorial application of the home country's human rights standards. Moreover, it extends duties to respect and protect such rights provided that the state has jurisdiction over the actor. Starting from the classical rule requiring each state to ensure that activity carried out within its own jurisdiction does not cause damages to another state one should add that TNCs today occupy much more space in contemporary international law than in the past. Insofar as they operate as partners of nation-states they bear an equivalent share of international responsibility in securing human rights in the territory in which they operate.

Of course, all approaches evidenced by Francioni should not be seen as alternatives. Rather, they may be combined together. Moreover, *Fabrizio Marrella* convincingly argues that they may also be combined with Corporate Social Responsibility (CSR) as a fifth 'legal avenue' for human rights protection.

The most important actors of globalisation are TNCs. International business affects almost every person in the world, in particular in industrialised countries. A multinational – *rectius* transnational – corporation has branches or affiliates or subsidiaries in different nations. Through its different components a TNC establishes a network of business-to-business contracts. Indeed, when a TNC enters a strategic contract or establishes a foreign investment, the decision is based mainly on business rather than legal factors. While most of a company's strategic decisions are grounded in business, such as to use cheaper labour or to establish a base in a foreign market (such as a free trade area) or even to minimise taxes, they have inevitably a legal dimension. This legal dimension is well evidenced by a growing number of resolutions of international organisations and by the latest interim report (E/CN.4/2006/97) of the Special Representative of the Secretary-General on the issue of human rights and TNCs and other business enterprises. But according to Marrella corporate social responsibility can hardly be imposed 'from above' by intergovernmental organisations through their non-binding resolutions. The turning point is when corporate social responsibility comes 'from below', i.e. when it is advanced by potential duty bearers and codified by international NGOs as codes of conduct representing the interests of the business community. CSR rules may thus become the new 'rules of the game' for competitors. Hence, although contracts are driven by purely commercial considerations, failure to address human rights impacts may have significant adverse consequences for corporate planning in the new global context.

Not surprisingly, introducing CSR rules has become, for certain firms, a moral need; for many others, a marketing tool to further their corporate image resulting in a better sales performance; and to others, again, a means to better access to financing and to a more positive corporate identity for their workers. Summing up it can be said that respecting human rights through corporate social responsibility produces economic value.

Conversely and from a legal standpoint, corporate activities linked to gross human rights abuses are likely to produce serious consequences in business to business contract law and in torts. Codes of conduct embodying CSR rules may be transmuted from soft law to hard law instruments whenever they are included in international contracts.

In international business transactions the main dispute resolution mechanism is arbitration. As a legal proceeding, arbitration operates within the limits set up by the application of procedural human rights standards including alleged violations of codes of conduct embodying CSR. The link between transnational arbitration and codes of conduct for CSR can thus be established. Marrella advances that arbitrations may become a new and unusual forum for 'contractualised human rights' litigation. Arbitral case law on the matter may contribute to shaping the scope of CSR, and, finally, to the application of human rights standards in the law of international trade.

As paradigms shift, human rights grow in importance

Cognisant of the paradigm shifts occurring in the context of economic globalisation the contributors to this volume have offered clarification of the impact a globalised economy has on human rights and of the increasing role human rights need to have, and have partly gained, in the process of globalisation. Combining different disciplinary perspectives, the contributors have shown that the dynamics of economic globalisation generated the development of a global ethics and a new perception of human rights which gives more attention to social and cultural rights, particularly affected by economic globalisation, but in a holistic approach together with civil and political rights. The processes in connection with economic globalisation result in a redefinition of the role of the state and of other actors in safeguarding human rights. Globalisation further requires the institutionalisation, if not the mainstreaming of human rights in the WTO and in the Bretton Woods institutions and their respective agreements in order to operationalise the human rights approach in practice, notably on the local level, where they matter most to people. Globalisation necessitates a stronger role for NGO advocacy in order to make international economic organisations more accountable and in order to enlarge the role of international law in finding ways to hold transnational corporations legally responsible.

As has been said by *Pascal Lamy*, director-general of the WTO in January 2006: 'Globalisation needs to be humanised: if solutions must often be global, the negative effects on individuals and societies must also be tackled.'[7]

Without doubt the increasing awareness of all stakeholders in the process of economic globalisation of the importance of the role of human rights has already generated significant results. Human rights today are an established concern, which cannot be ignored by the different actors. However, the translation of awareness into new institutions, mechanisms and rules and their operation in daily realities remains on the agenda for the future. The evolving nature of globalisation does not permit a final statement on its relationship with human rights. However, while traditional structures of authority are changing, human rights are evolving to a central governance principle for the global world. In conclusion, it is our hope that this publication will provide a fresh approach to ensuring that human rights take up the strong, central and crucial position in the process of economic globalisation that they deserve. Only by respecting human rights can economic globalisation serve its final purpose: ensuring sustainable human development.

Bibliography

Arangio-Ruiz, G., 'Dualism Revisited: International Law and Interindividual Law', *Rivista di diritto internazionale* (2003), 909–999

Benedek, W., 'The Emerging Global Civil Society: Achievements and Prospects', in Rittberger V. and Nettesheim, M., (eds.), *Changing Patterns of Authority in the Global Political Economy* (Houndmills: Palgrave Macmillan Publishers, 2007), in print

Carreau, D., *Droit international*, 8th ed. (Paris: Pedone, 2004)

Habermas, J., *The Postnational Constellation: Political Essays* (Cambridge: MIT Press, 2001)

Höffe, O., 'Globalität statt Globalismus. Über eine subsidiäre und föderale Weltrepublik' [Globality or Globalism. On a Subsidiary and Federal World republic] in Lutz-Bachmann, M. and Bohman, J. (eds.), *Weltstaat oder Staatenwelt. Für und wider die Idee einer Weltrepublik* [*World State or World of States. Pro and Contra the Idea of a World Republic*] (Frankfurt: Suhrkamp, 2002)

---

[7] P. Lamy, 'Humanising Globalisation', Speech in Santiago de Chile, 30 January 2006, http://wto.org/english/news_e/sppl_e/sppl16_e.htm (last accessed: 25 September 2006).

Keohane, R. O. and Nye, J. S., 'The Club Model of Multilateral Cooperation and the WTO: Problems of Democratic Legitimacy', Harvard University Center for Business and Government, available at: www.ksg.harvard.edu/visions/publication/keohane_nye.pdf (last accessed: 1 July 2006)

Lamy, P., 'Humanising Globalisation', Speech in Santiago de Chile, 30 January 2006, http://wto.org/english/news_e/sppl_e/sppl16_e.htm (last accessed: 25 September 2006)

Schachter, O., 'The decline of the nation-state and its implications for international law', *Columbia Journal of Transnational Law* (1998), 7–23